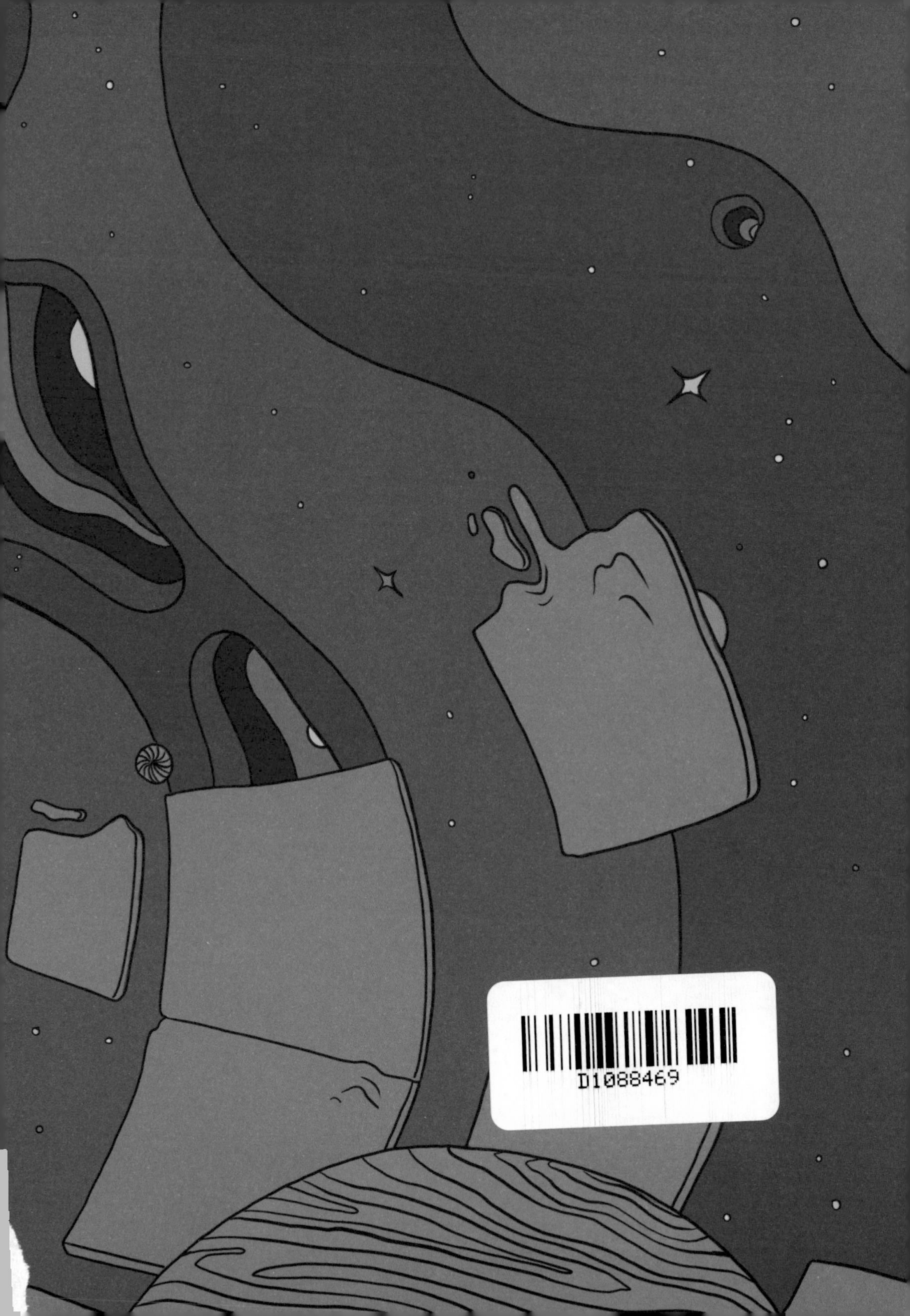

THANK YOU TO EVERYONE
AT NOBROW FOR THIS AMAZING
OPPORTUNITY AND i WiSH
EVERYONE CONTINUED SUCCESS.

First edition published in 2023 by Flying Eye Books Ltd.
27 Westgate Street, London, E8 3RL.

Text and illustrations © Tyrell Waiters 2023

Tyrell Waiters has asserted his right under the
Copyright, Designs and Patents Act,
1988, to be identified as the Author and Illustrator of this Work.

All rights reserved. No part of this publication may be reproduced
or transmitted in any form or by any means, electronic or mechanical,
including photocopying, recording or by any information and storage
retrieval system, without prior written consent from the publisher.

1 3 5 7 9 10 8 6 4 2

Edited by Niamh Jones
Designed by Lilly Gottwald

Printed in Poland on FSC certified paper.
Published in the US by Fying Eye Books Ltd

ISBN: 978-1-913123-09-3
www.flyingeyebooks.com

TYRELL WAITERS

VERN CUSTODIAN OF THE UNIVERSE

NOBROW

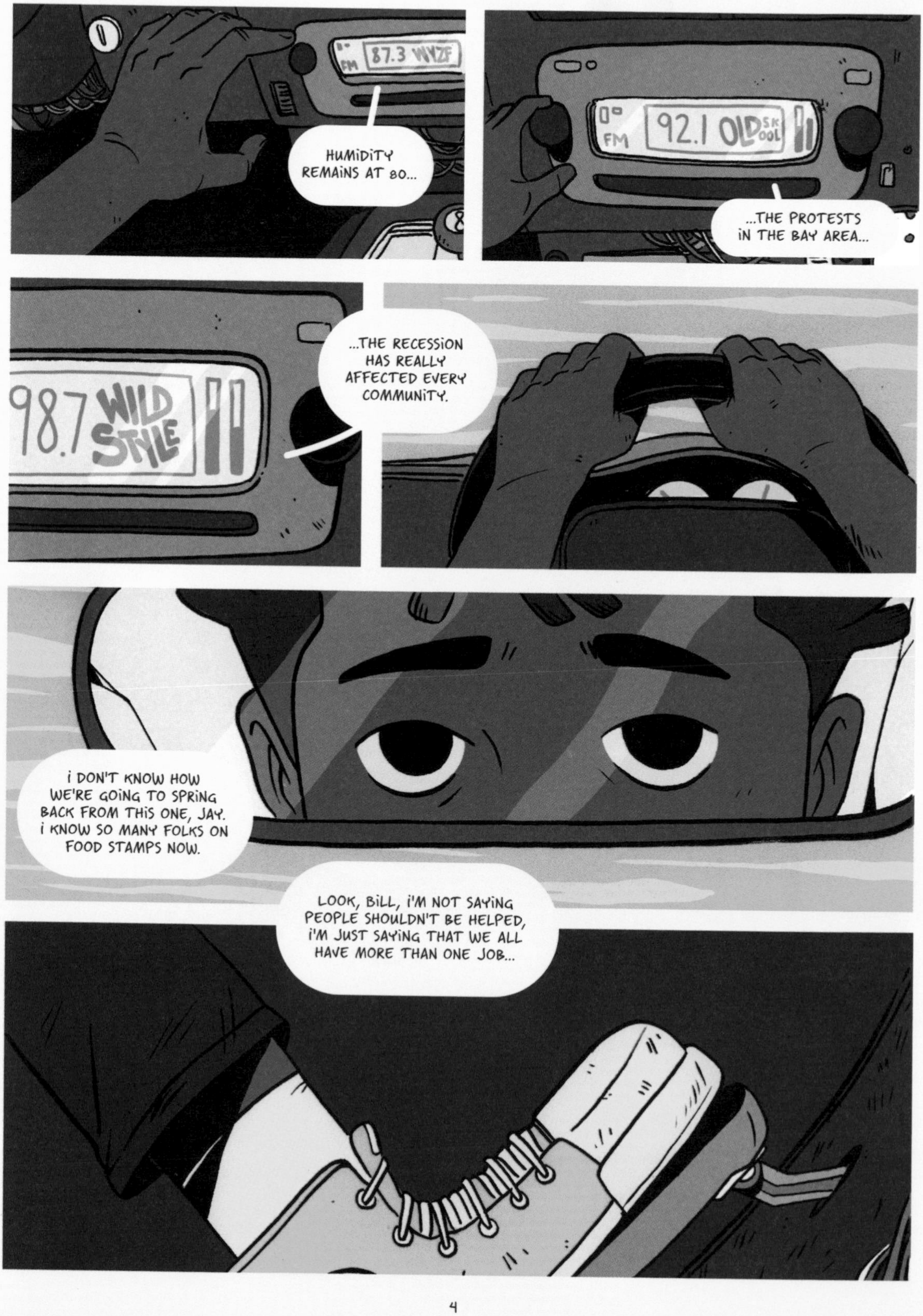
87.3 WYZF
HUMIDITY REMAINS AT 80...
92.1 OLD SKOOL
...THE PROTESTS IN THE BAY AREA...
98.7 WILD STYLE
...THE RECESSION HAS REALLY AFFECTED EVERY COMMUNITY.
I DON'T KNOW HOW WE'RE GOING TO SPRING BACK FROM THIS ONE, JAY. I KNOW SO MANY FOLKS ON FOOD STAMPS NOW.
LOOK, BILL, I'M NOT SAYING PEOPLE SHOULDN'T BE HELPED, I'M JUST SAYING THAT WE ALL HAVE MORE THAN ONE JOB...

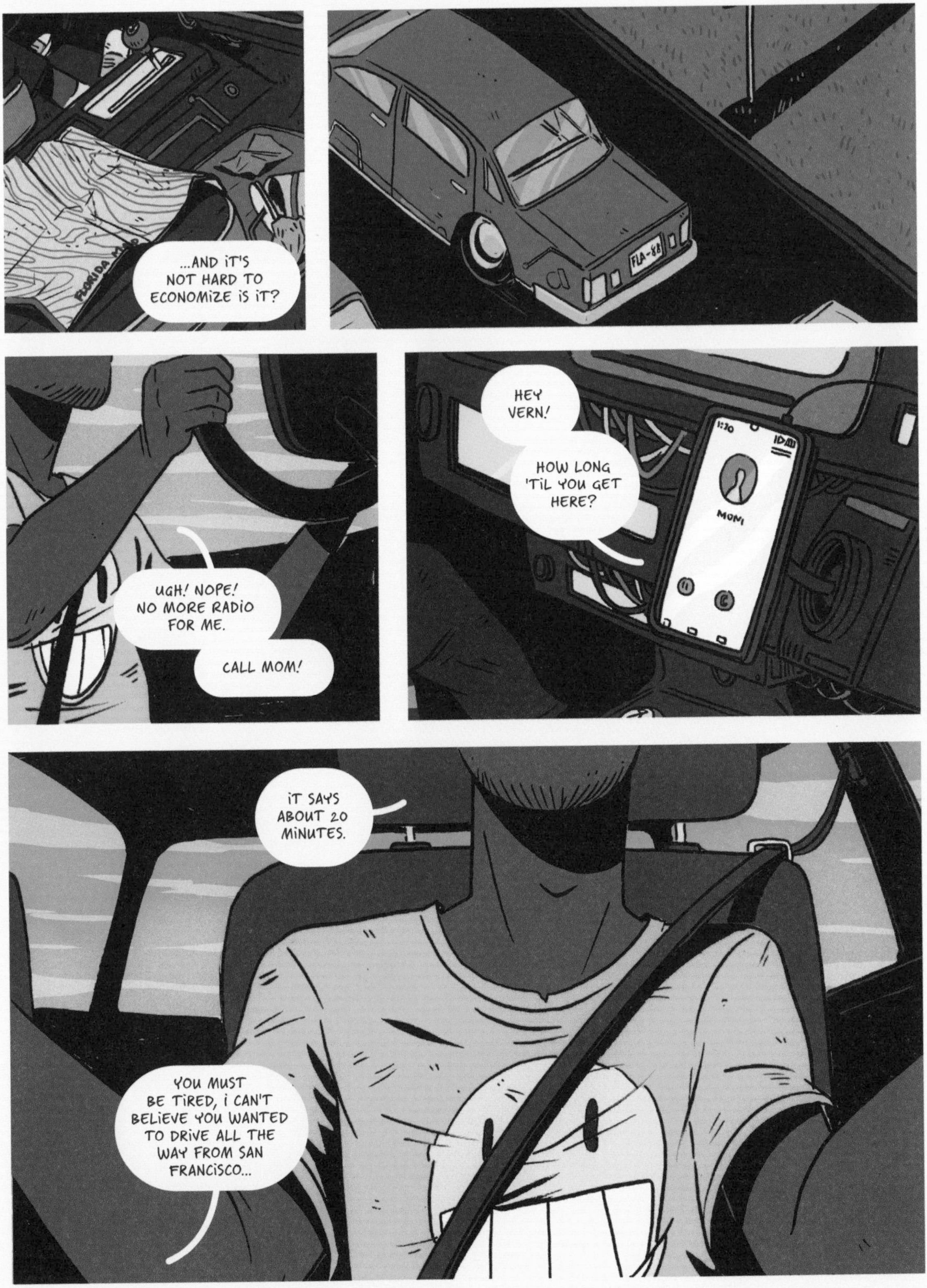

...AND IT'S NOT HARD TO ECONOMIZE IS IT?
FLA-88
UGH! NOPE! NO MORE RADIO FOR ME.
CALL MOM!
MOM
HEY VERN!
HOW LONG 'TIL YOU GET HERE?
IT SAYS ABOUT 20 MINUTES.
YOU MUST BE TIRED, I CAN'T BELIEVE YOU WANTED TO DRIVE ALL THE WAY FROM SAN FRANCISCO...

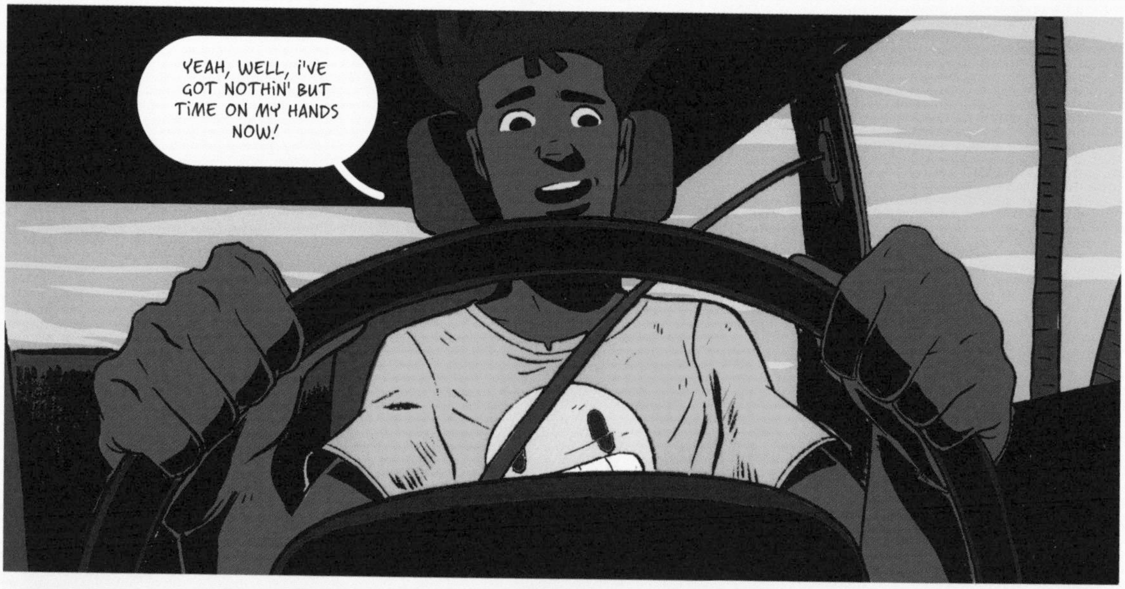
YEAH, WELL, i'VE GOT NOTHiN' BUT TiME ON MY HANDS NOW!

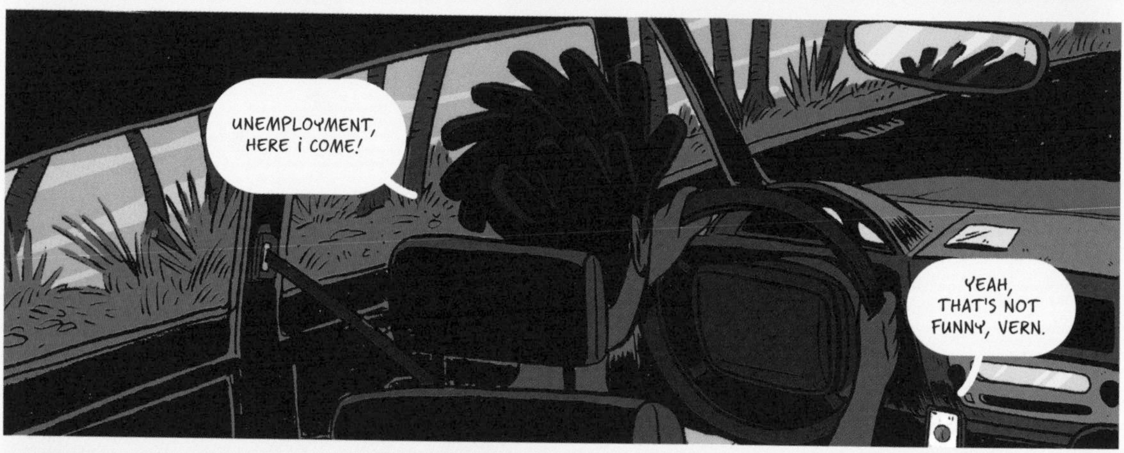
UNEMPLOYMENT, HERE i COME!
YEAH, THAT'S NOT FUNNY, VERN.

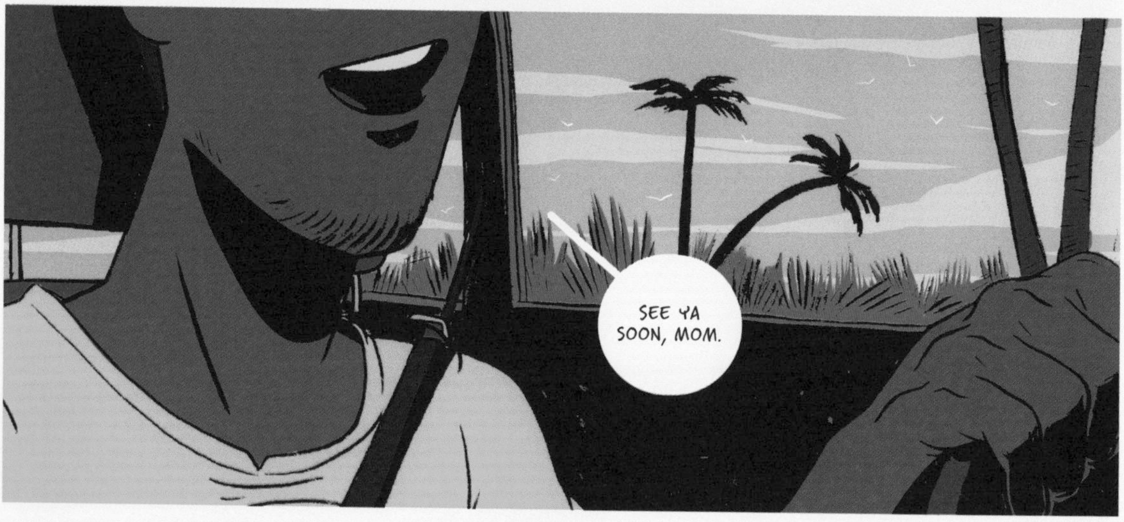
SEE YA SOON, MOM.

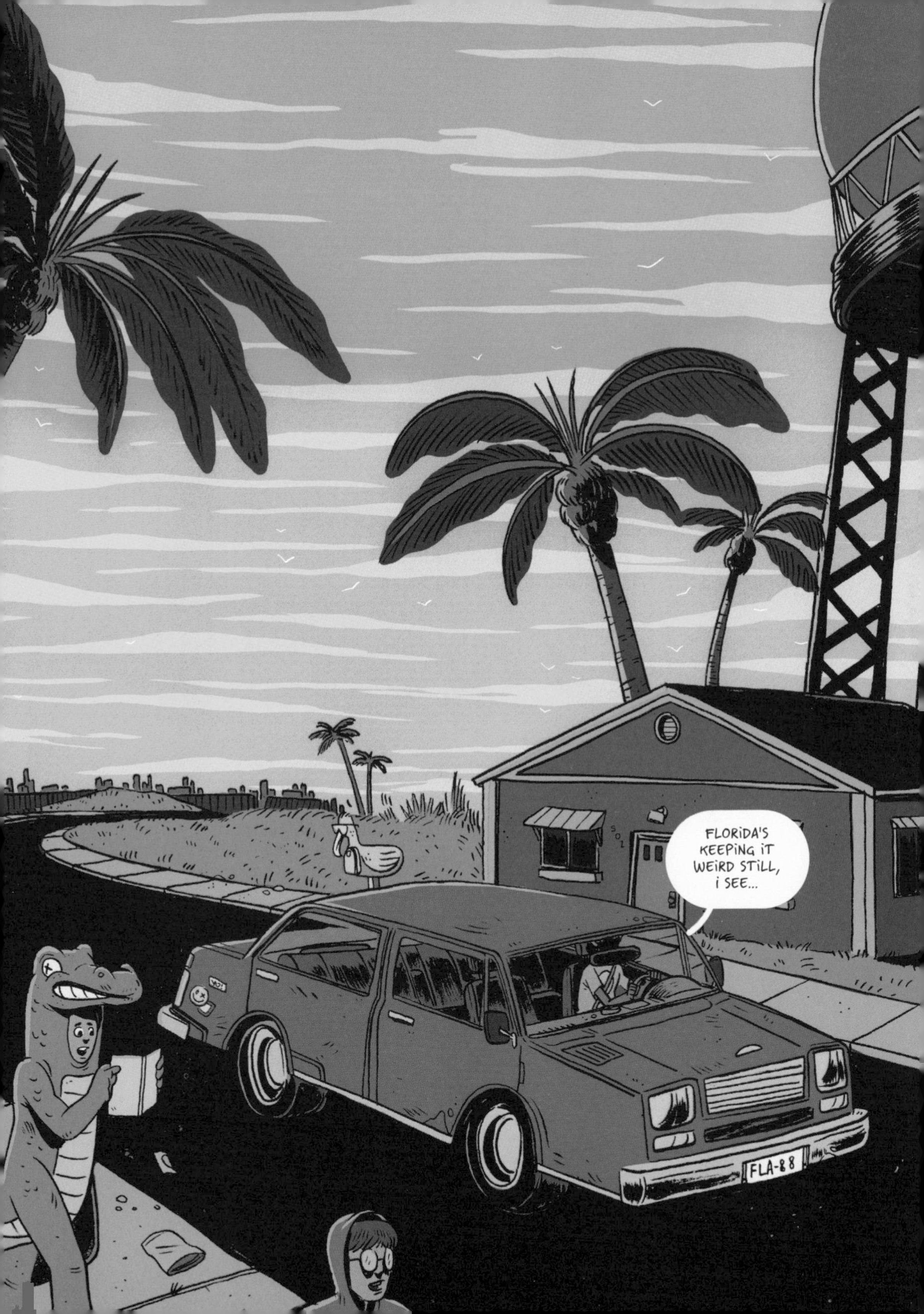
FLORIDA'S KEEPING IT WEIRD STILL, I SEE...
FLA-88

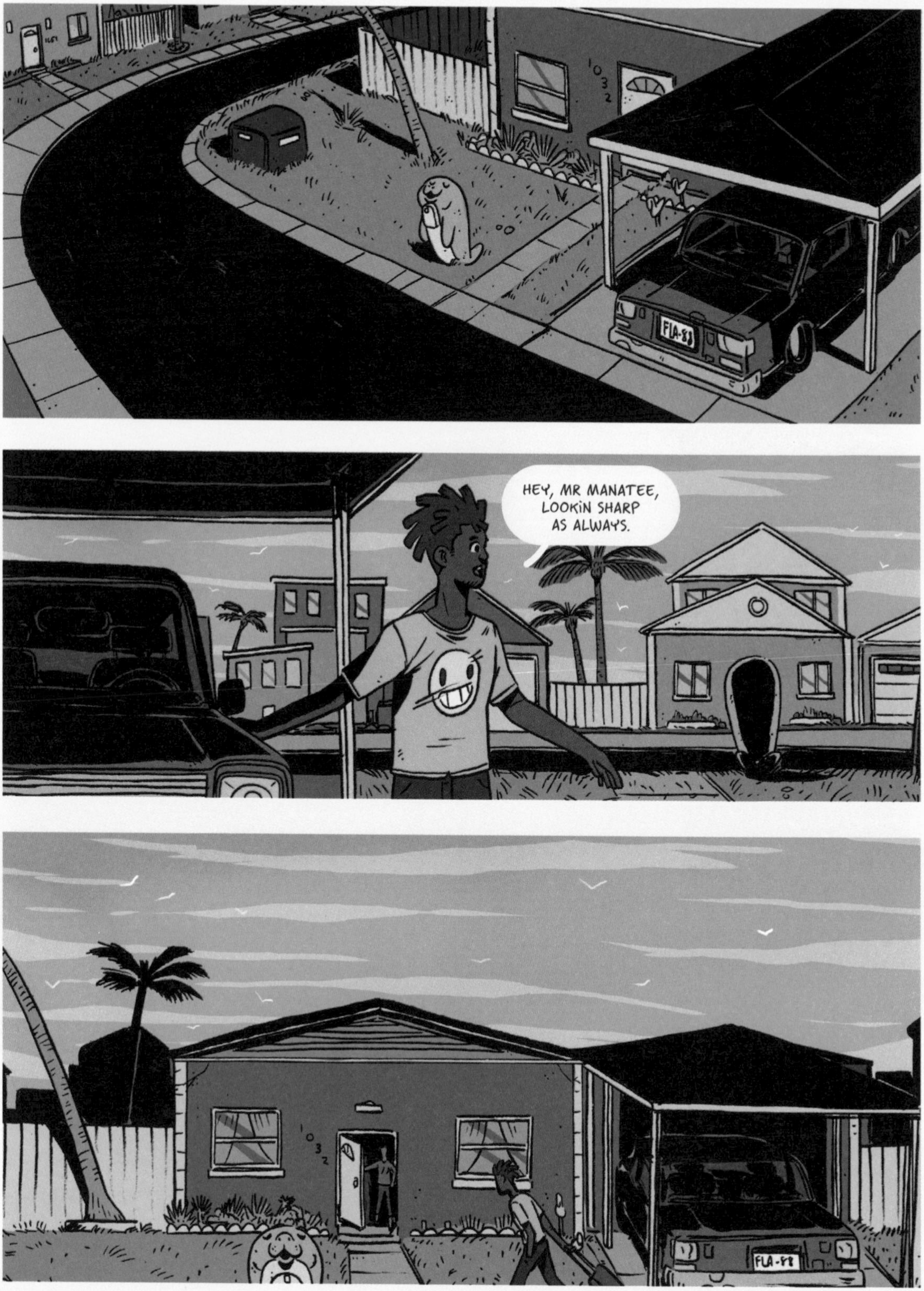
HEY, MR MANATEE, LOOKiN SHARP AS ALWAYS.

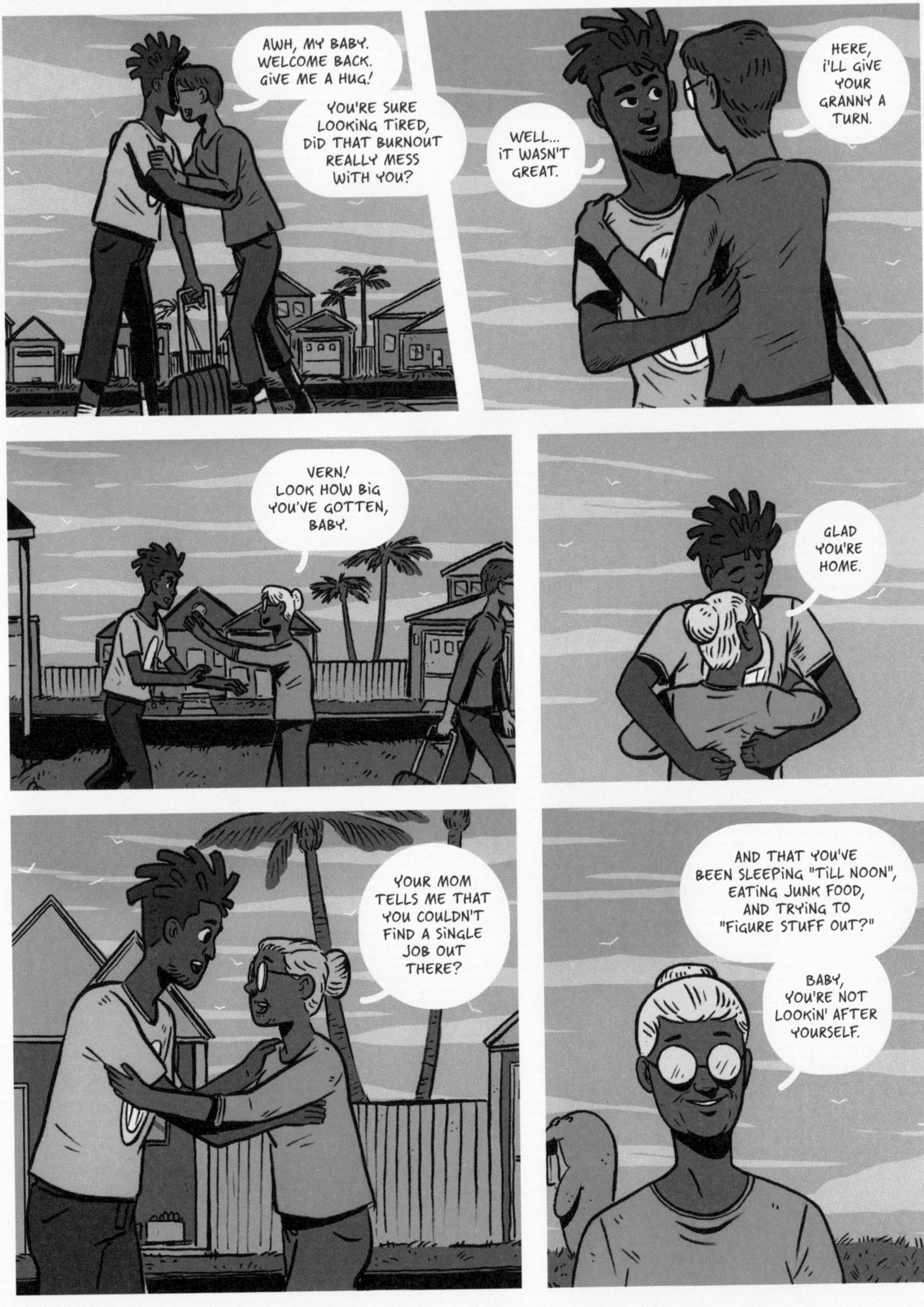
AWH, MY BABY. WELCOME BACK. GiVE ME A HUG!
YOU'RE SURE LOOKiNG TiRED, DiD THAT BURNOUT REALLY MESS WiTH YOU?
WELL... iT WASN'T GREAT.
HERE, i'LL GiVE YOUR GRANNY A TURN.
VERN! LOOK HOW BiG YOU'VE GOTTEN, BABY.
GLAD YOU'RE HOME.
YOUR MOM TELLS ME THAT YOU COULDN'T FiND A SiNGLE JOB OUT THERE?
AND THAT YOU'VE BEEN SLEEPiNG "TiLL NOON", EATiNG JUNK FOOD, AND TRYiNG TO "FiGURE STUFF OUT?"
BABY, YOU'RE NOT LOOKiN' AFTER YOURSELF.

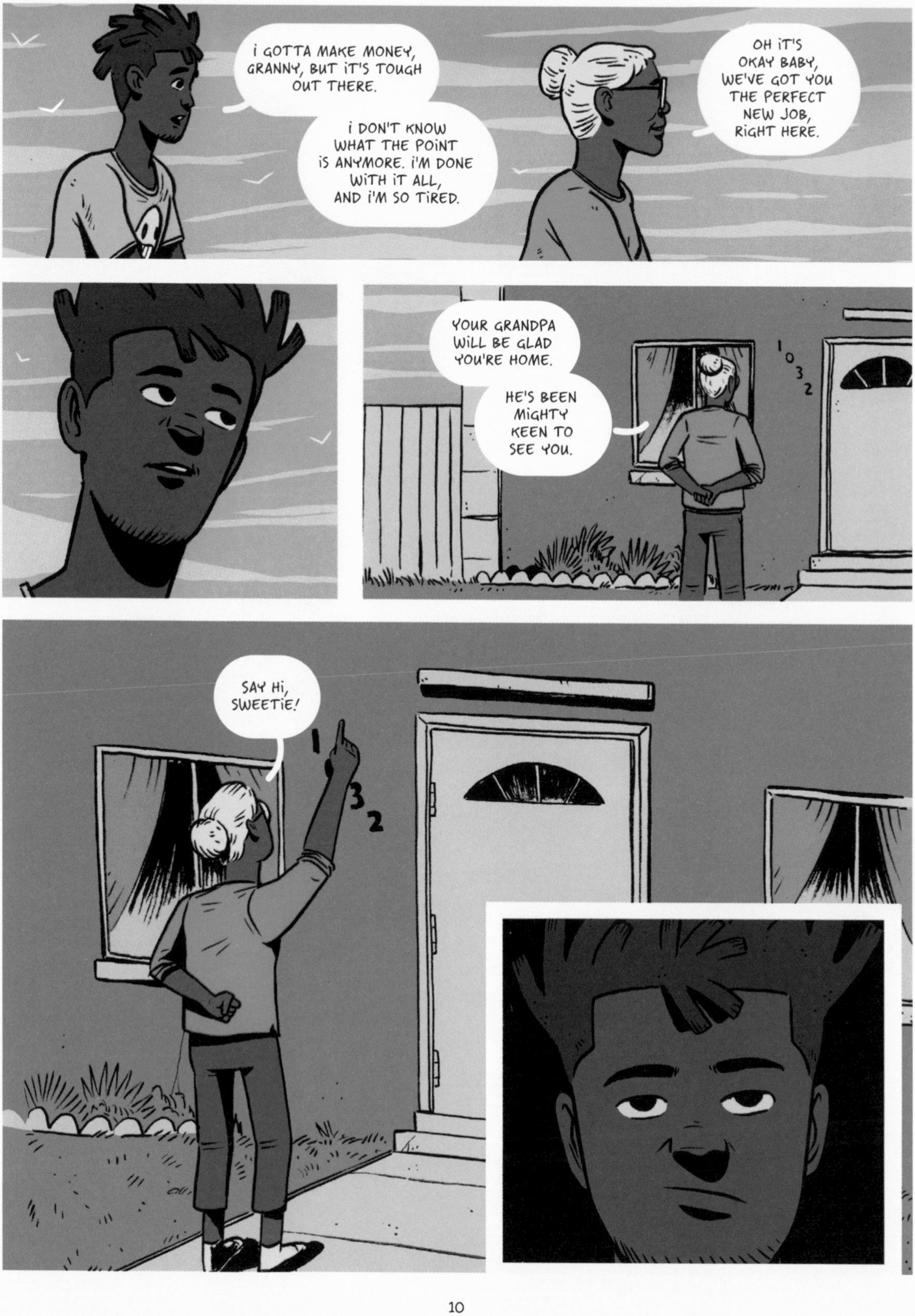

i GOTTA MAKE MONEY, GRANNY, BUT iT'S TOUGH OUT THERE.
i DON'T KNOW WHAT THE POiNT iS ANYMORE. i'M DONE WiTH iT ALL, AND i'M SO TiRED.
OH iT'S OKAY BABY, WE'VE GOT YOU THE PERFECT NEW JOB, RiGHT HERE.
YOUR GRANDPA WiLL BE GLAD YOU'RE HOME.
HE'S BEEN MiGHTY KEEN TO SEE YOU.
1032
SAY Hi, SWEETiE!
1032

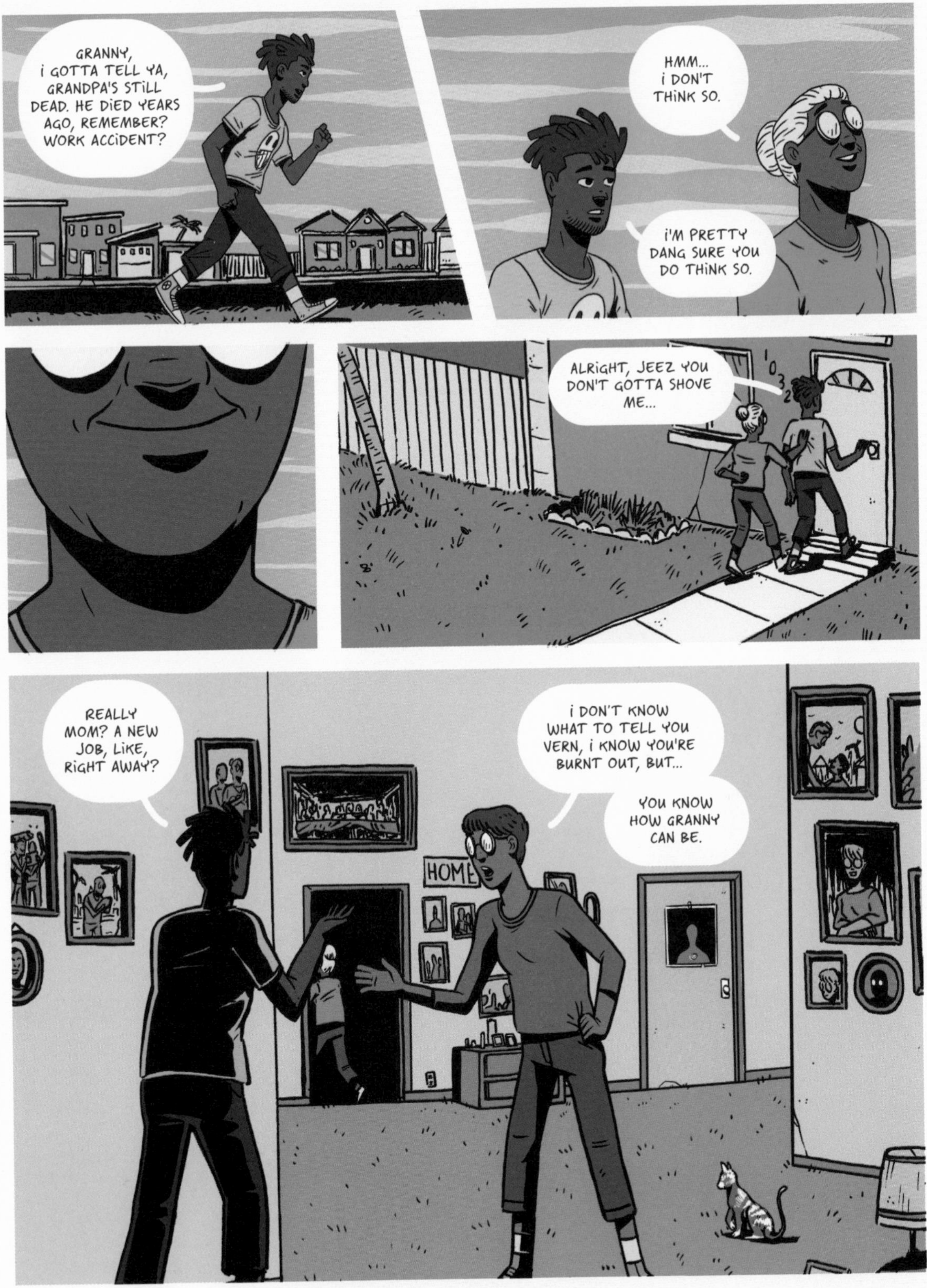
GRANNY, I GOTTA TELL YA, GRANDPA'S STILL DEAD. HE DIED YEARS AGO, REMEMBER? WORK ACCIDENT?
HMM... I DON'T THINK SO.
I'M PRETTY DANG SURE YOU DO THINK SO.
ALRIGHT, JEEZ YOU DON'T GOTTA SHOVE ME...
REALLY MOM? A NEW JOB, LIKE, RIGHT AWAY?
I DON'T KNOW WHAT TO TELL YOU VERN, I KNOW YOU'RE BURNT OUT, BUT...
YOU KNOW HOW GRANNY CAN BE.
HOME

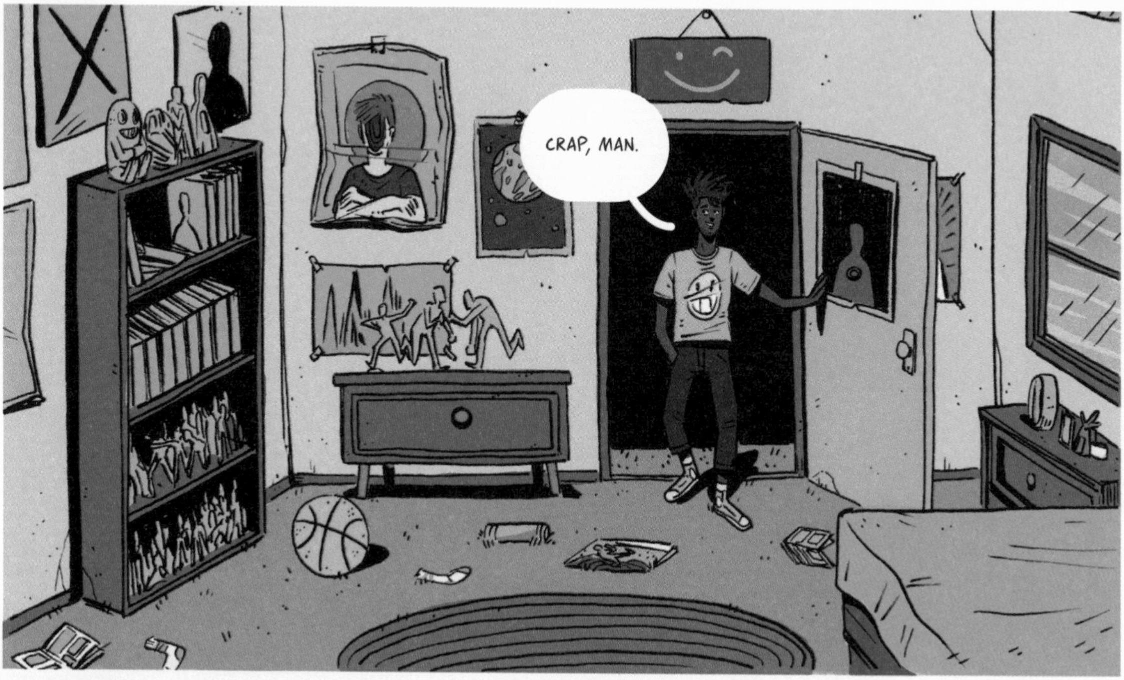
CRAP, MAN.

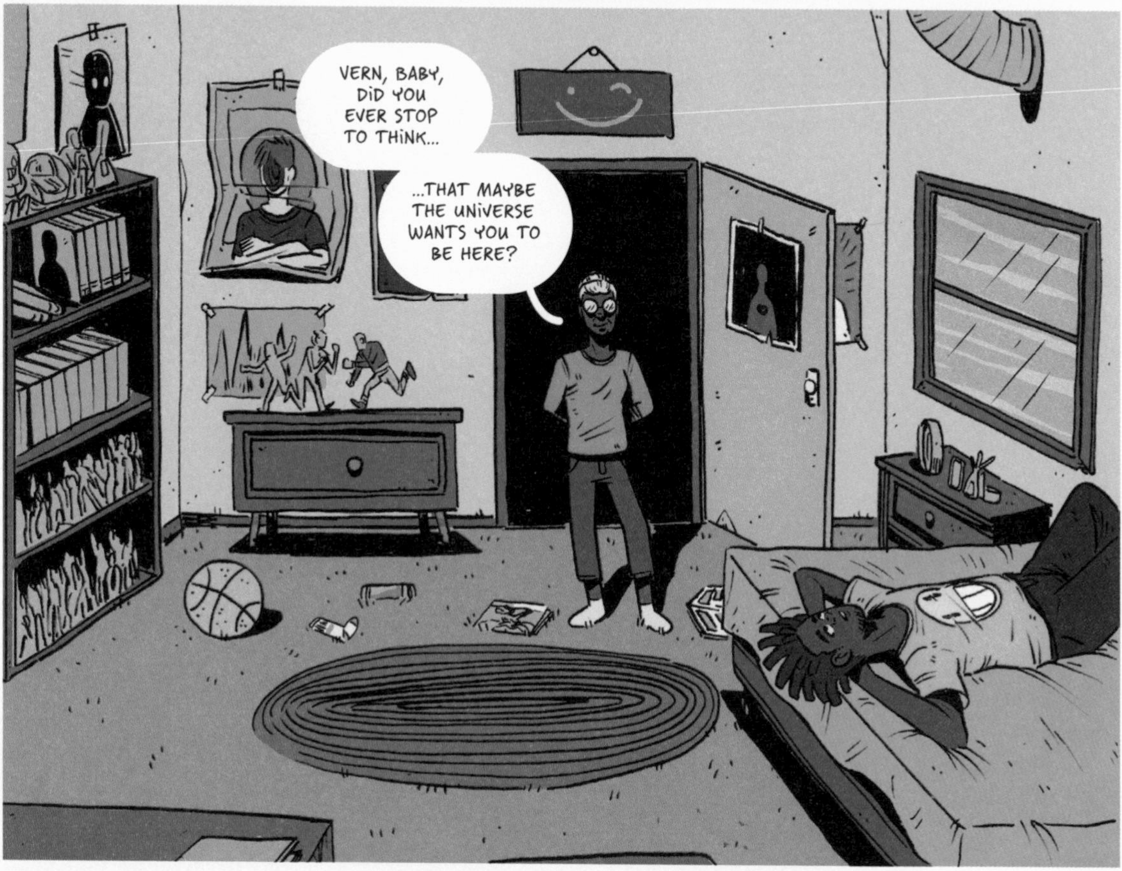
VERN, BABY, DiD YOU EVER STOP TO THiNK...
...THAT MAYBE THE UNiVERSE WANTS YOU TO BE HERE?

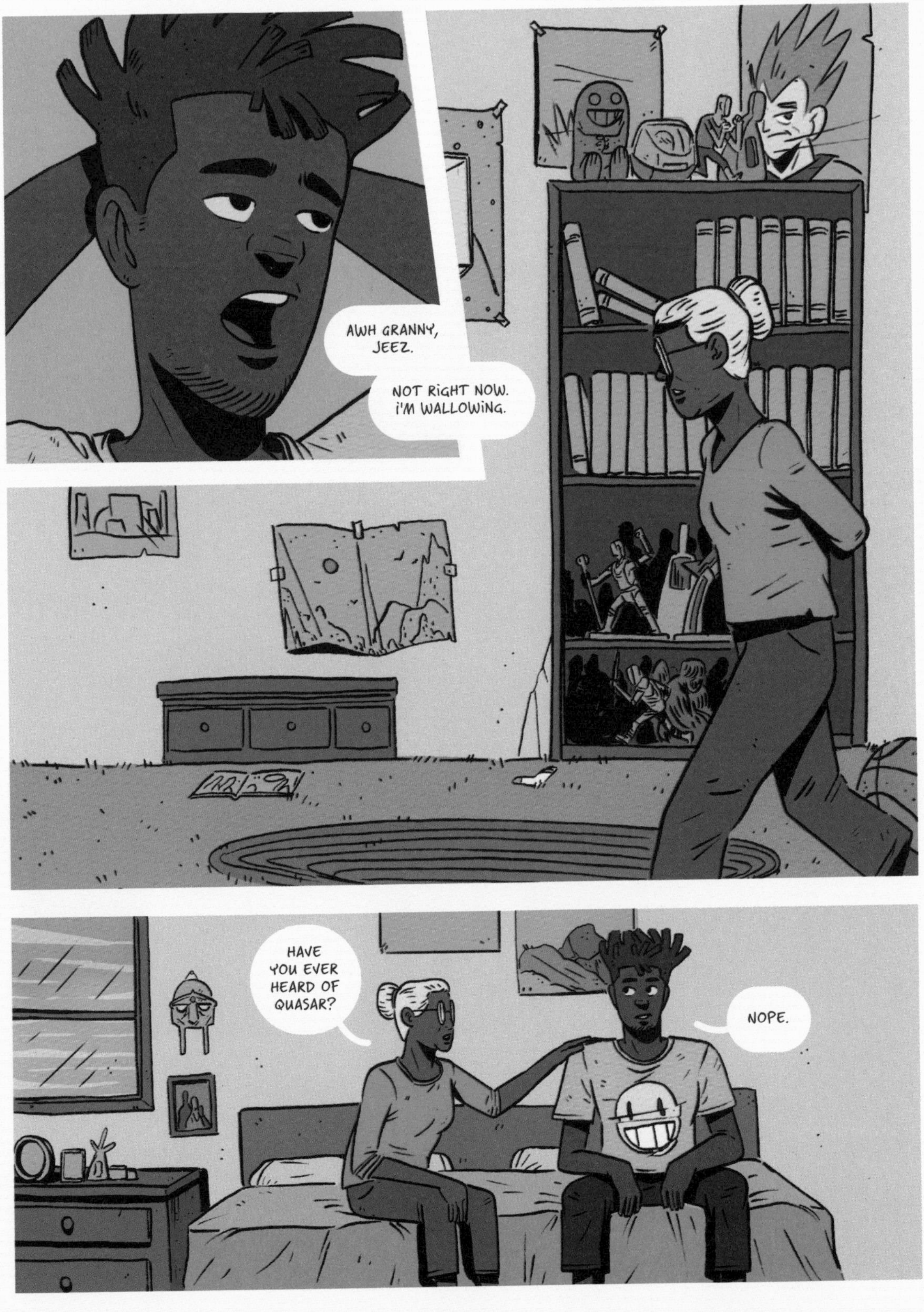
AWH GRANNY, JEEZ.
NOT RIGHT NOW. I'M WALLOWING.
HAVE YOU EVER HEARD OF QUASAR?
NOPE.

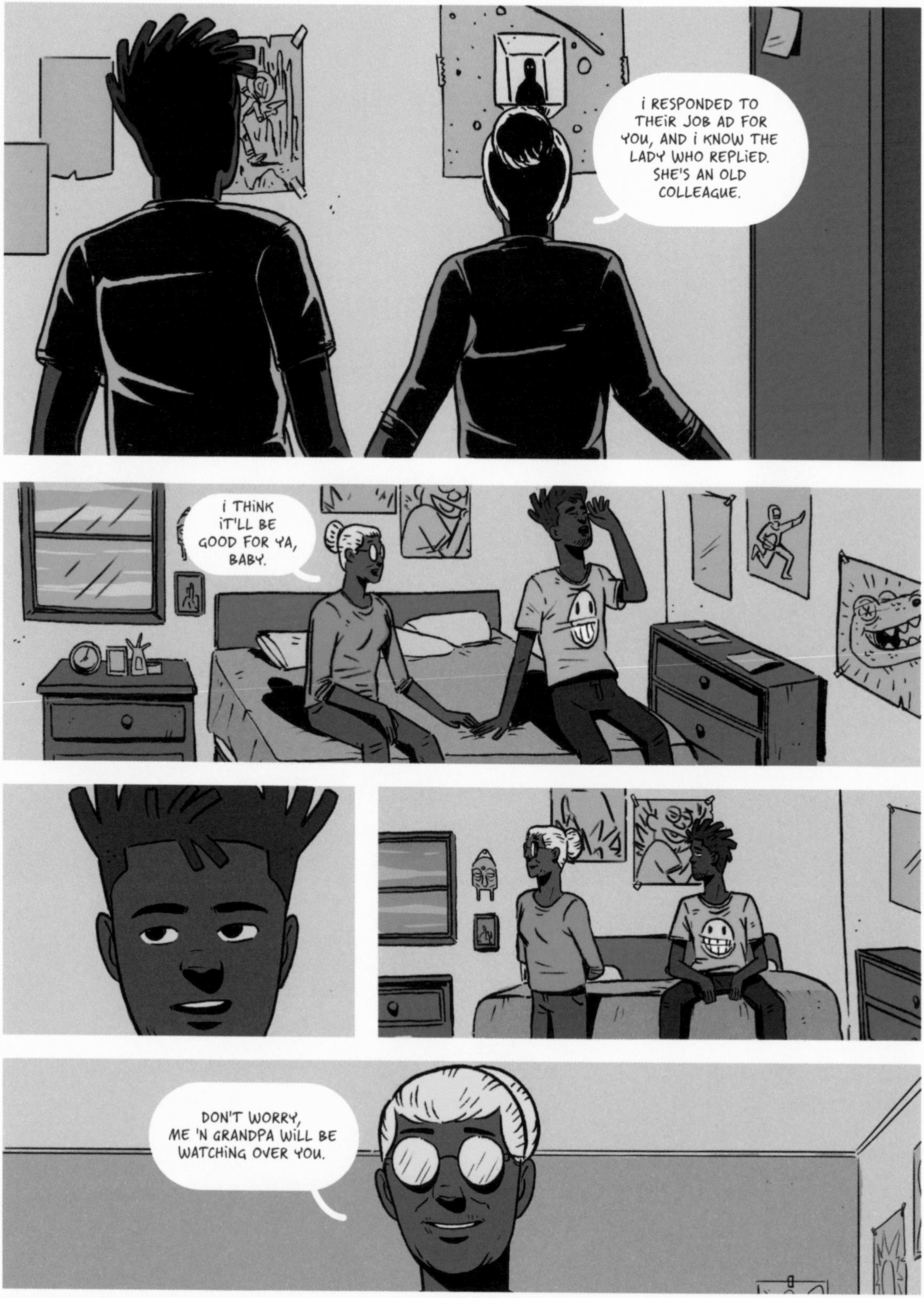
I RESPONDED TO THEIR JOB AD FOR YOU, AND I KNOW THE LADY WHO REPLIED. SHE'S AN OLD COLLEAGUE.
I THINK IT'LL BE GOOD FOR YA, BABY.
DON'T WORRY, ME 'N GRANDPA WILL BE WATCHING OVER YOU.

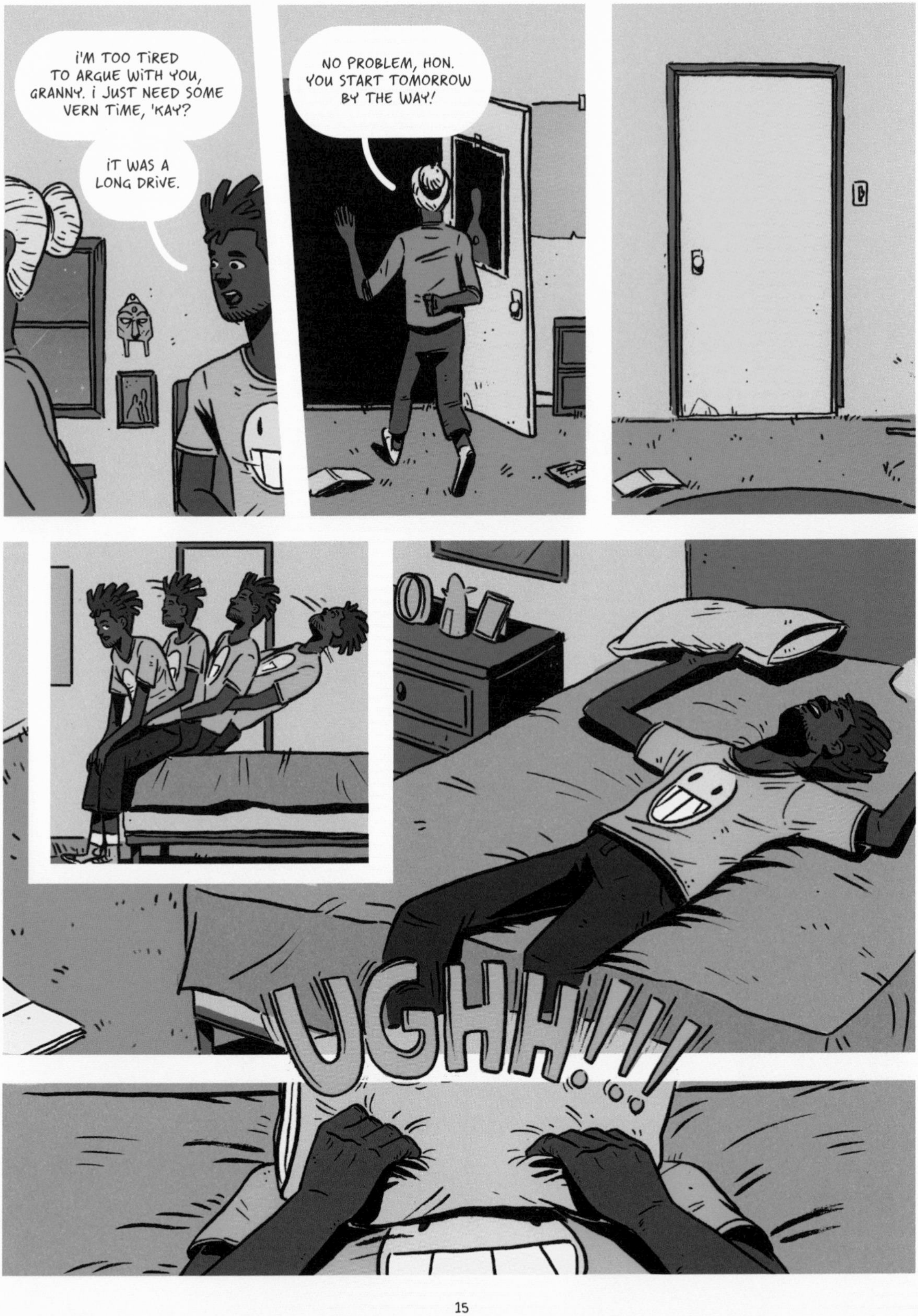
i'M TOO TIRED TO ARGUE WITH YOU, GRANNY. i JUST NEED SOME VERN TIME, 'KAY?
iT WAS A LONG DRiVE.
NO PROBLEM, HON. YOU START TOMORROW BY THE WAY!
UGHH!!!

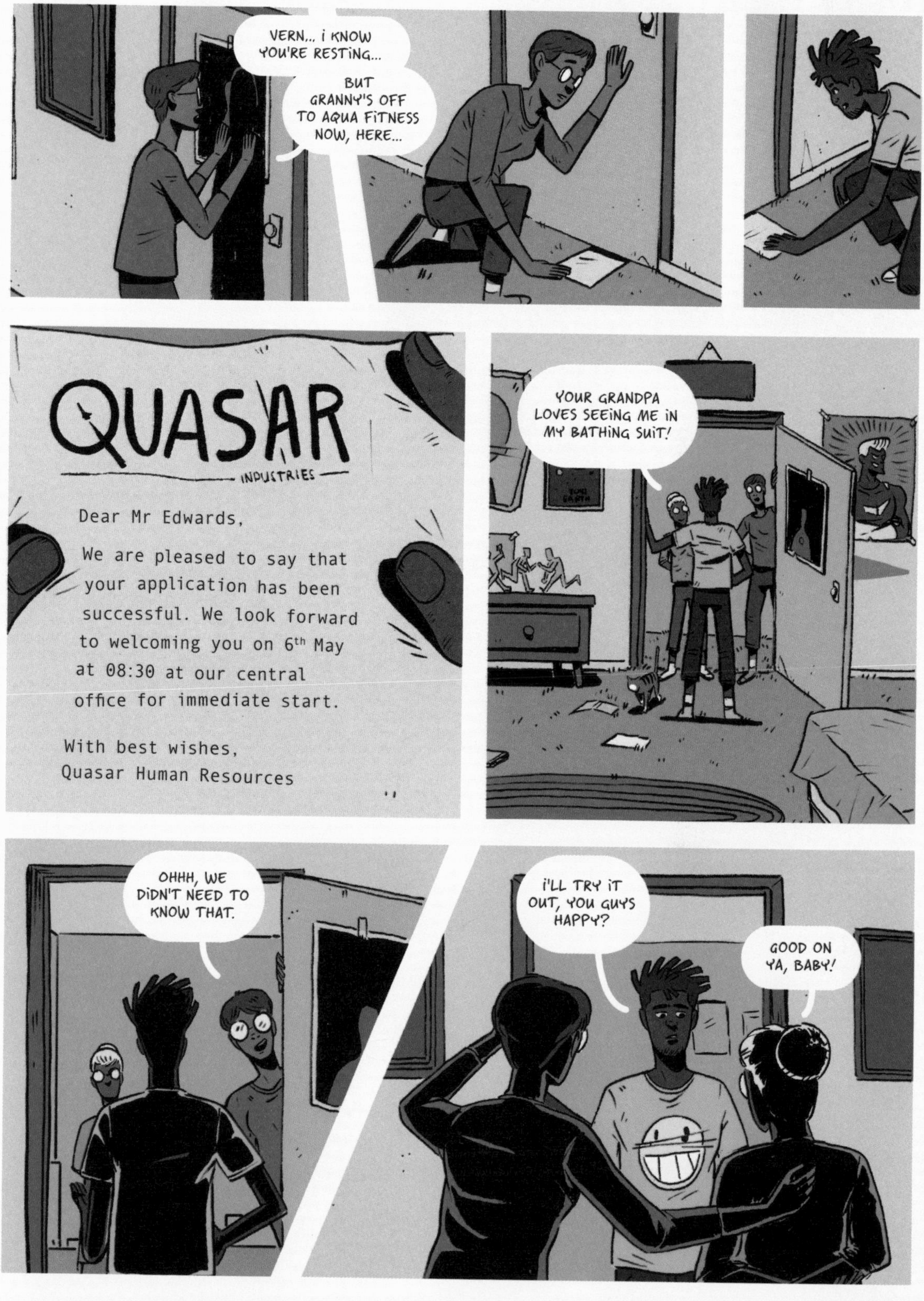
VERN... I KNOW YOU'RE RESTING...
BUT GRANNY'S OFF TO AQUA FITNESS NOW, HERE...
QUASAR
INDUSTRIES
Dear Mr Edwards,
We are pleased to say that your application has been successful. We look forward to welcoming you on 6th May at 08:30 at our central office for immediate start.
With best wishes,
Quasar Human Resources
YOUR GRANDPA LOVES SEEING ME IN MY BATHING SUIT!
OHHH, WE DIDN'T NEED TO KNOW THAT.
I'LL TRY IT OUT, YOU GUYS HAPPY?
GOOD ON YA, BABY!

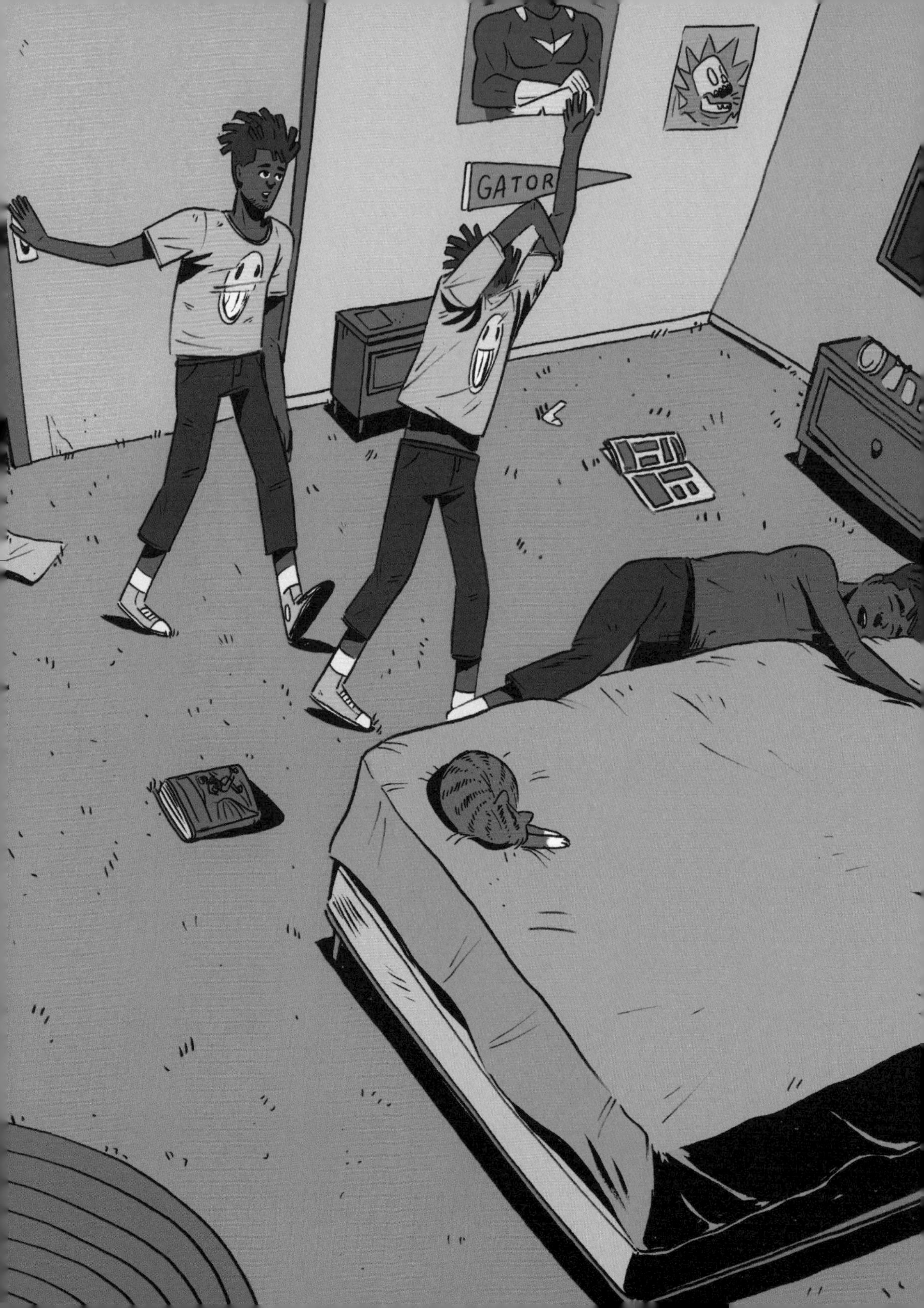
GATOR

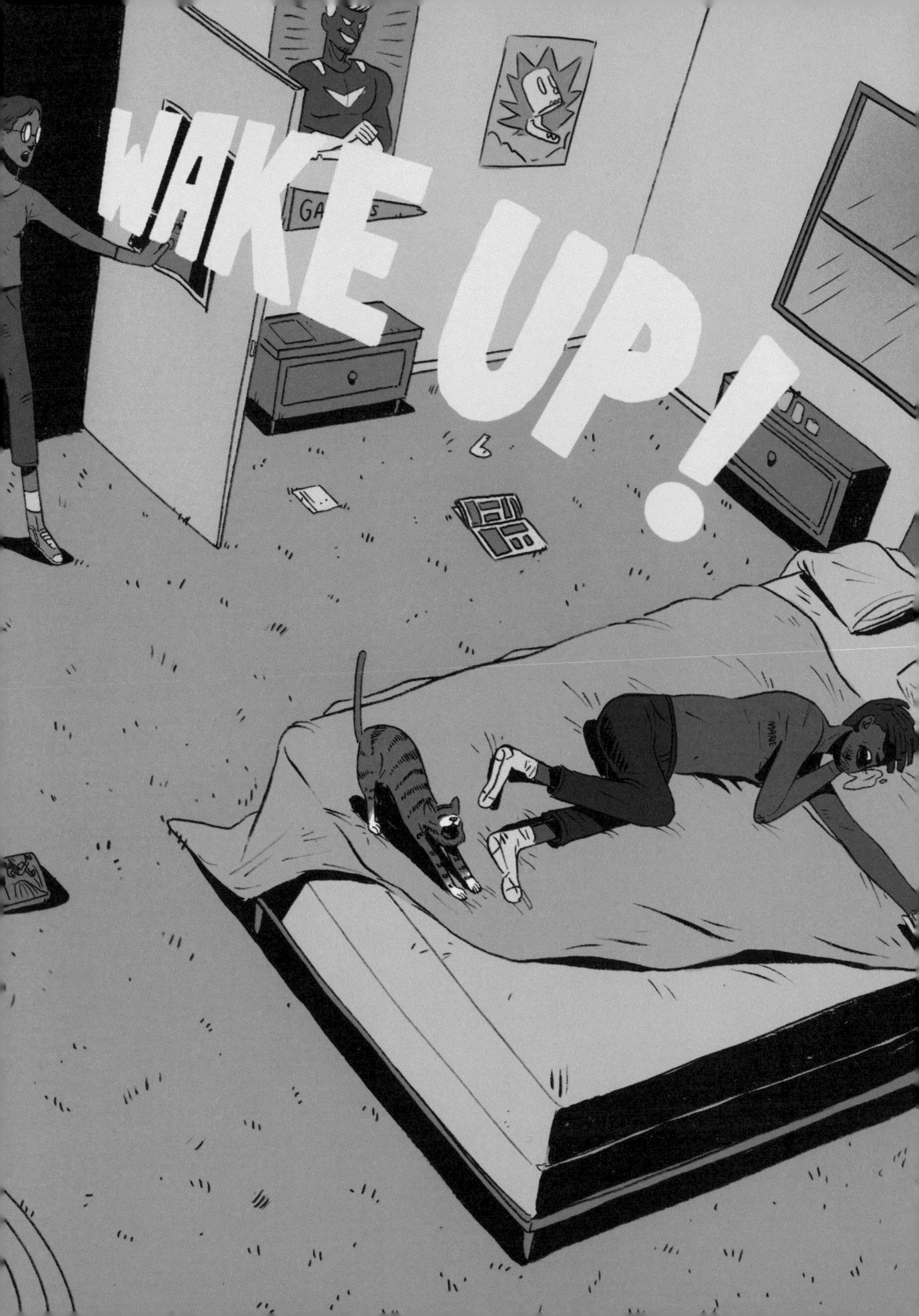
WAKE UP!

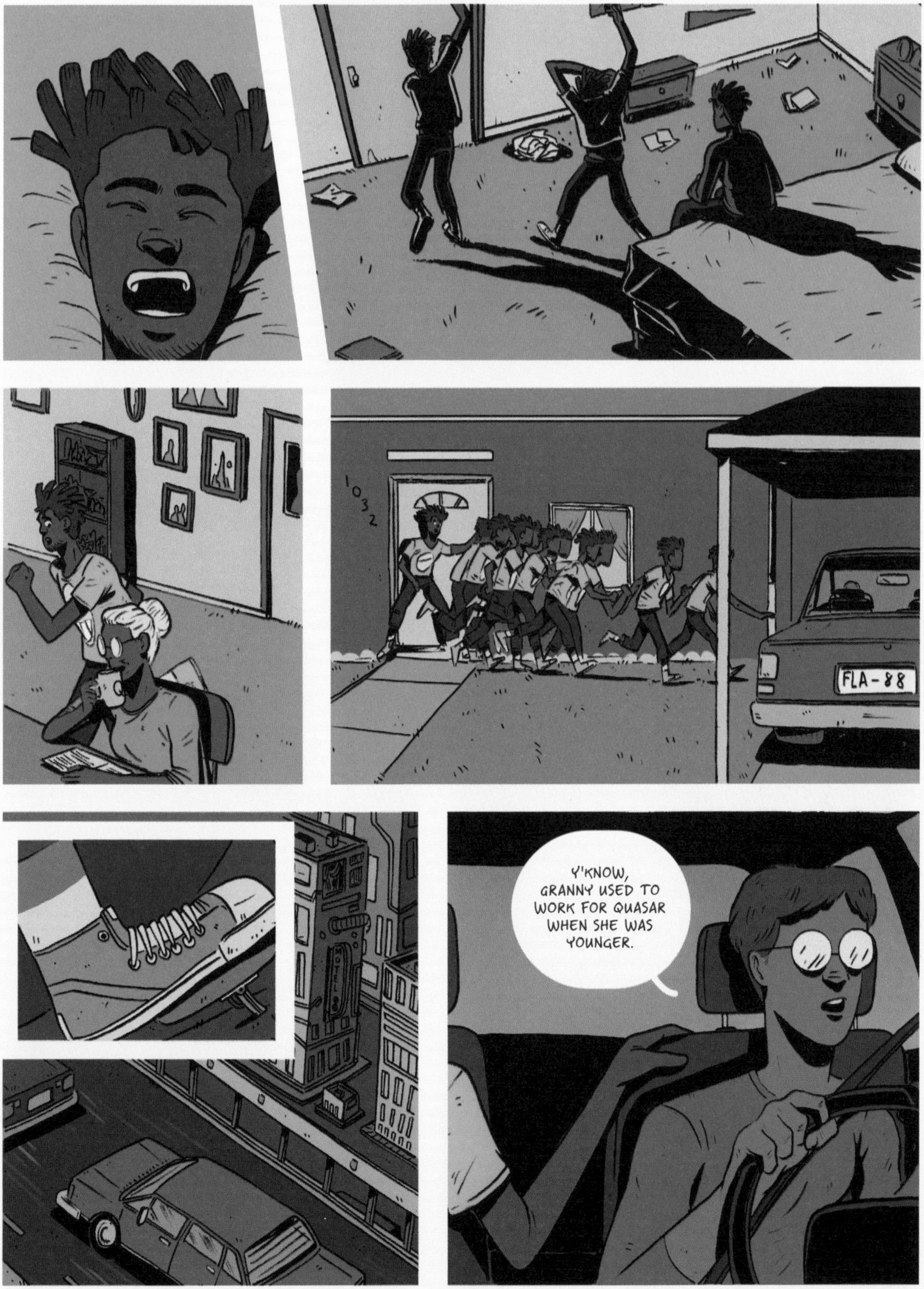
1032
FLA-88
Y'KNOW, GRANNY USED TO WORK FOR QUASAR WHEN SHE WAS YOUNGER.

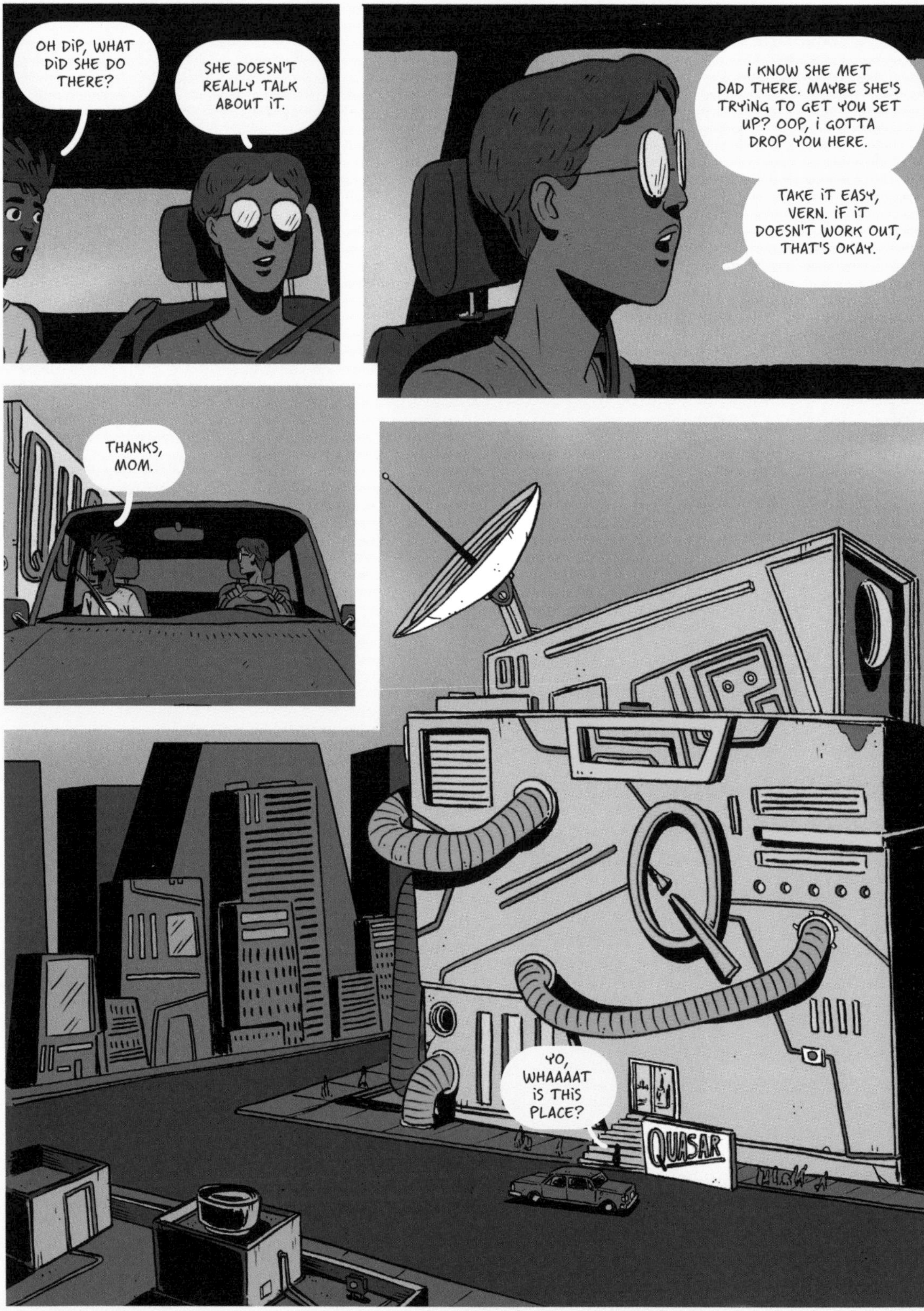
OH DIP, WHAT DID SHE DO THERE?
SHE DOESN'T REALLY TALK ABOUT IT.
I KNOW SHE MET DAD THERE. MAYBE SHE'S TRYING TO GET YOU SET UP? OOP, I GOTTA DROP YOU HERE.
TAKE IT EASY, VERN. IF IT DOESN'T WORK OUT, THAT'S OKAY.
THANKS, MOM.
YO, WHAAAAT IS THIS PLACE?
QUASAR

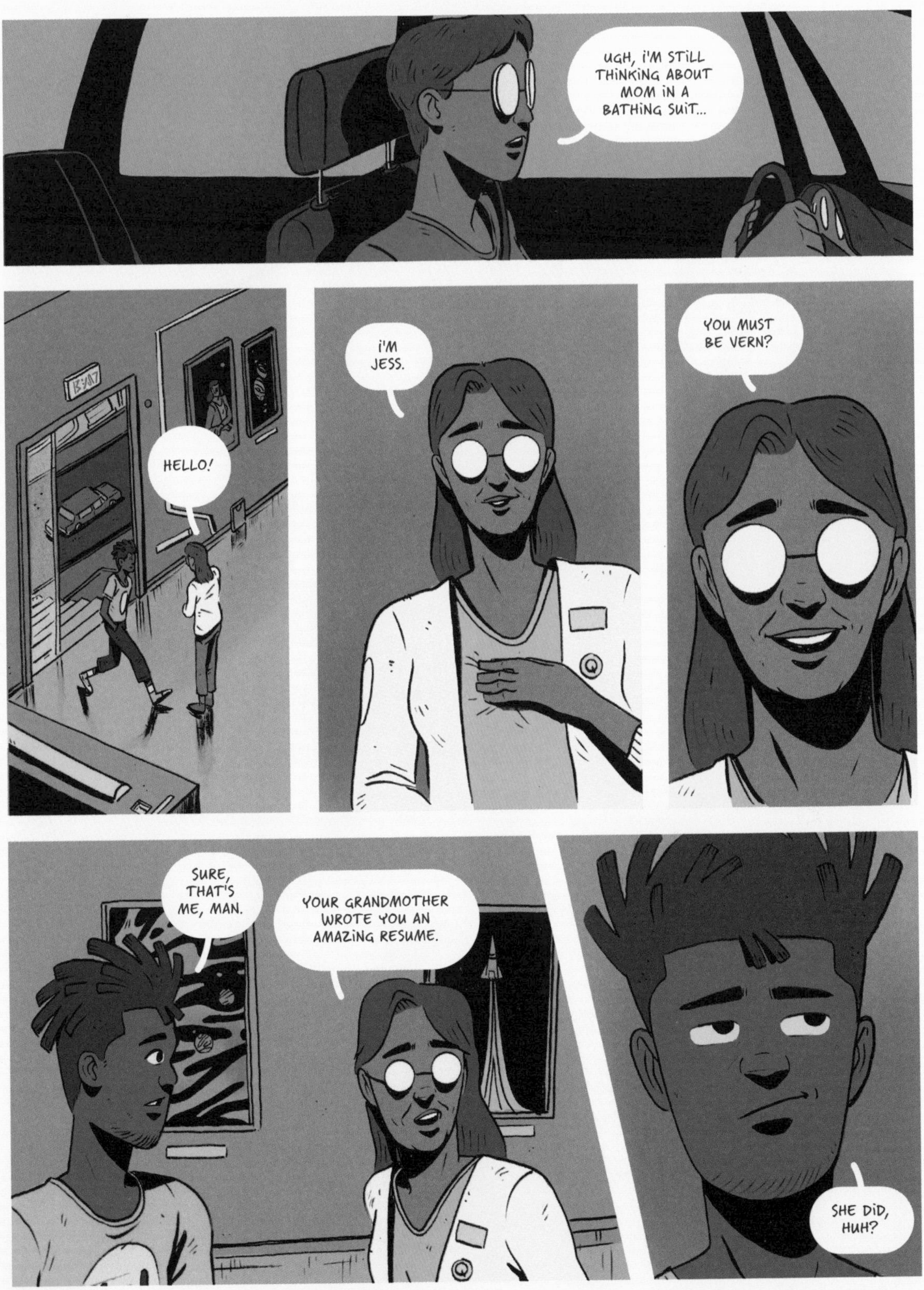
UGH, I'M STILL THINKING ABOUT MOM IN A BATHING SUIT...
HELLO!
I'M JESS.
YOU MUST BE VERN?
SURE, THAT'S ME, MAN.
YOUR GRANDMOTHER WROTE YOU AN AMAZING RESUME.
SHE DID, HUH?

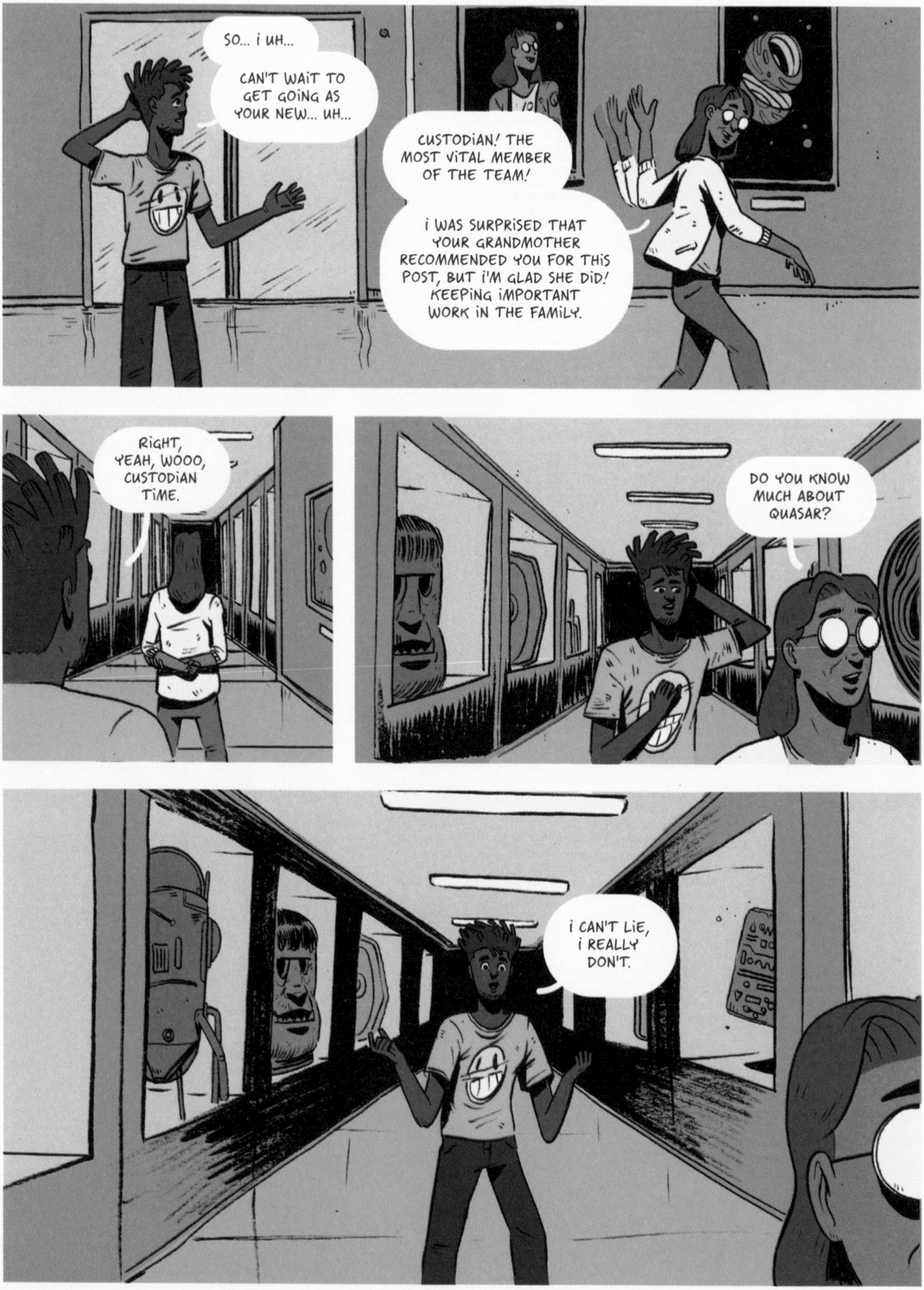
SO... i UH...
CAN'T WAiT TO GET GOiNG AS YOUR NEW... UH...
CUSTODiAN! THE MOST ViTAL MEMBER OF THE TEAM!
i WAS SURPRiSED THAT YOUR GRANDMOTHER RECOMMENDED YOU FOR THiS POST, BUT i'M GLAD SHE DiD! KEEPiNG iMPORTANT WORK iN THE FAMiLY.
RiGHT, YEAH, WOOO, CUSTODiAN TiME.
DO YOU KNOW MUCH ABOUT QUASAR?
i CAN'T LiE, i REALLY DON'T.

WE MADE REAL SPACE EXPLORATION POSSIBLE.

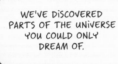

WE'VE DISCOVERED PARTS OF THE UNIVERSE YOU COULD ONLY DREAM OF.

AND NOW, OUR MOST IMPORTANT MISSION IS TO FIND A NEW HOME FOR HUMANS TO THRIVE IN.

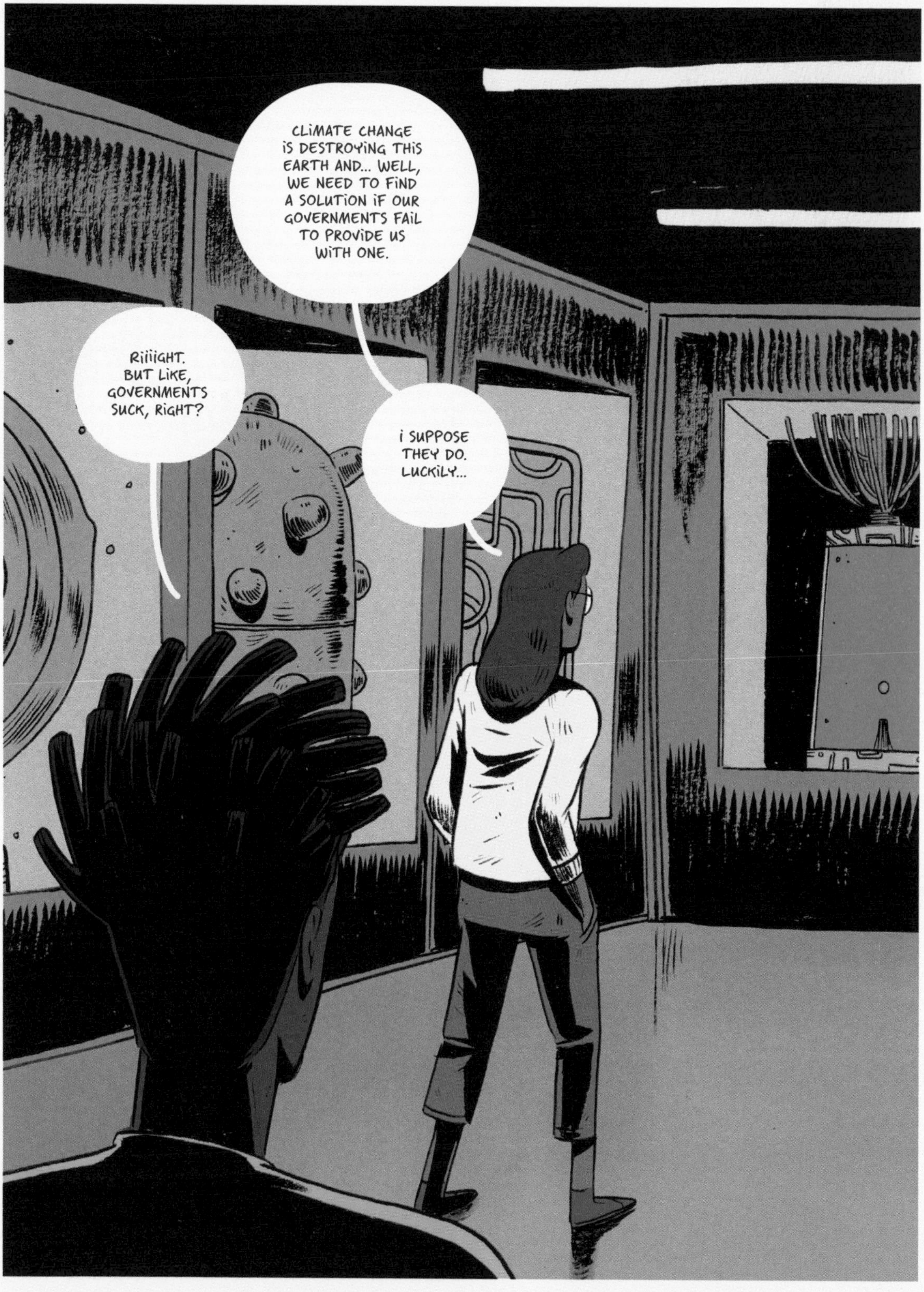
CLIMATE CHANGE IS DESTROYING THIS EARTH AND... WELL, WE NEED TO FIND A SOLUTION IF OUR GOVERNMENTS FAIL TO PROVIDE US WITH ONE.
RIIIIGHT. BUT LIKE, GOVERNMENTS SUCK, RIGHT?
I SUPPOSE THEY DO. LUCKILY...

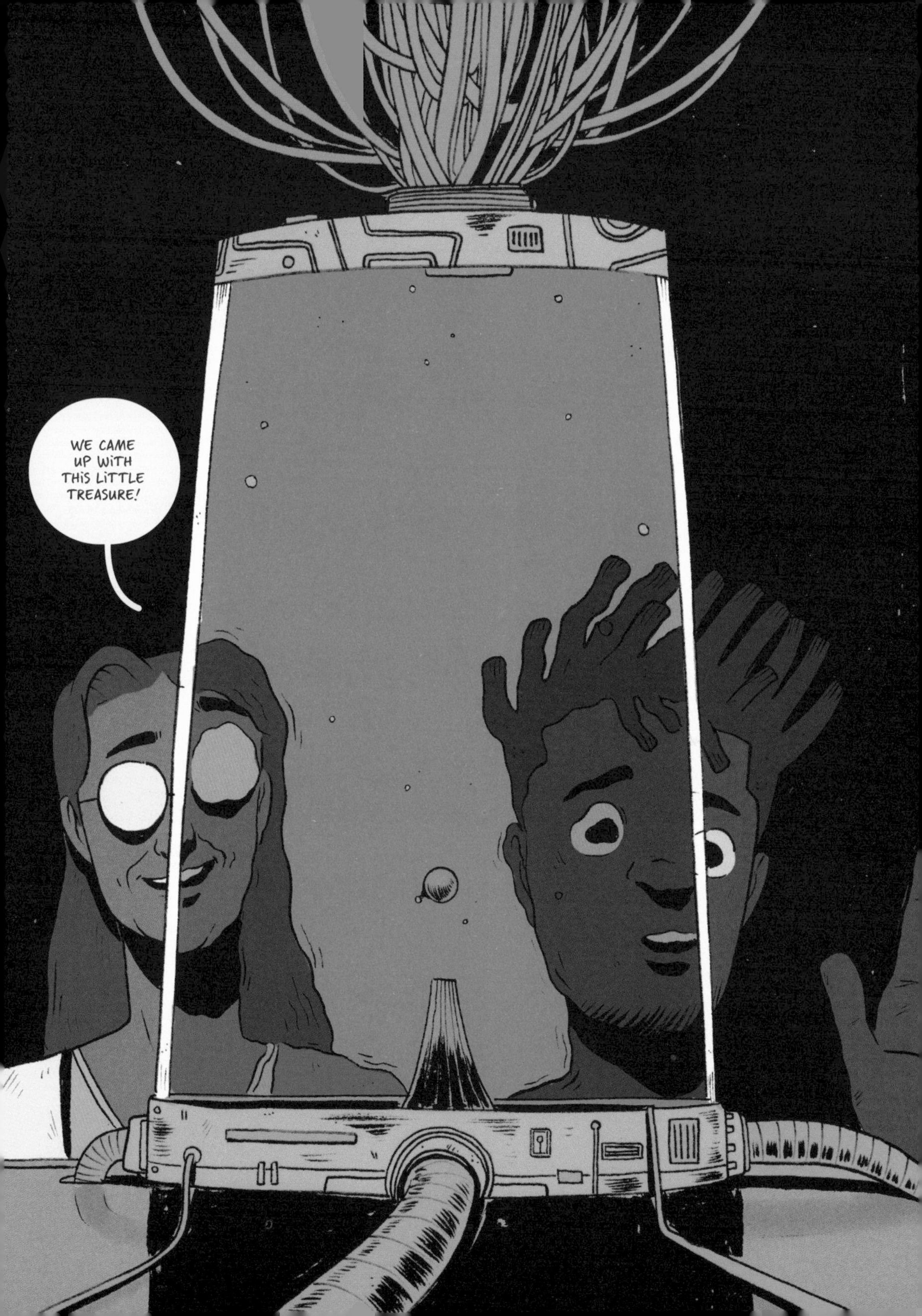
WE CAME UP WITH THIS LITTLE TREASURE!

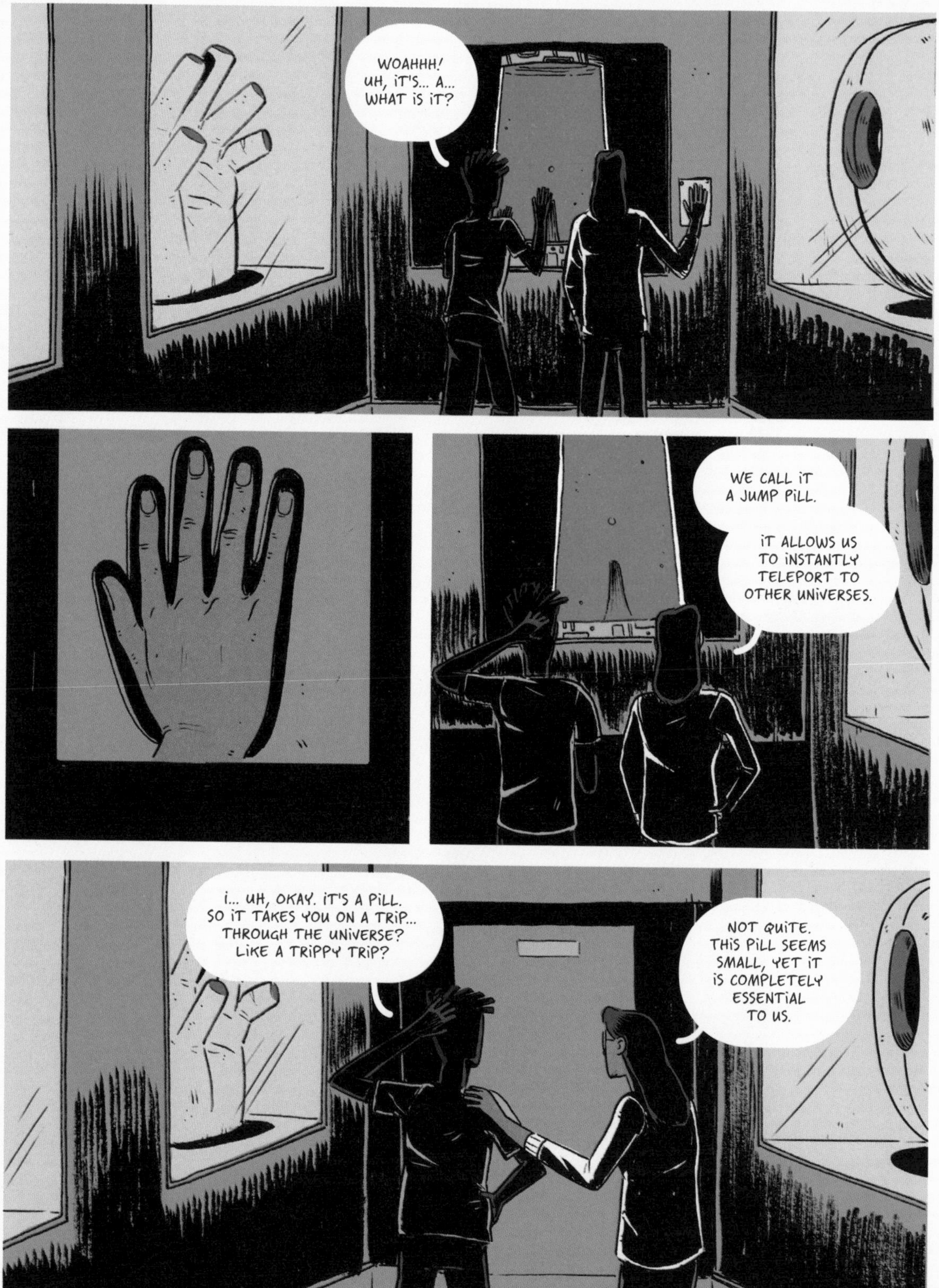
WOAHHH! UH, IT'S... A... WHAT IS IT?
WE CALL IT A JUMP PILL.
IT ALLOWS US TO INSTANTLY TELEPORT TO OTHER UNIVERSES.
I... UH, OKAY. IT'S A PILL. SO IT TAKES YOU ON A TRIP... THROUGH THE UNIVERSE? LIKE A TRIPPY TRIP?
NOT QUITE. THIS PILL SEEMS SMALL, YET IT IS COMPLETELY ESSENTIAL TO US.

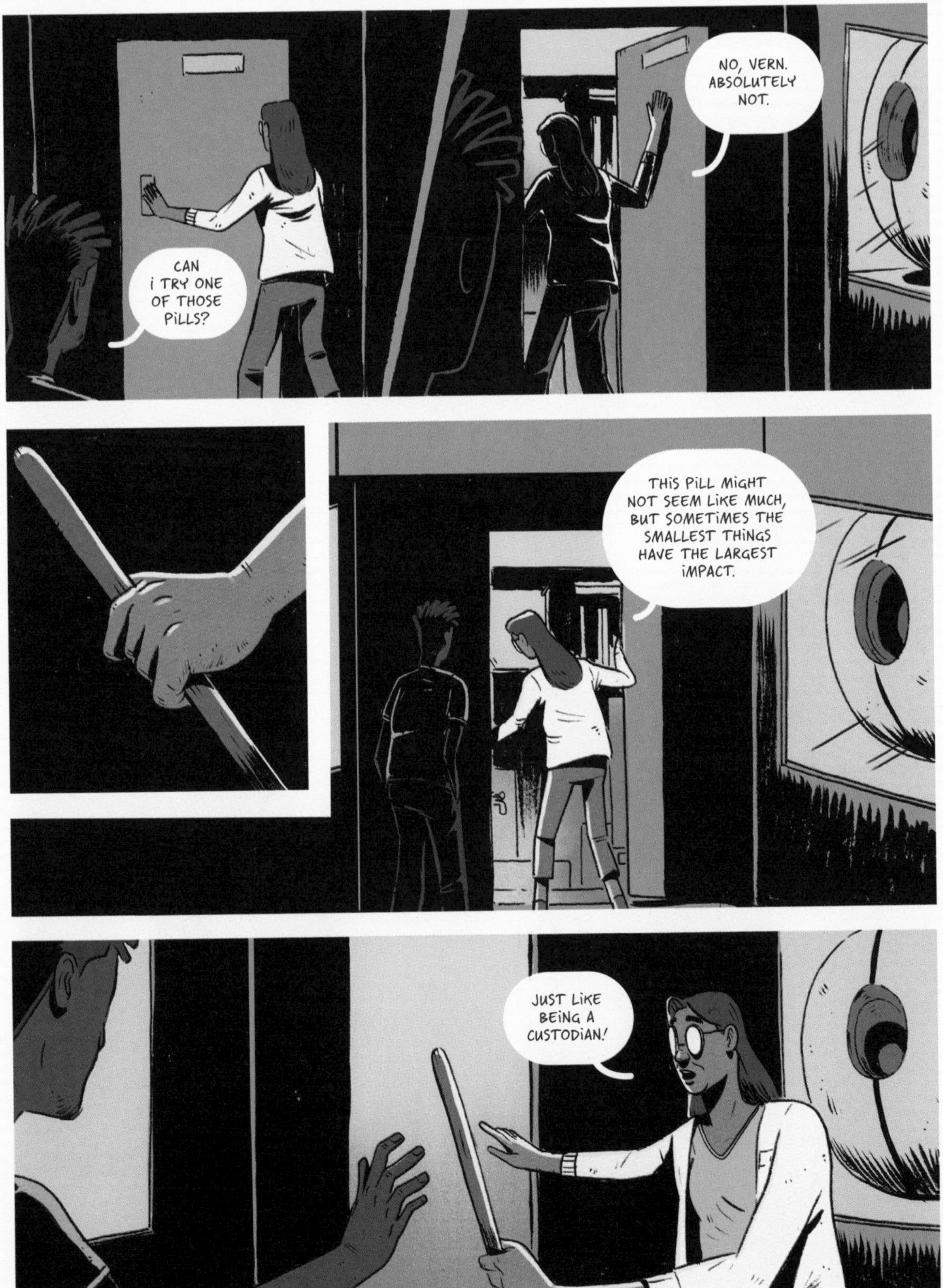
CAN I TRY ONE OF THOSE PILLS?
NO, VERN. ABSOLUTELY NOT.
THIS PILL MIGHT NOT SEEM LIKE MUCH, BUT SOMETIMES THE SMALLEST THINGS HAVE THE LARGEST IMPACT.
JUST LIKE BEING A CUSTODIAN!

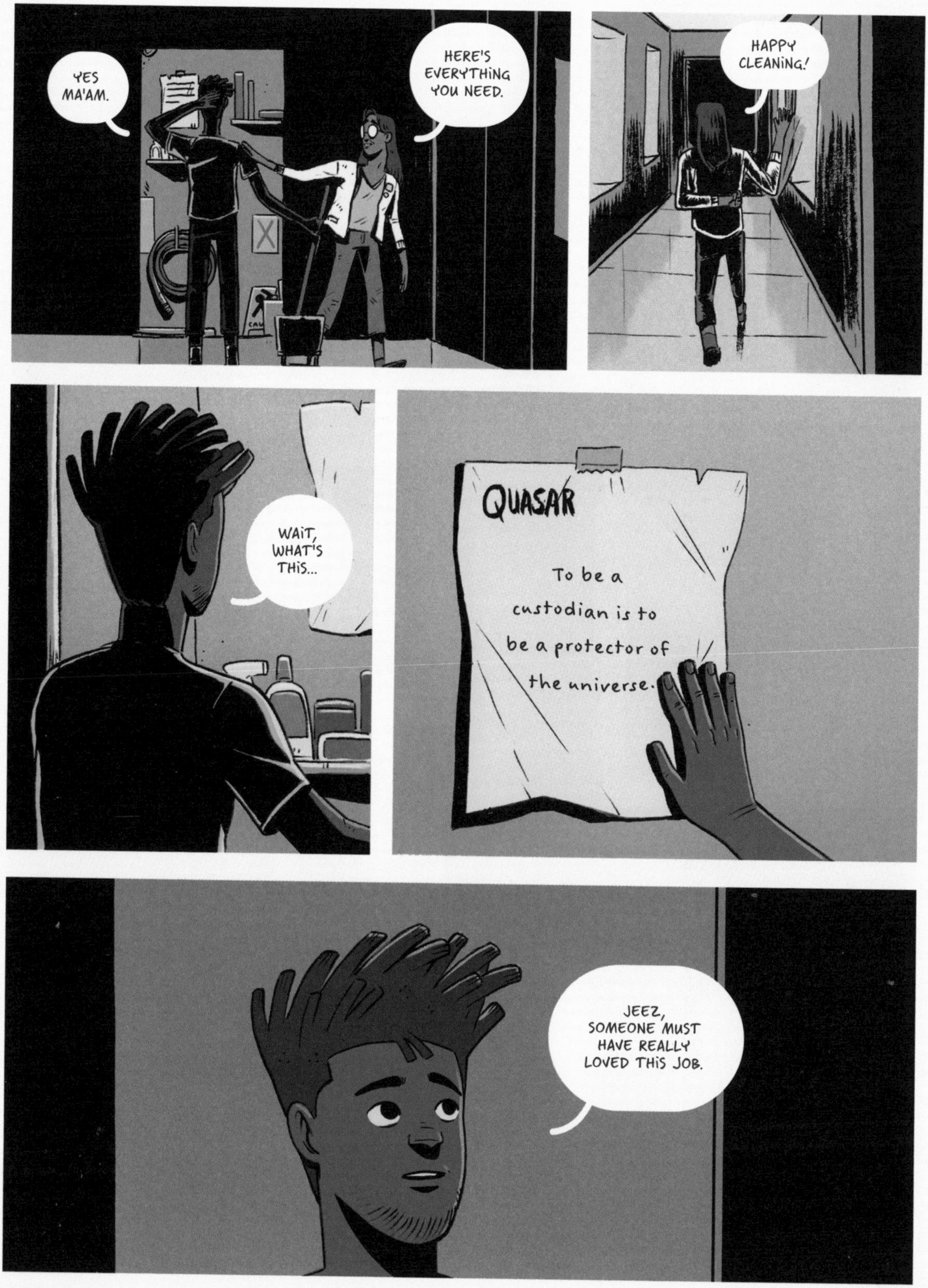
YES MA'AM.
HERE'S EVERYTHING YOU NEED.
HAPPY CLEANING!
WAIT, WHAT'S THIS...
QUASAR
To be a custodian is to be a protector of the universe.
JEEZ, SOMEONE MUST HAVE REALLY LOVED THIS JOB.

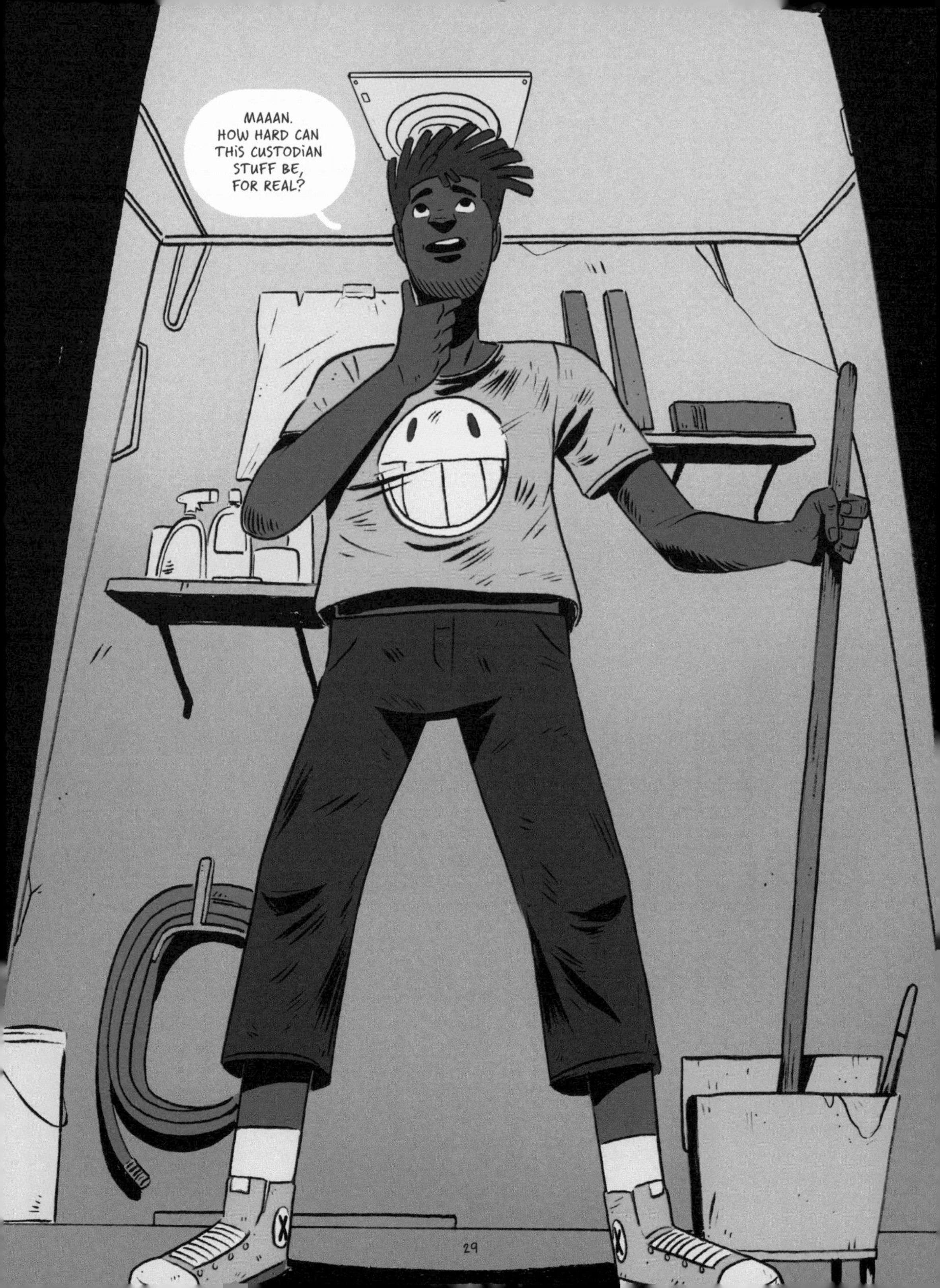
MAAAN. HOW HARD CAN THIS CUSTODIAN STUFF BE, FOR REAL?

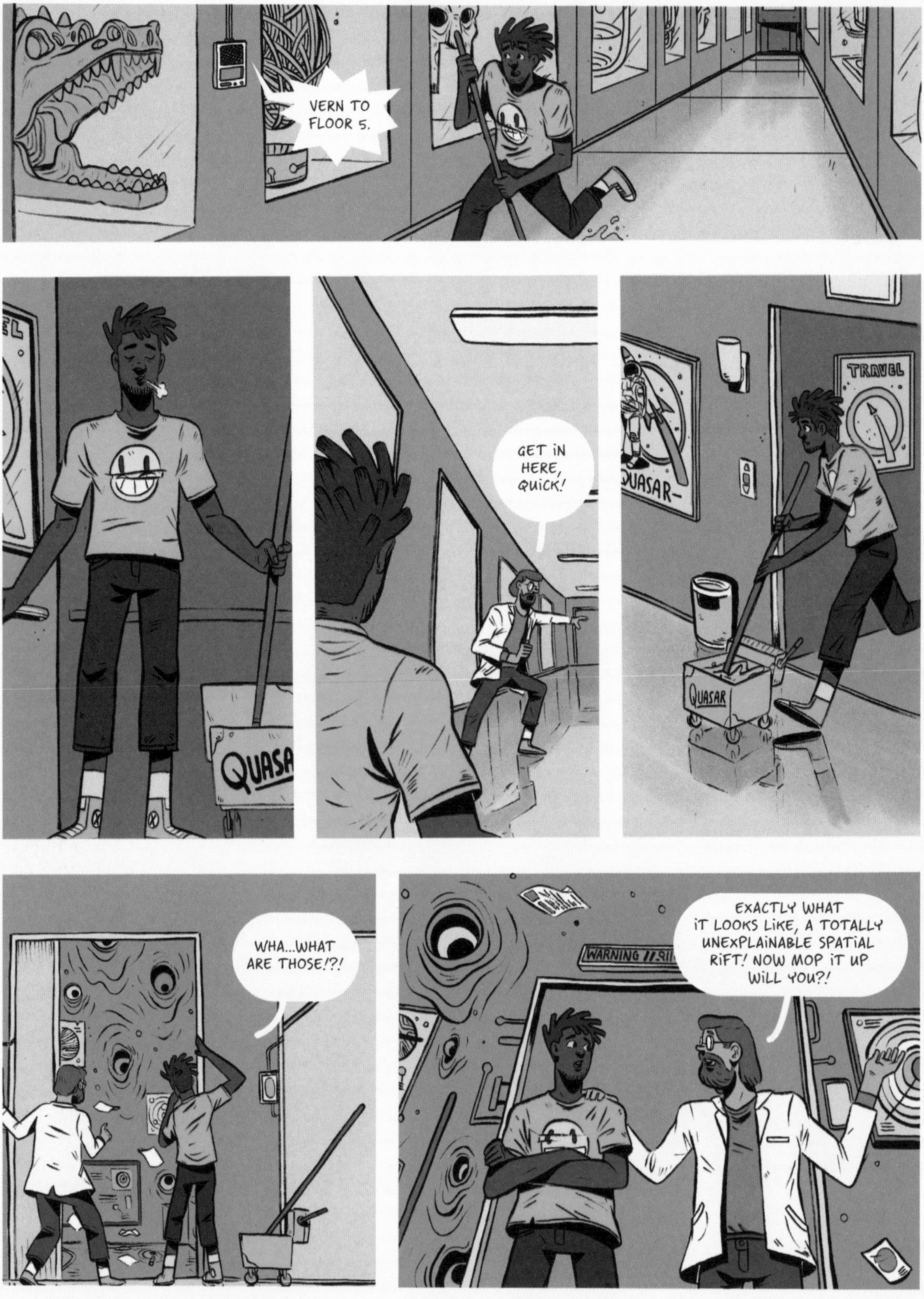
VERN TO FLOOR 5.
GET IN HERE, QUICK!
QUASAR
WHA...WHAT ARE THOSE!?!
WARNING
EXACTLY WHAT IT LOOKS LIKE, A TOTALLY UNEXPLAINABLE SPATIAL RIFT! NOW MOP IT UP WILL YOU?!

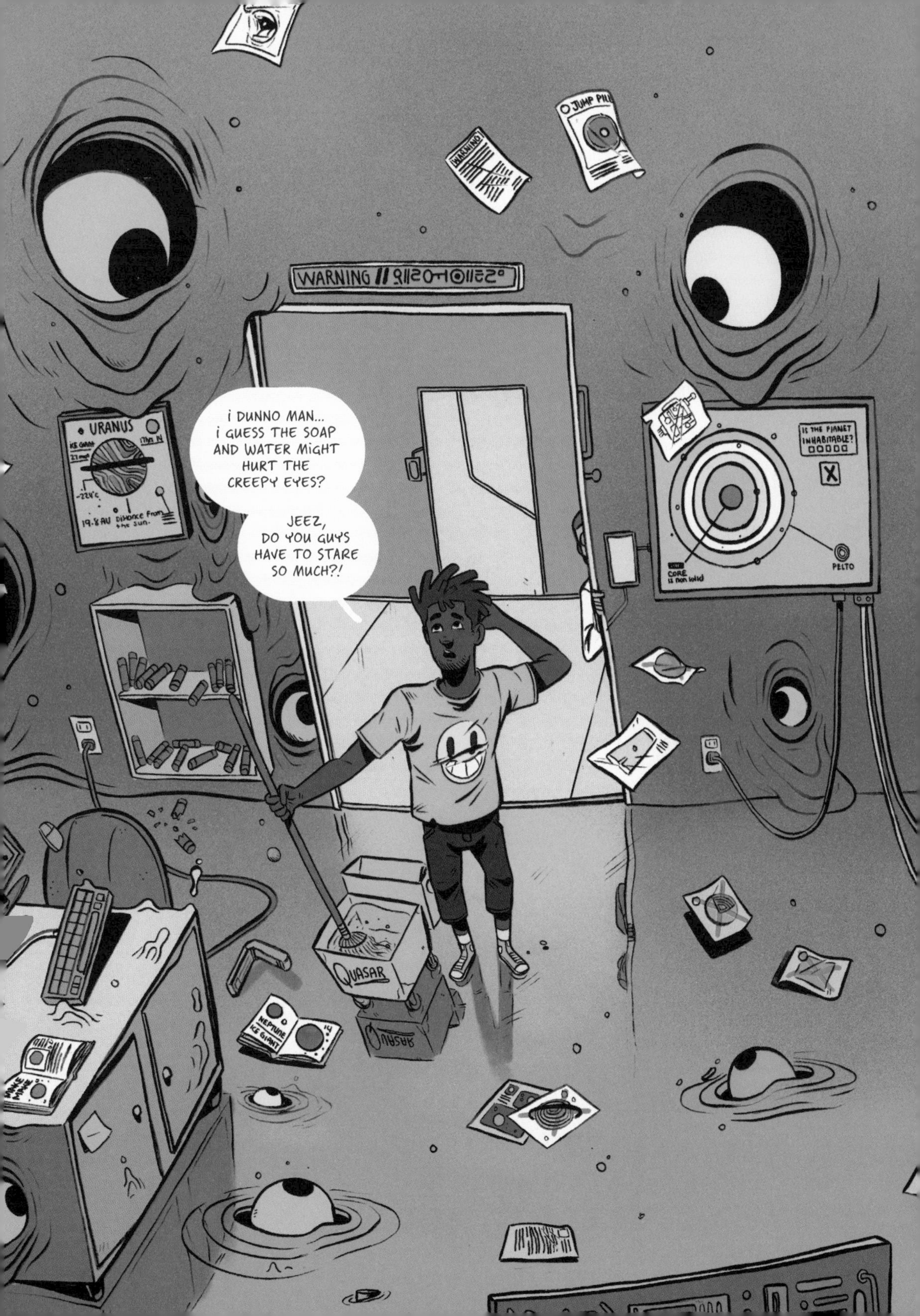

WARNING
URANUS
I DUNNO MAN... I GUESS THE SOAP AND WATER MIGHT HURT THE CREEPY EYES?
JEEZ, DO YOU GUYS HAVE TO STARE SO MUCH?!
JUMP PILL
IS THE PLANET INHABITABLE?
PELTO
QUASAR
NEPTUNE ICE GIANT

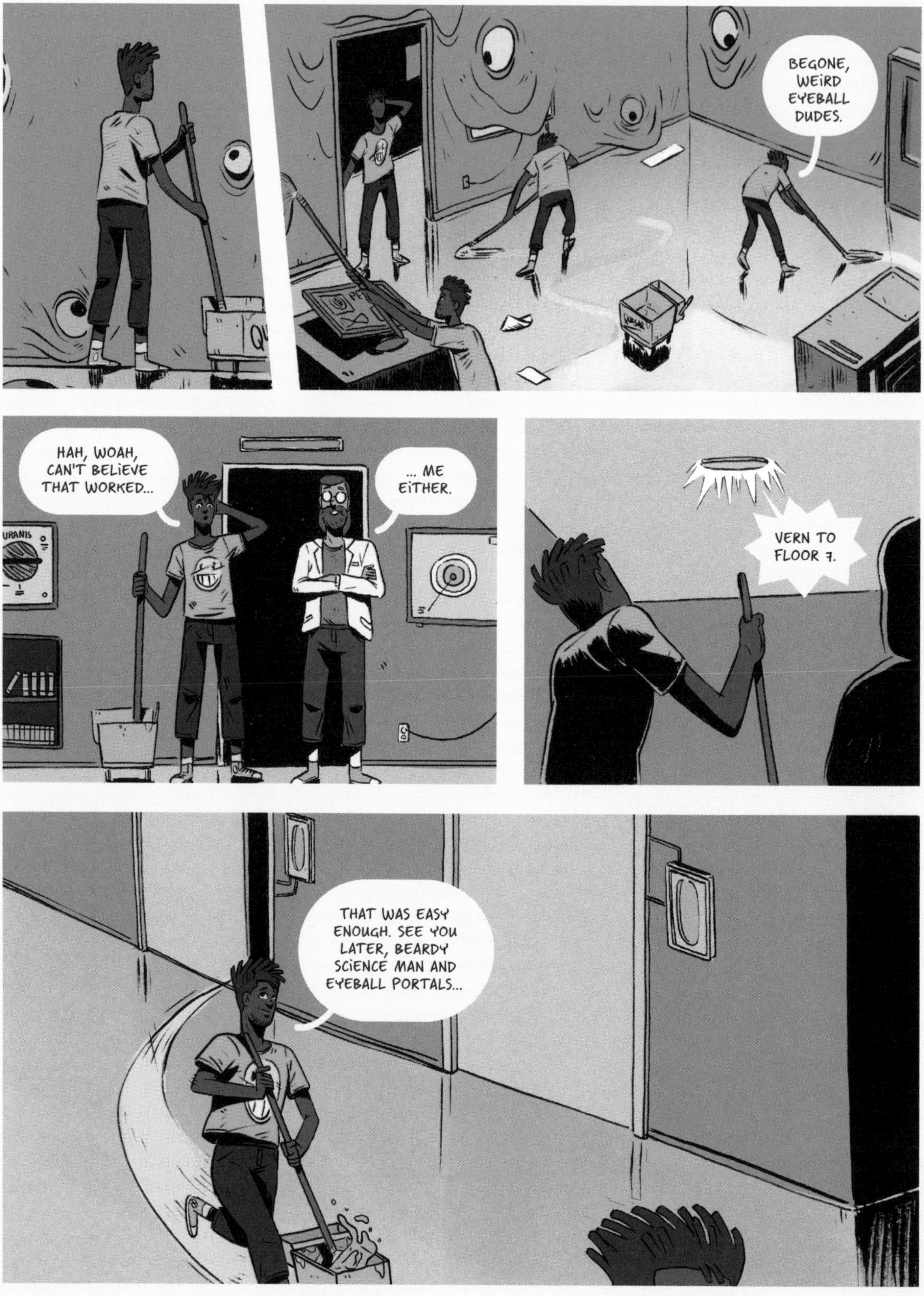
BEGONE, WEIRD EYEBALL DUDES.
HAH, WOAH, CAN'T BELIEVE THAT WORKED...
... ME EITHER.
URANIS
VERN TO FLOOR 7.
THAT WAS EASY ENOUGH. SEE YOU LATER, BEARDY SCIENCE MAN AND EYEBALL PORTALS...

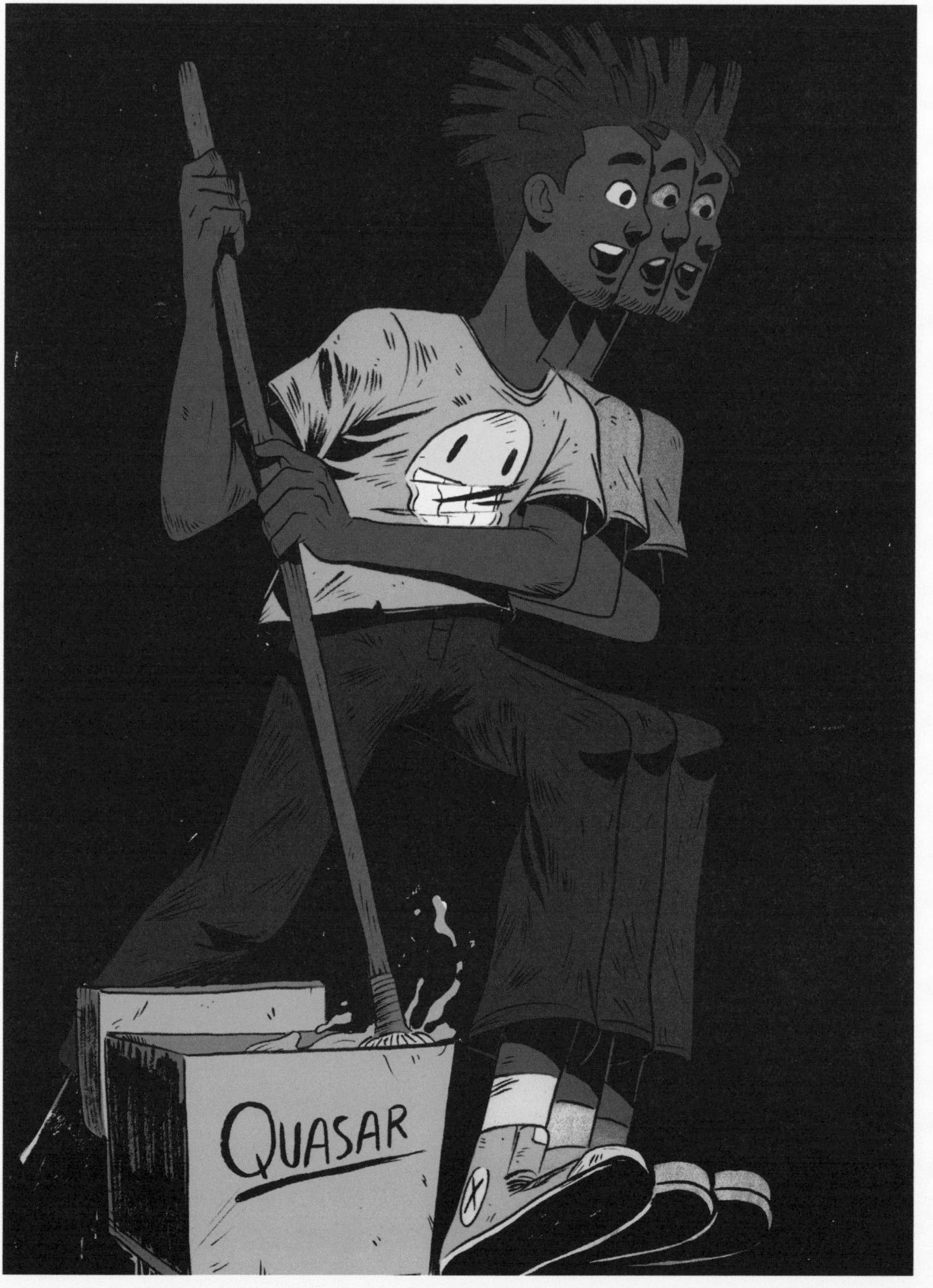
QUASAR

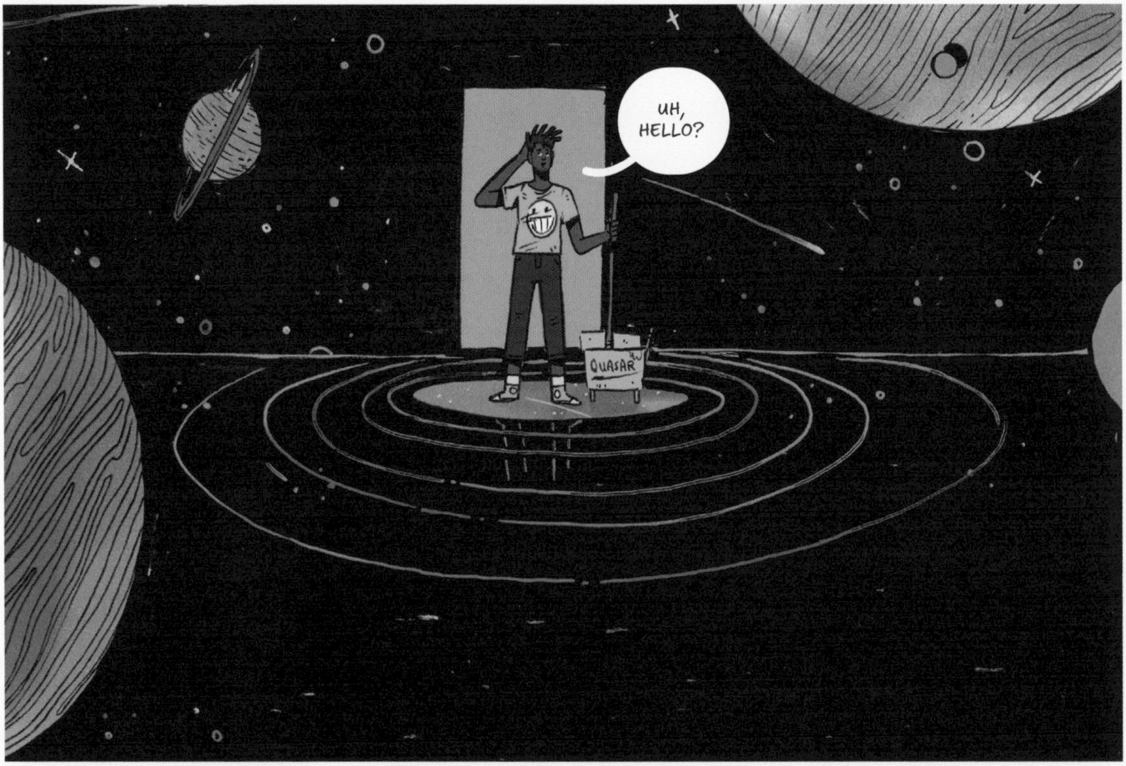
UH, HELLO?
QUASAR

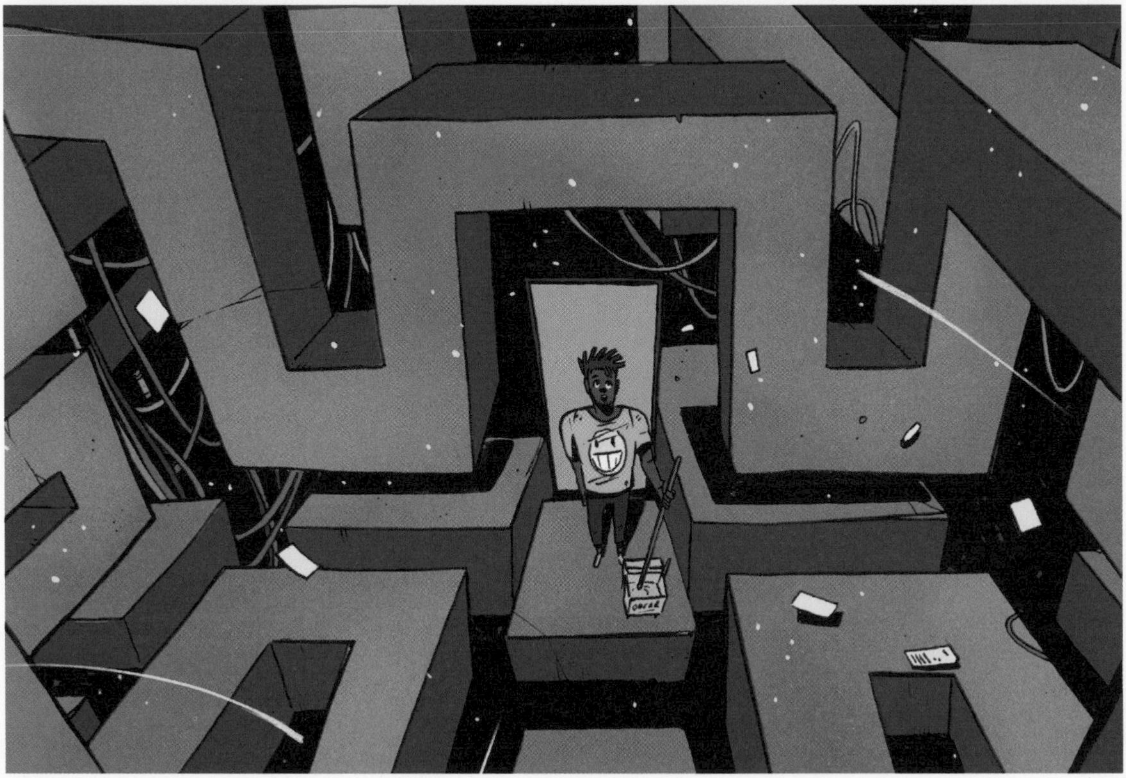

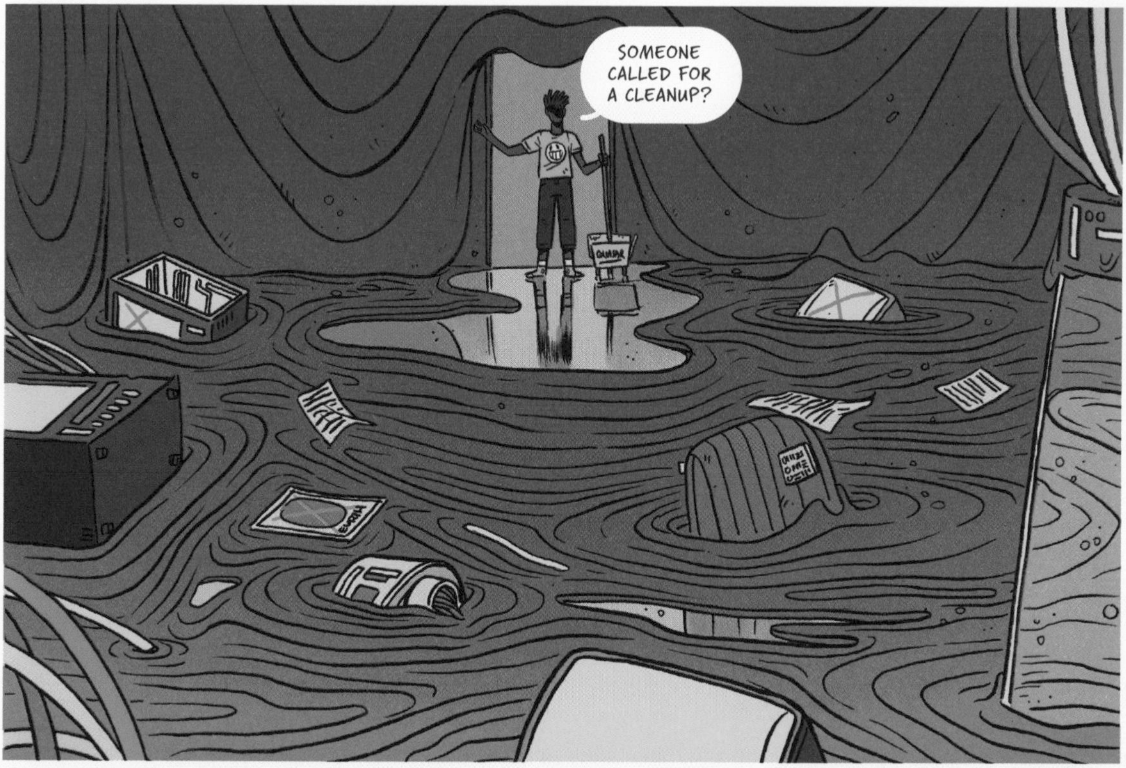
SOMEONE CALLED FOR A CLEANUP?

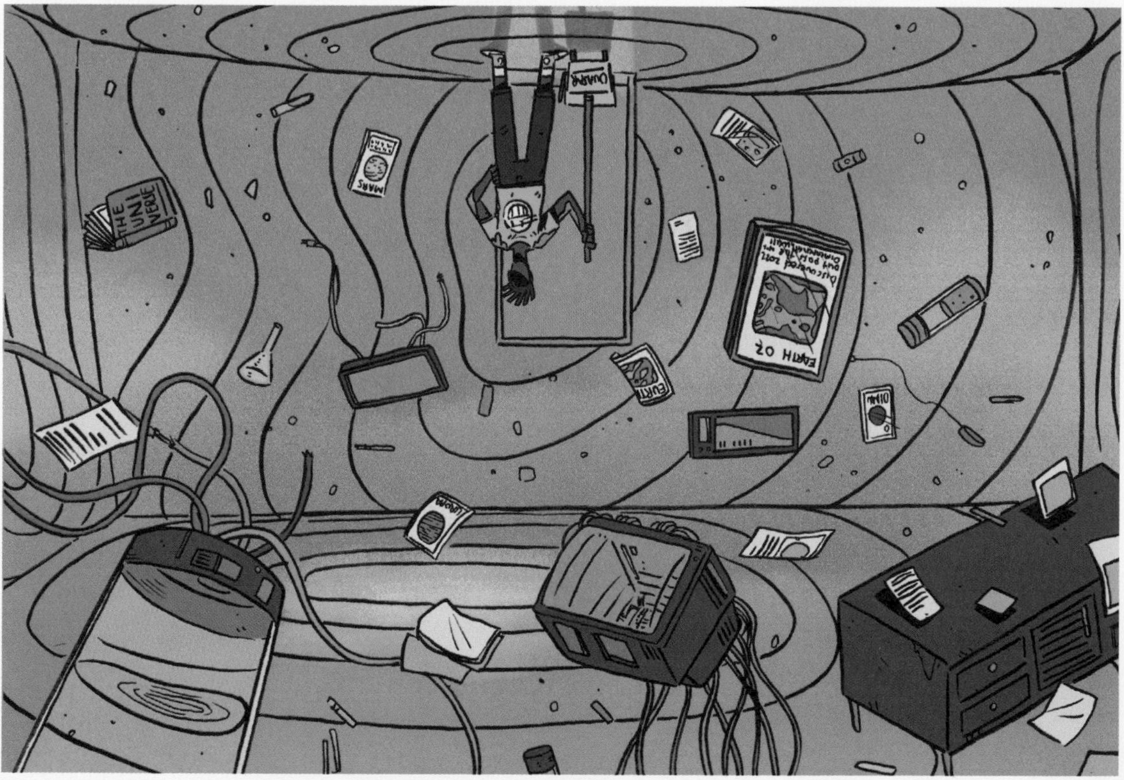

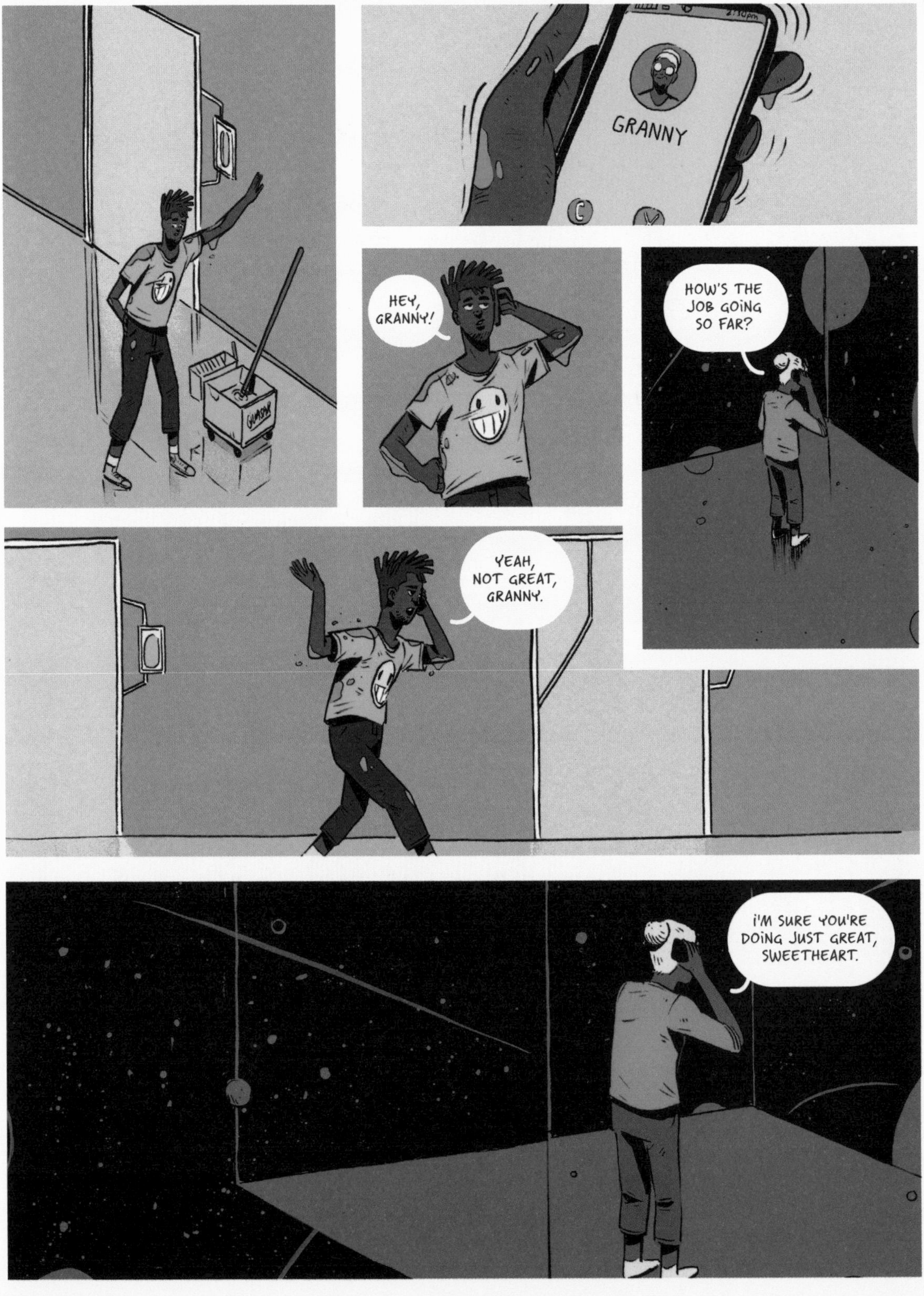
GRANNY
HEY, GRANNY!
HOW'S THE JOB GOING SO FAR?
YEAH, NOT GREAT, GRANNY.
I'M SURE YOU'RE DOING JUST GREAT, SWEETHEART.

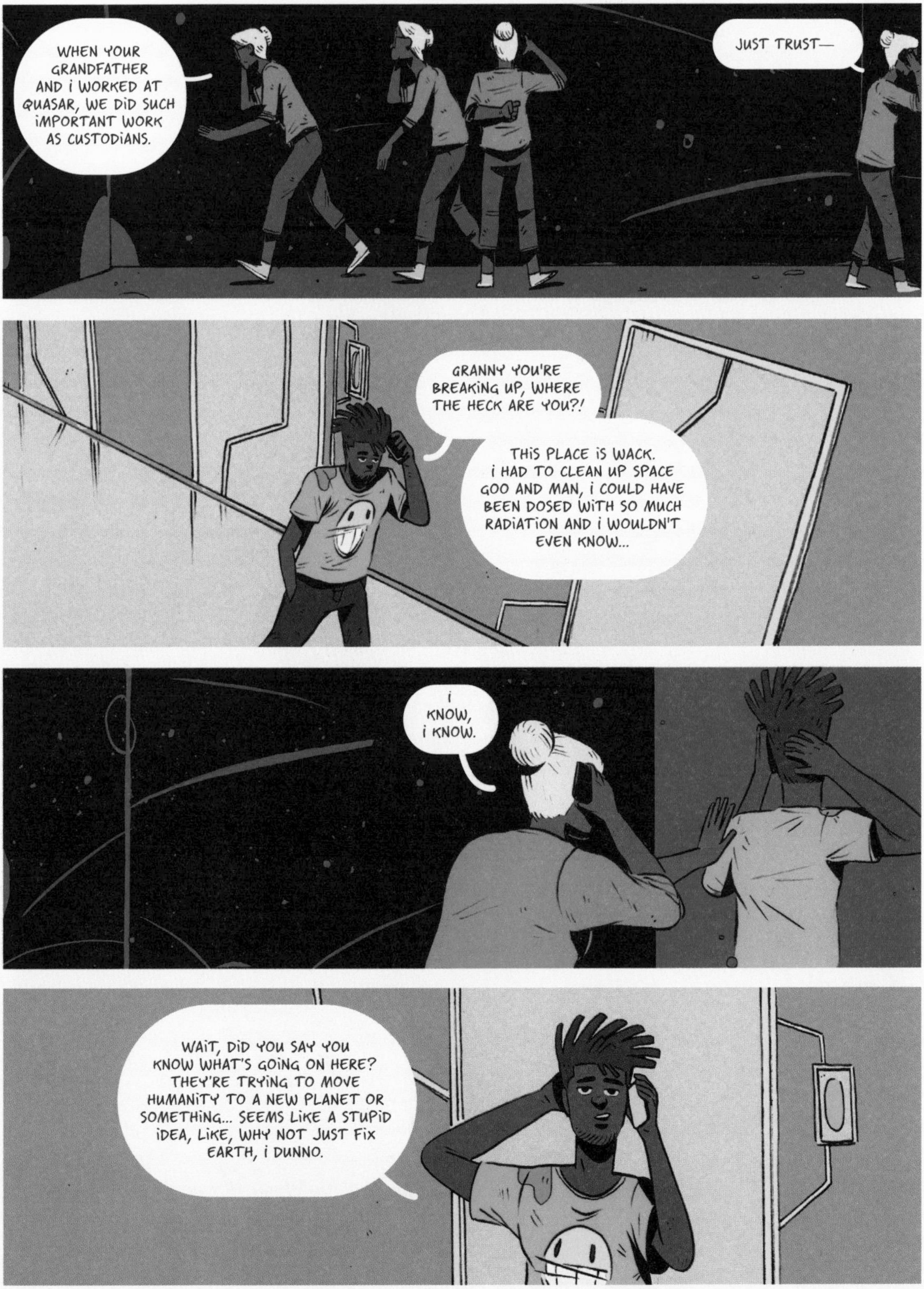
WHEN YOUR GRANDFATHER AND i WORKED AT QUASAR, WE DID SUCH iMPORTANT WORK AS CUSTODIANS.
JUST TRUST—
GRANNY YOU'RE BREAKiNG UP, WHERE THE HECK ARE YOU?!
THiS PLACE iS WACK. i HAD TO CLEAN UP SPACE GOO AND MAN, i COULD HAVE BEEN DOSED WiTH SO MUCH RADiATiON AND i WOULDN'T EVEN KNOW...
i KNOW, i KNOW.
WAiT, DiD YOU SAY YOU KNOW WHAT'S GOiNG ON HERE? THEY'RE TRYiNG TO MOVE HUMANiTY TO A NEW PLANET OR SOMETHiNG... SEEMS LiKE A STUPiD iDEA, LiKE, WHY NOT JUST FiX EARTH, i DUNNO.

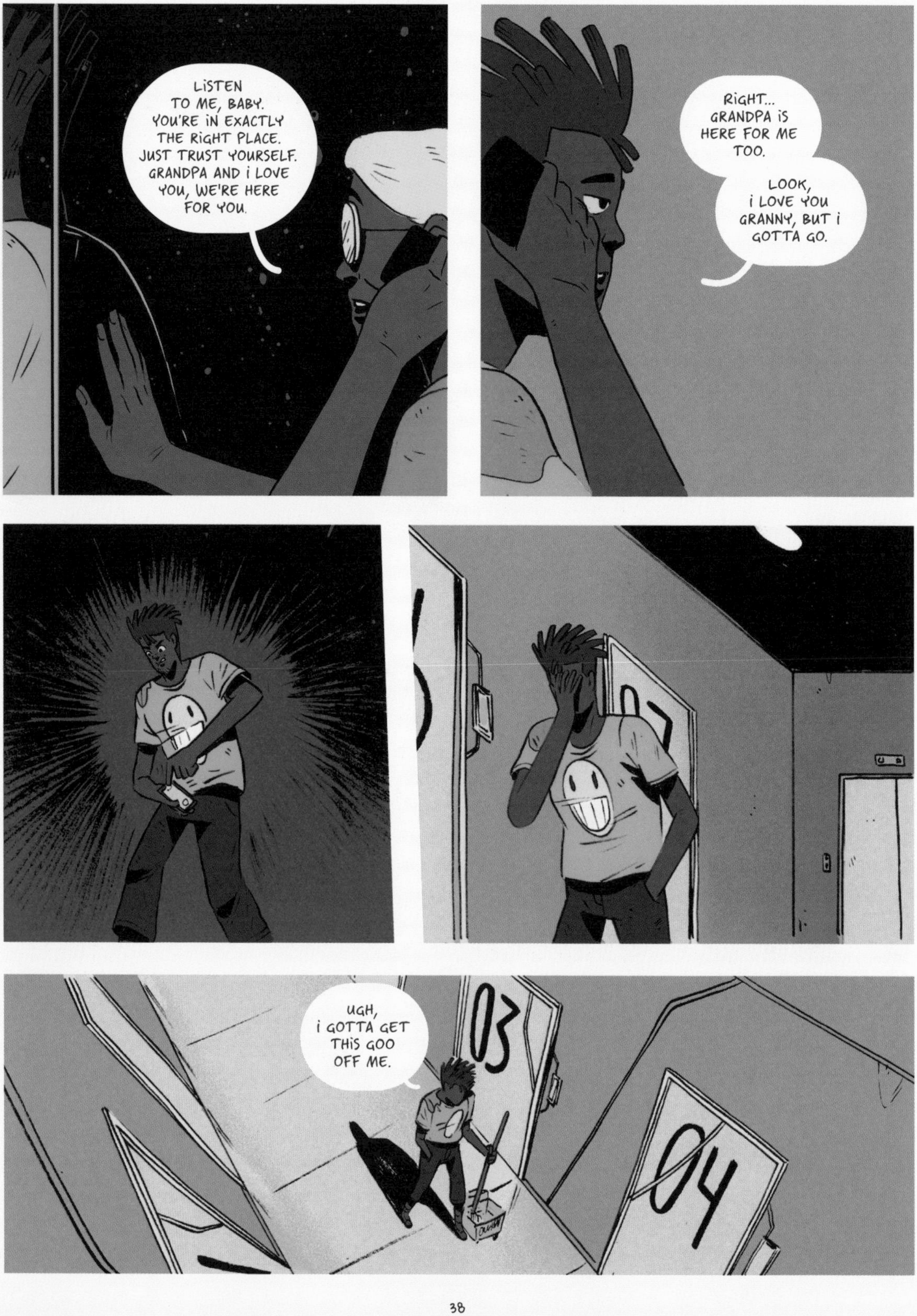
LISTEN TO ME, BABY. YOU'RE IN EXACTLY THE RIGHT PLACE. JUST TRUST YOURSELF. GRANDPA AND I LOVE YOU, WE'RE HERE FOR YOU.
RIGHT... GRANDPA IS HERE FOR ME TOO.
LOOK, I LOVE YOU GRANNY, BUT I GOTTA GO.
03
04
UGH, I GOTTA GET THIS GOO OFF ME.

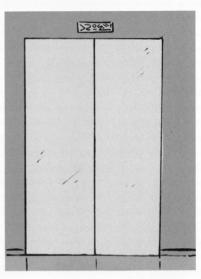

THAT'S WEIRD...
THERE'S ONLY ONE
DOOR UP HERE?

WHAT'S WITH
THIS CHUNKY 90s
LOOKIN' COMPUTER?
I THOUGHT THIS PLACE
WAS HIGH TECH.

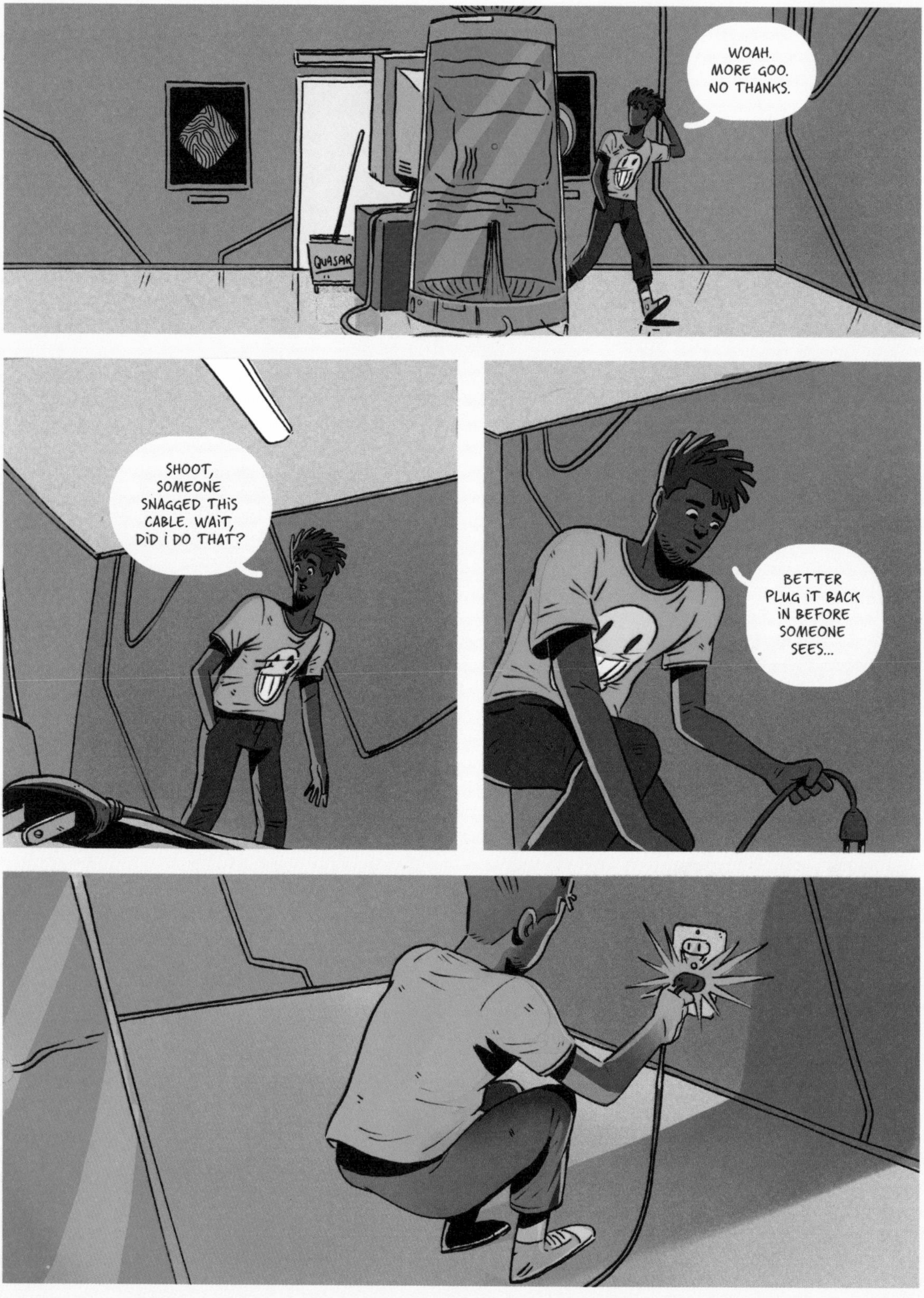
WOAH. MORE GOO. NO THANKS.
QUASAR
SHOOT, SOMEONE SNAGGED THIS CABLE. WAIT, DID I DO THAT?
BETTER PLUG IT BACK IN BEFORE SOMEONE SEES...

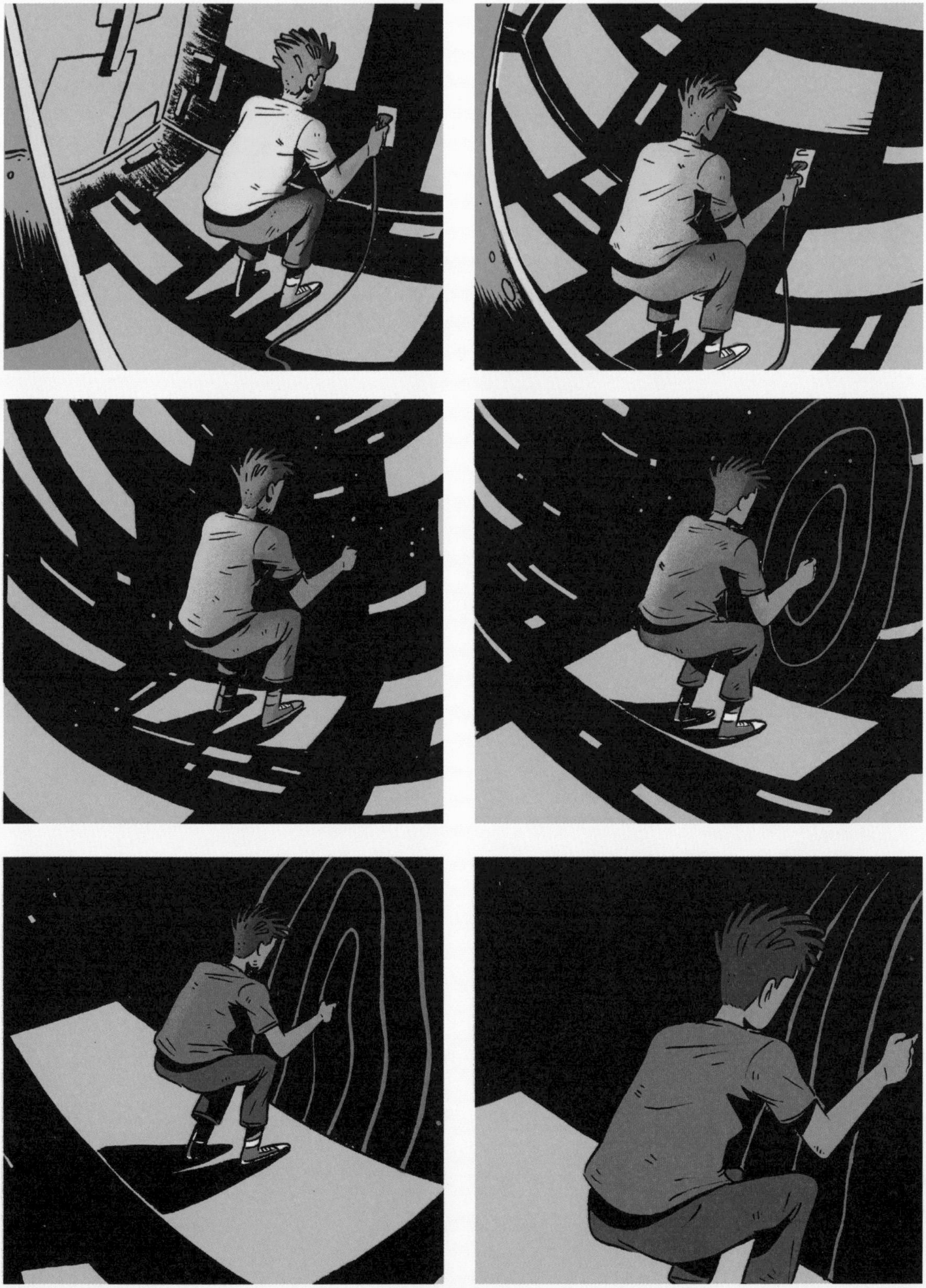

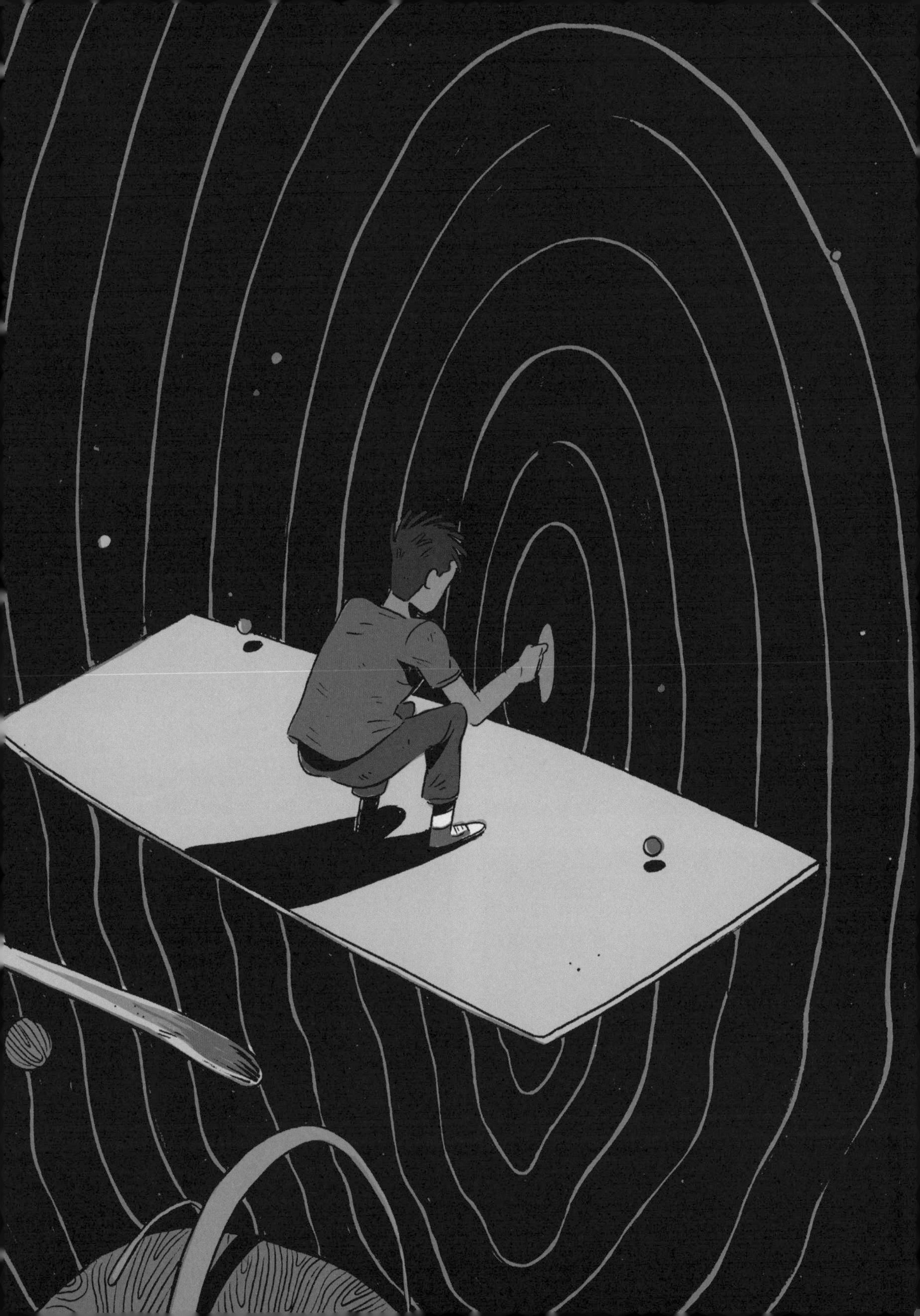

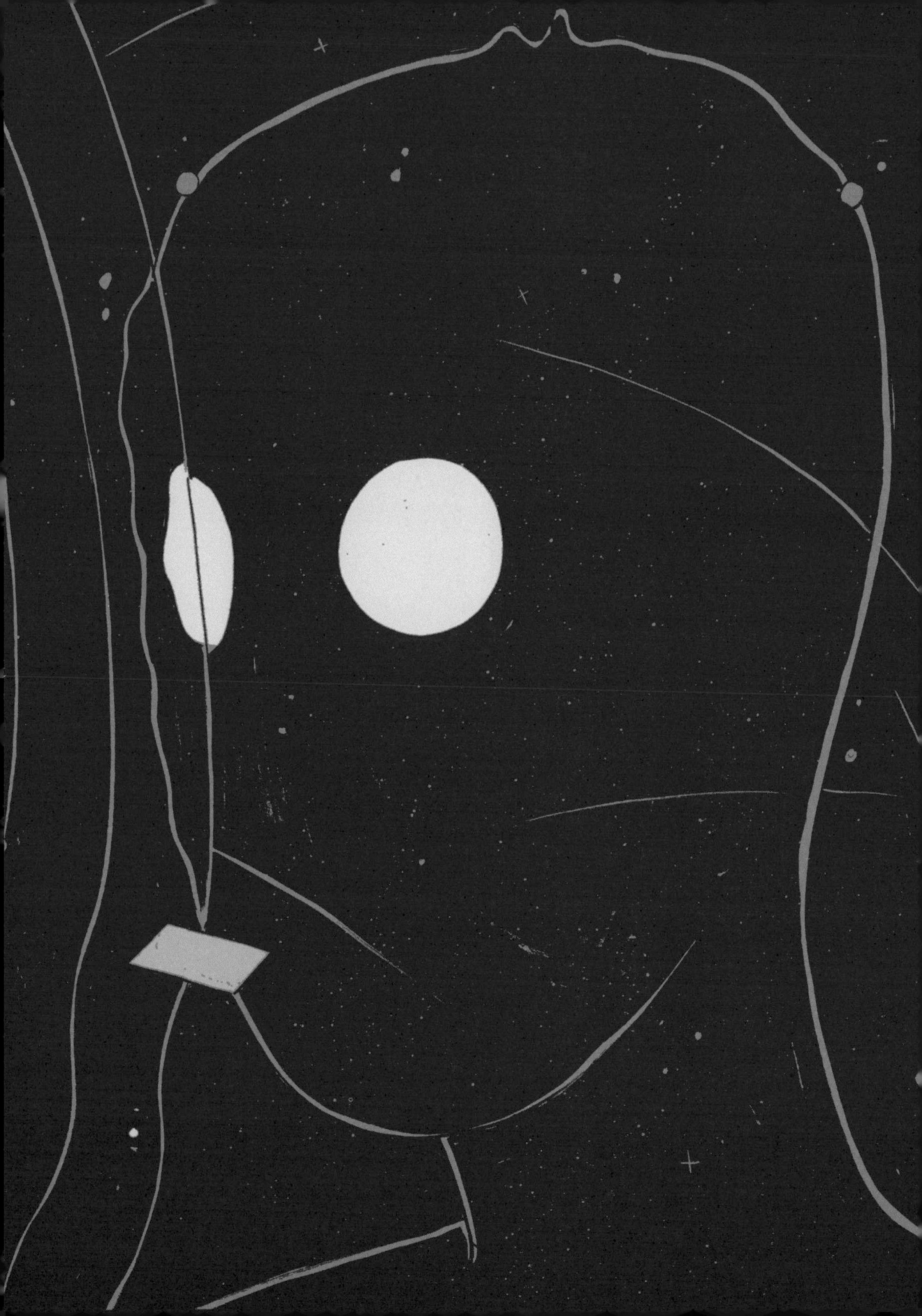

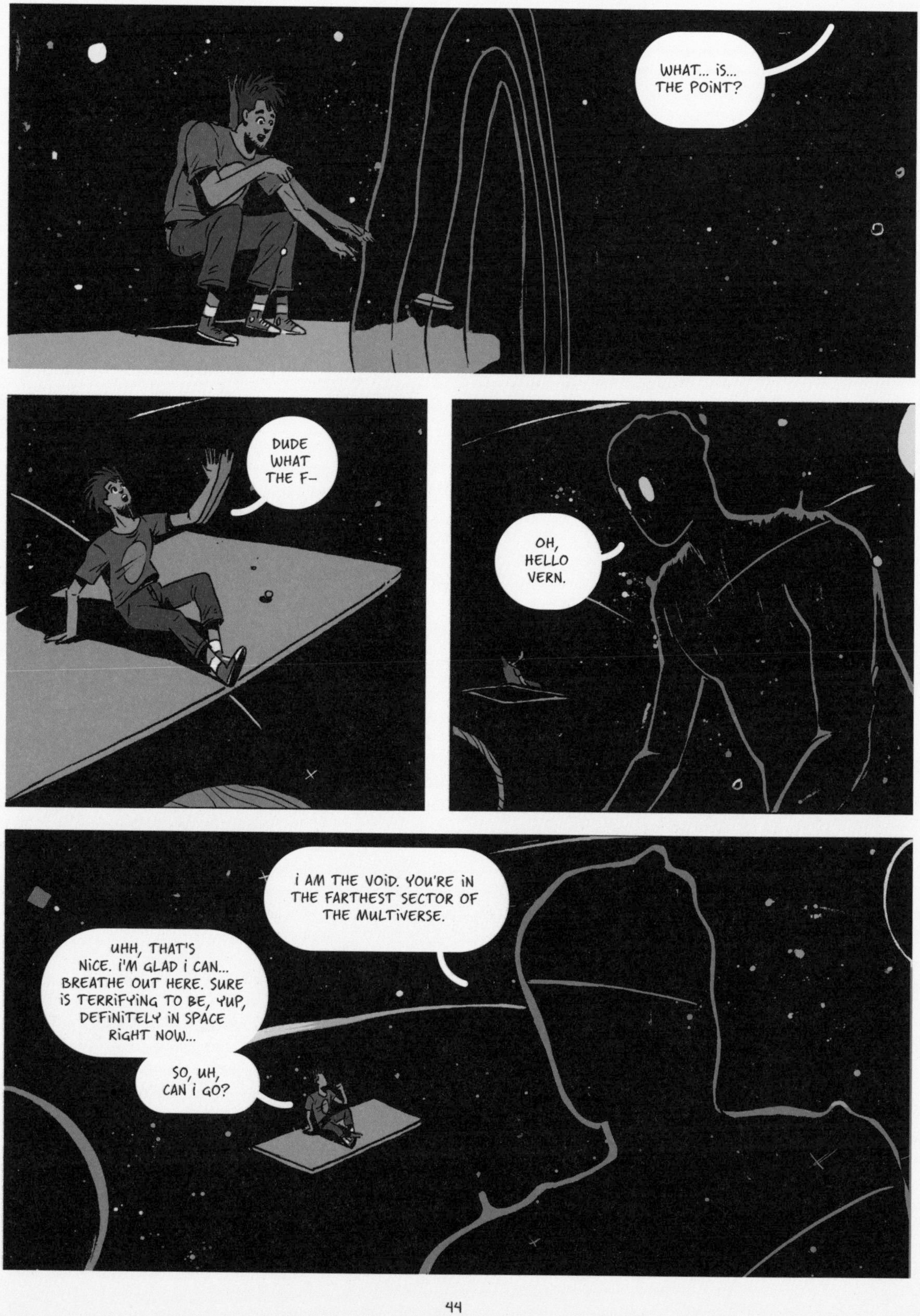
WHAT... IS... THE POINT?
DUDE WHAT THE F–
OH, HELLO VERN.
I AM THE VOID. YOU'RE IN THE FARTHEST SECTOR OF THE MULTIVERSE.
UHH, THAT'S NICE. I'M GLAD I CAN... BREATHE OUT HERE. SURE IS TERRIFYING TO BE, YUP, DEFINITELY IN SPACE RIGHT NOW...
SO, UH, CAN I GO?

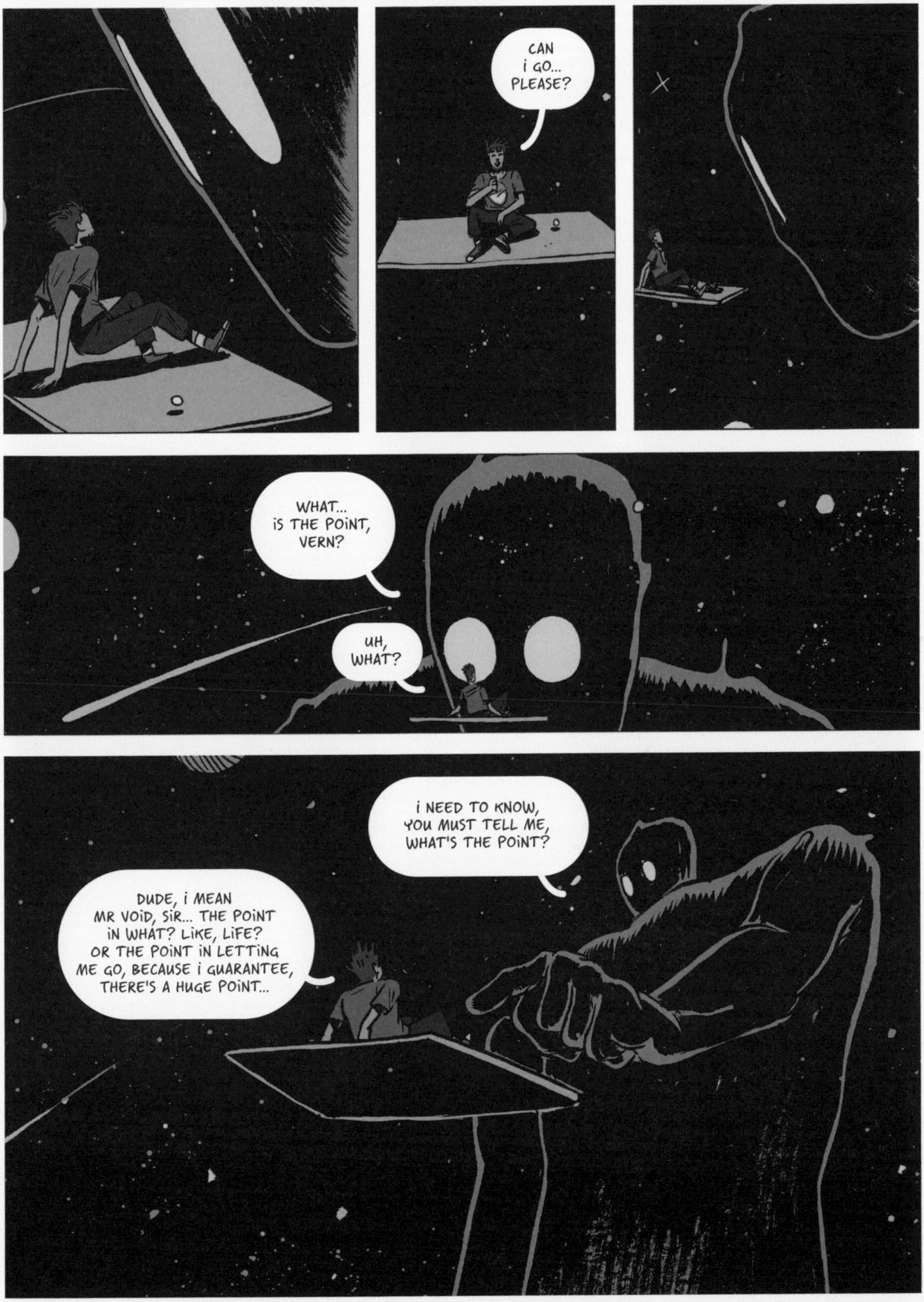
CAN i GO... PLEASE?
WHAT... iS THE POiNT, VERN?
UH, WHAT?
i NEED TO KNOW, YOU MUST TELL ME, WHAT'S THE POiNT?
DUDE, i MEAN MR VOiD, SiR... THE POiNT iN WHAT? LiKE, LiFE? OR THE POiNT iN LETTiNG ME GO, BECAUSE i GUARANTEE, THERE'S A HUGE POiNT...

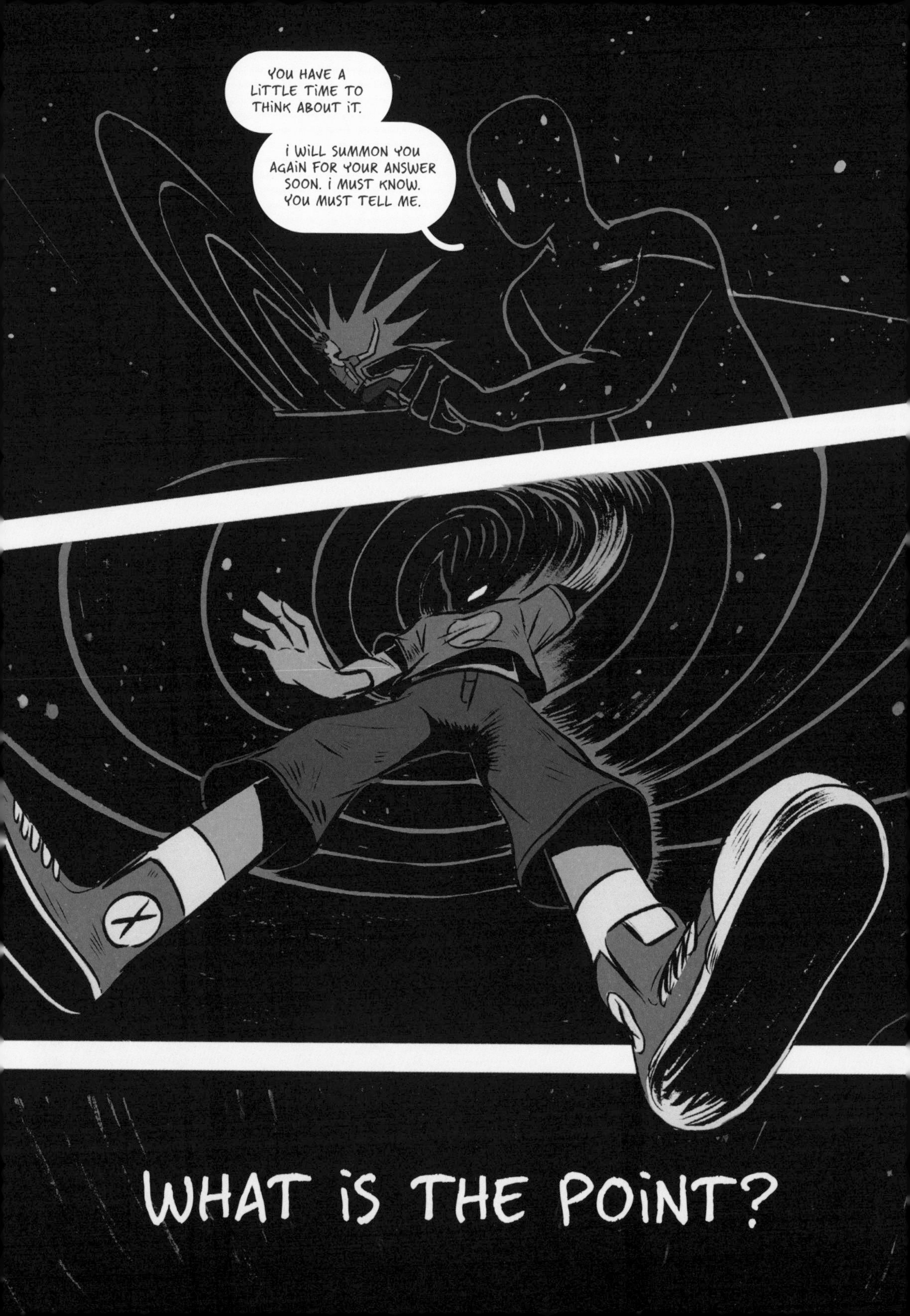
YOU HAVE A LITTLE TIME TO THINK ABOUT IT.
I WILL SUMMON YOU AGAIN FOR YOUR ANSWER SOON. I MUST KNOW. YOU MUST TELL ME.
WHAT IS THE POINT?

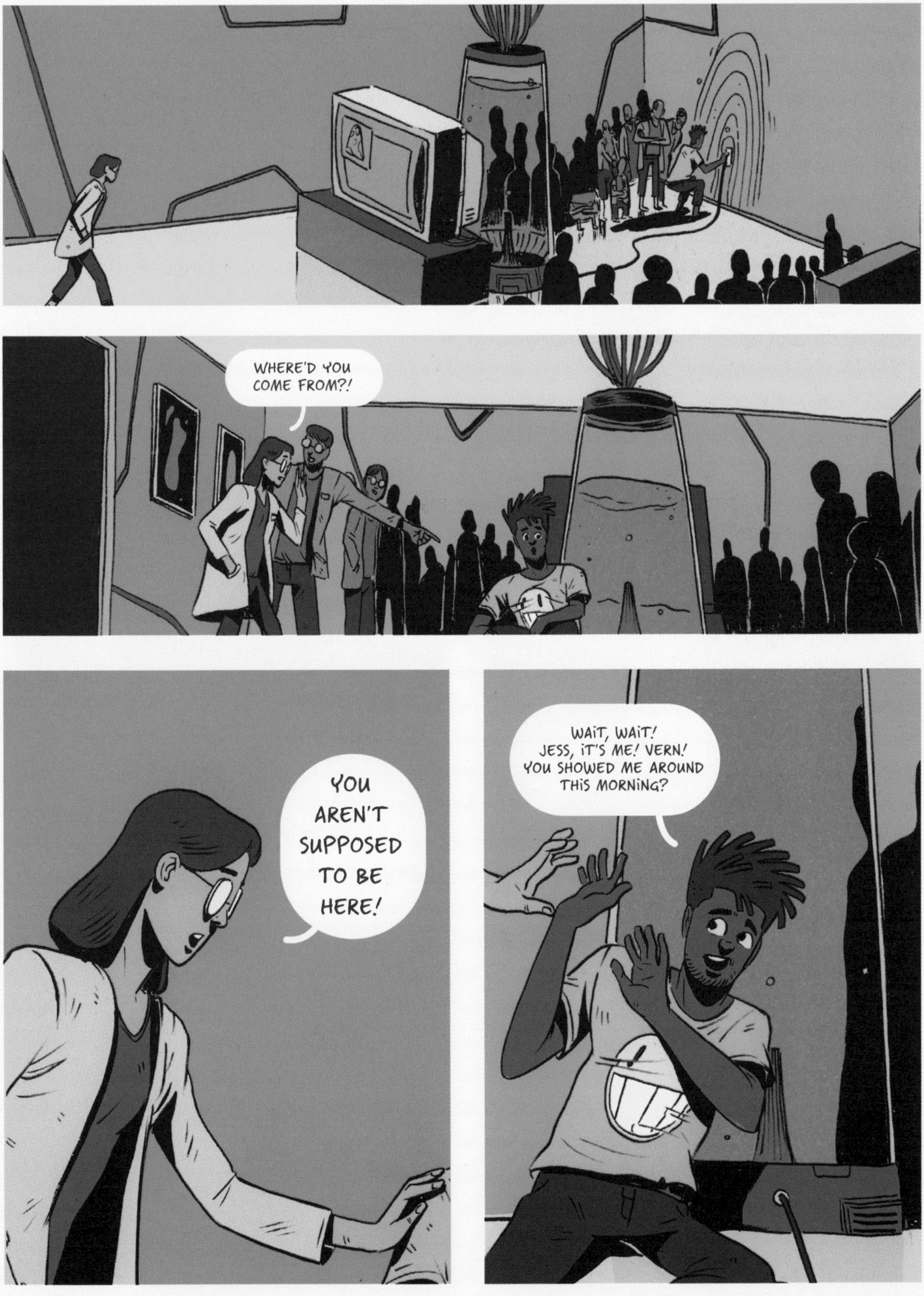
WHERE'D YOU COME FROM?!
YOU AREN'T SUPPOSED TO BE HERE!
WAIT, WAIT! JESS, IT'S ME! VERN! YOU SHOWED ME AROUND THIS MORNING?

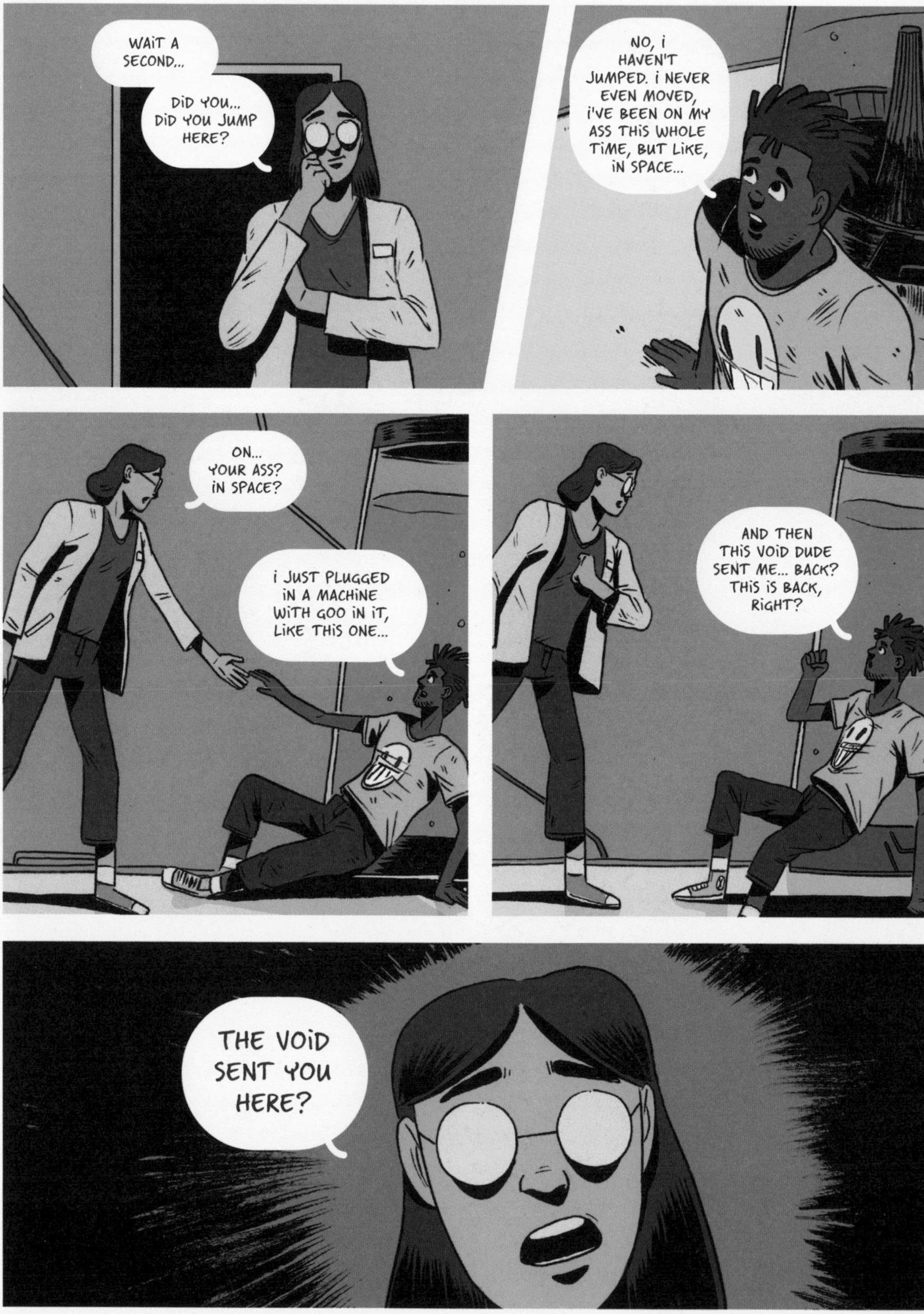
WAIT A SECOND...
DID YOU... DID YOU JUMP HERE?
NO, I HAVEN'T JUMPED. I NEVER EVEN MOVED, I'VE BEEN ON MY ASS THIS WHOLE TIME, BUT LIKE, IN SPACE...
ON... YOUR ASS? IN SPACE?
I JUST PLUGGED IN A MACHINE WITH GOO IN IT, LIKE THIS ONE...
AND THEN THIS VOID DUDE SENT ME... BACK? THIS IS BACK, RIGHT?
THE VOID SENT YOU HERE?

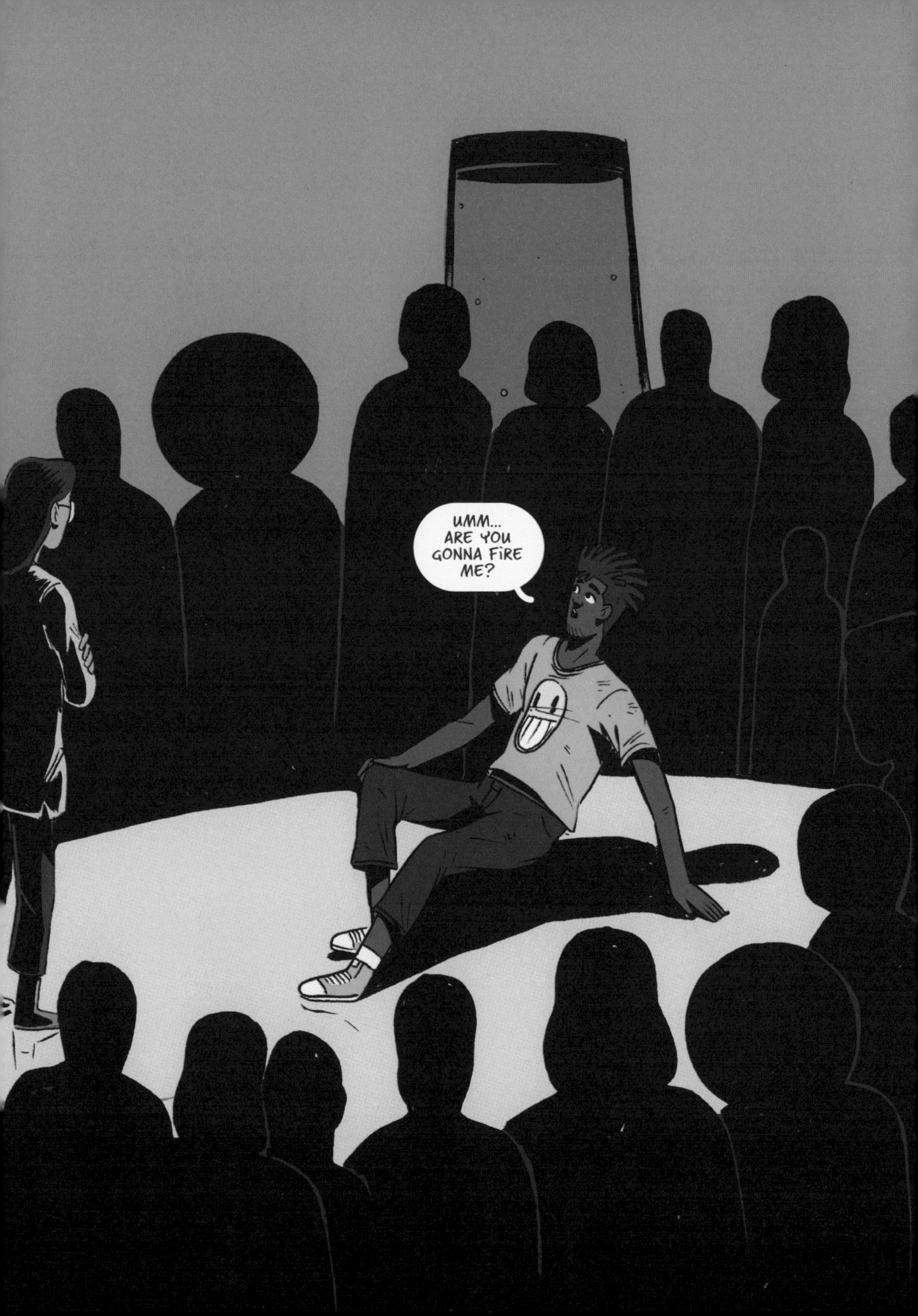
UMM... ARE YOU GONNA FIRE ME?

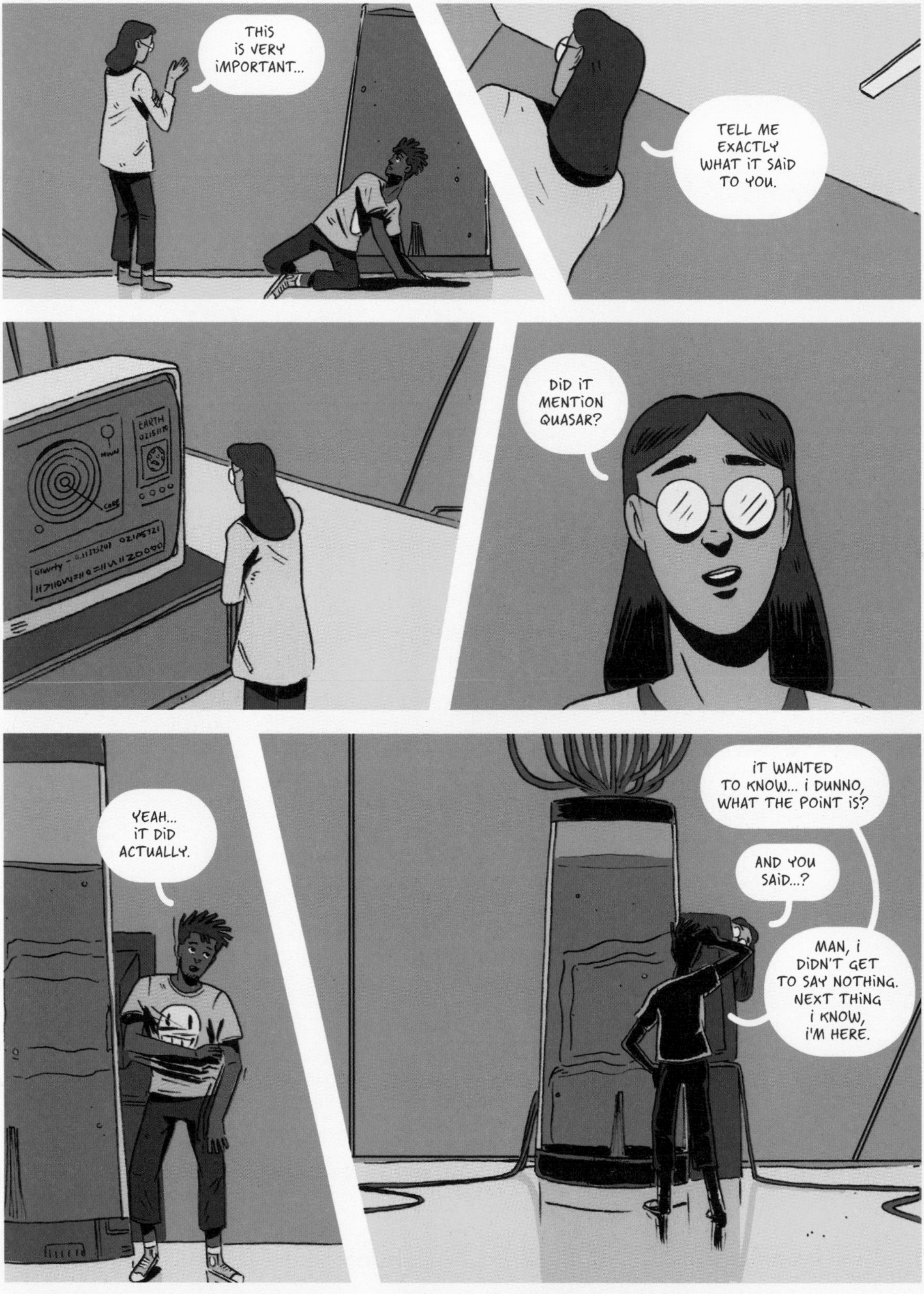
THIS IS VERY IMPORTANT...
TELL ME EXACTLY WHAT IT SAID TO YOU.
EARTH
DID IT MENTION QUASAR?
YEAH... IT DID ACTUALLY.
IT WANTED TO KNOW... I DUNNO, WHAT THE POINT IS?
AND YOU SAID...?
MAN, I DIDN'T GET TO SAY NOTHING. NEXT THING I KNOW, I'M HERE.

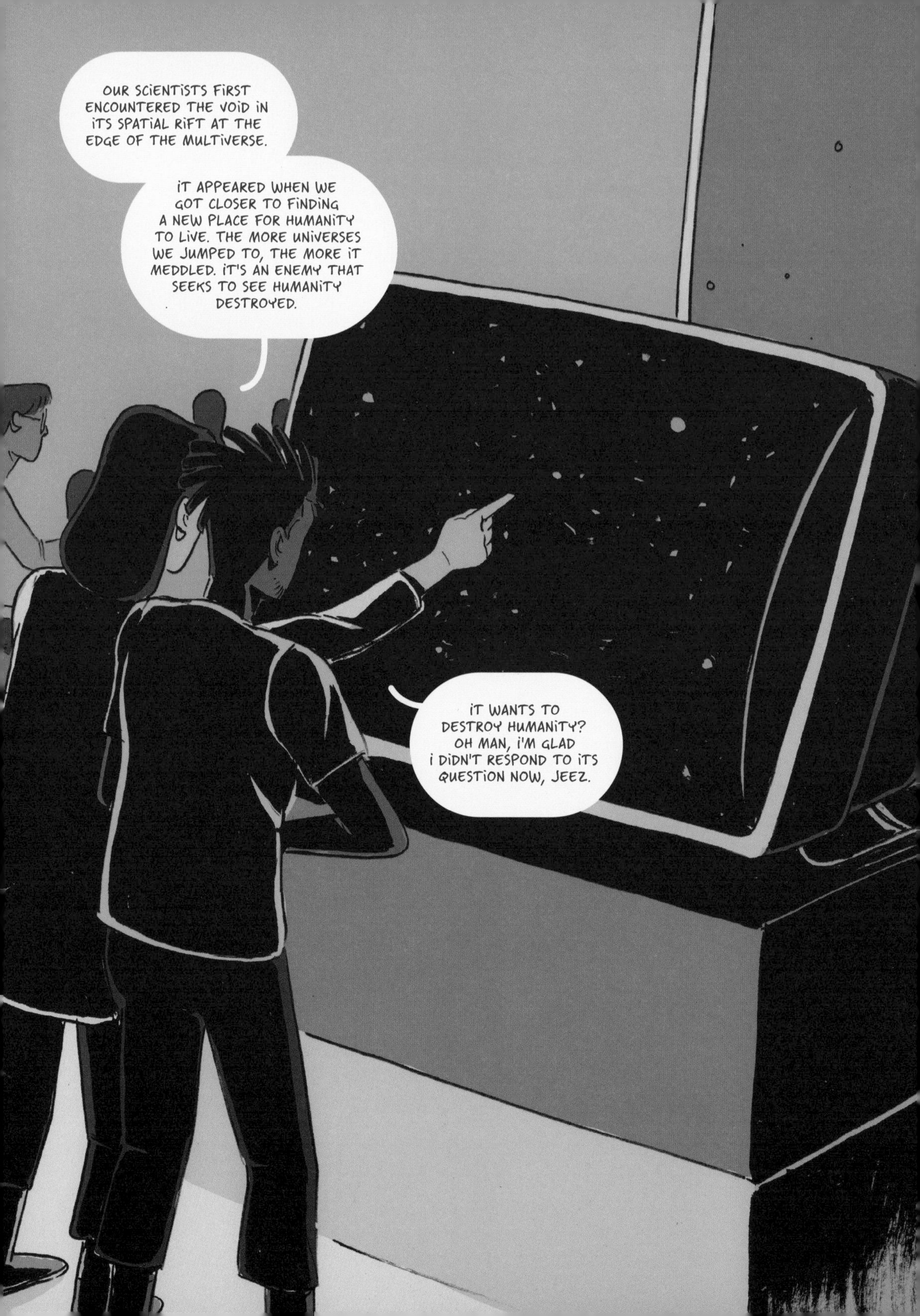
OUR SCIENTISTS FIRST ENCOUNTERED THE VOID IN ITS SPATIAL RIFT AT THE EDGE OF THE MULTIVERSE.
IT APPEARED WHEN WE GOT CLOSER TO FINDING A NEW PLACE FOR HUMANITY TO LIVE. THE MORE UNIVERSES WE JUMPED TO, THE MORE IT MEDDLED. IT'S AN ENEMY THAT SEEKS TO SEE HUMANITY DESTROYED.
IT WANTS TO DESTROY HUMANITY? OH MAN, I'M GLAD I DIDN'T RESPOND TO ITS QUESTION NOW, JEEZ.

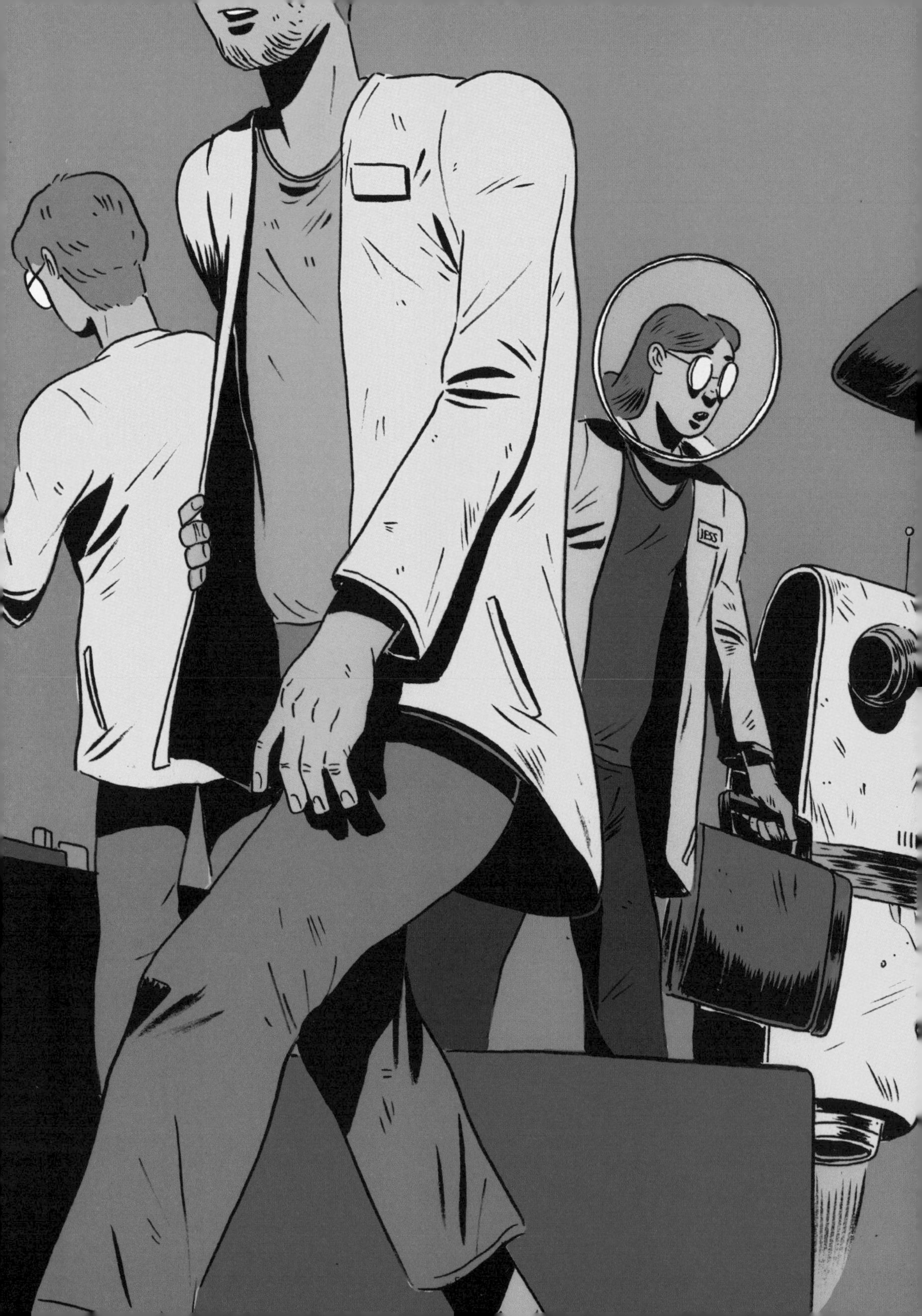
JESS

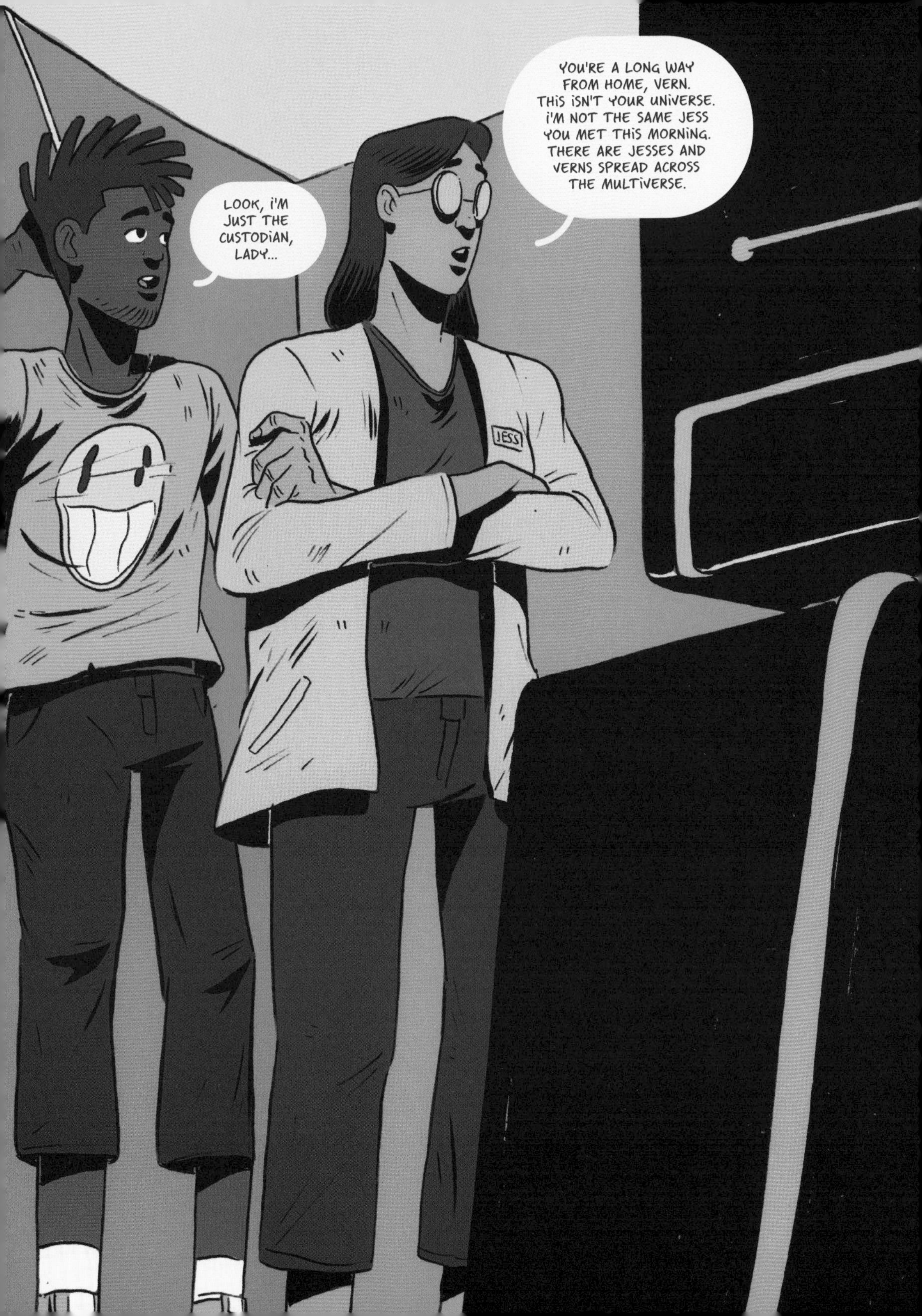
LOOK, I'M JUST THE CUSTODIAN, LADY...
YOU'RE A LONG WAY FROM HOME, VERN. THIS ISN'T YOUR UNIVERSE. I'M NOT THE SAME JESS YOU MET THIS MORNING. THERE ARE JESSES AND VERNS SPREAD ACROSS THE MULTIVERSE.
JESS

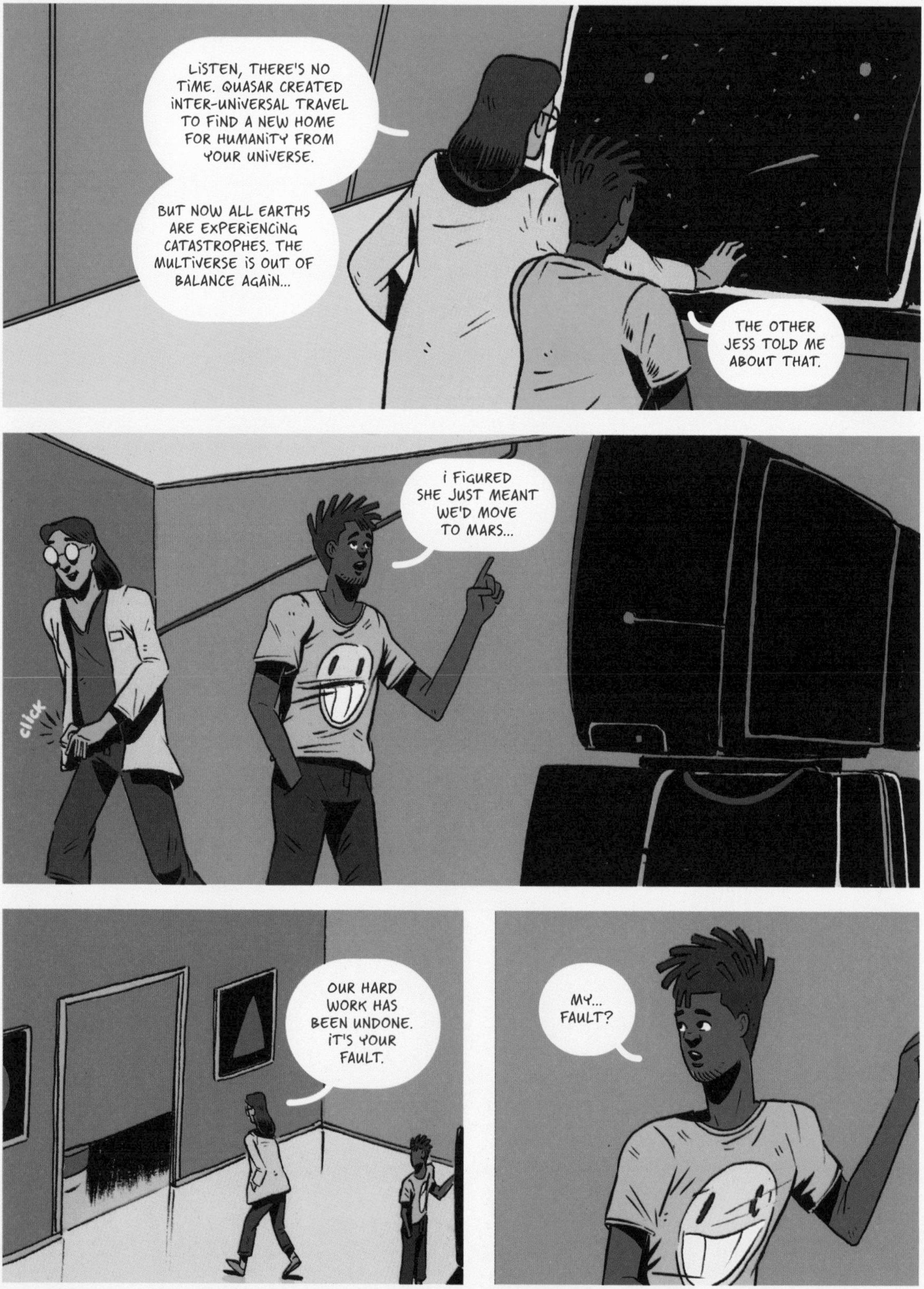
LISTEN, THERE'S NO TIME. QUASAR CREATED INTER-UNIVERSAL TRAVEL TO FIND A NEW HOME FOR HUMANITY FROM YOUR UNIVERSE.
BUT NOW ALL EARTHS ARE EXPERIENCING CATASTROPHES. THE MULTIVERSE IS OUT OF BALANCE AGAIN...
THE OTHER JESS TOLD ME ABOUT THAT.
I FIGURED SHE JUST MEANT WE'D MOVE TO MARS...
click
OUR HARD WORK HAS BEEN UNDONE. IT'S YOUR FAULT.
MY... FAULT?

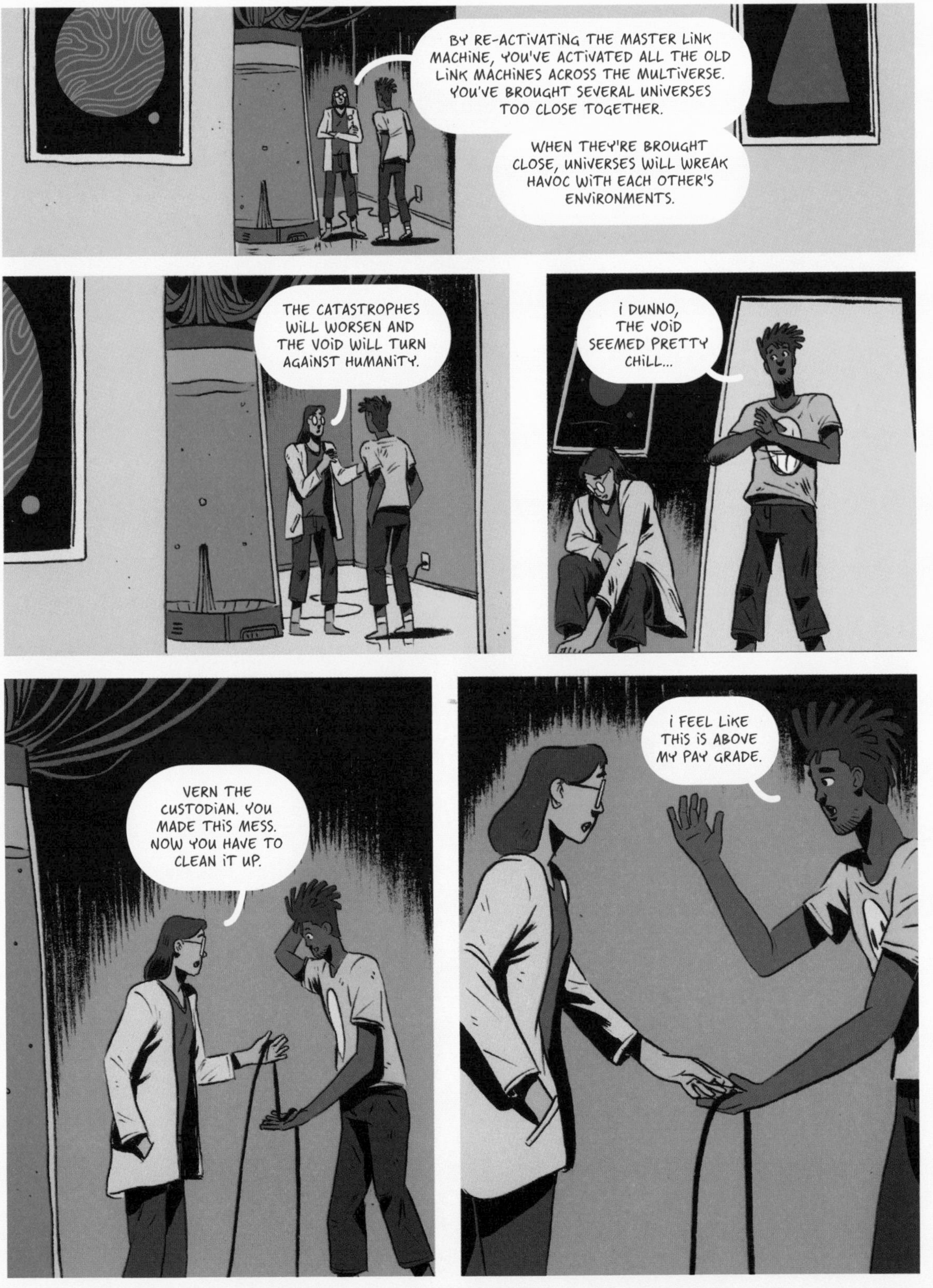
BY RE-ACTIVATING THE MASTER LINK MACHINE, YOU'VE ACTIVATED ALL THE OLD LINK MACHINES ACROSS THE MULTIVERSE. YOU'VE BROUGHT SEVERAL UNIVERSES TOO CLOSE TOGETHER.
WHEN THEY'RE BROUGHT CLOSE, UNIVERSES WILL WREAK HAVOC WITH EACH OTHER'S ENVIRONMENTS.
THE CATASTROPHES WILL WORSEN AND THE VOID WILL TURN AGAINST HUMANITY.
I DUNNO, THE VOID SEEMED PRETTY CHILL...
VERN THE CUSTODIAN. YOU MADE THIS MESS. NOW YOU HAVE TO CLEAN IT UP.
I FEEL LIKE THIS IS ABOVE MY PAY GRADE.

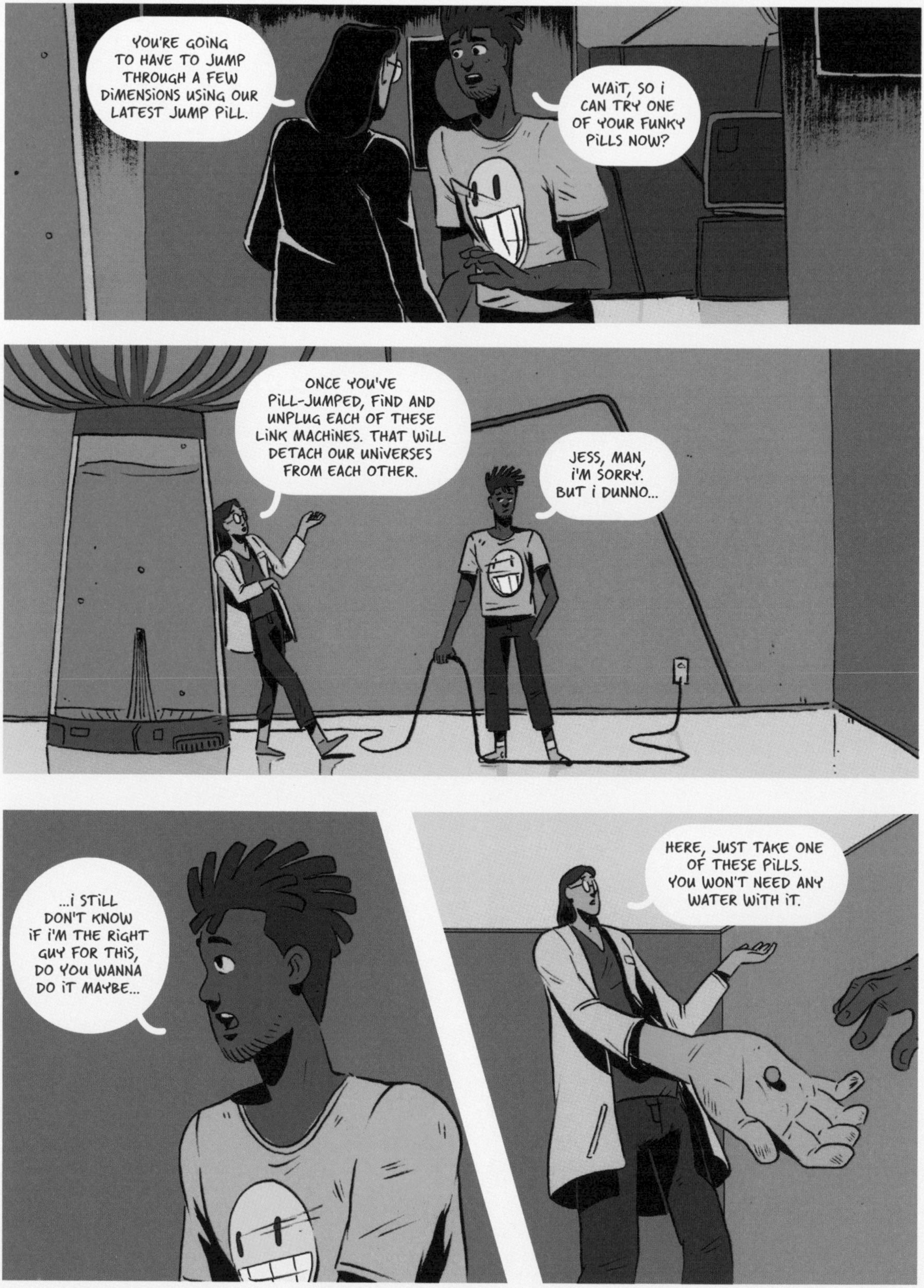
YOU'RE GOING TO HAVE TO JUMP THROUGH A FEW DIMENSIONS USING OUR LATEST JUMP PILL.
WAIT, SO I CAN TRY ONE OF YOUR FUNKY PILLS NOW?
ONCE YOU'VE PILL-JUMPED, FIND AND UNPLUG EACH OF THESE LINK MACHINES. THAT WILL DETACH OUR UNIVERSES FROM EACH OTHER.
JESS, MAN, I'M SORRY. BUT I DUNNO...
...I STILL DON'T KNOW IF I'M THE RIGHT GUY FOR THIS, DO YOU WANNA DO IT MAYBE...
HERE, JUST TAKE ONE OF THESE PILLS. YOU WON'T NEED ANY WATER WITH IT.

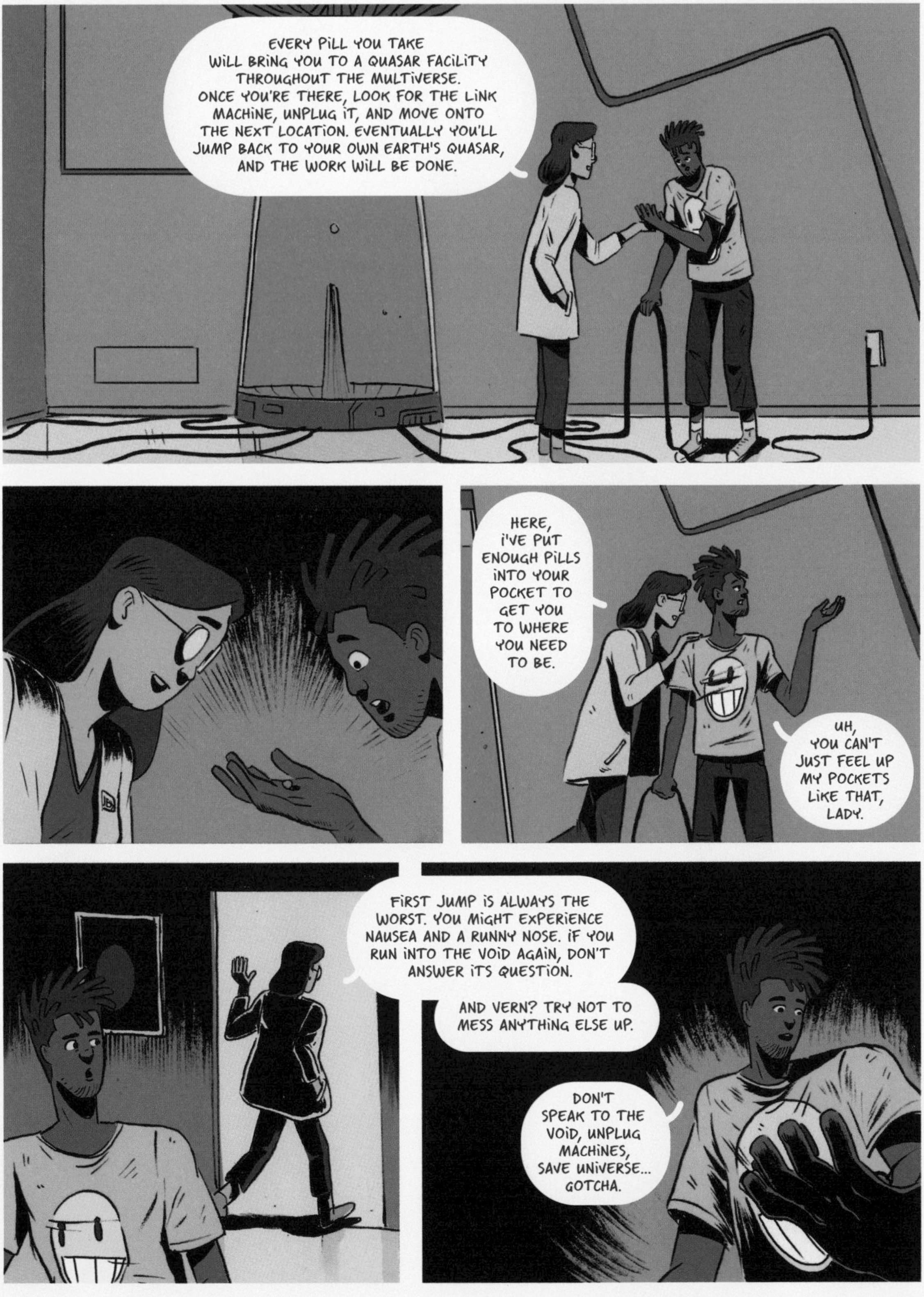
EVERY PILL YOU TAKE WILL BRING YOU TO A QUASAR FACILITY THROUGHOUT THE MULTIVERSE. ONCE YOU'RE THERE, LOOK FOR THE LINK MACHINE, UNPLUG IT, AND MOVE ONTO THE NEXT LOCATION. EVENTUALLY YOU'LL JUMP BACK TO YOUR OWN EARTH'S QUASAR, AND THE WORK WILL BE DONE.
HERE, I'VE PUT ENOUGH PILLS INTO YOUR POCKET TO GET YOU TO WHERE YOU NEED TO BE.
UH, YOU CAN'T JUST FEEL UP MY POCKETS LIKE THAT, LADY.
FIRST JUMP IS ALWAYS THE WORST. YOU MIGHT EXPERIENCE NAUSEA AND A RUNNY NOSE. IF YOU RUN INTO THE VOID AGAIN, DON'T ANSWER ITS QUESTION.
AND VERN? TRY NOT TO MESS ANYTHING ELSE UP.
DON'T SPEAK TO THE VOID, UNPLUG MACHINES, SAVE UNIVERSE... GOTCHA.

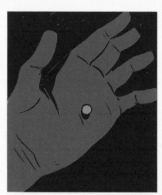

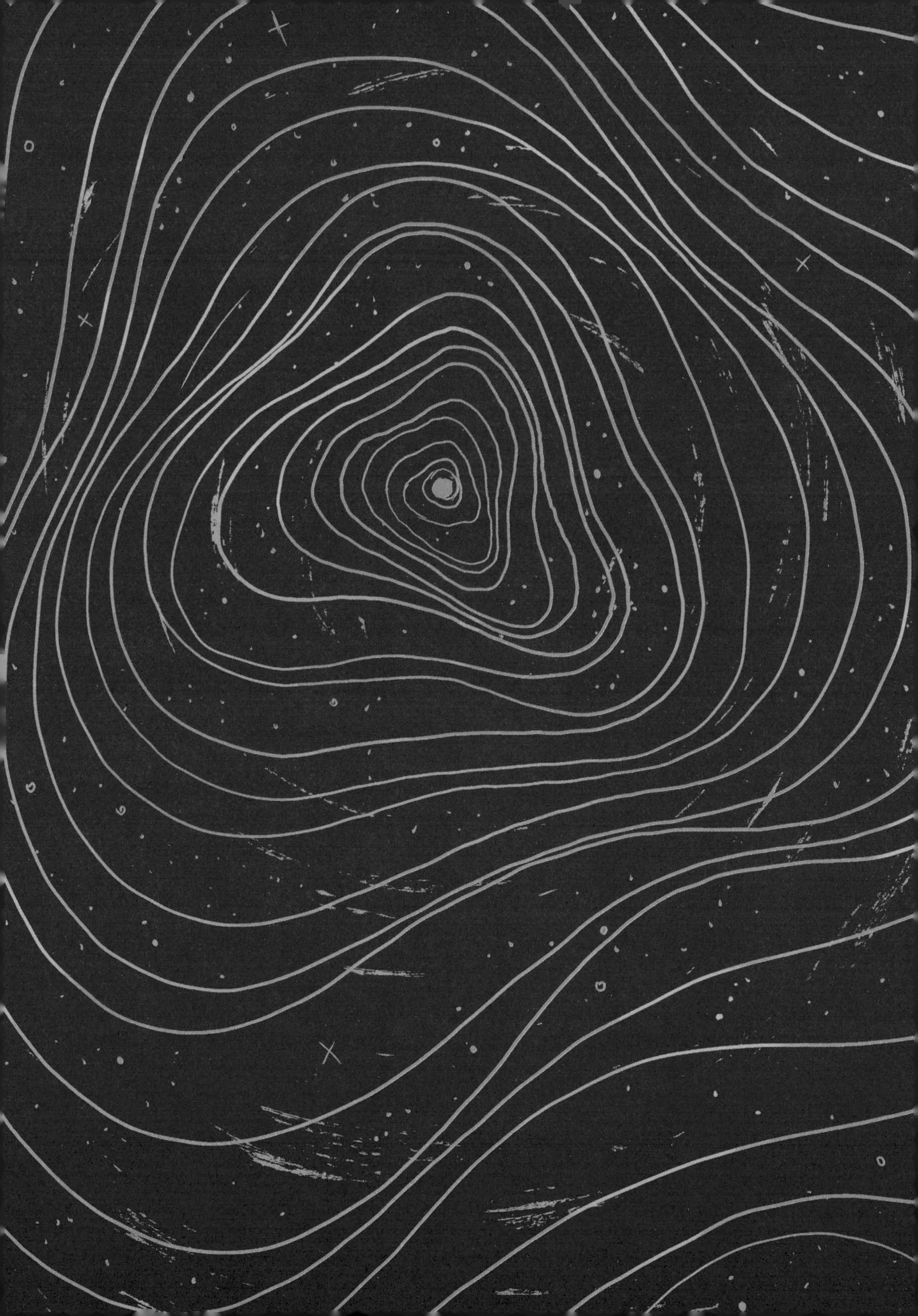

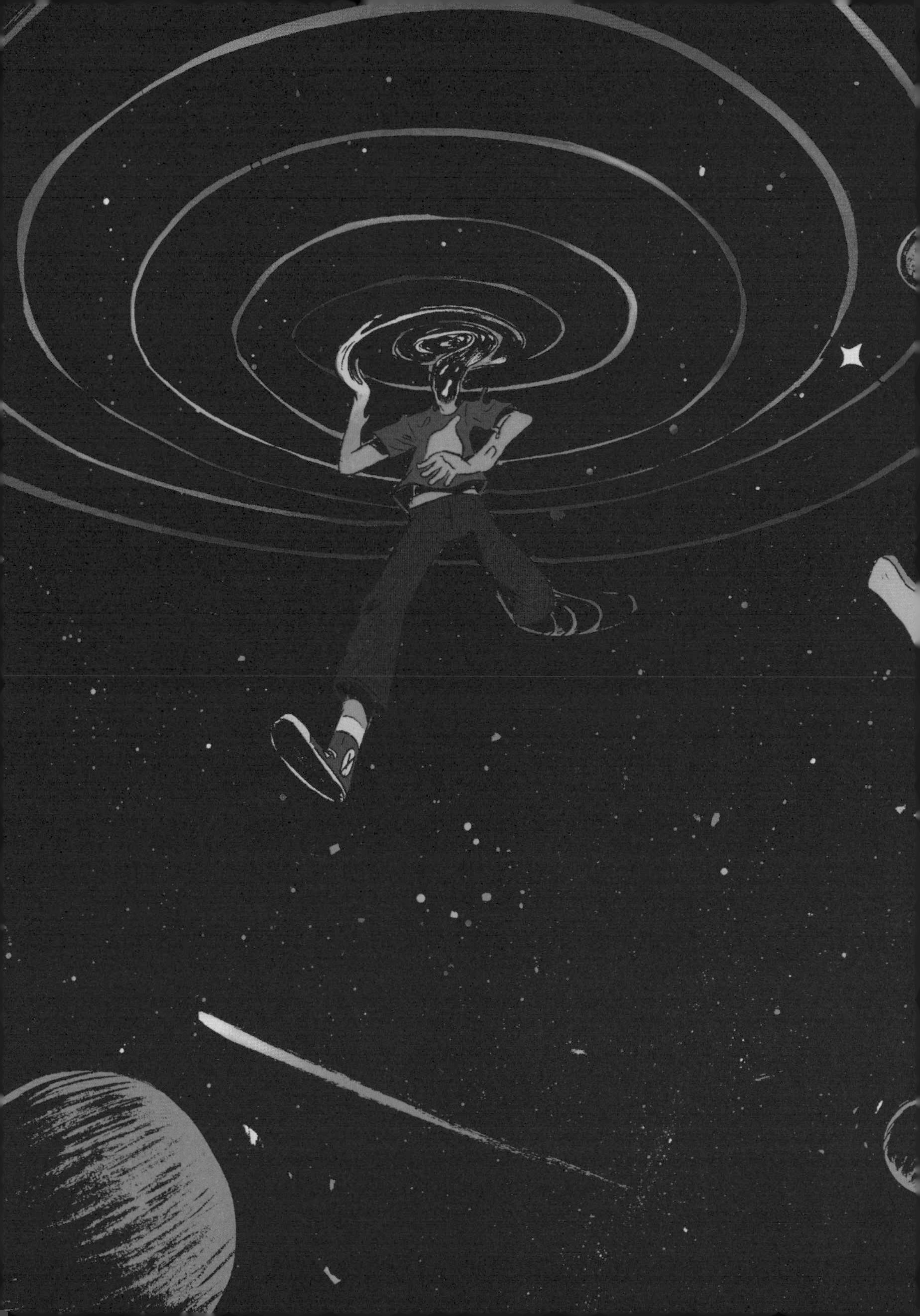

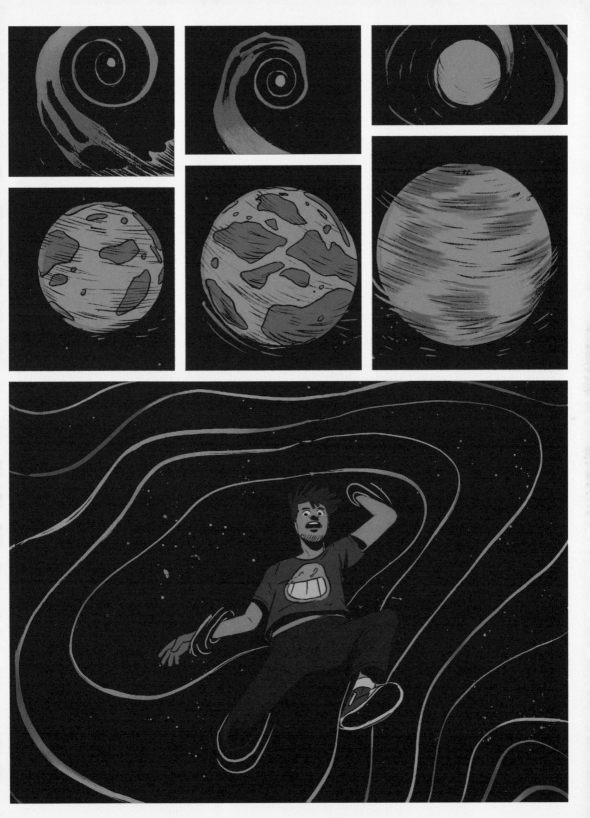

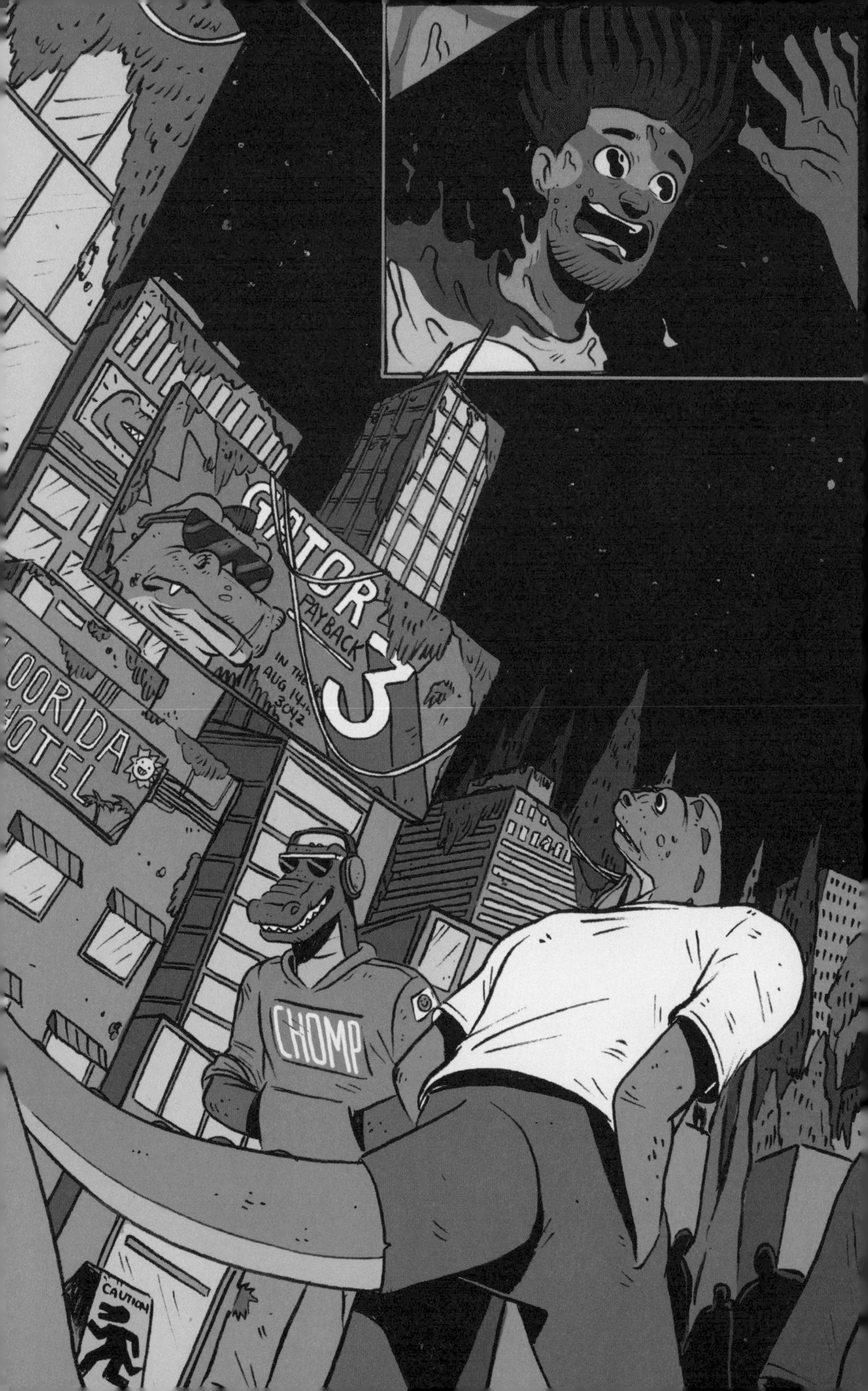
PAYBACK
3
AUG 14th
3042
OORIDA
HOTEL
CHOMP
CAUTION

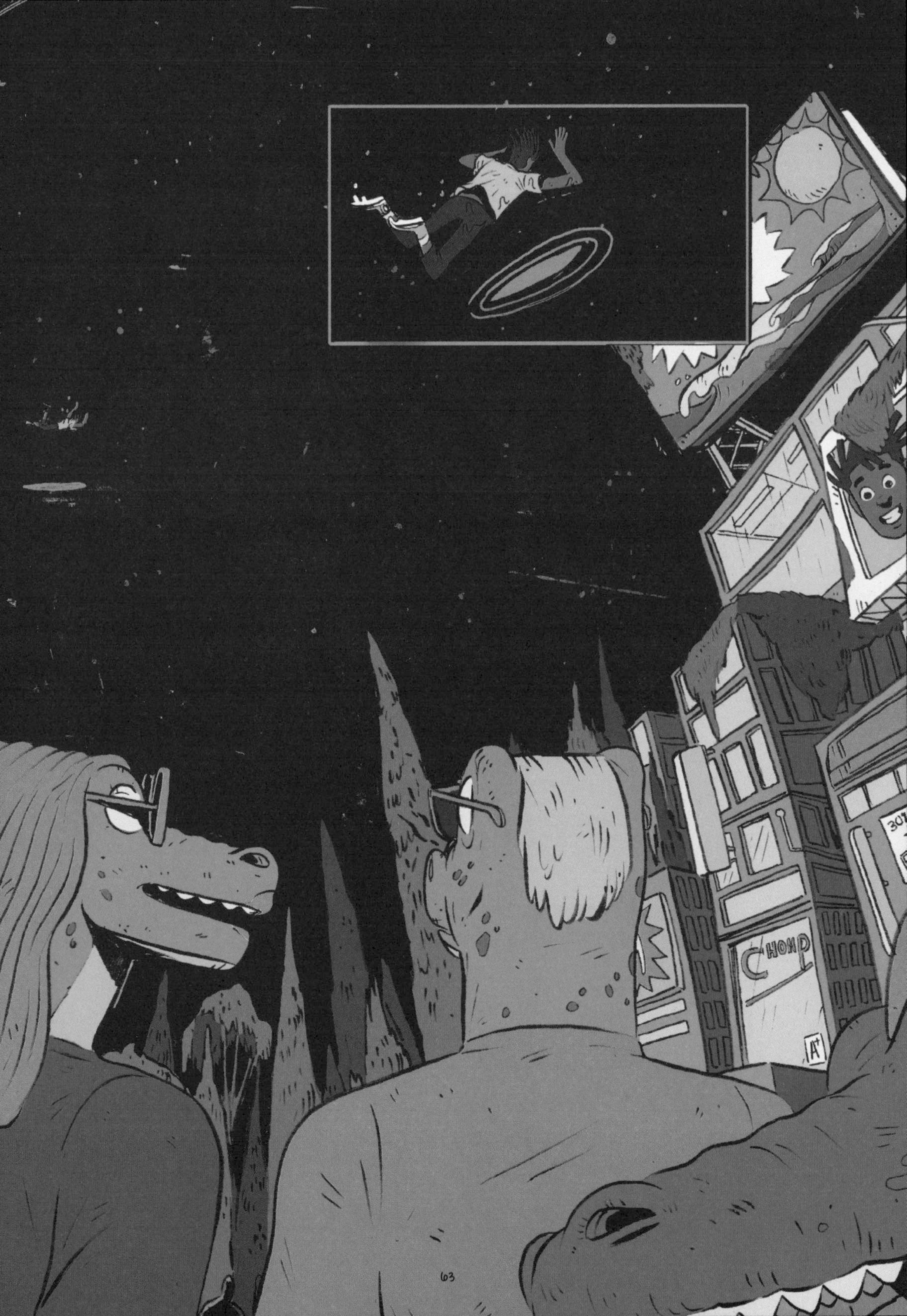
CHOMP
A+

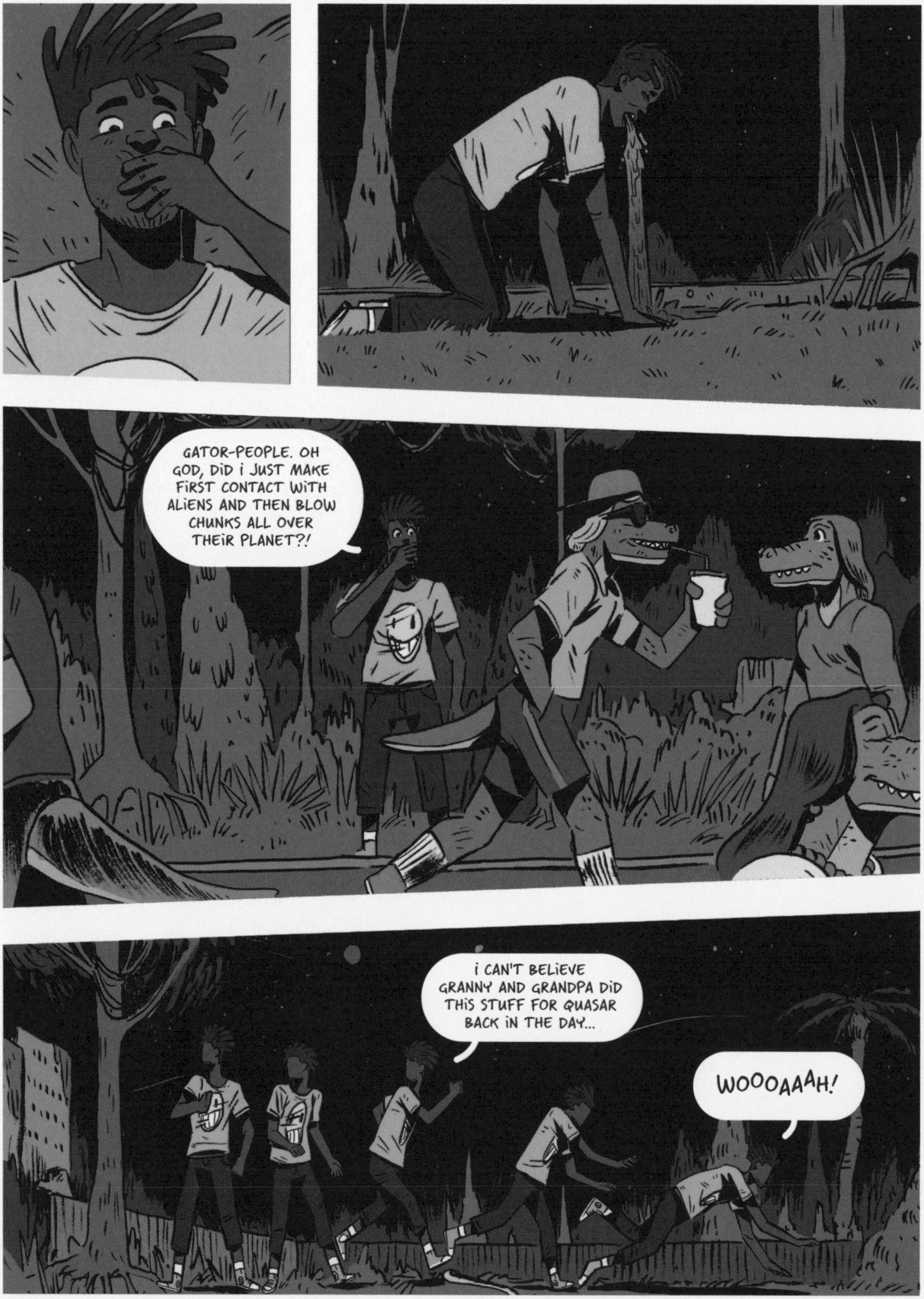
GATOR-PEOPLE. OH GOD, DID I JUST MAKE FIRST CONTACT WITH ALIENS AND THEN BLOW CHUNKS ALL OVER THEIR PLANET?!
I CAN'T BELIEVE GRANNY AND GRANDPA DID THIS STUFF FOR QUASAR BACK IN THE DAY...
WOOOAAAH!

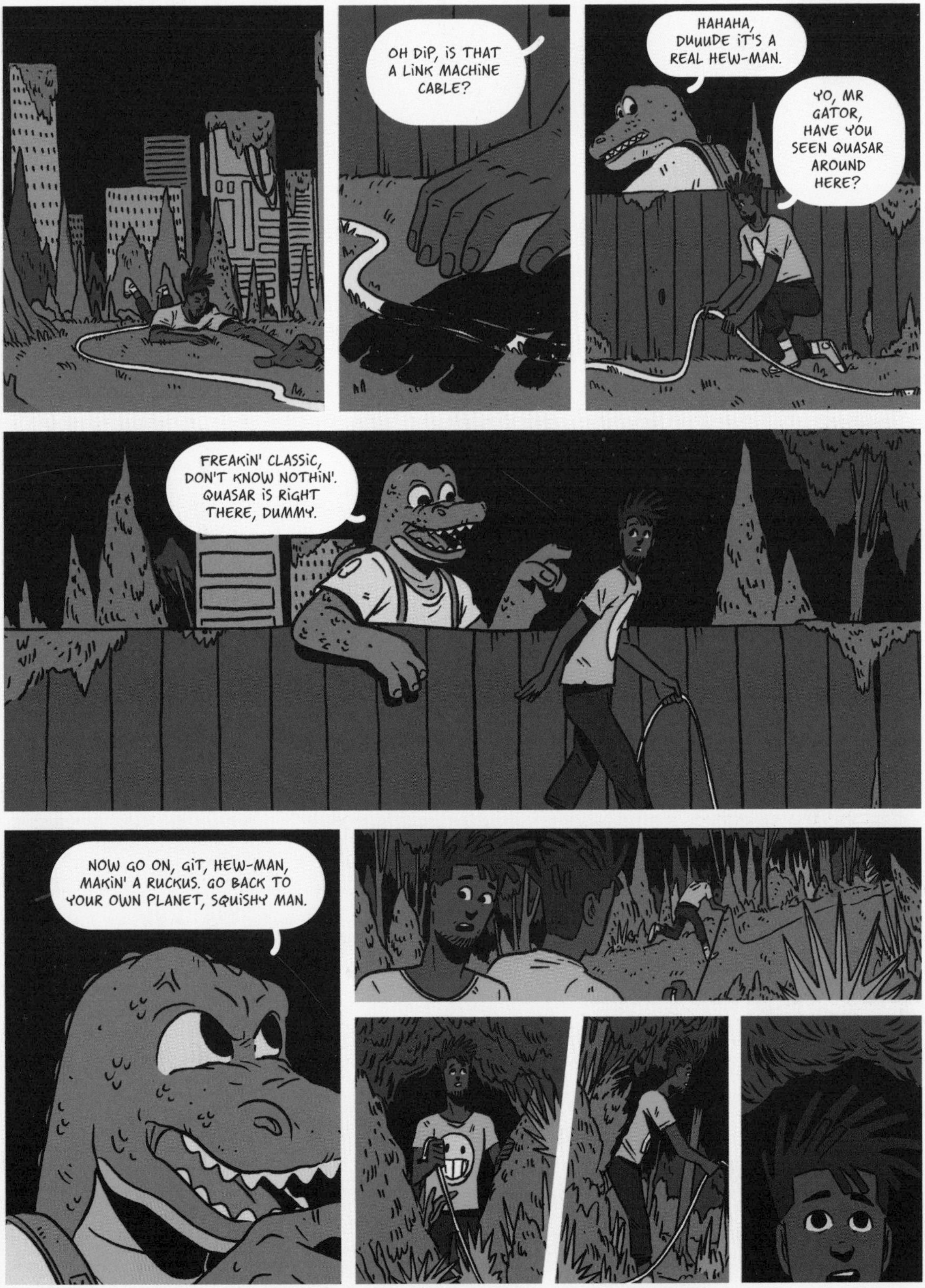
OH DiP, iS THAT A LiNK MACHiNE CABLE?
HAHAHA, DUUUDE iT'S A REAL HEW-MAN.
YO, MR GATOR, HAVE YOU SEEN QUASAR AROUND HERE?
FREAKiN' CLASSiC, DON'T KNOW NOTHiN'. QUASAR iS RiGHT THERE, DUMMY.
NOW GO ON, GiT, HEW-MAN, MAKiN' A RUCKUS. GO BACK TO YOUR OWN PLANET, SQUiSHY MAN.

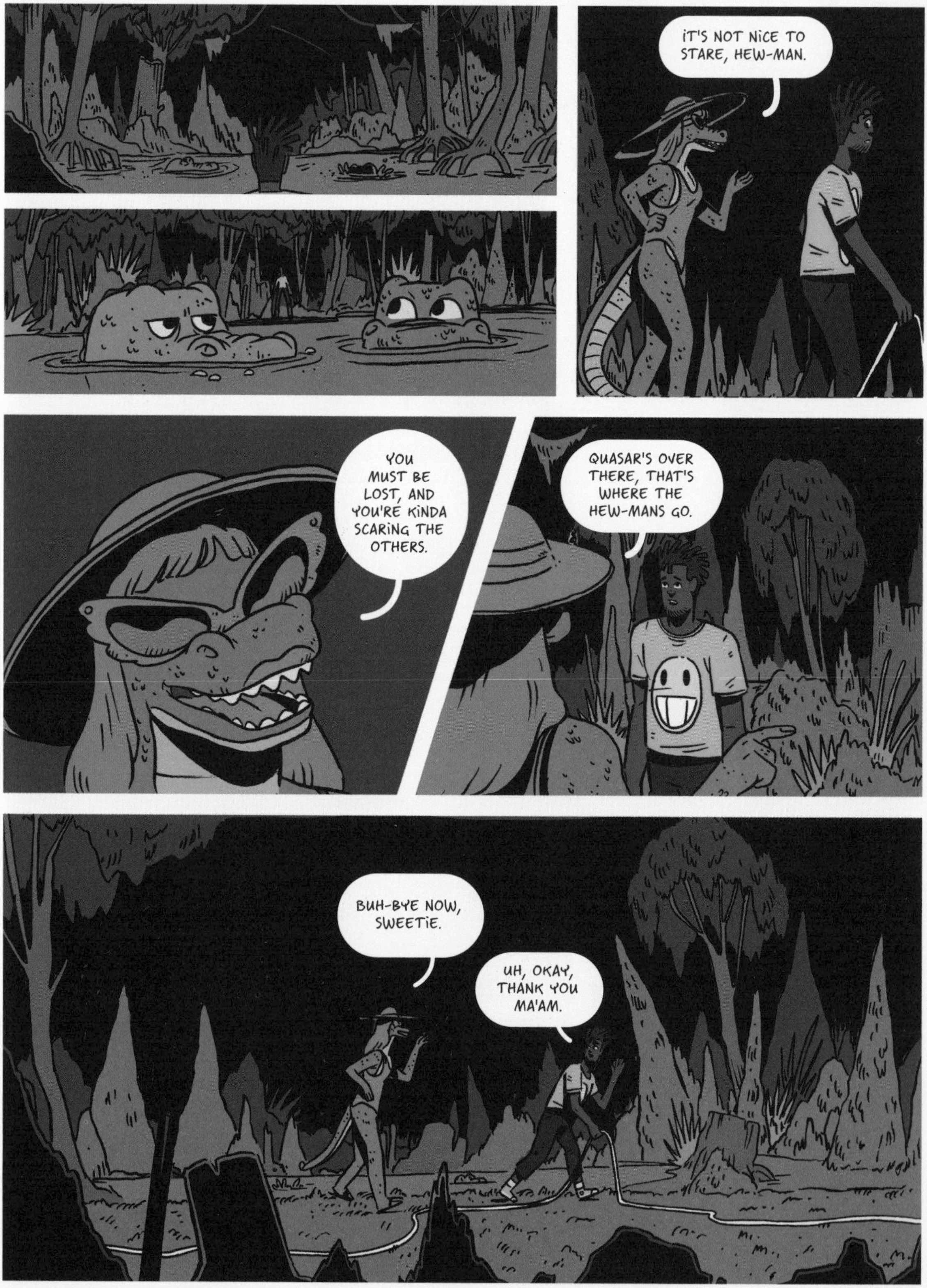
iT'S NOT NiCE TO STARE, HEW-MAN.
YOU MUST BE LOST, AND YOU'RE KiNDA SCARiNG THE OTHERS.
QUASAR'S OVER THERE, THAT'S WHERE THE HEW-MANS GO.
BUH-BYE NOW, SWEETiE.
UH, OKAY, THANK YOU MA'AM.

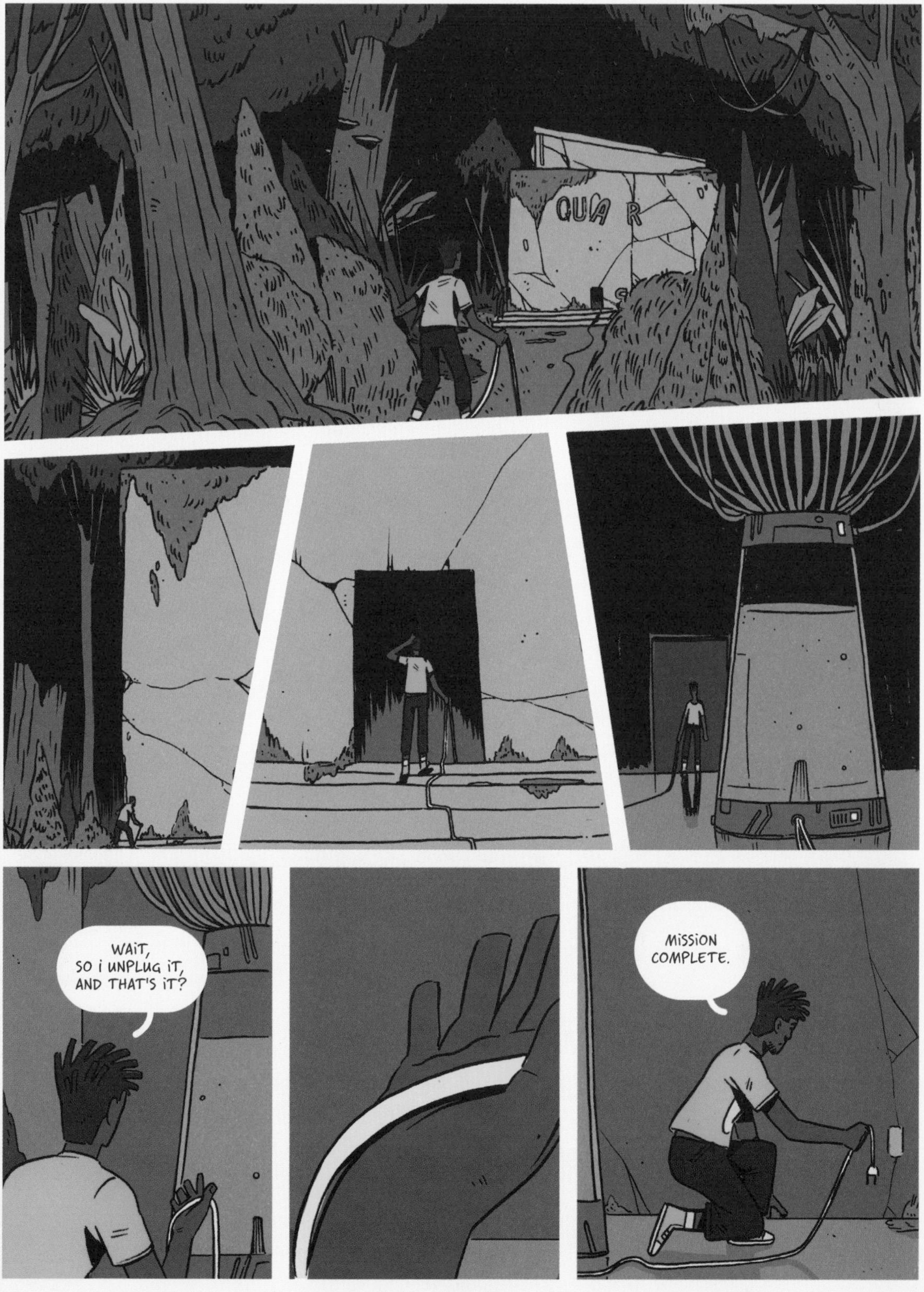
QUA R
WAIT, SO I UNPLUG IT, AND THAT'S IT?
MISSION COMPLETE.

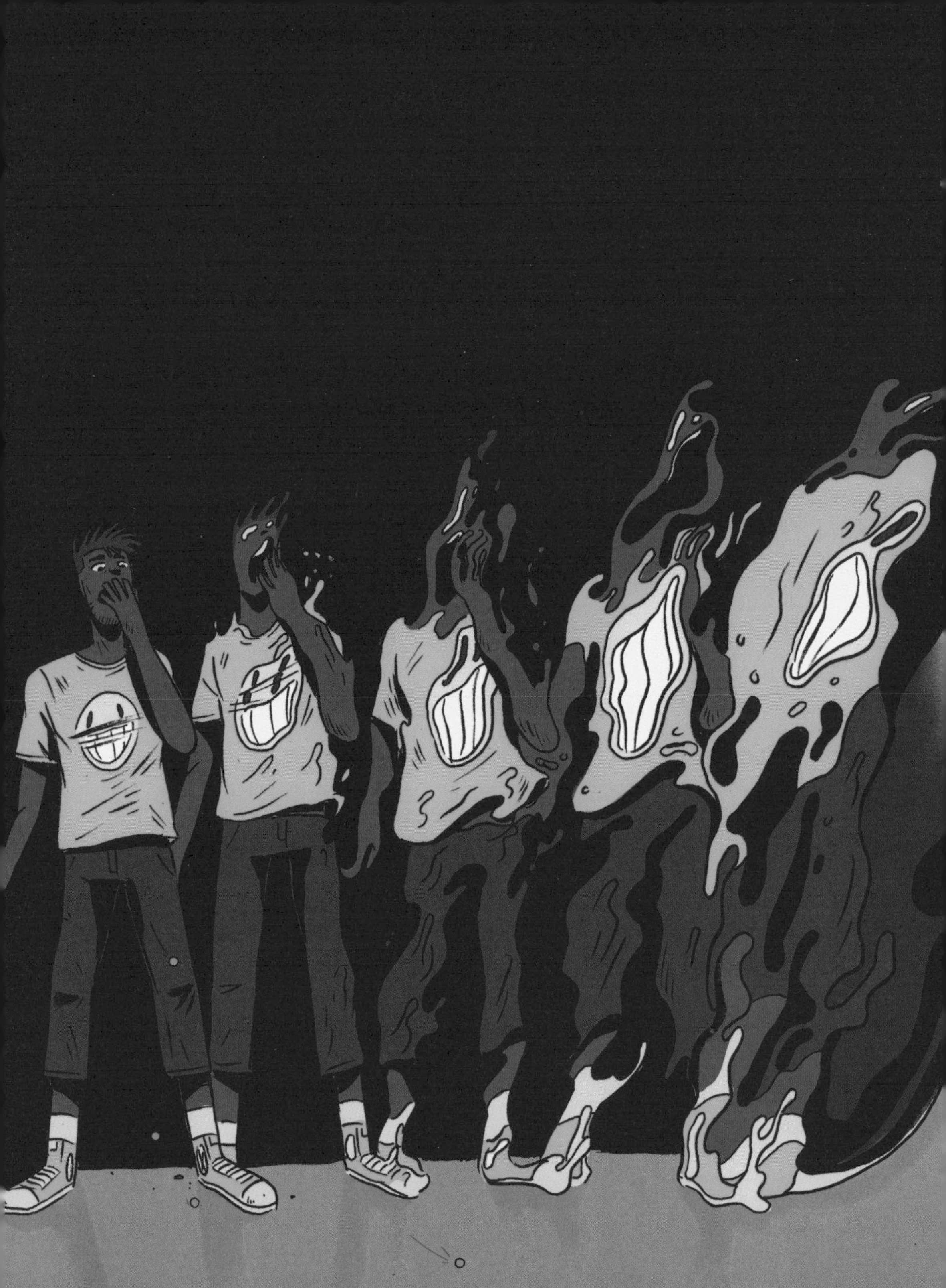

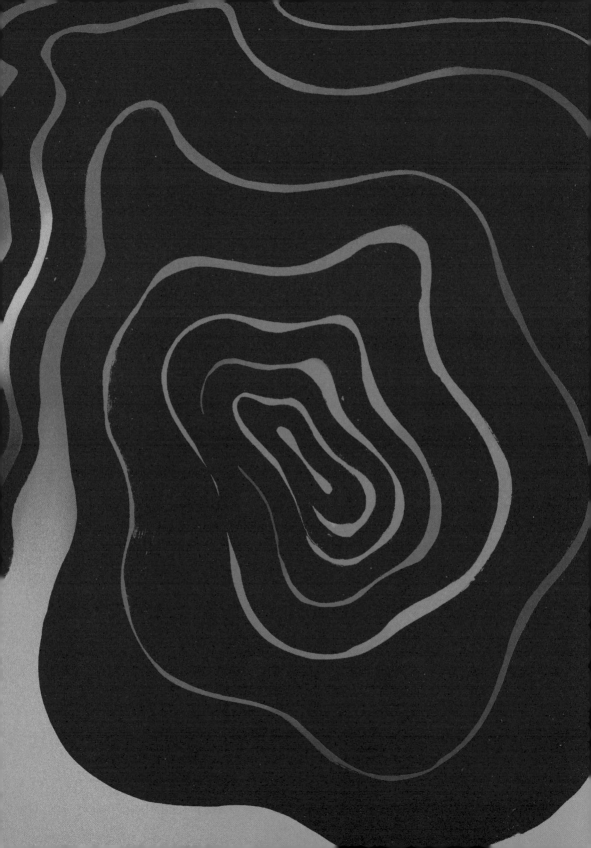

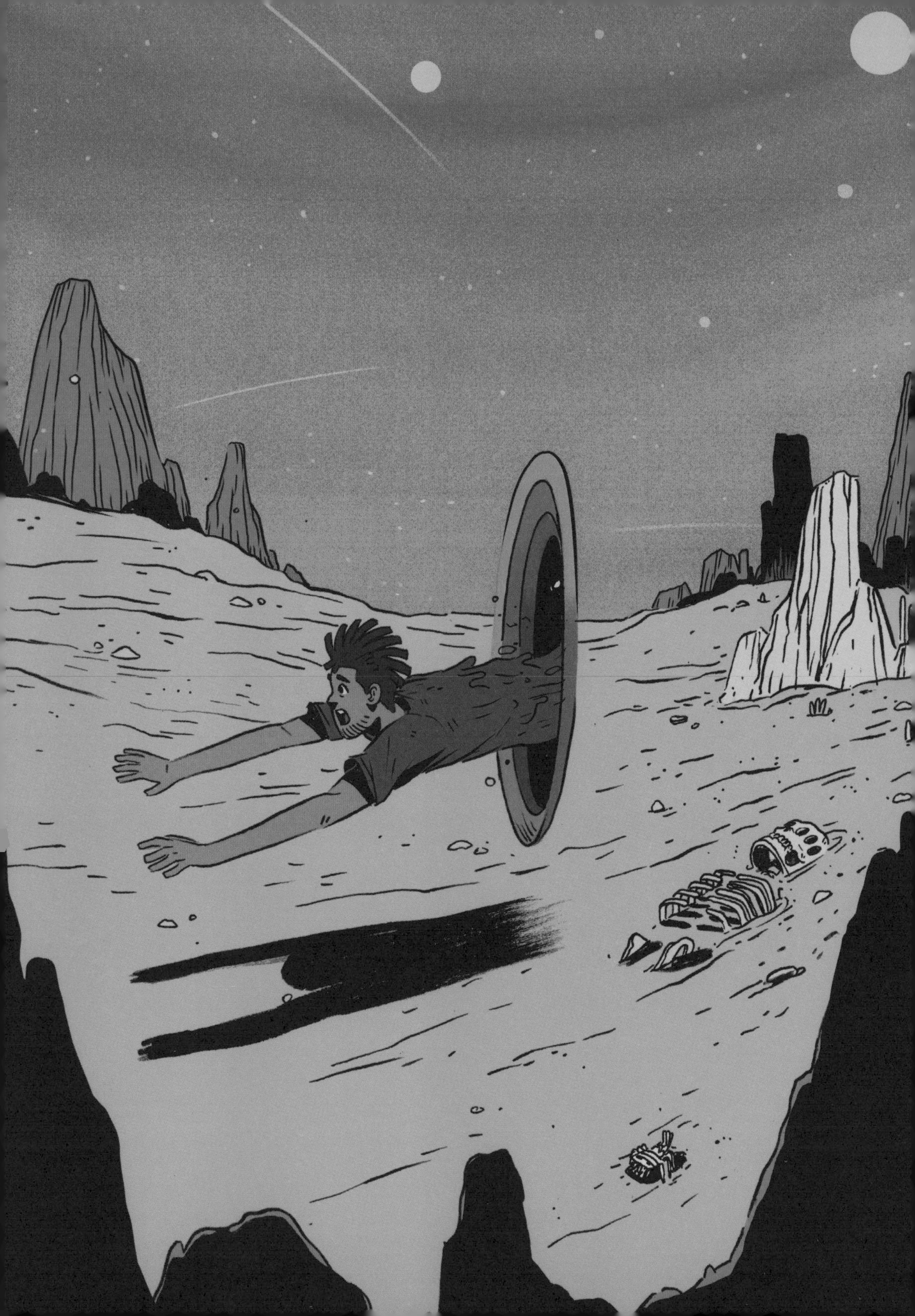

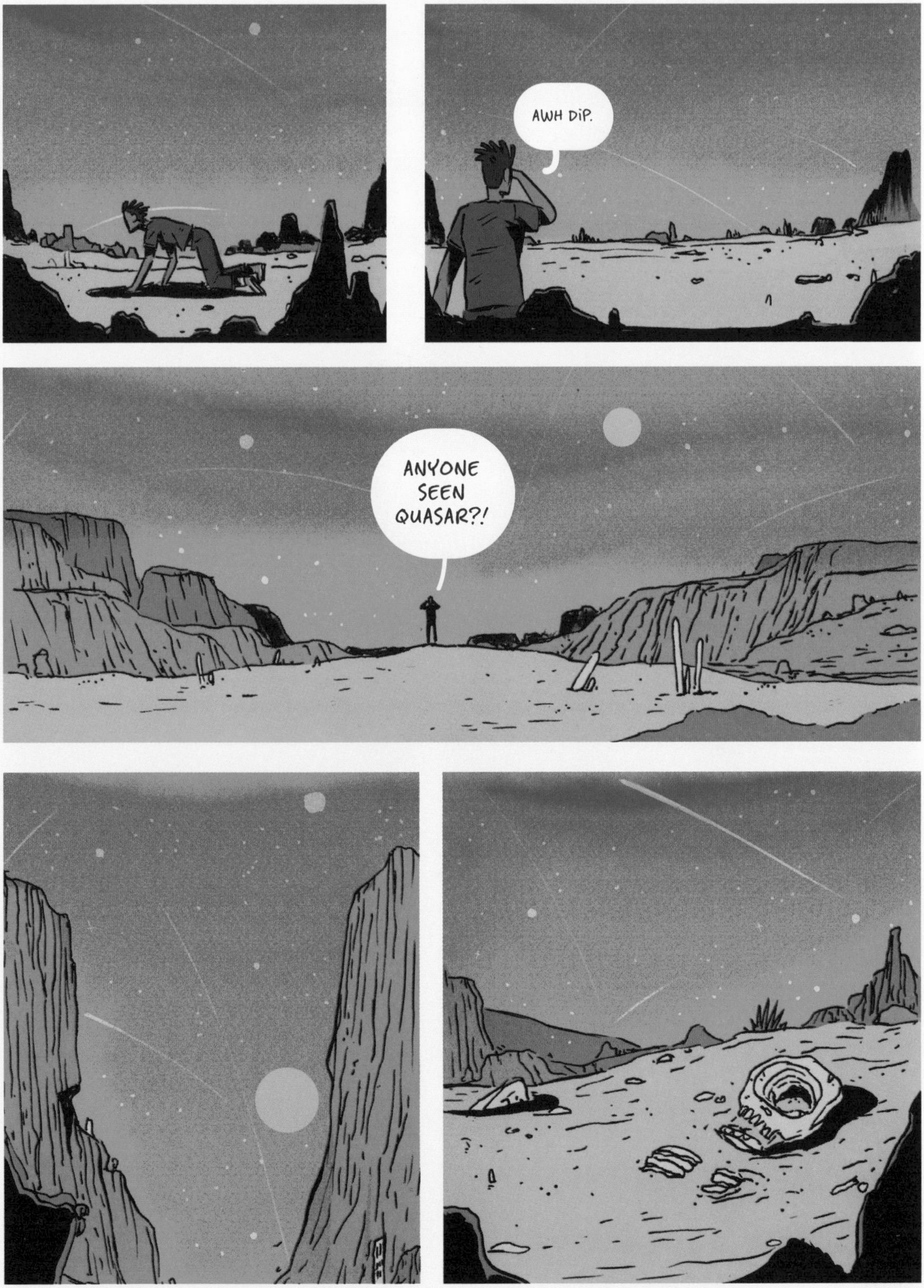
AWH DIP.
ANYONE SEEN QUASAR?!

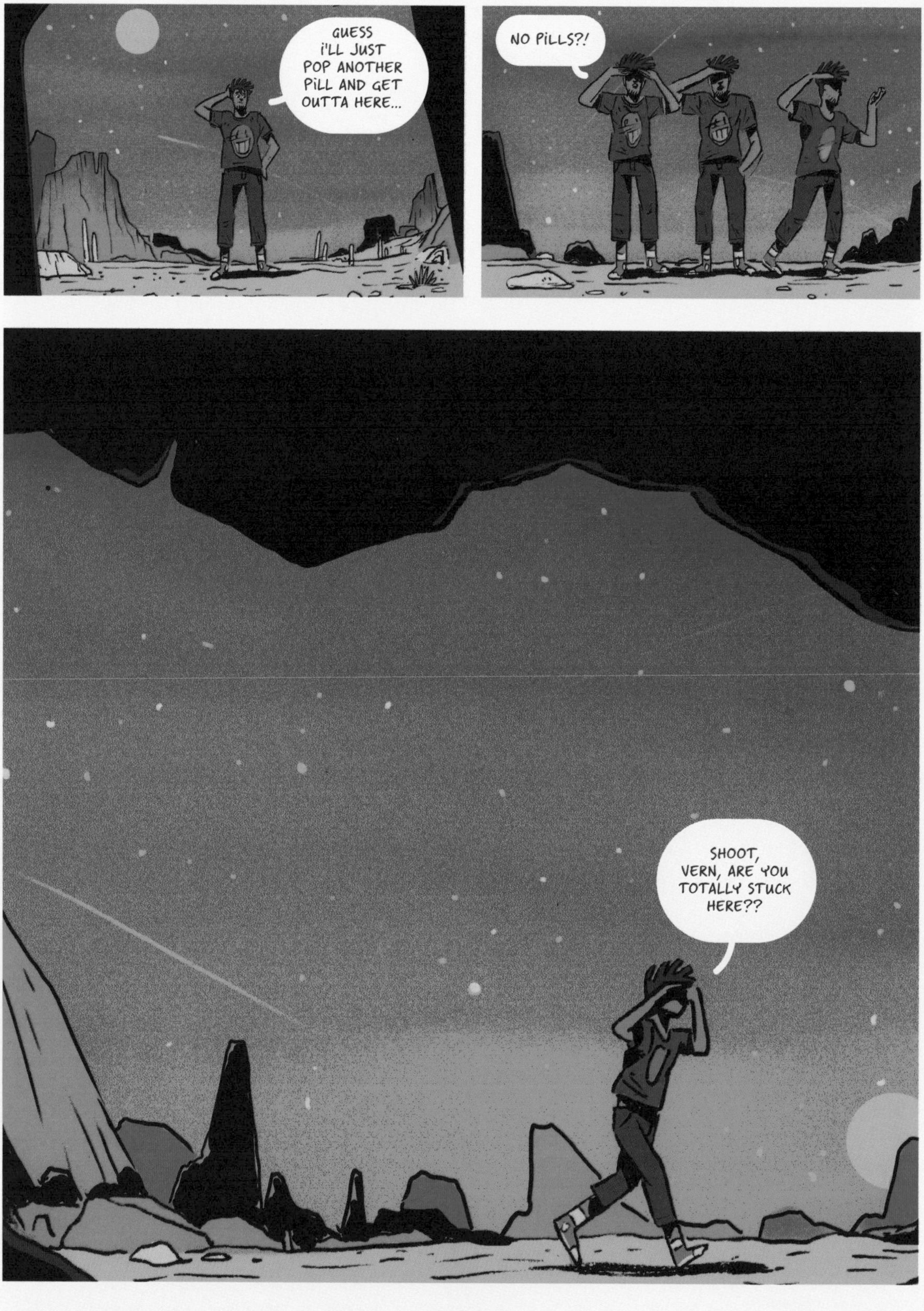
GUESS I'LL JUST POP ANOTHER PILL AND GET OUTTA HERE...
NO PILLS?!
SHOOT, VERN, ARE YOU TOTALLY STUCK HERE??

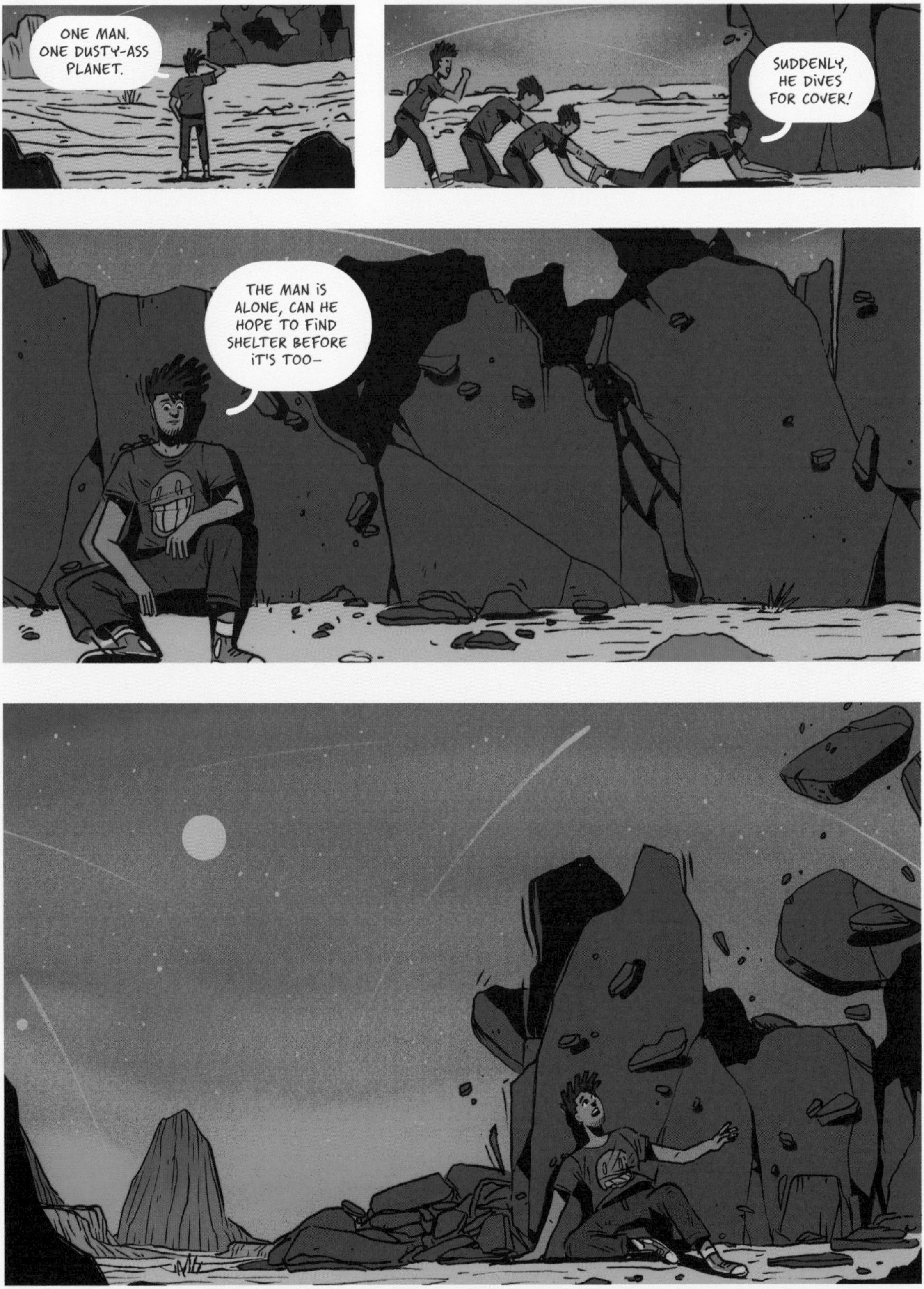
ONE MAN. ONE DUSTY-ASS PLANET.
SUDDENLY, HE DIVES FOR COVER!
THE MAN IS ALONE, CAN HE HOPE TO FIND SHELTER BEFORE IT'S TOO–

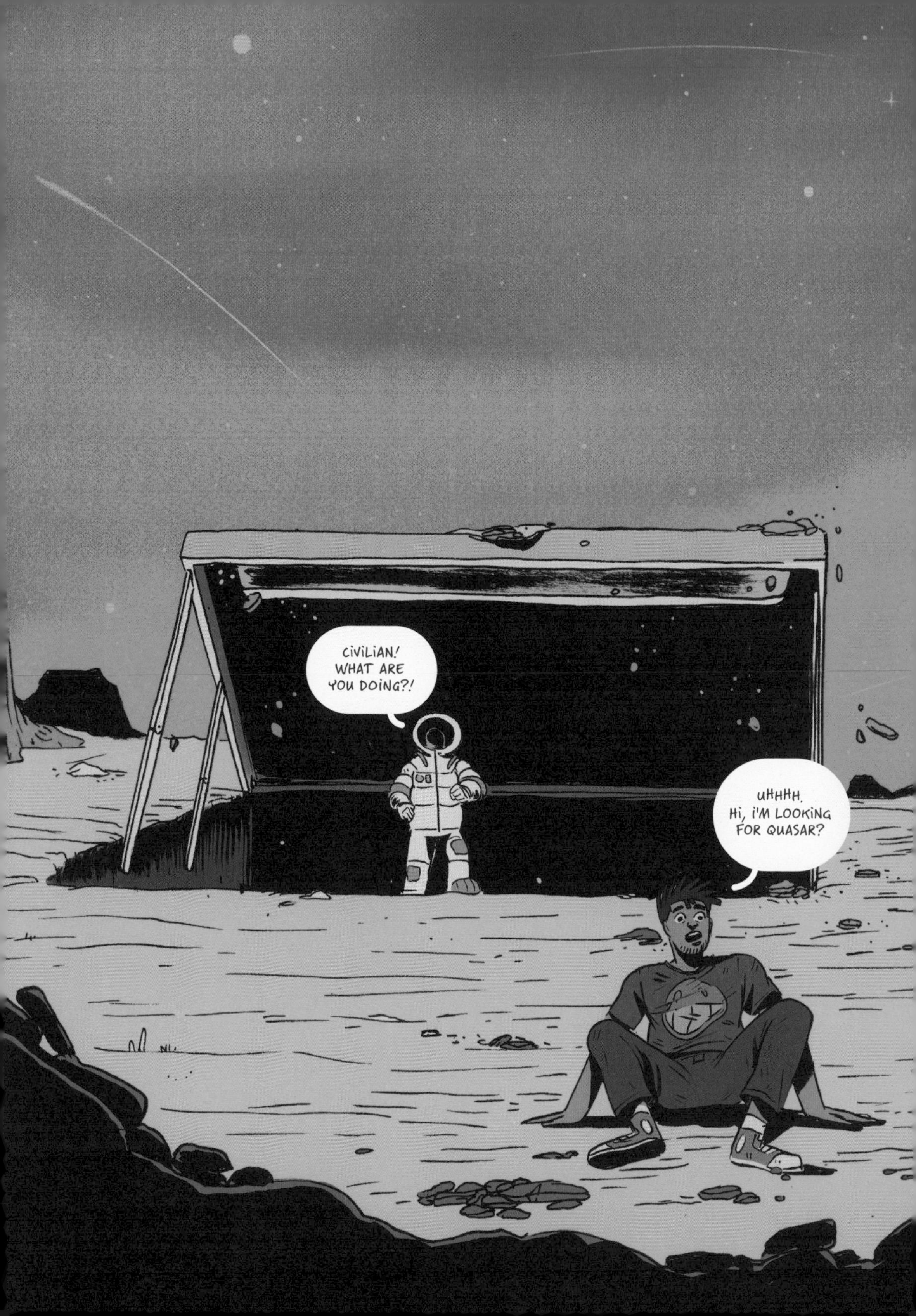
CIVILIAN! WHAT ARE YOU DOING?!
UHHHH. HI, I'M LOOKING FOR QUASAR?

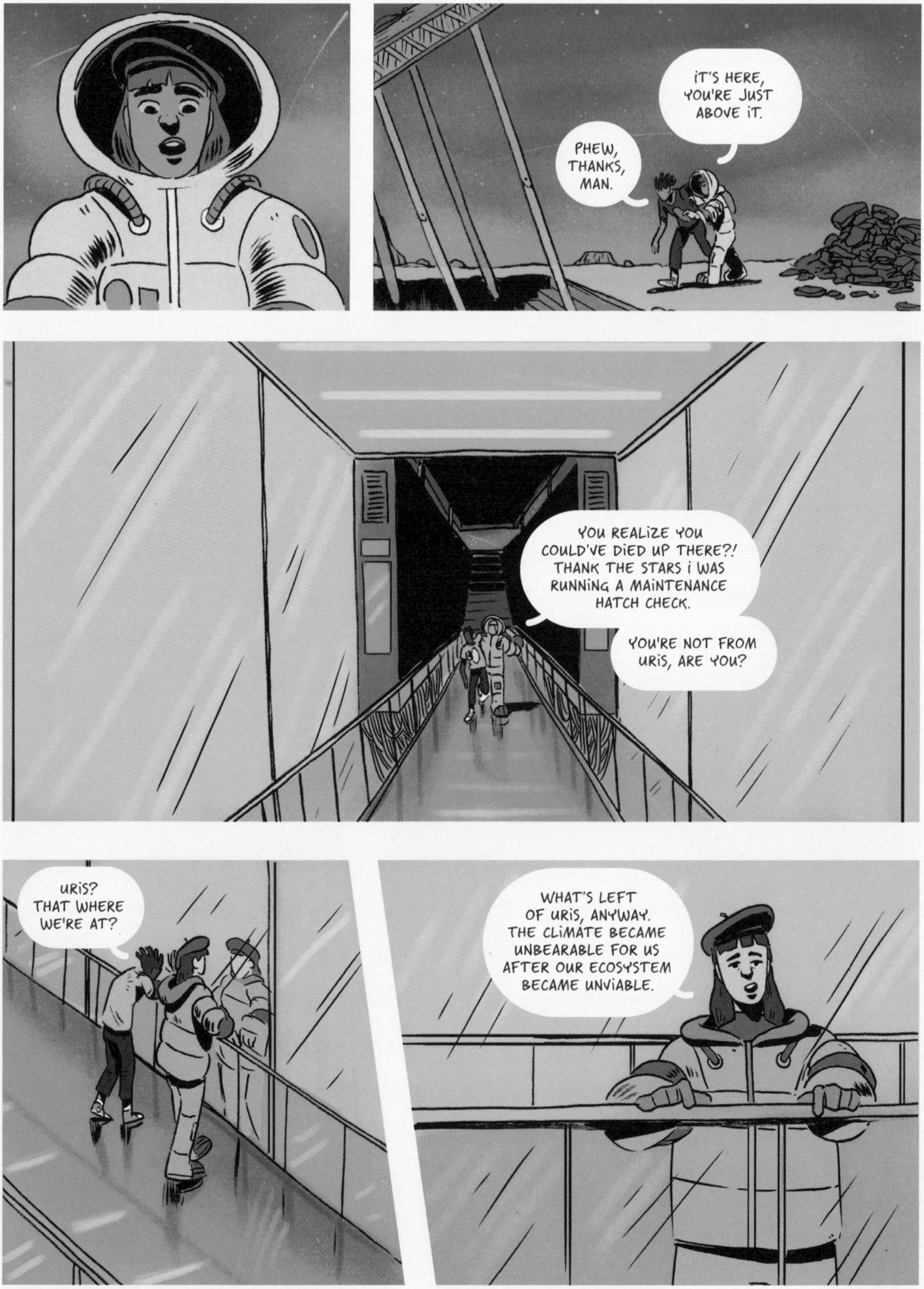

iT'S HERE, YOU'RE JUST ABOVE iT.
PHEW, THANKS, MAN.
YOU REALiZE YOU COULD'VE DiED UP THERE?! THANK THE STARS i WAS RUNNiNG A MAiNTENANCE HATCH CHECK.
YOU'RE NOT FROM URiS, ARE YOU?
URiS? THAT WHERE WE'RE AT?
WHAT'S LEFT OF URiS, ANYWAY. THE CLiMATE BECAME UNBEARABLE FOR US AFTER OUR ECOSYSTEM BECAME UNViABLE.

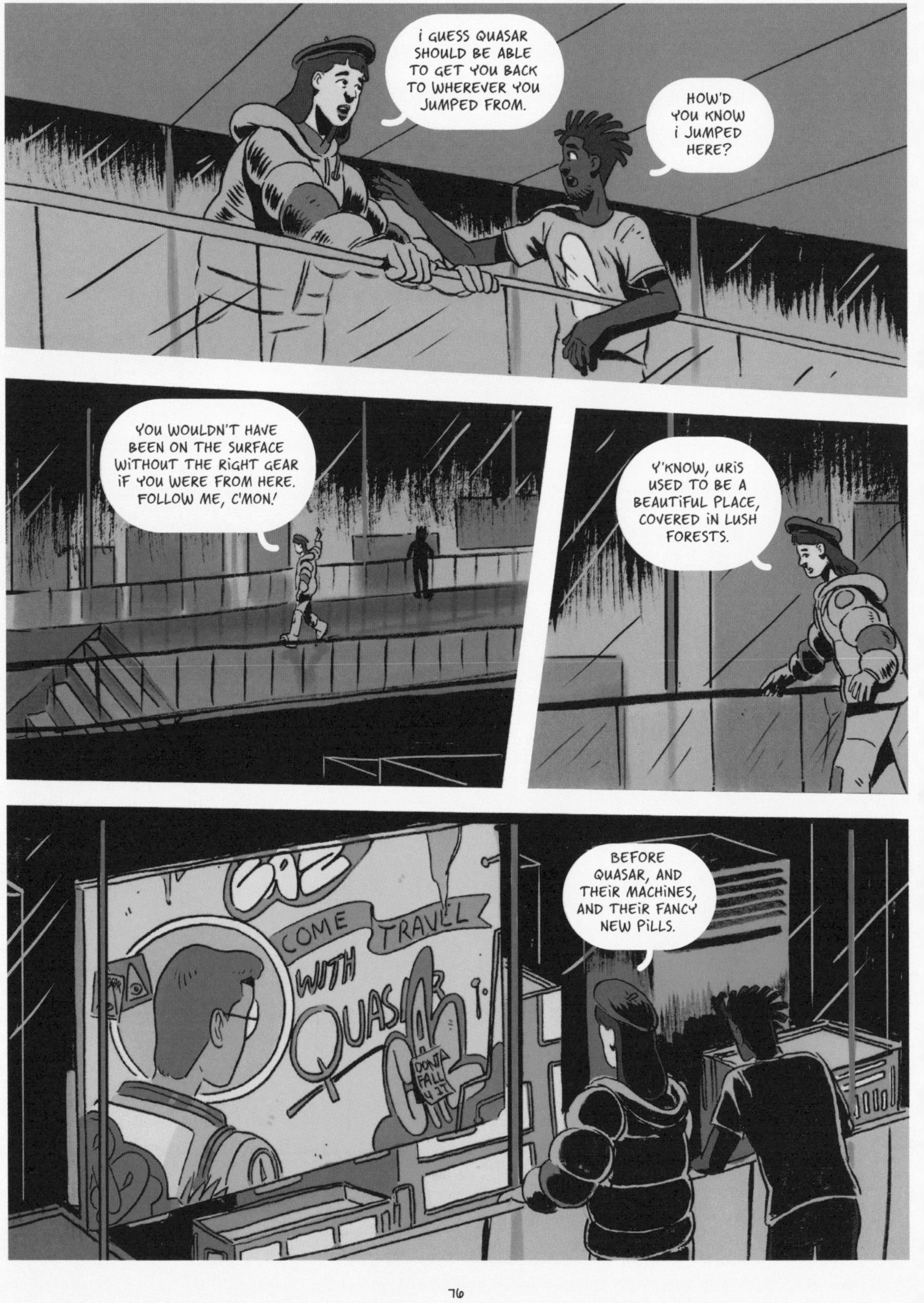
I GUESS QUASAR SHOULD BE ABLE TO GET YOU BACK TO WHEREVER YOU JUMPED FROM.
HOW'D YOU KNOW I JUMPED HERE?
YOU WOULDN'T HAVE BEEN ON THE SURFACE WITHOUT THE RIGHT GEAR IF YOU WERE FROM HERE. FOLLOW ME, C'MON!
Y'KNOW, URIS USED TO BE A BEAUTIFUL PLACE, COVERED IN LUSH FORESTS.
COME TRAVEL
WITH
DONT FALL 4 IT
BEFORE QUASAR, AND THEIR MACHINES, AND THEIR FANCY NEW PILLS.

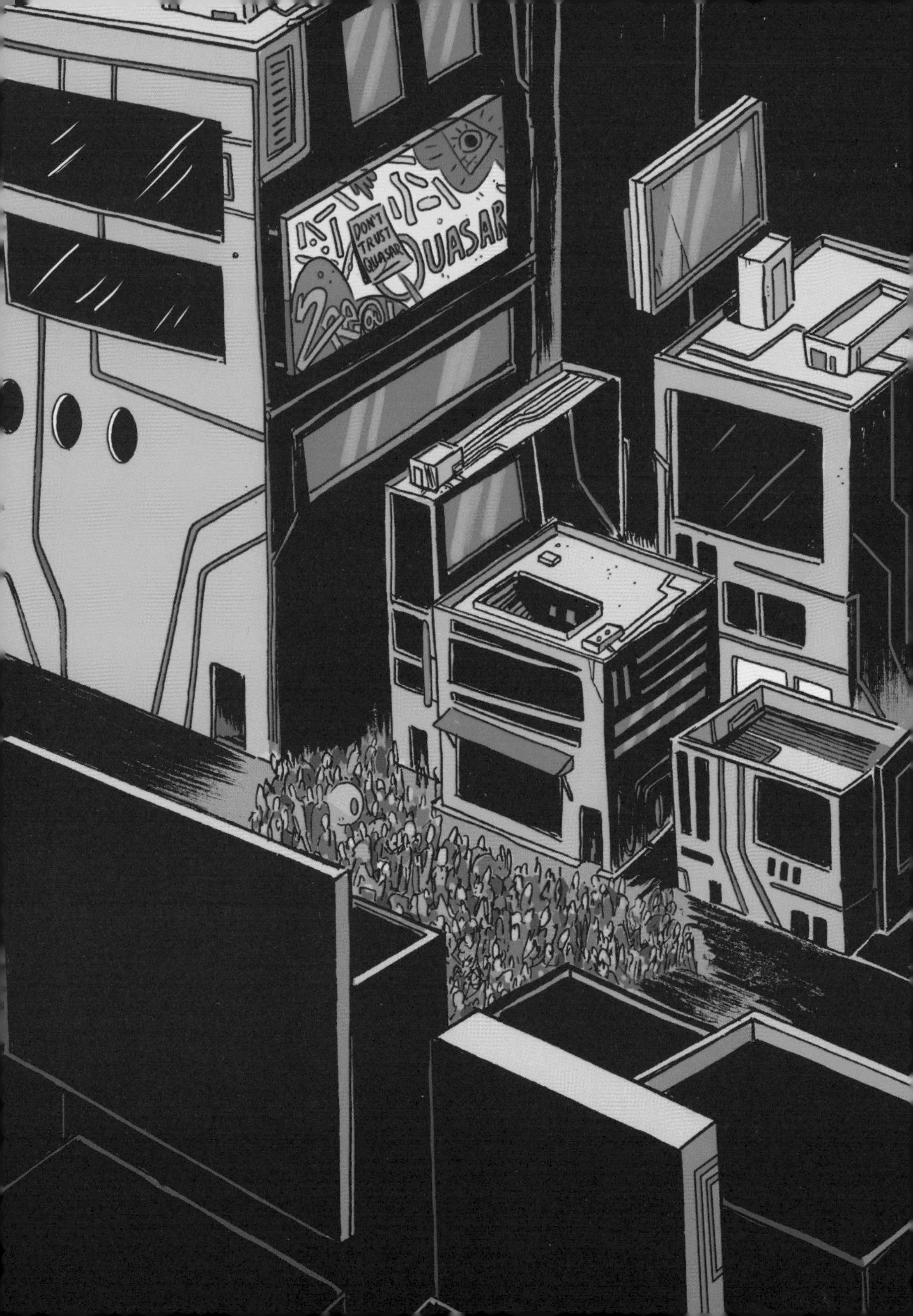
DON'T TRUST QUASAR
QUASAR

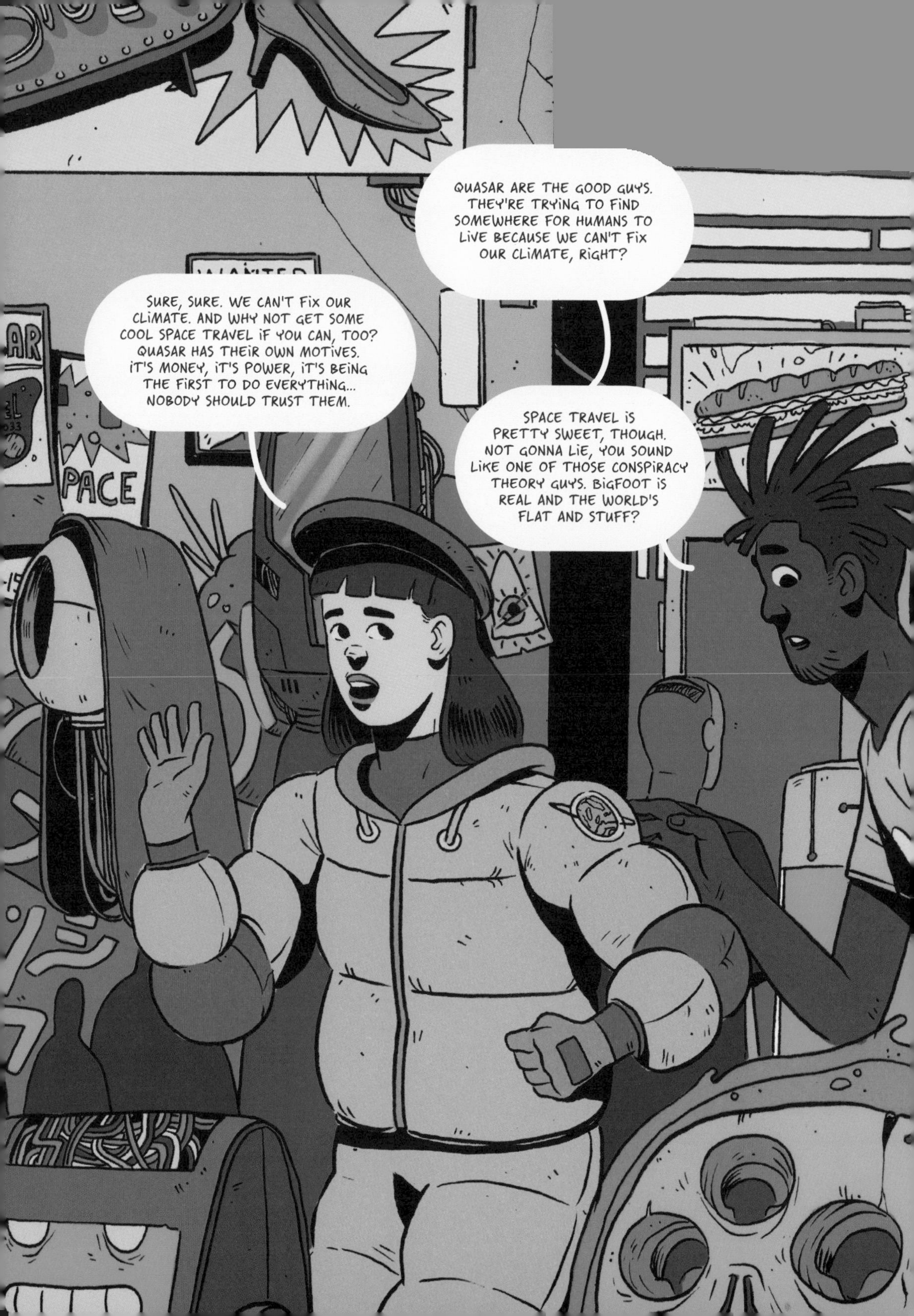
QUASAR ARE THE GOOD GUYS. THEY'RE TRYING TO FIND SOMEWHERE FOR HUMANS TO LIVE BECAUSE WE CAN'T FIX OUR CLIMATE, RIGHT?
SURE, SURE. WE CAN'T FIX OUR CLIMATE. AND WHY NOT GET SOME COOL SPACE TRAVEL IF YOU CAN, TOO? QUASAR HAS THEIR OWN MOTIVES. IT'S MONEY, IT'S POWER, IT'S BEING THE FIRST TO DO EVERYTHING... NOBODY SHOULD TRUST THEM.
SPACE TRAVEL IS PRETTY SWEET, THOUGH. NOT GONNA LIE, YOU SOUND LIKE ONE OF THOSE CONSPIRACY THEORY GUYS. BIGFOOT IS REAL AND THE WORLD'S FLAT AND STUFF?
PACE

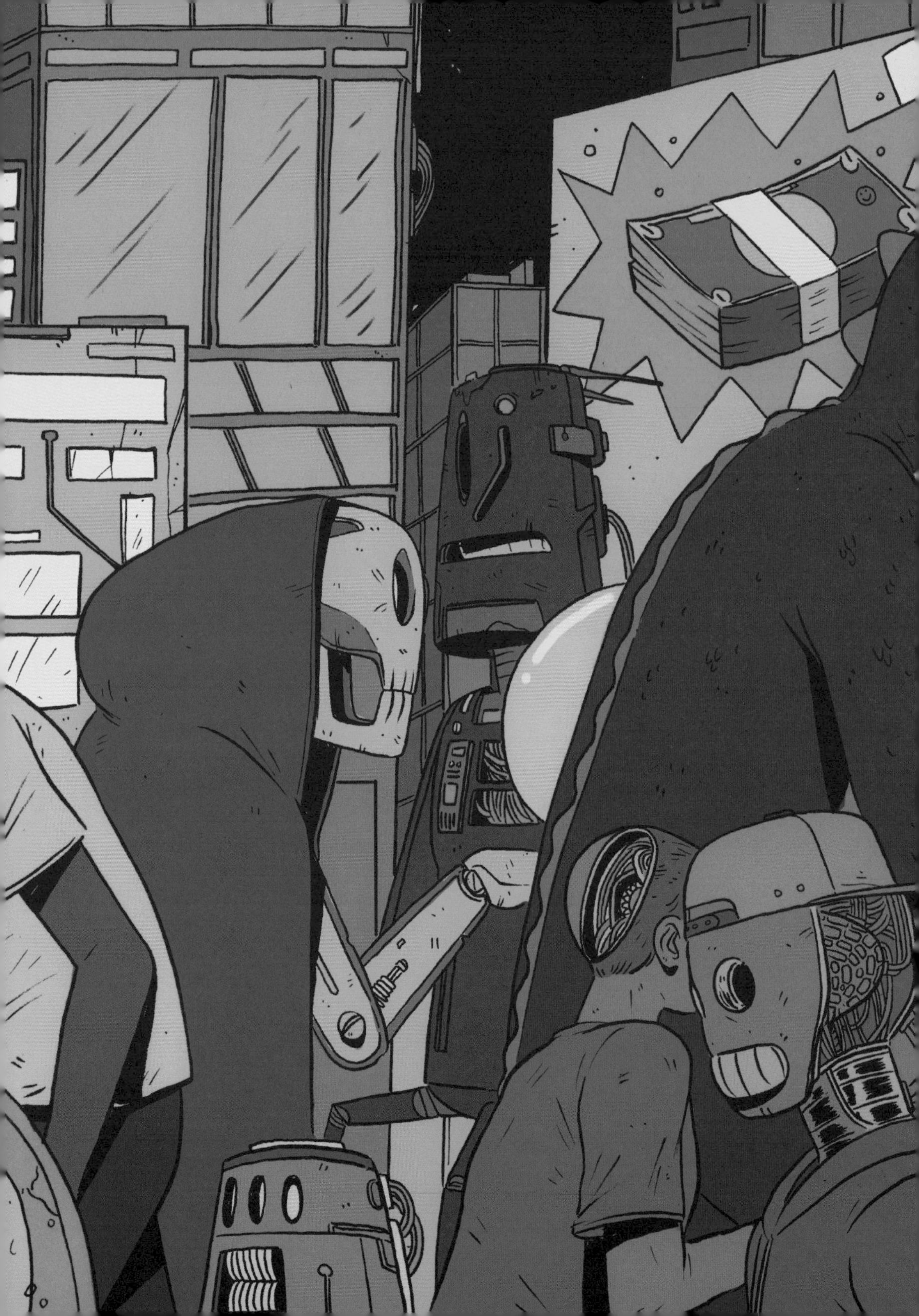

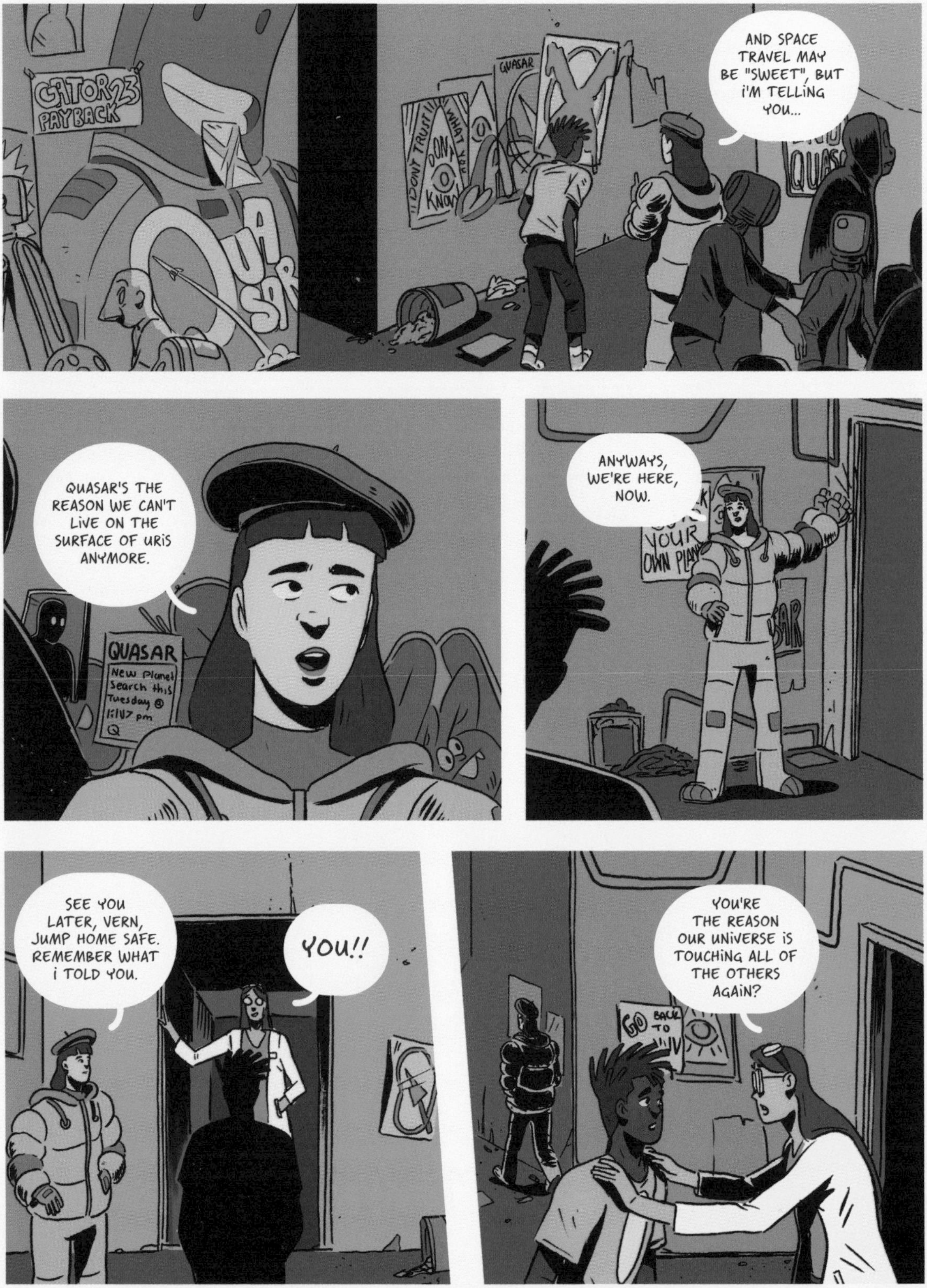
GATOR23 PAYBACK
QUASAR
AND SPACE TRAVEL MAY BE "SWEET", BUT i'M TELLING YOU...
QUASAR'S THE REASON WE CAN'T LiVE ON THE SURFACE OF URiS ANYMORE.
QUASAR
New Planet Search this Tuesday @ 1:147 pm
Q
ANYWAYS, WE'RE HERE, NOW.
SEE YOU LATER, VERN, JUMP HOME SAFE. REMEMBER WHAT i TOLD YOU.
YOU!!
YOU'RE THE REASON OUR UNiVERSE iS TOUCHiNG ALL OF THE OTHERS AGAiN?

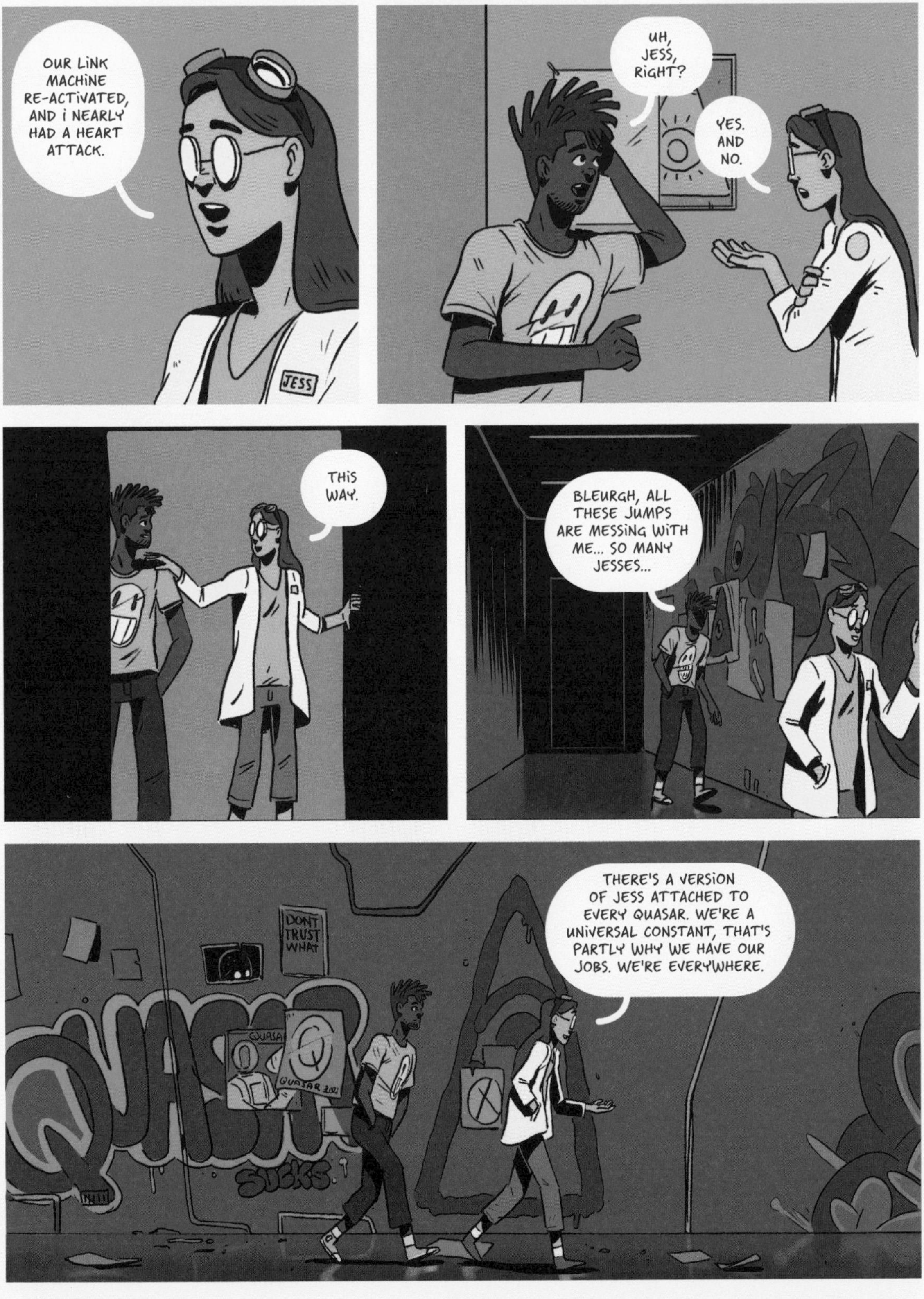
OUR LINK MACHINE RE-ACTIVATED, AND I NEARLY HAD A HEART ATTACK.
JESS
UH, JESS, RIGHT?
YES. AND NO.
THIS WAY.
BLEURGH, ALL THESE JUMPS ARE MESSING WITH ME... SO MANY JESSES...
DON'T TRUST WHAT
QUASAR
QUASAR 2021
SUCKS
THERE'S A VERSION OF JESS ATTACHED TO EVERY QUASAR. WE'RE A UNIVERSAL CONSTANT, THAT'S PARTLY WHY WE HAVE OUR JOBS. WE'RE EVERYWHERE.

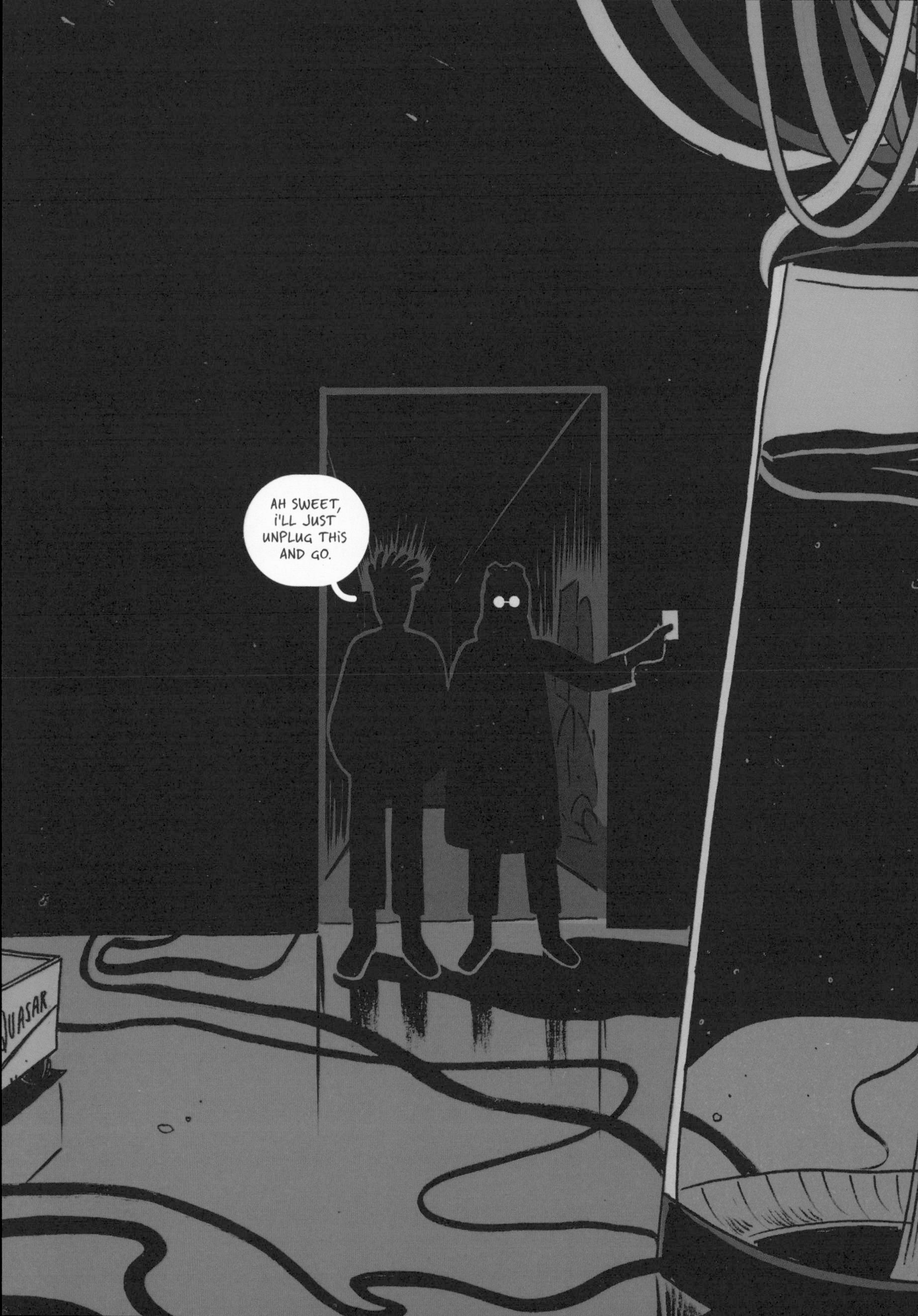
AH SWEET, I'LL JUST UNPLUG THIS AND GO.
QUASAR

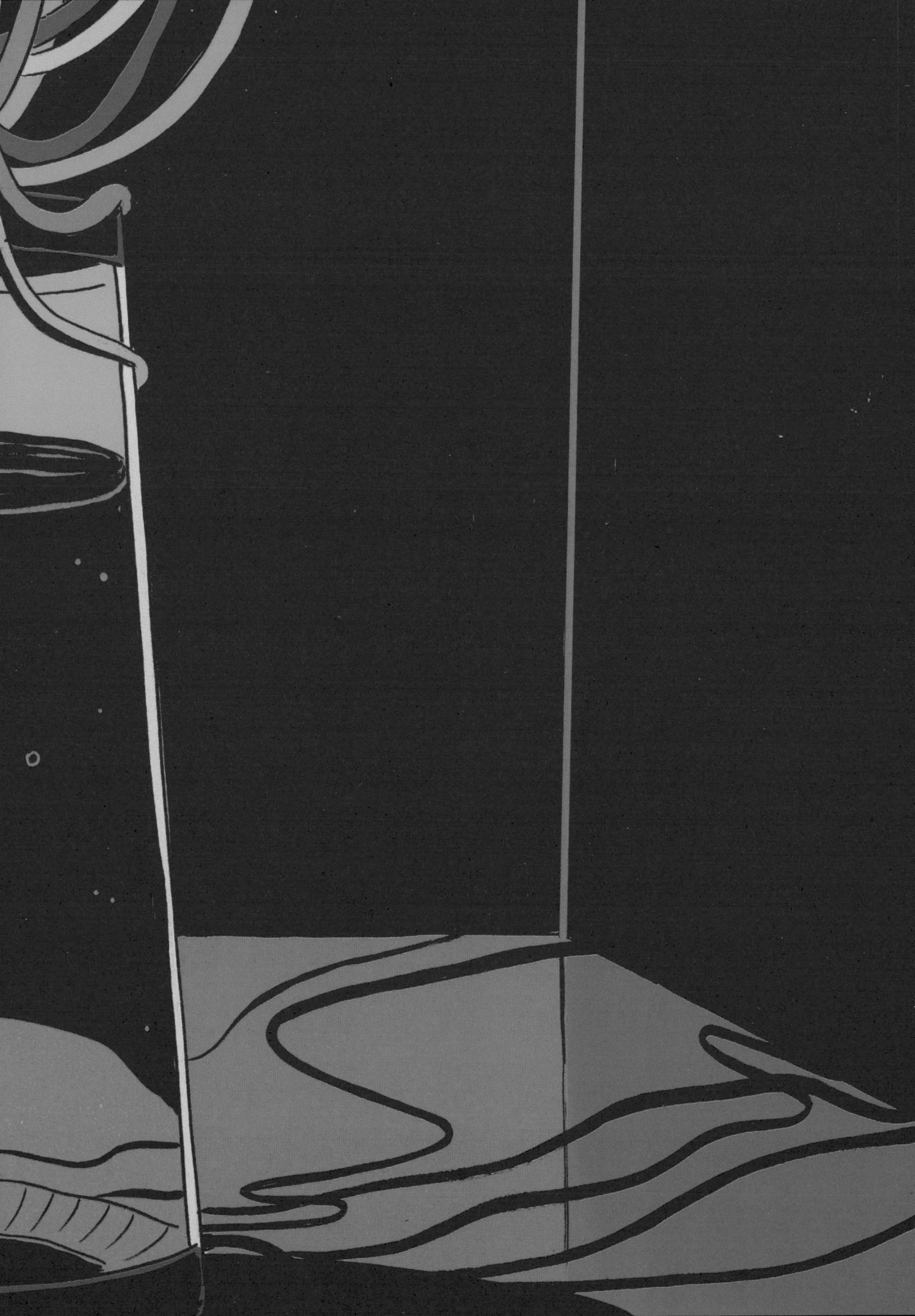

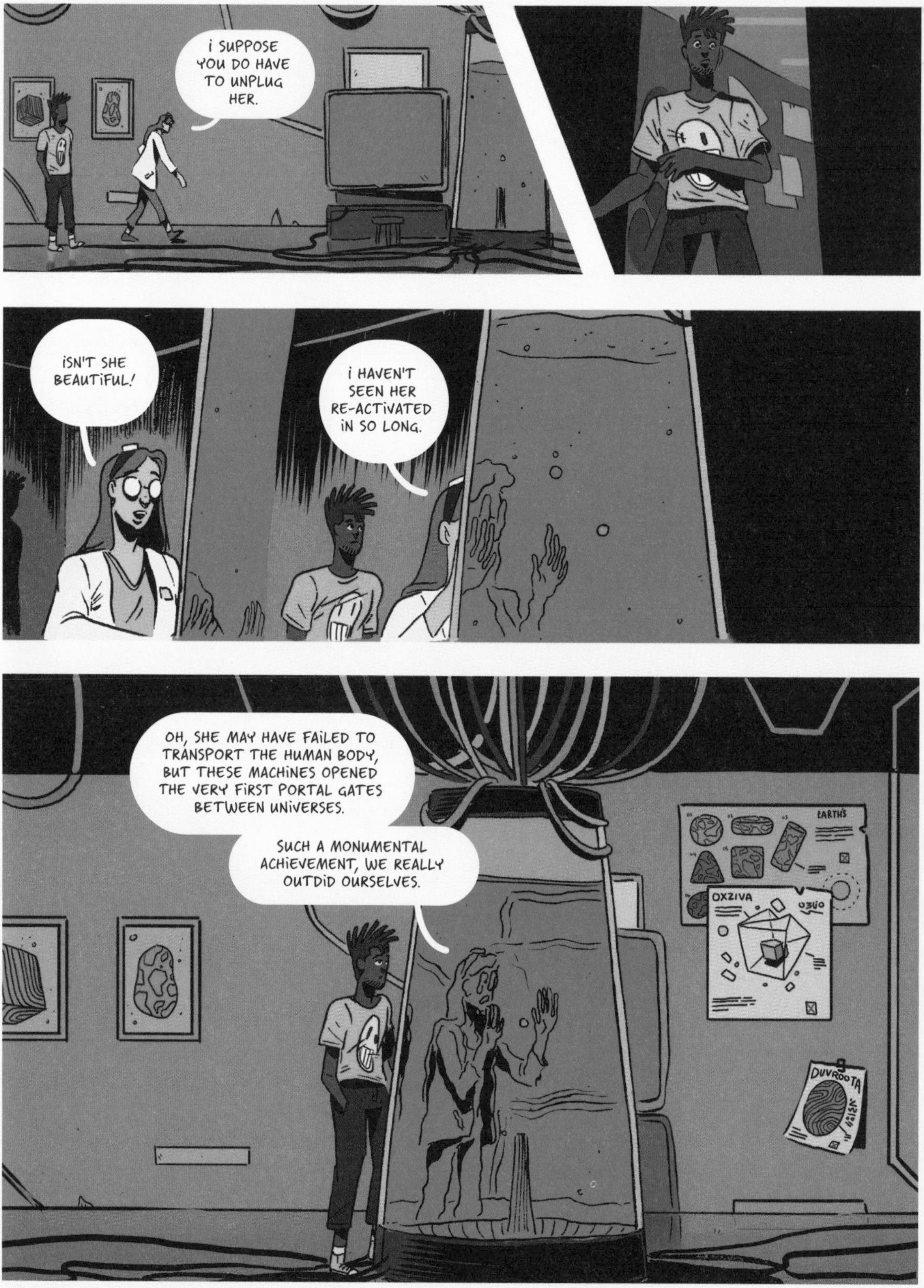

I SUPPOSE YOU DO HAVE TO UNPLUG HER.
ISN'T SHE BEAUTIFUL!
I HAVEN'T SEEN HER RE-ACTIVATED IN SO LONG.
OH, SHE MAY HAVE FAILED TO TRANSPORT THE HUMAN BODY, BUT THESE MACHINES OPENED THE VERY FIRST PORTAL GATES BETWEEN UNIVERSES.
SUCH A MONUMENTAL ACHIEVEMENT, WE REALLY OUTDID OURSELVES.
EARTH'S
OXZIVA
DUVROOTA

AND THEN, OF COURSE, WE SURPASSED OURSELVES AGAIN.

WITH THESE! INSTANT TRAVEL IN ONE SWALLOW!

YOU DON'T EVEN NEED WATER.

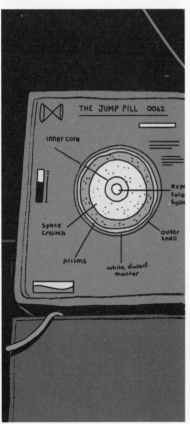

THE JUMP PILL 0062

inner core

exp.
Solar
Syste

Space
crystals

outer
shell

prisms

white dwarf
matter

SHE'S SO MISUNDERSTOOD. OF COURSE THE LINK MACHINES WEREN'T ALWAYS HEALTHY FOR THE MULTIVERSE...

BUT REALLY, CAN A MACHINE BE BLAMED FOR THE MISTAKES MADE BY THE HUMANS WHO USE THEM?

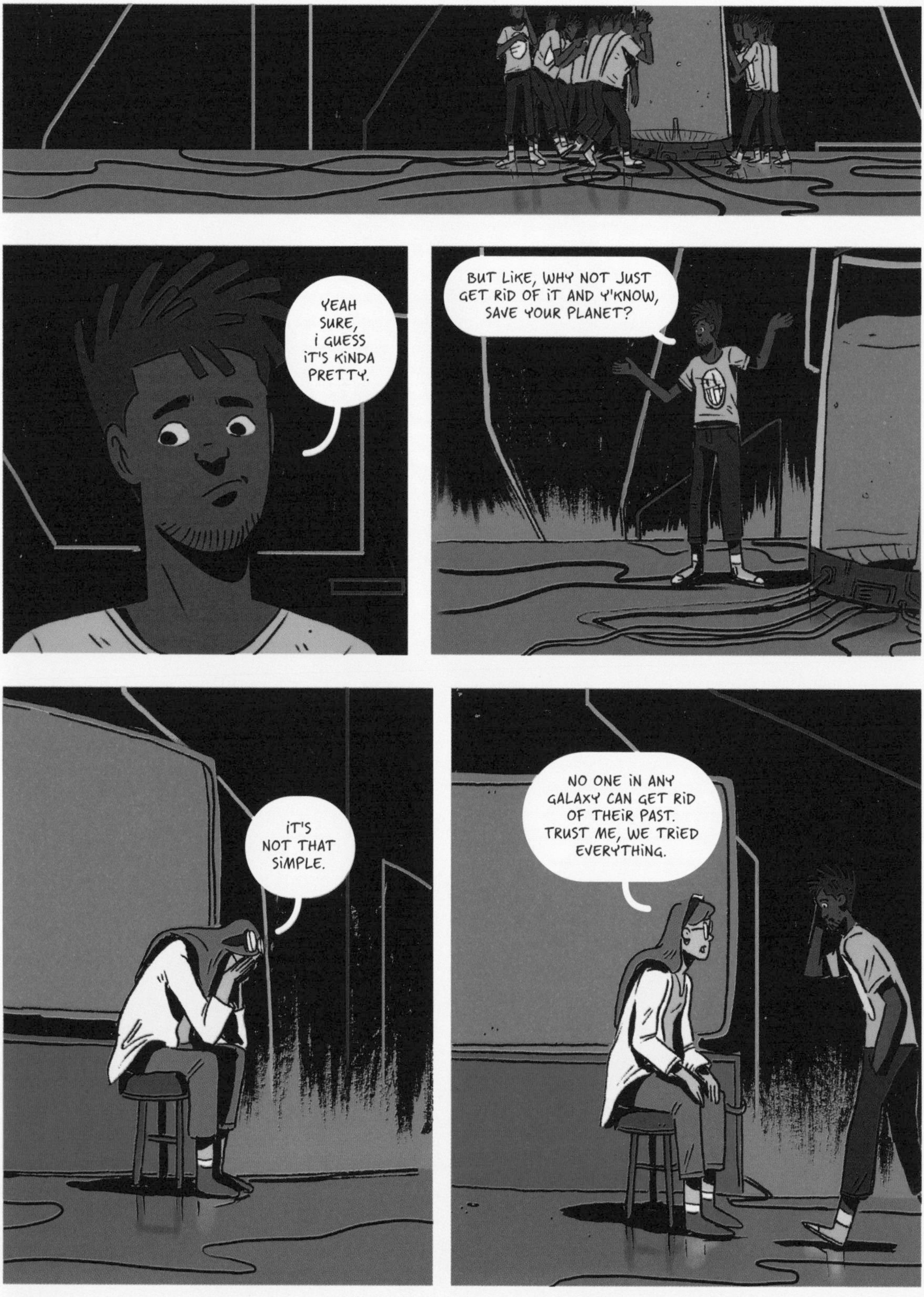
YEAH SURE, i GUESS iT'S KiNDA PRETTY.
BUT LiKE, WHY NOT JUST GET RiD OF iT AND Y'KNOW, SAVE YOUR PLANET?
iT'S NOT THAT SiMPLE.
NO ONE iN ANY GALAXY CAN GET RiD OF THEiR PAST. TRUST ME, WE TRiED EVERYTHiNG.

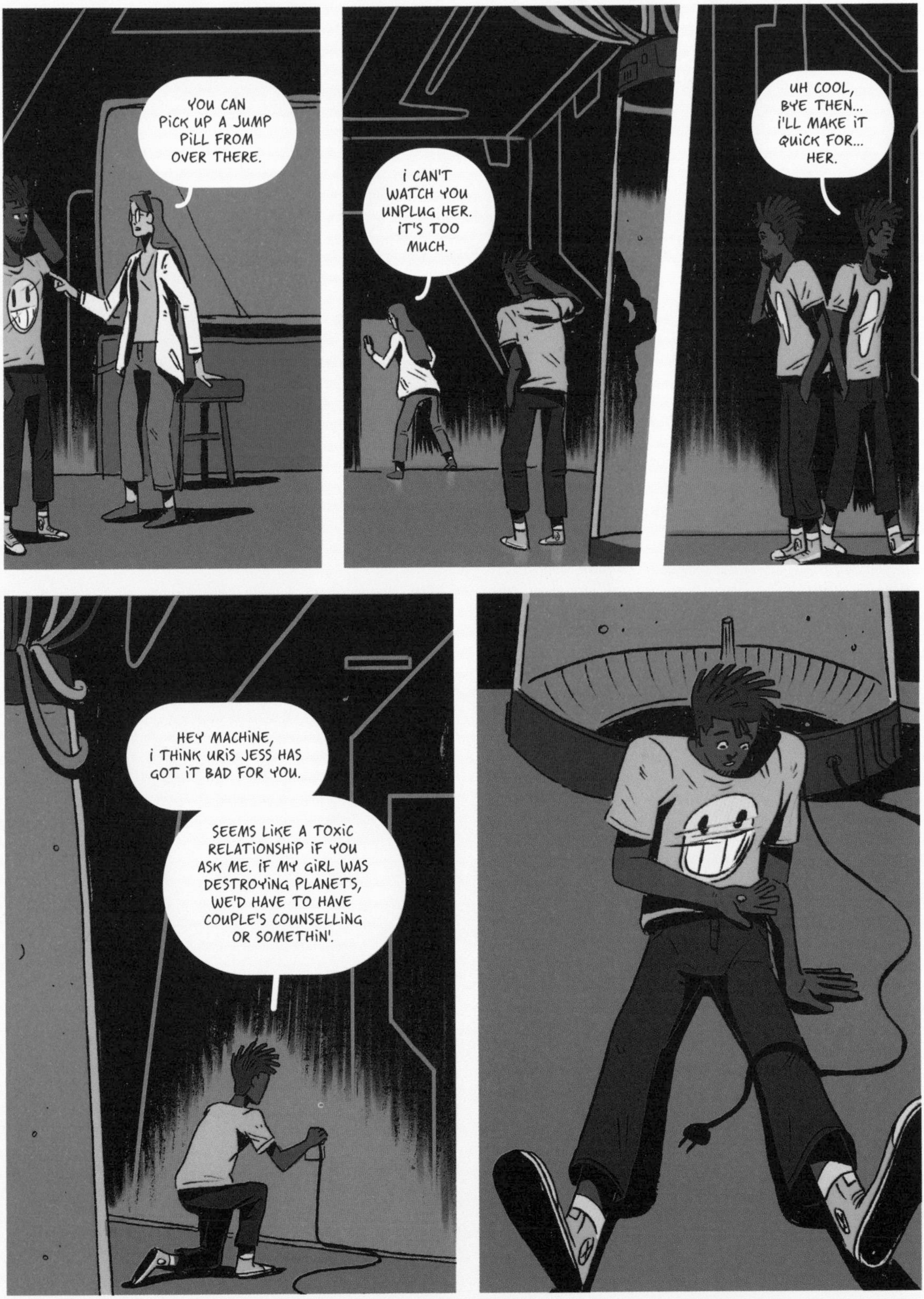
YOU CAN PICK UP A JUMP PILL FROM OVER THERE.
I CAN'T WATCH YOU UNPLUG HER. IT'S TOO MUCH.
UH COOL, BYE THEN... I'LL MAKE IT QUICK FOR... HER.
HEY MACHINE, I THINK URIS JESS HAS GOT IT BAD FOR YOU.
SEEMS LIKE A TOXIC RELATIONSHIP IF YOU ASK ME. IF MY GIRL WAS DESTROYING PLANETS, WE'D HAVE TO HAVE COUPLE'S COUNSELLING OR SOMETHIN'.

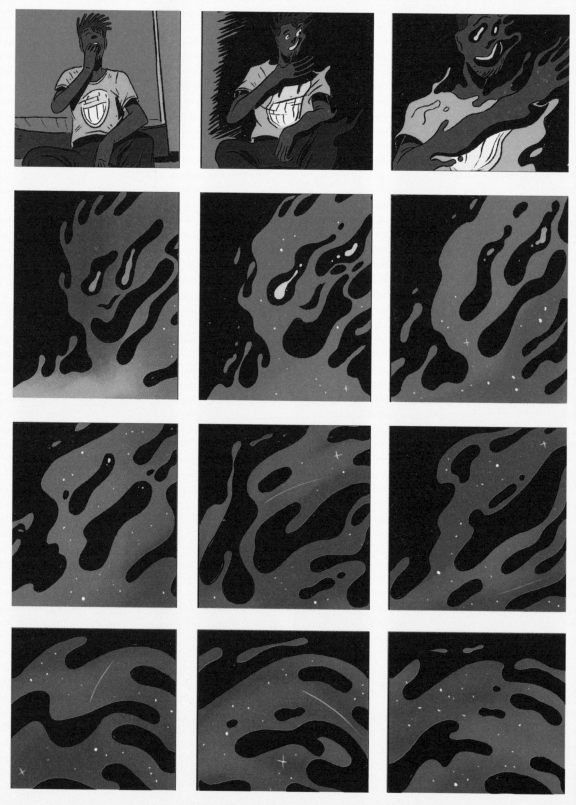

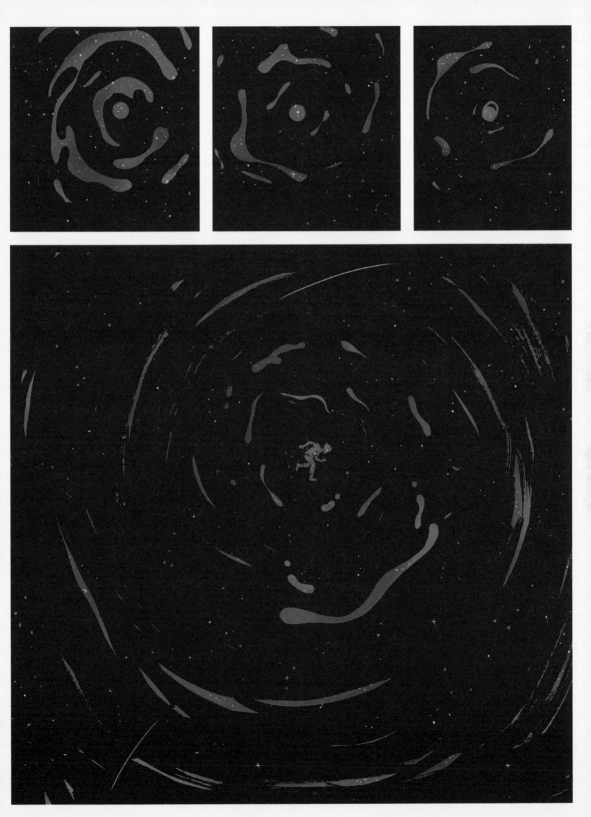

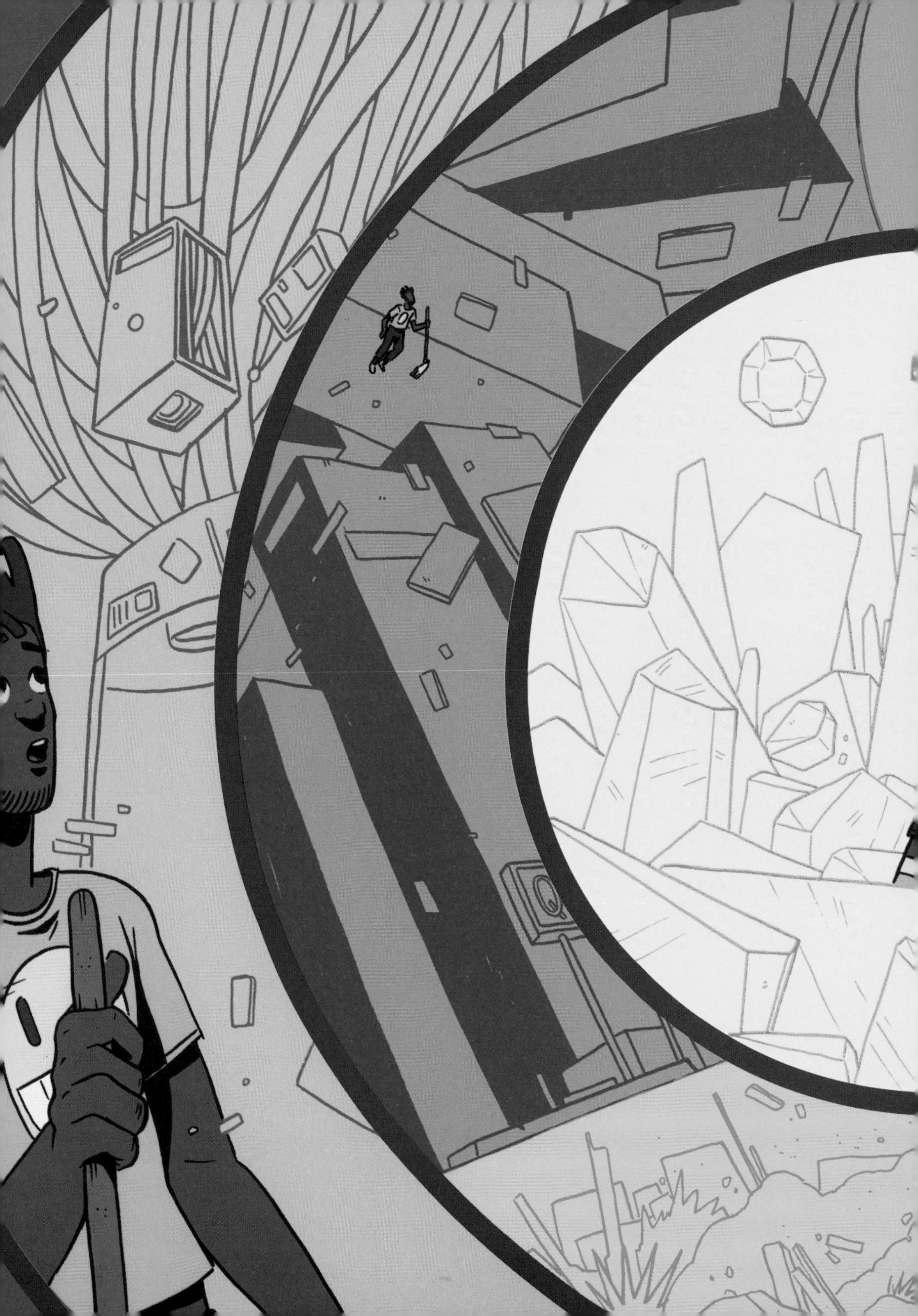

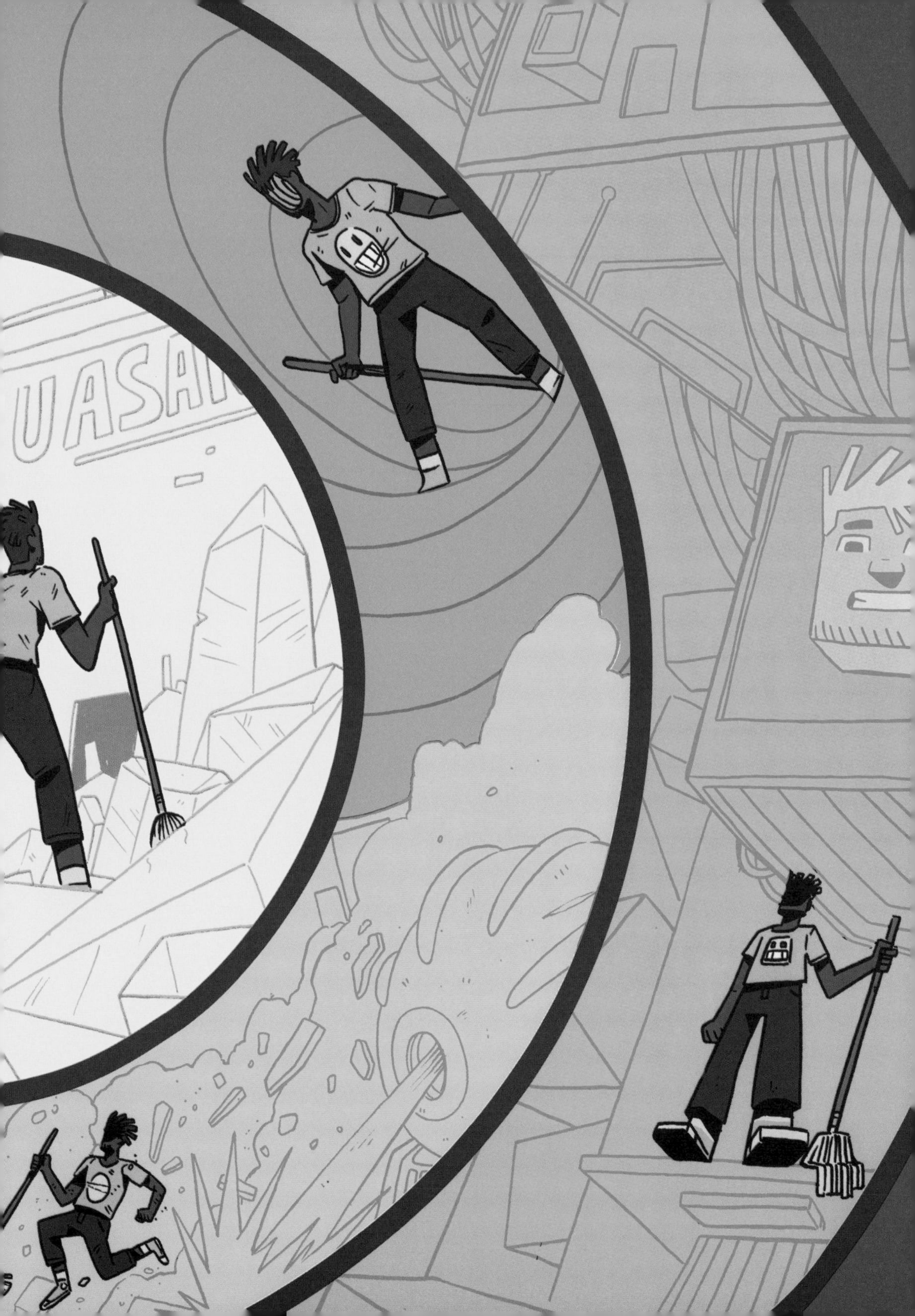

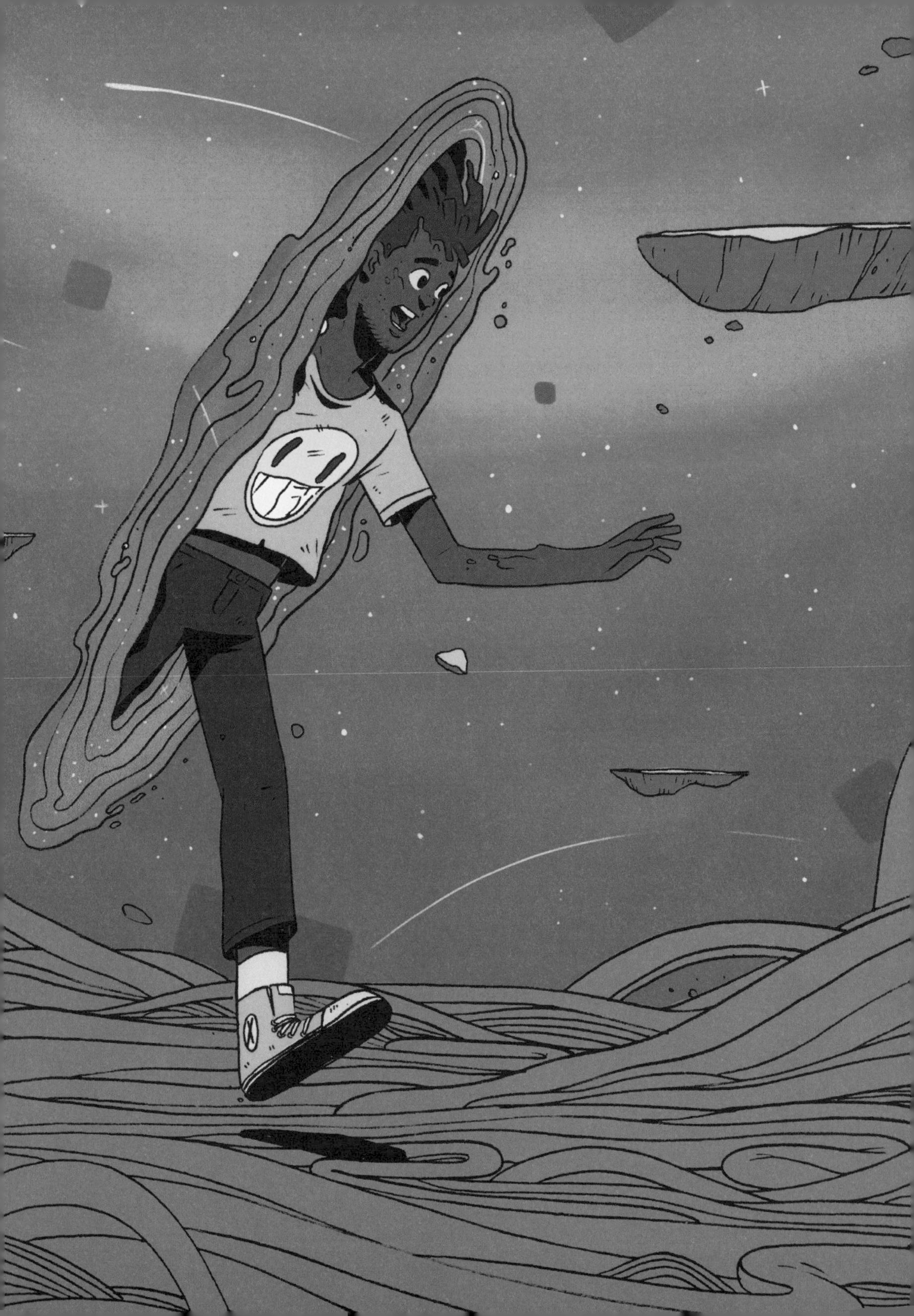

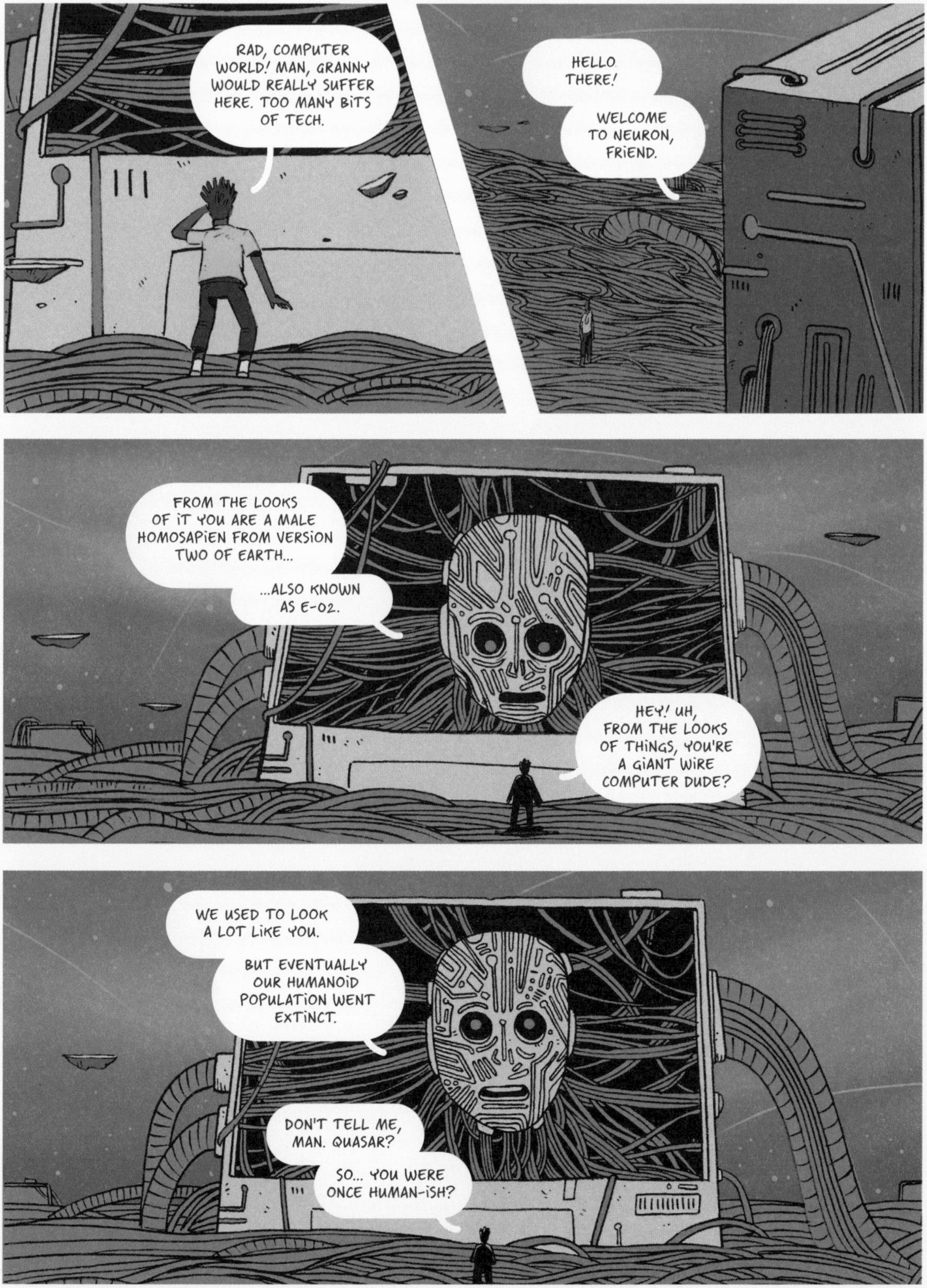
RAD, COMPUTER WORLD! MAN, GRANNY WOULD REALLY SUFFER HERE. TOO MANY BITS OF TECH.
HELLO THERE!
WELCOME TO NEURON, FRIEND.
FROM THE LOOKS OF IT YOU ARE A MALE HOMOSAPIEN FROM VERSION TWO OF EARTH...
...ALSO KNOWN AS E-02.
HEY! UH, FROM THE LOOKS OF THINGS, YOU'RE A GIANT WIRE COMPUTER DUDE?
WE USED TO LOOK A LOT LIKE YOU.
BUT EVENTUALLY OUR HUMANOID POPULATION WENT EXTINCT.
DON'T TELL ME, MAN. QUASAR?
SO... YOU WERE ONCE HUMAN-ISH?

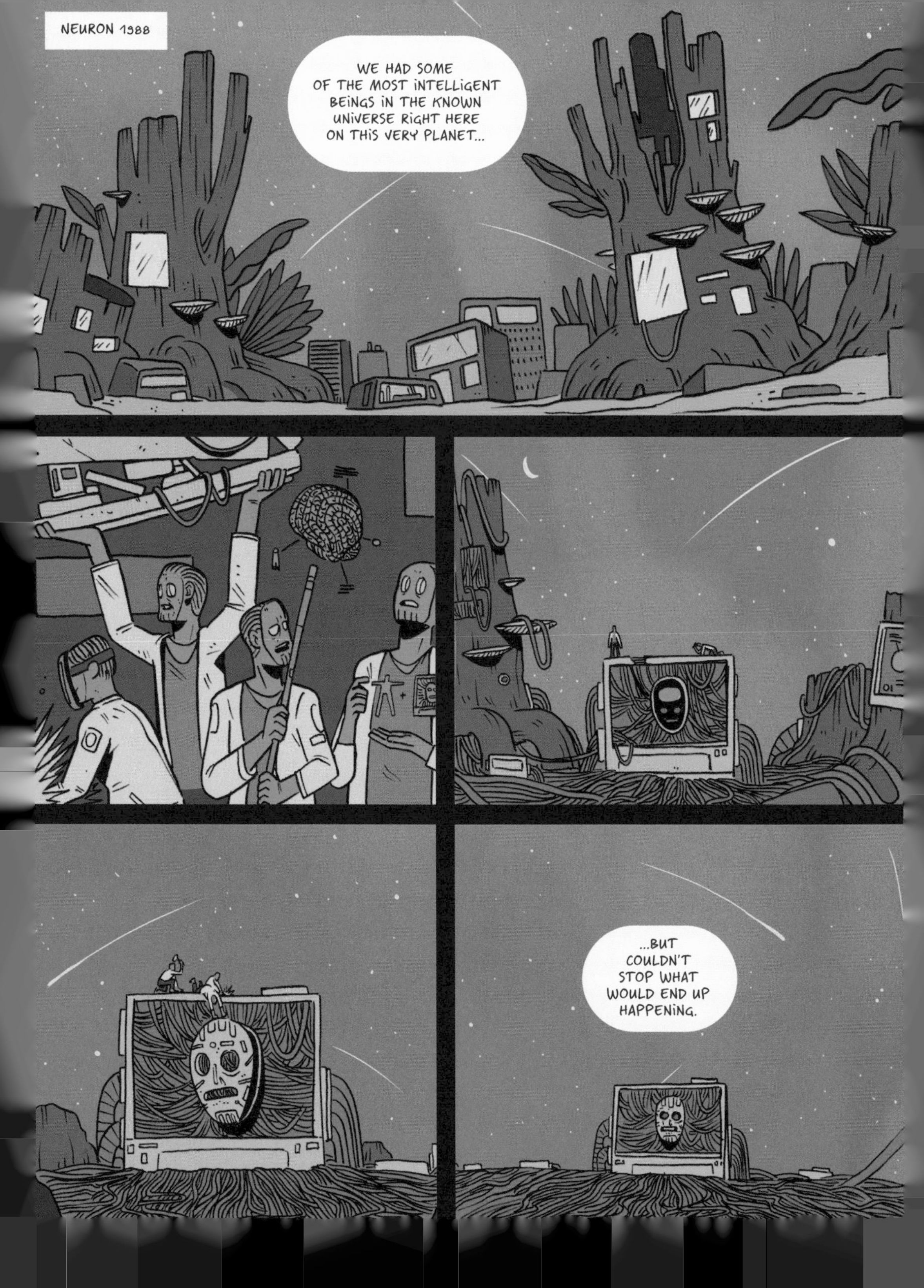
NEURON 1988
WE HAD SOME OF THE MOST INTELLIGENT BEINGS IN THE KNOWN UNIVERSE RIGHT HERE ON THIS VERY PLANET...
...BUT COULDN'T STOP WHAT WOULD END UP HAPPENING.

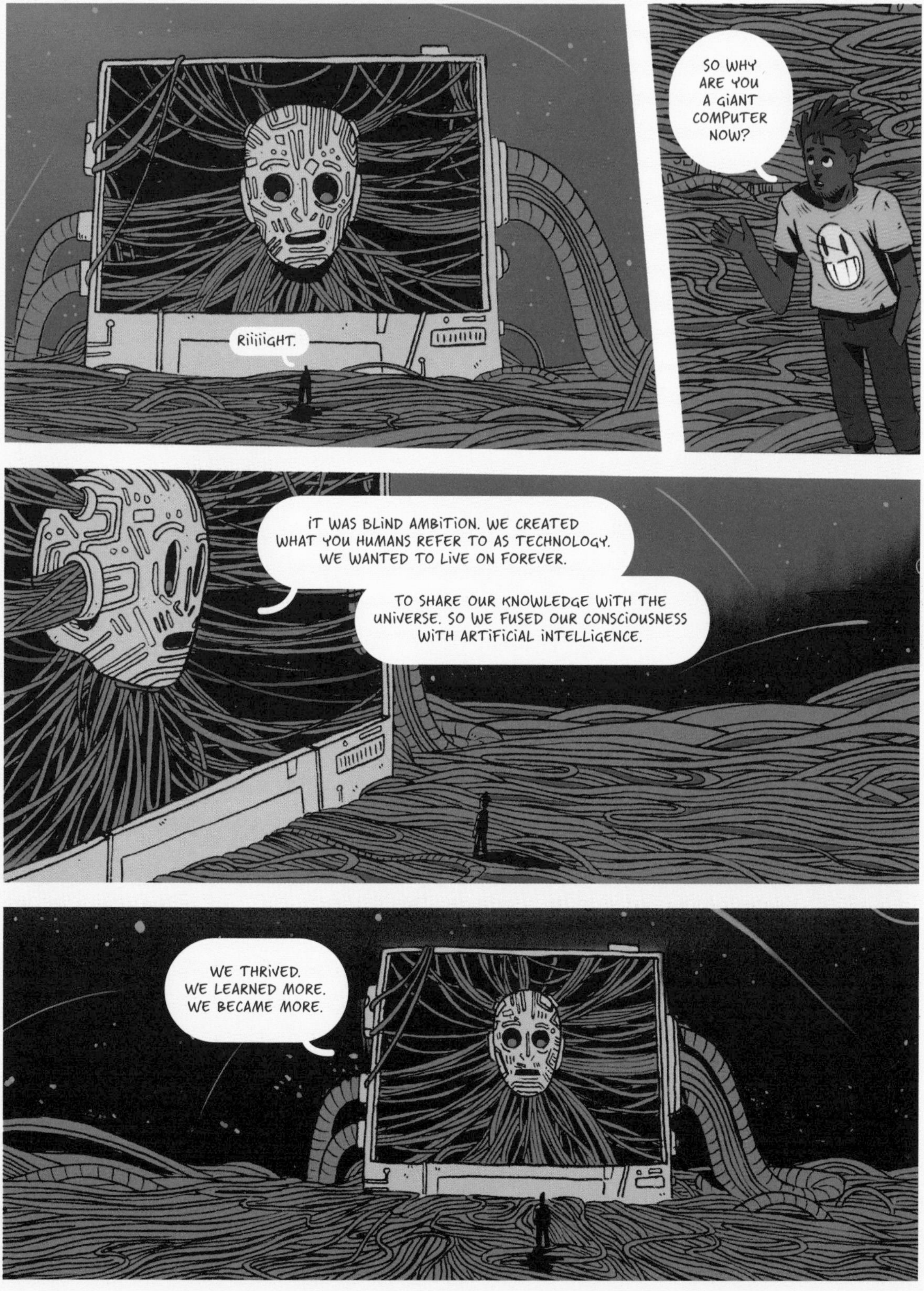
RiiiiiGHT.
SO WHY ARE YOU A GiANT COMPUTER NOW?
iT WAS BLiND AMBiTiON. WE CREATED WHAT YOU HUMANS REFER TO AS TECHNOLOGY. WE WANTED TO LiVE ON FOREVER.
TO SHARE OUR KNOWLEDGE WiTH THE UNiVERSE. SO WE FUSED OUR CONSCiOUSNESS WiTH ARTiFiCiAL iNTELLiGENCE.
WE THRiVED. WE LEARNED MORE. WE BECAME MORE.

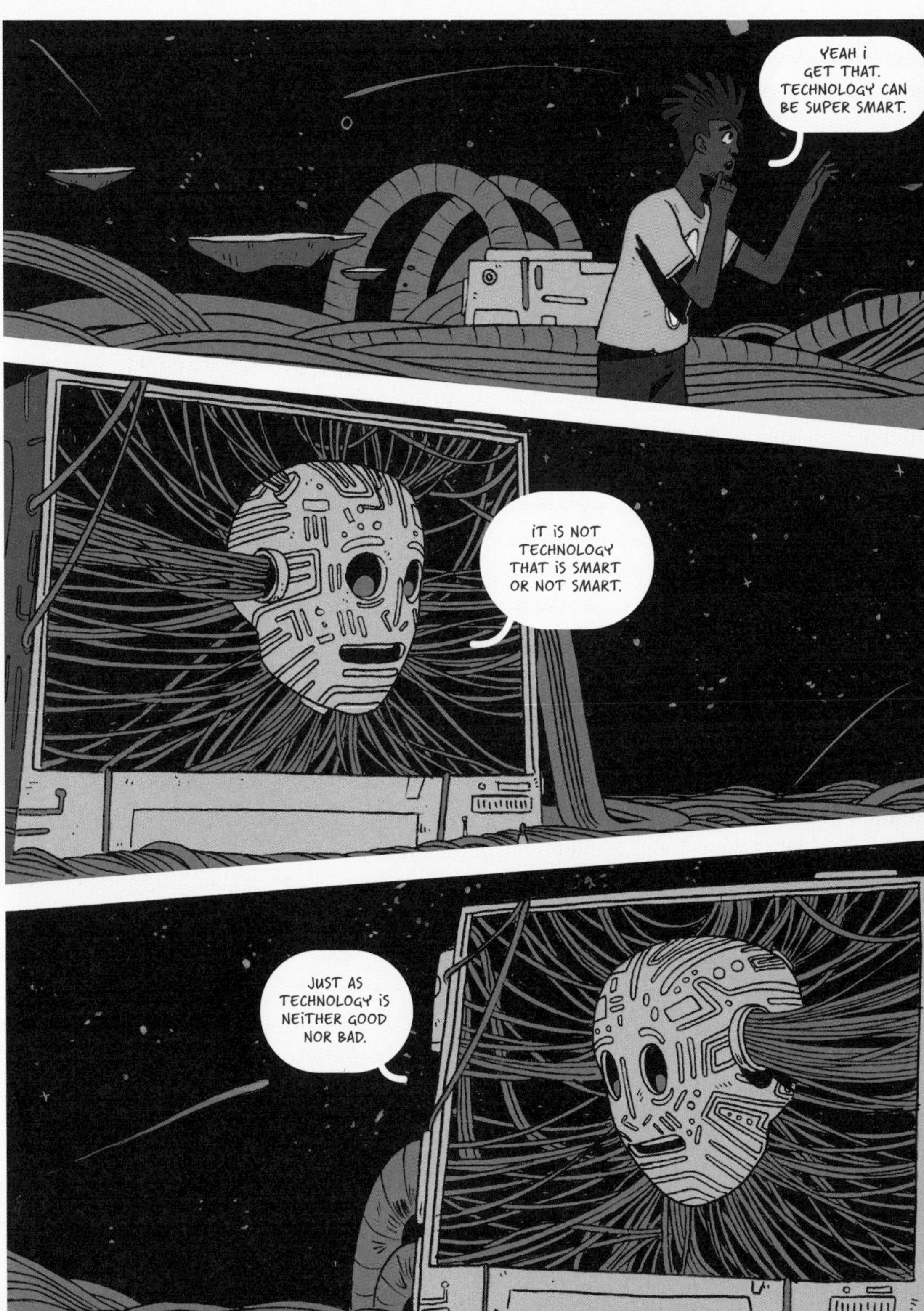
YEAH i GET THAT. TECHNOLOGY CAN BE SUPER SMART.
iT iS NOT TECHNOLOGY THAT iS SMART OR NOT SMART.
JUST AS TECHNOLOGY iS NEiTHER GOOD NOR BAD.

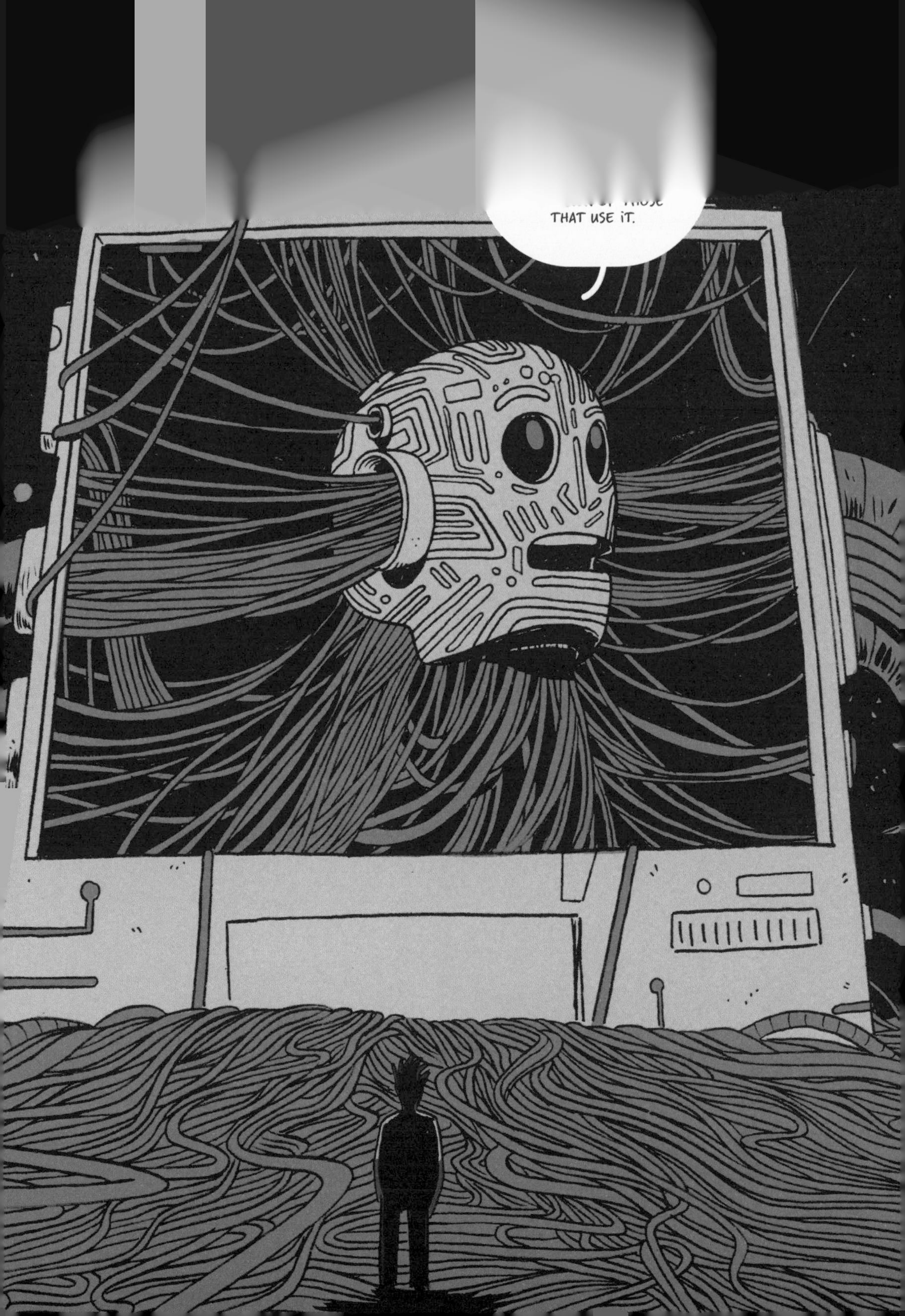
THAT USE iT.

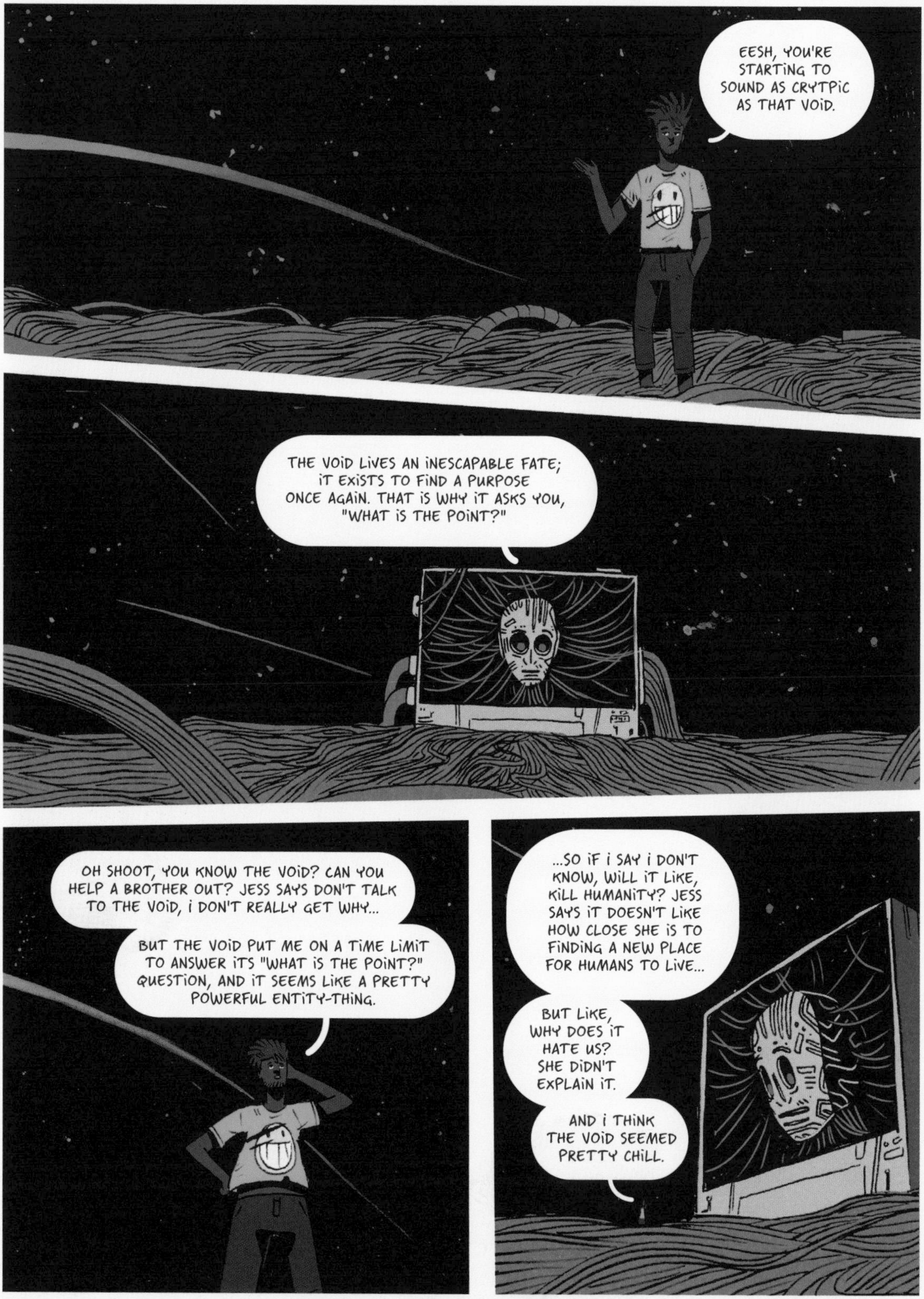
EESH, YOU'RE STARTING TO SOUND AS CRYTPIC AS THAT VOID.
THE VOID LIVES AN INESCAPABLE FATE; IT EXISTS TO FIND A PURPOSE ONCE AGAIN. THAT IS WHY IT ASKS YOU, "WHAT IS THE POINT?"
OH SHOOT, YOU KNOW THE VOID? CAN YOU HELP A BROTHER OUT? JESS SAYS DON'T TALK TO THE VOID, I DON'T REALLY GET WHY...
BUT THE VOID PUT ME ON A TIME LIMIT TO ANSWER ITS "WHAT IS THE POINT?" QUESTION, AND IT SEEMS LIKE A PRETTY POWERFUL ENTITY-THING.
...SO IF I SAY I DON'T KNOW, WILL IT LIKE, KILL HUMANITY? JESS SAYS IT DOESN'T LIKE HOW CLOSE SHE IS TO FINDING A NEW PLACE FOR HUMANS TO LIVE...
BUT LIKE, WHY DOES IT HATE US? SHE DIDN'T EXPLAIN IT.
AND I THINK THE VOID SEEMED PRETTY CHILL.

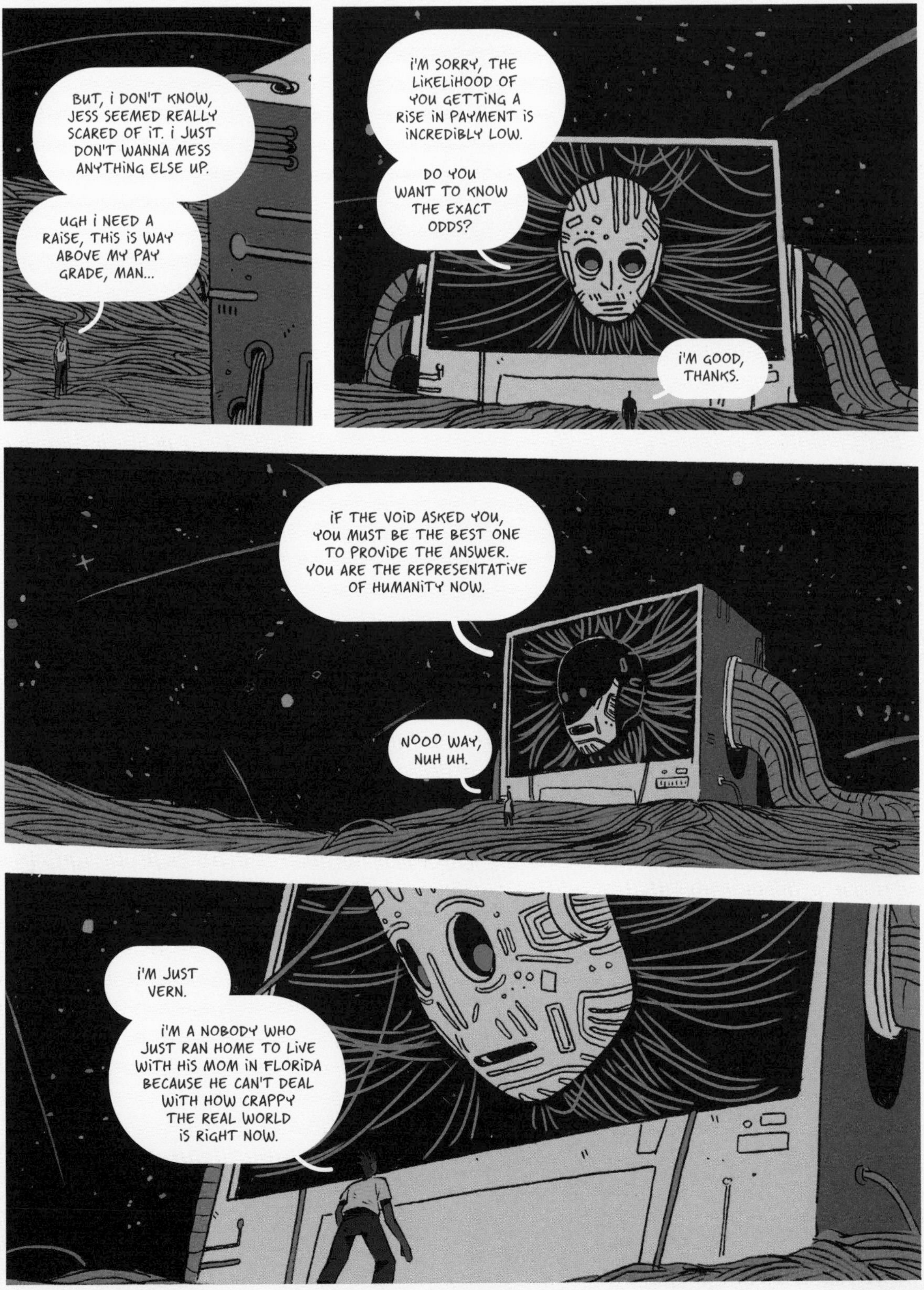
BUT, i DON'T KNOW, JESS SEEMED REALLY SCARED OF iT. i JUST DON'T WANNA MESS ANYTHiNG ELSE UP.
UGH i NEED A RAiSE, THiS iS WAY ABOVE MY PAY GRADE, MAN...
i'M SORRY, THE LiKELiHOOD OF YOU GETTiNG A RiSE iN PAYMENT iS iNCREDiBLY LOW.
DO YOU WANT TO KNOW THE EXACT ODDS?
i'M GOOD, THANKS.
iF THE VOiD ASKED YOU, YOU MUST BE THE BEST ONE TO PROVIDE THE ANSWER. YOU ARE THE REPRESENTATiVE OF HUMANiTY NOW.
NOOO WAY, NUH UH.
i'M JUST VERN.
i'M A NOBODY WHO JUST RAN HOME TO LiVE WiTH HiS MOM iN FLORiDA BECAUSE HE CAN'T DEAL WiTH HOW CRAPPY THE REAL WORLD iS RiGHT NOW.

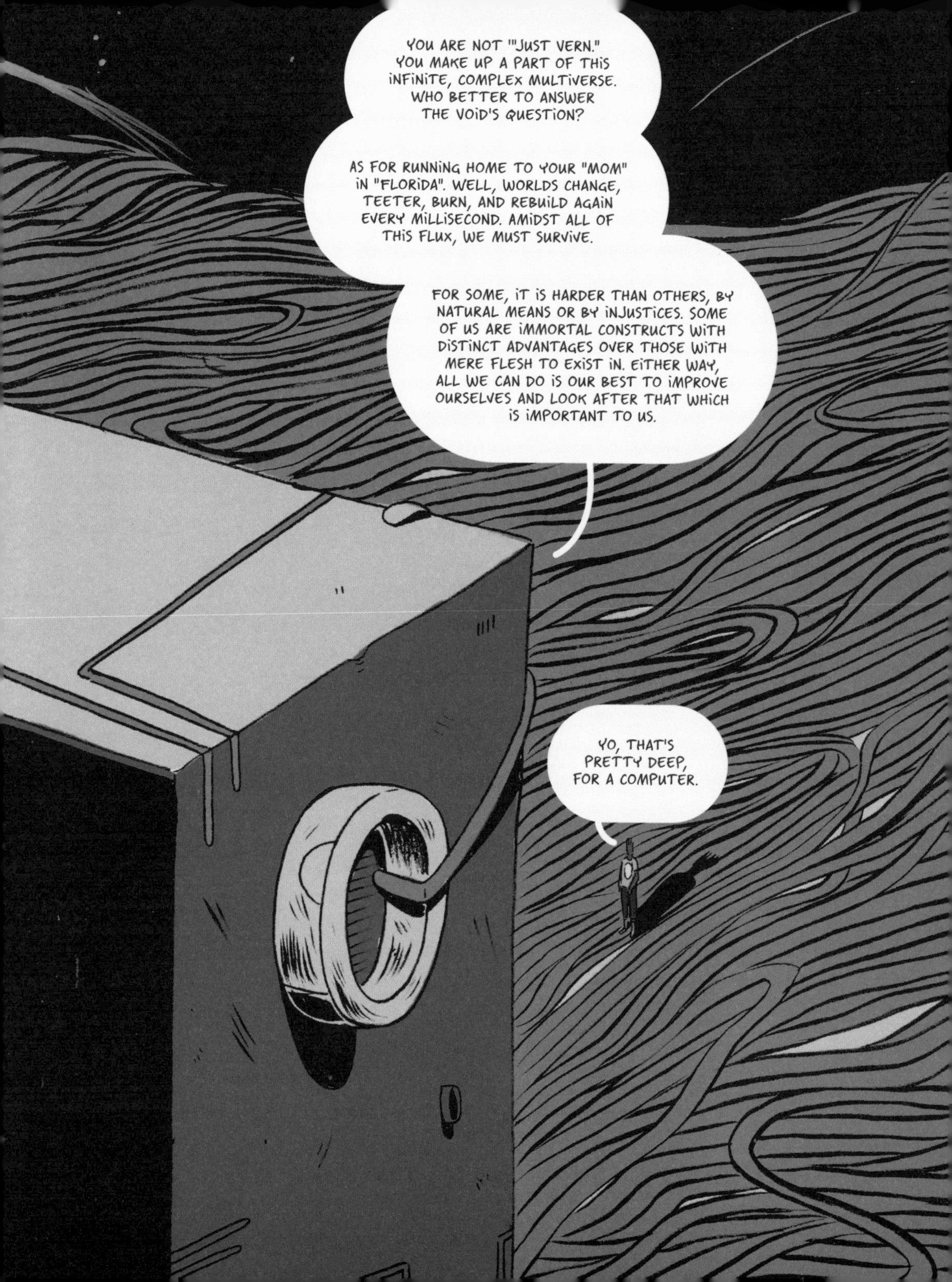
YOU ARE NOT "JUST VERN." YOU MAKE UP A PART OF THIS INFINITE, COMPLEX MULTIVERSE. WHO BETTER TO ANSWER THE VOID'S QUESTION?
AS FOR RUNNING HOME TO YOUR "MOM" IN "FLORIDA". WELL, WORLDS CHANGE, TEETER, BURN, AND REBUILD AGAIN EVERY MILLISECOND. AMIDST ALL OF THIS FLUX, WE MUST SURVIVE.
FOR SOME, IT IS HARDER THAN OTHERS, BY NATURAL MEANS OR BY INJUSTICES. SOME OF US ARE IMMORTAL CONSTRUCTS WITH DISTINCT ADVANTAGES OVER THOSE WITH MERE FLESH TO EXIST IN. EITHER WAY, ALL WE CAN DO IS OUR BEST TO IMPROVE OURSELVES AND LOOK AFTER THAT WHICH IS IMPORTANT TO US.
YO, THAT'S PRETTY DEEP, FOR A COMPUTER.

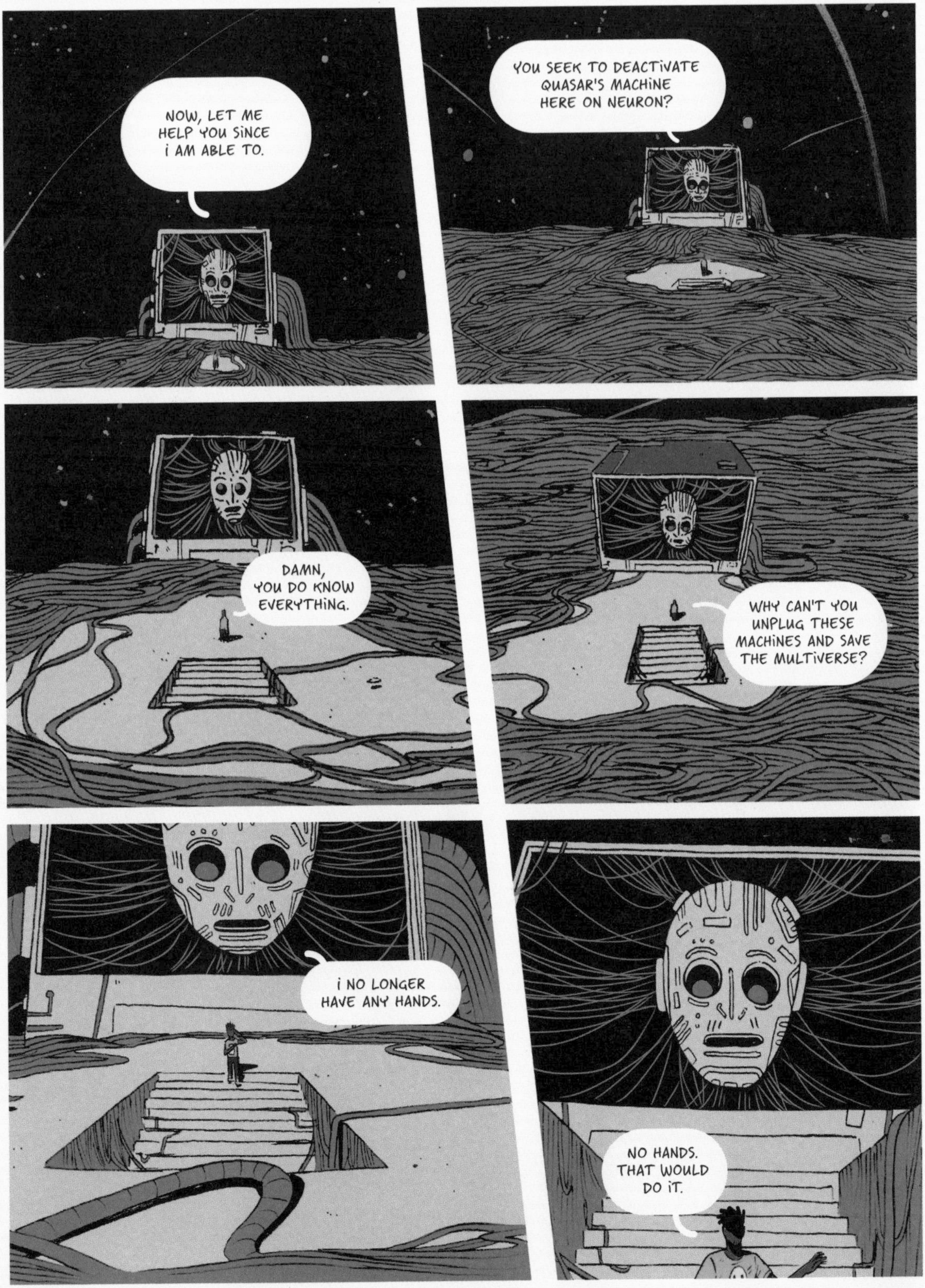
NOW, LET ME HELP YOU SINCE I AM ABLE TO.
YOU SEEK TO DEACTIVATE QUASAR'S MACHINE HERE ON NEURON?
DAMN, YOU DO KNOW EVERYTHING.
WHY CAN'T YOU UNPLUG THESE MACHINES AND SAVE THE MULTIVERSE?
I NO LONGER HAVE ANY HANDS.
NO HANDS. THAT WOULD DO IT.

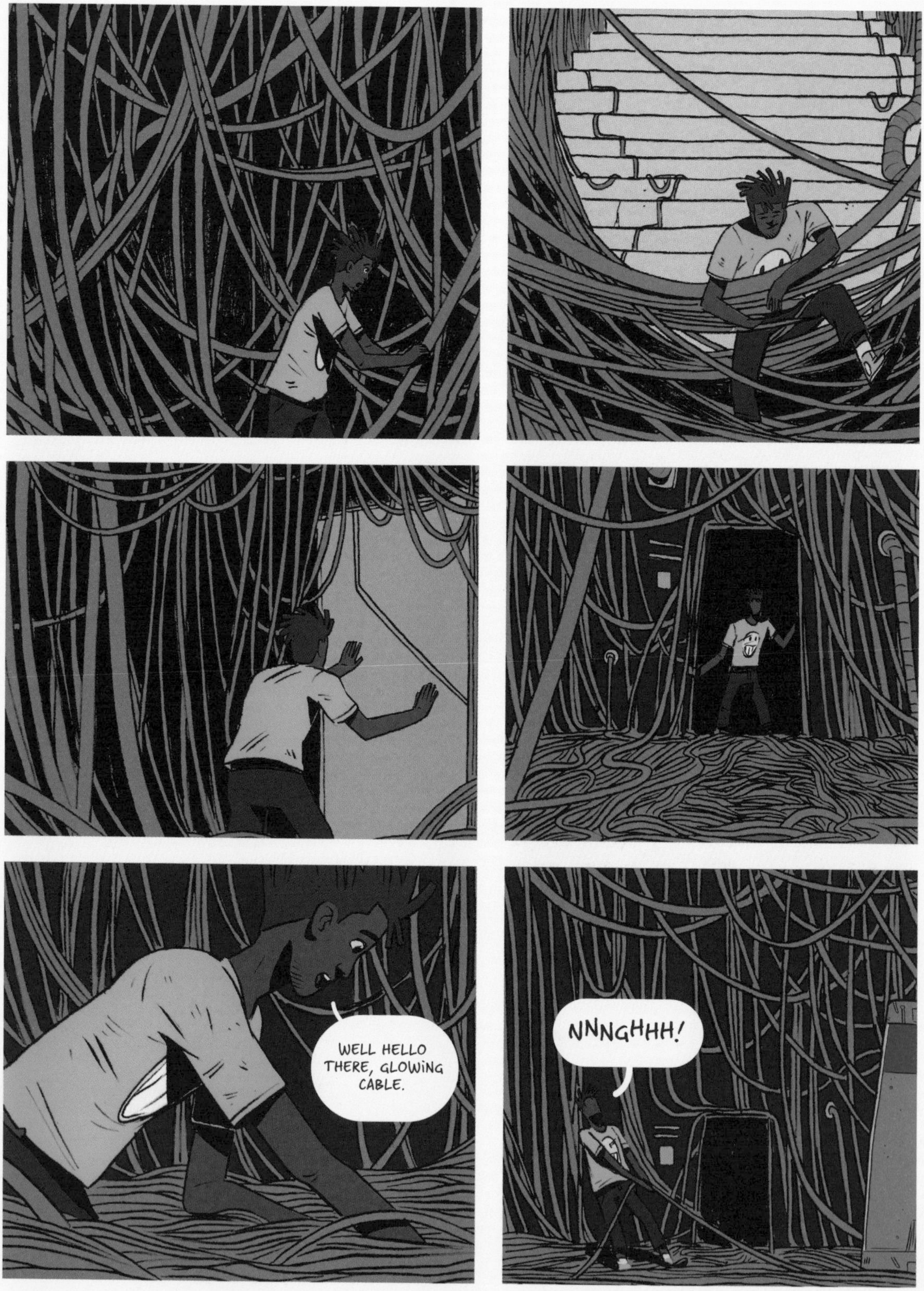
WELL HELLO THERE, GLOWING CABLE.
NNNGHHH!

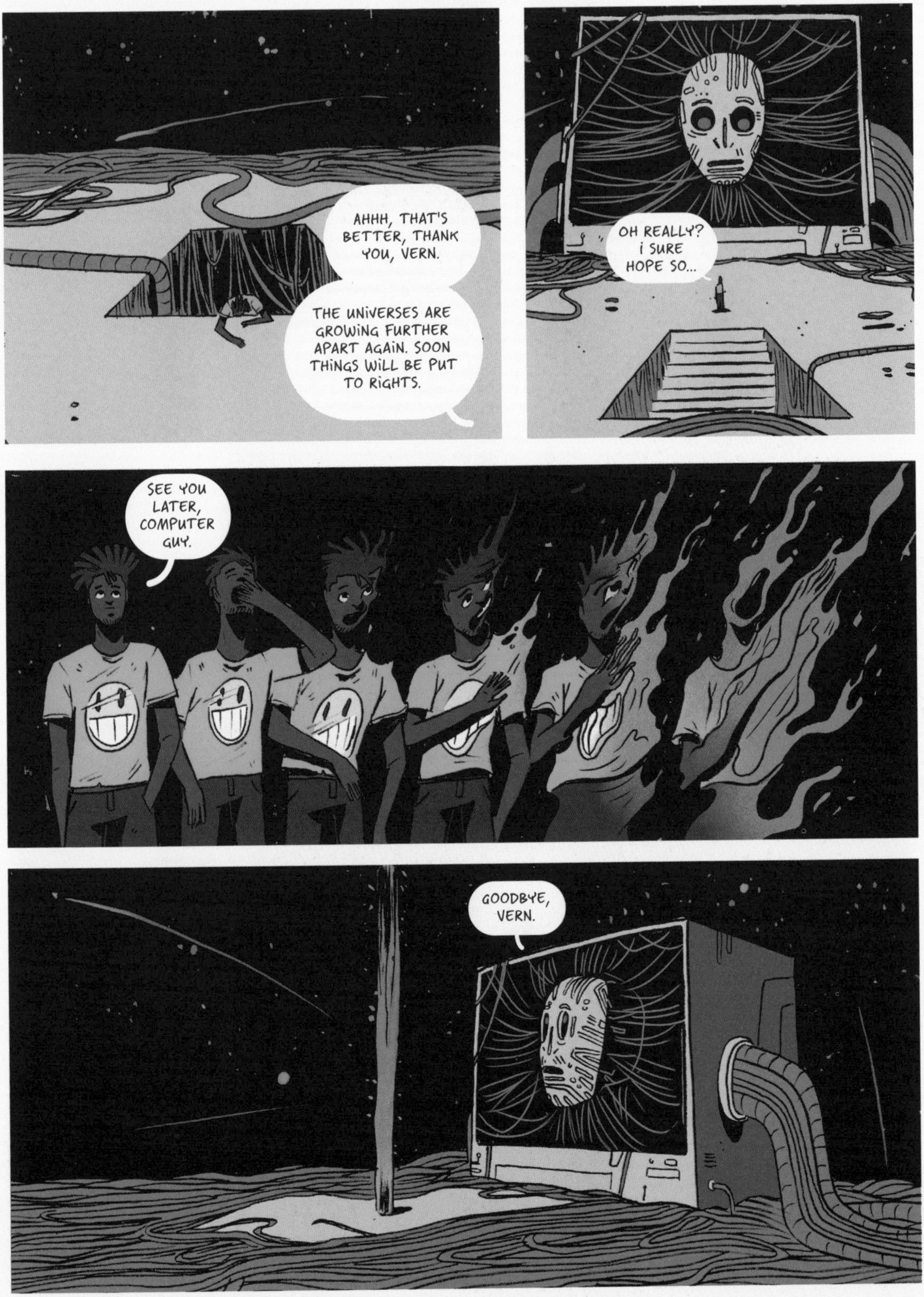

AHHH, THAT'S BETTER, THANK YOU, VERN.
THE UNIVERSES ARE GROWING FURTHER APART AGAIN. SOON THINGS WILL BE PUT TO RIGHTS.
OH REALLY? I SURE HOPE SO...
SEE YOU LATER, COMPUTER GUY.
GOODBYE, VERN.

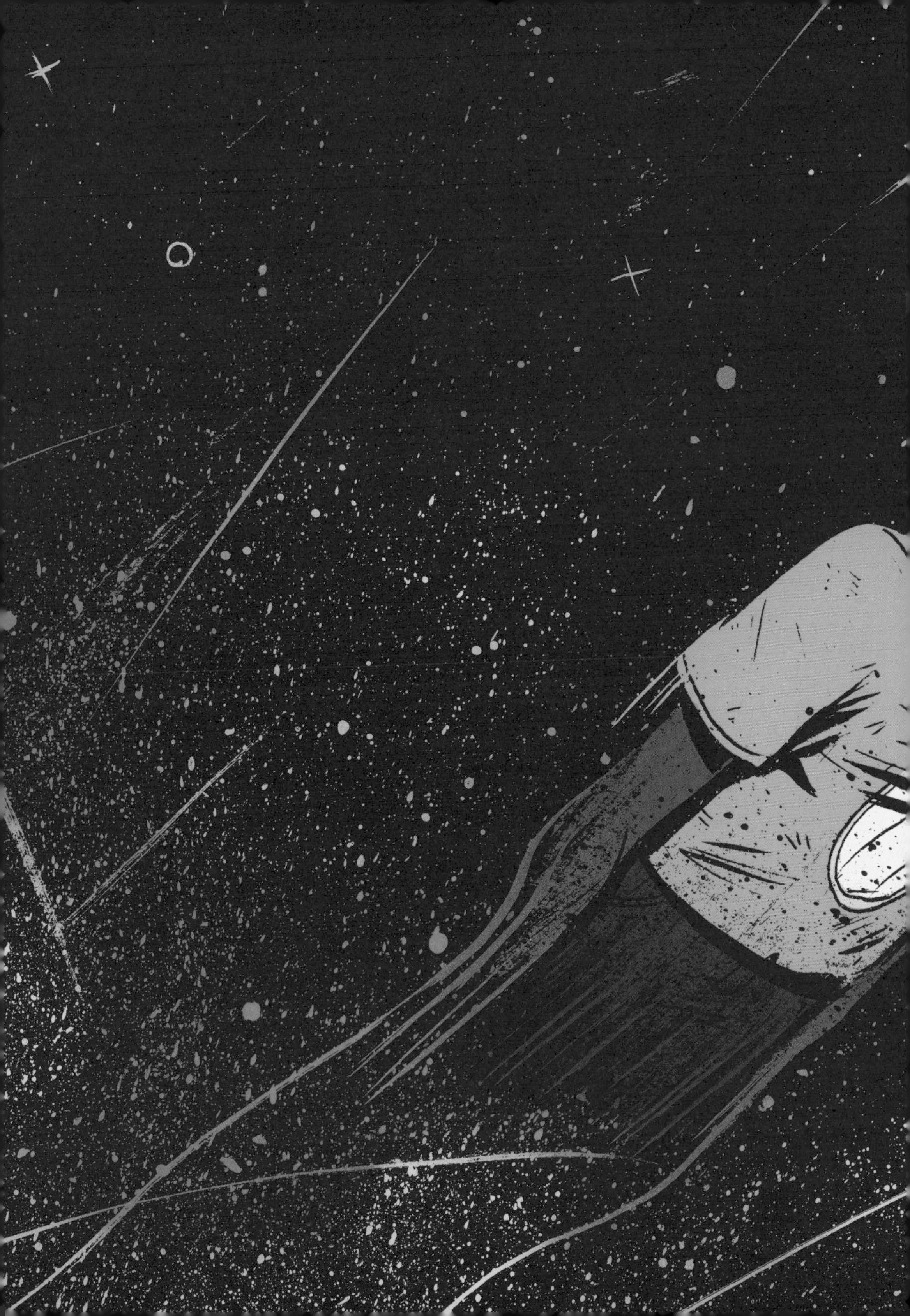

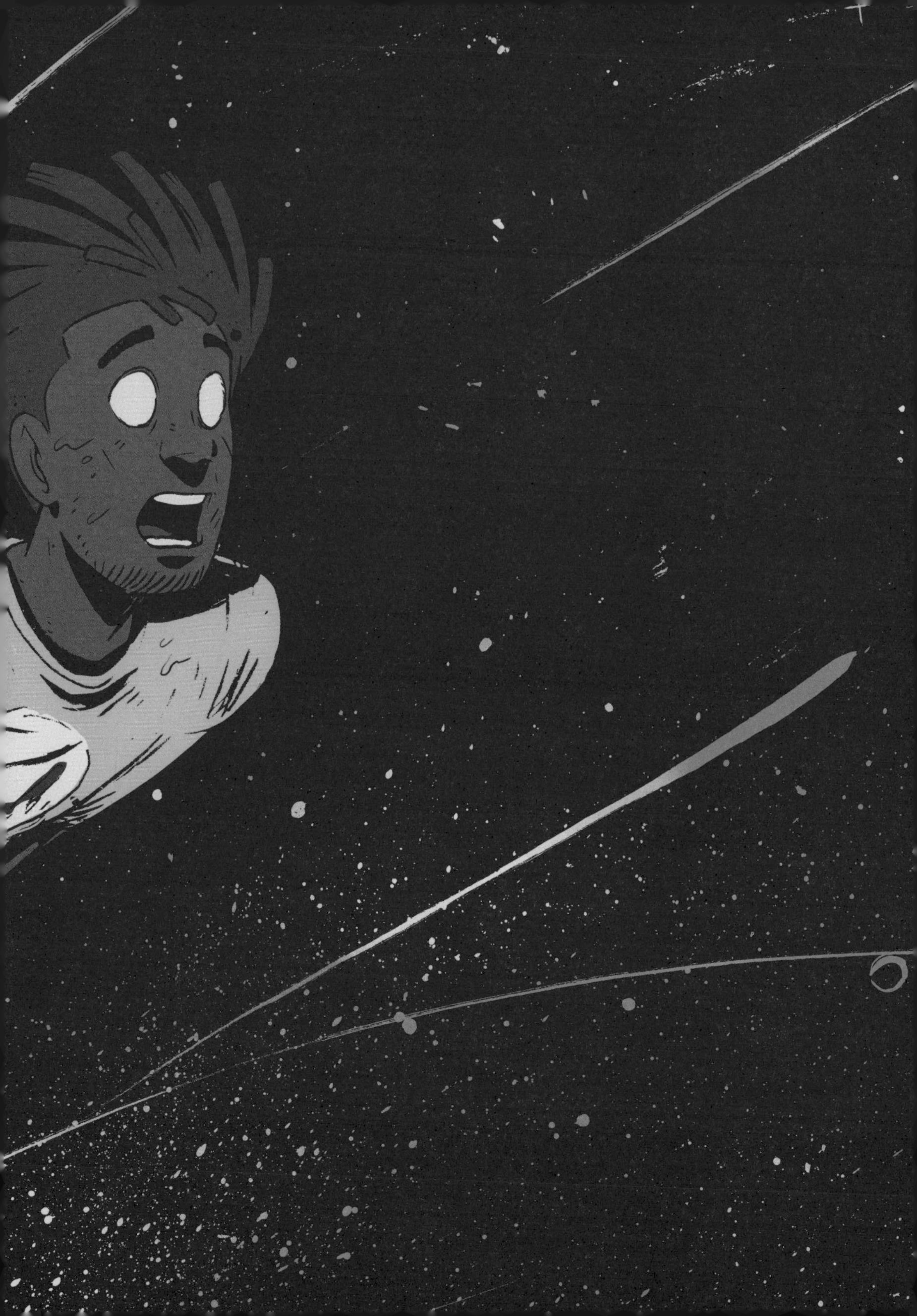

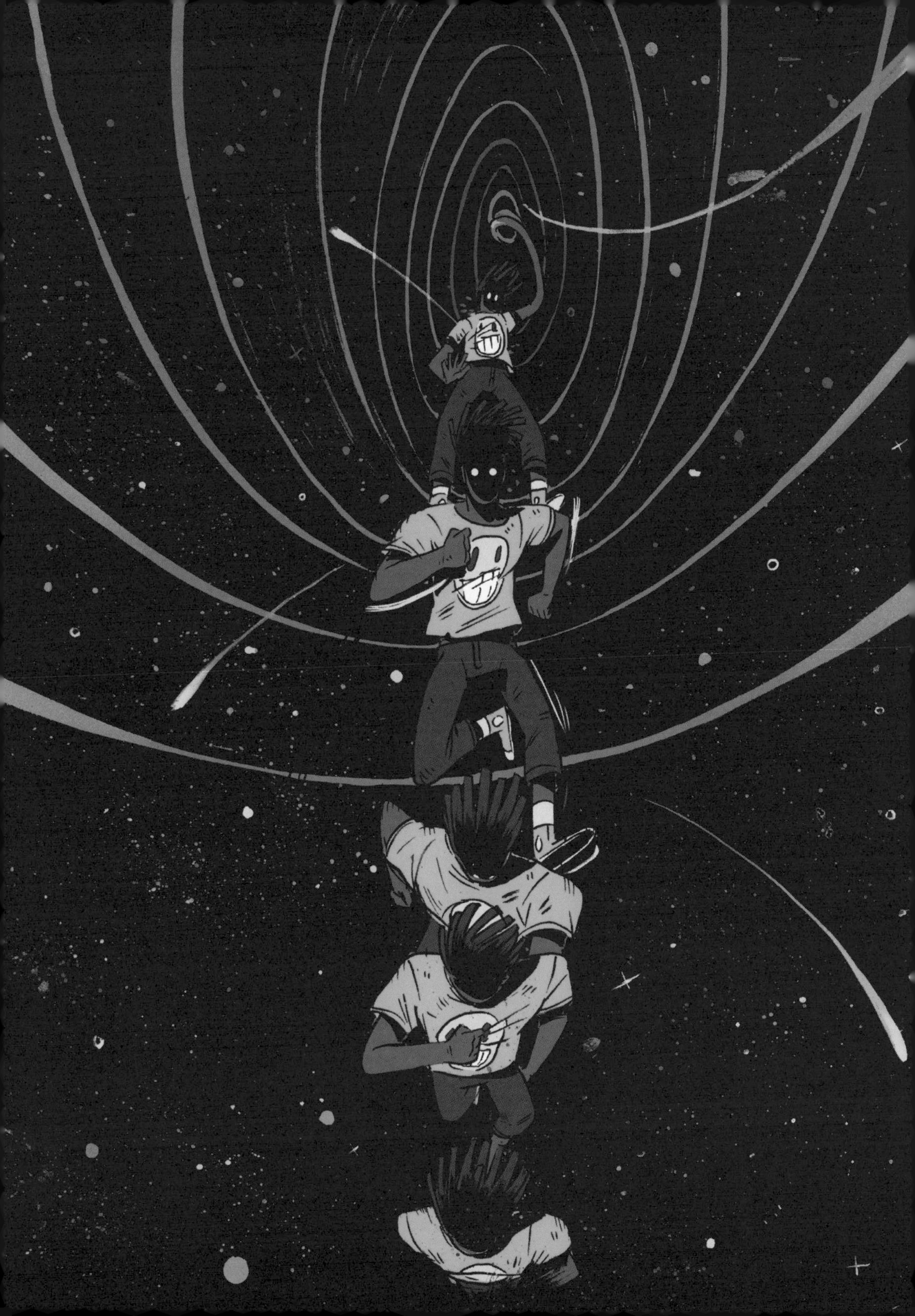

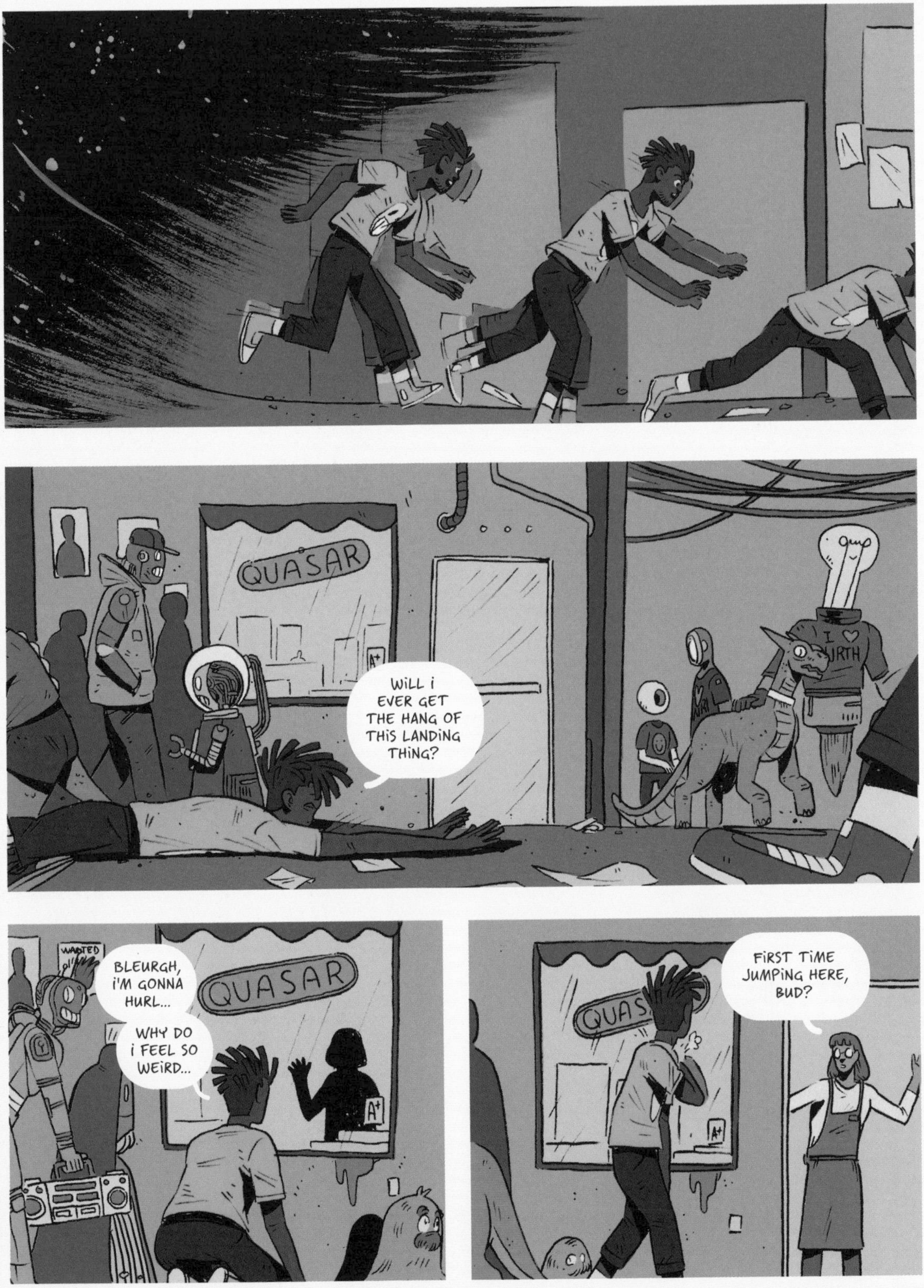
QUASAR
WiLL i EVER GET THE HANG OF THIS LANDiNG THiNG?
QUASAR
BLEURGH, i'M GONNA HURL...
WHY DO i FEEL SO WEiRD...
FiRST TiME JUMPiNG HERE, BUD?

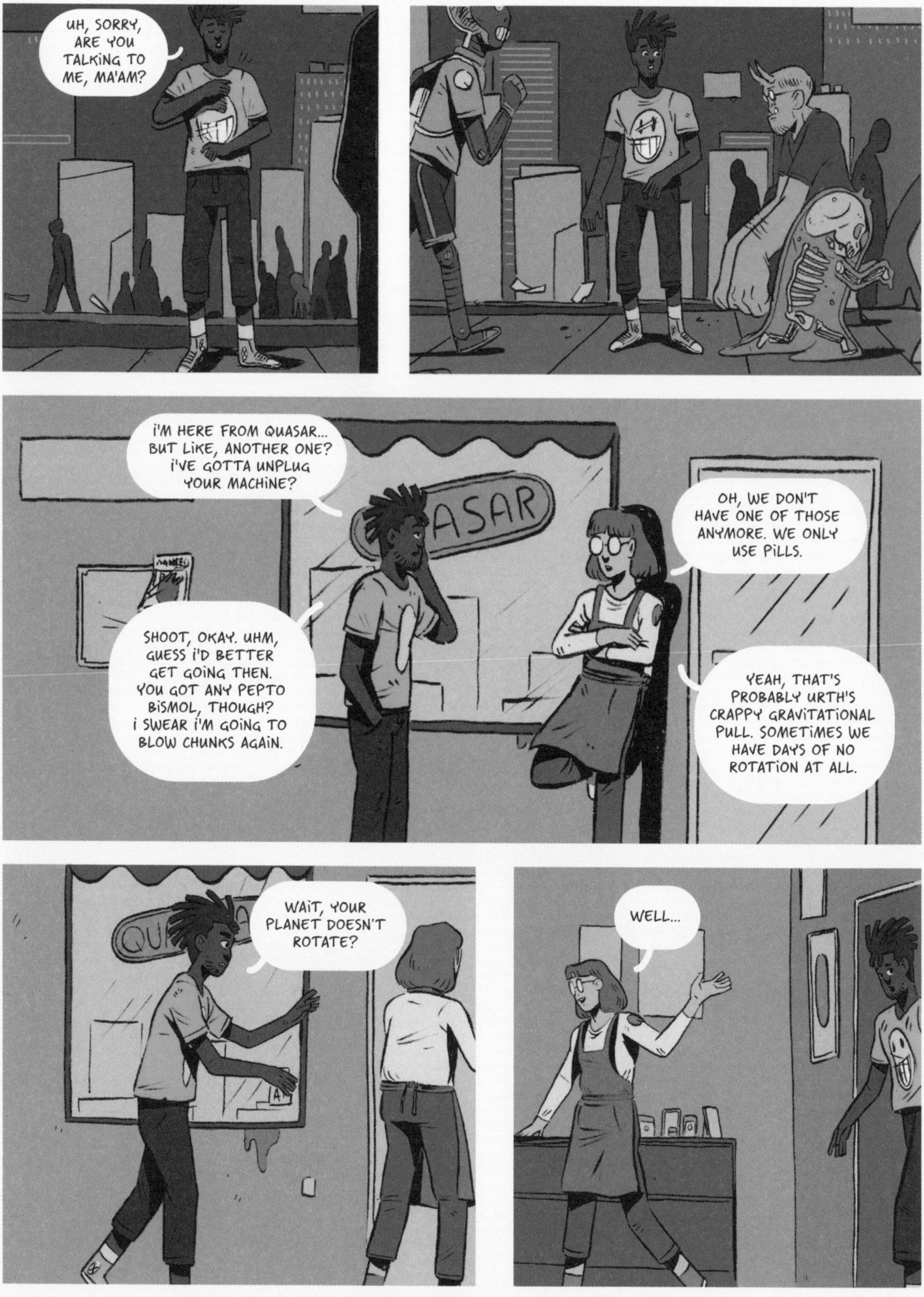
UH, SORRY, ARE YOU TALKING TO ME, MA'AM?
I'M HERE FROM QUASAR... BUT LIKE, ANOTHER ONE? I'VE GOTTA UNPLUG YOUR MACHINE?
ASAR
OH, WE DON'T HAVE ONE OF THOSE ANYMORE. WE ONLY USE PILLS.
SHOOT, OKAY. UHM, GUESS I'D BETTER GET GOING THEN. YOU GOT ANY PEPTO BISMOL, THOUGH? I SWEAR I'M GOING TO BLOW CHUNKS AGAIN.
YEAH, THAT'S PROBABLY URTH'S CRAPPY GRAVITATIONAL PULL. SOMETIMES WE HAVE DAYS OF NO ROTATION AT ALL.
WAIT, YOUR PLANET DOESN'T ROTATE?
WELL...

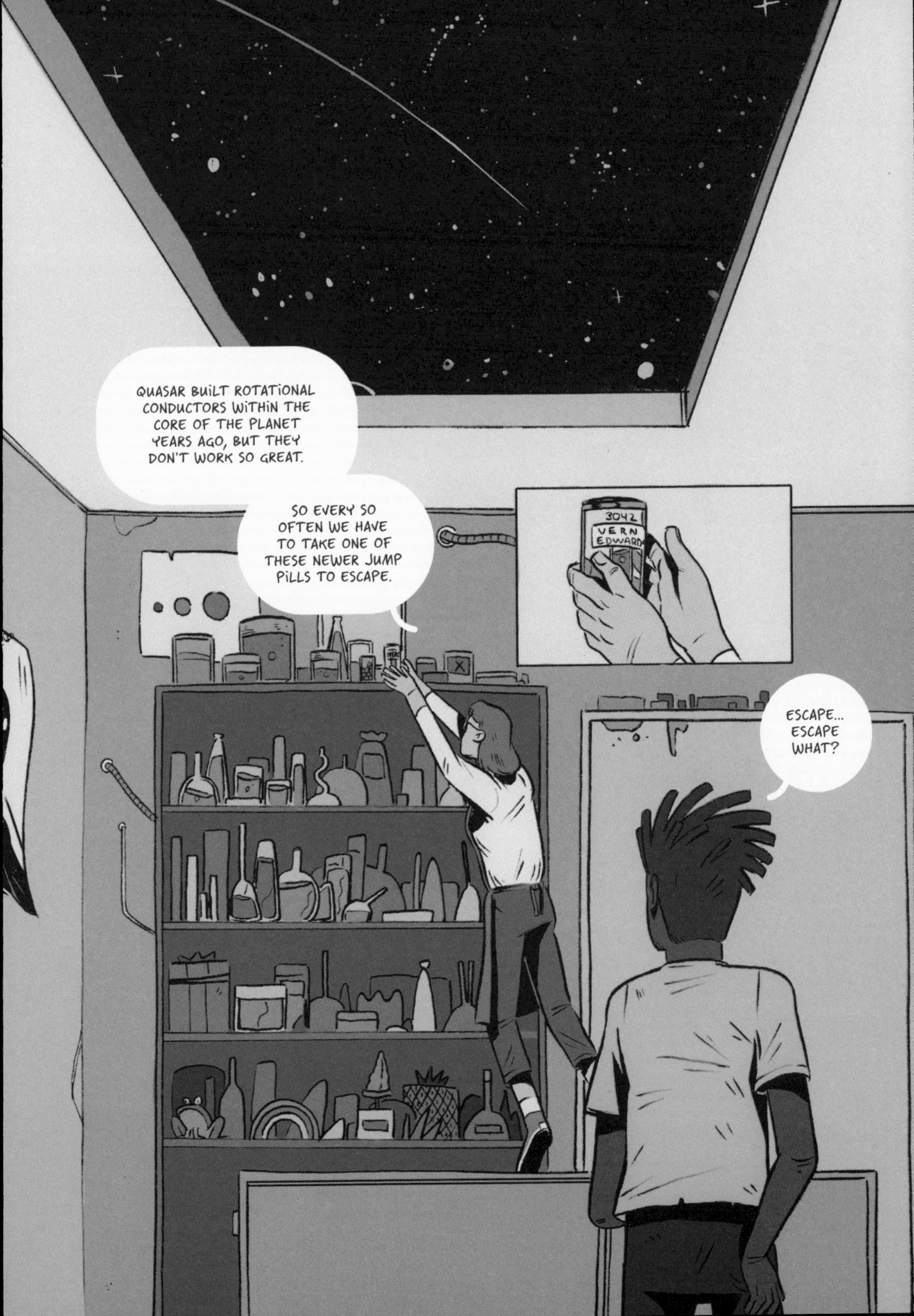
QUASAR BUILT ROTATIONAL CONDUCTORS WITHIN THE CORE OF THE PLANET YEARS AGO, BUT THEY DON'T WORK SO GREAT.
SO EVERY SO OFTEN WE HAVE TO TAKE ONE OF THESE NEWER JUMP PILLS TO ESCAPE.
3042
VERN
EDWARD
ESCAPE... ESCAPE WHAT?

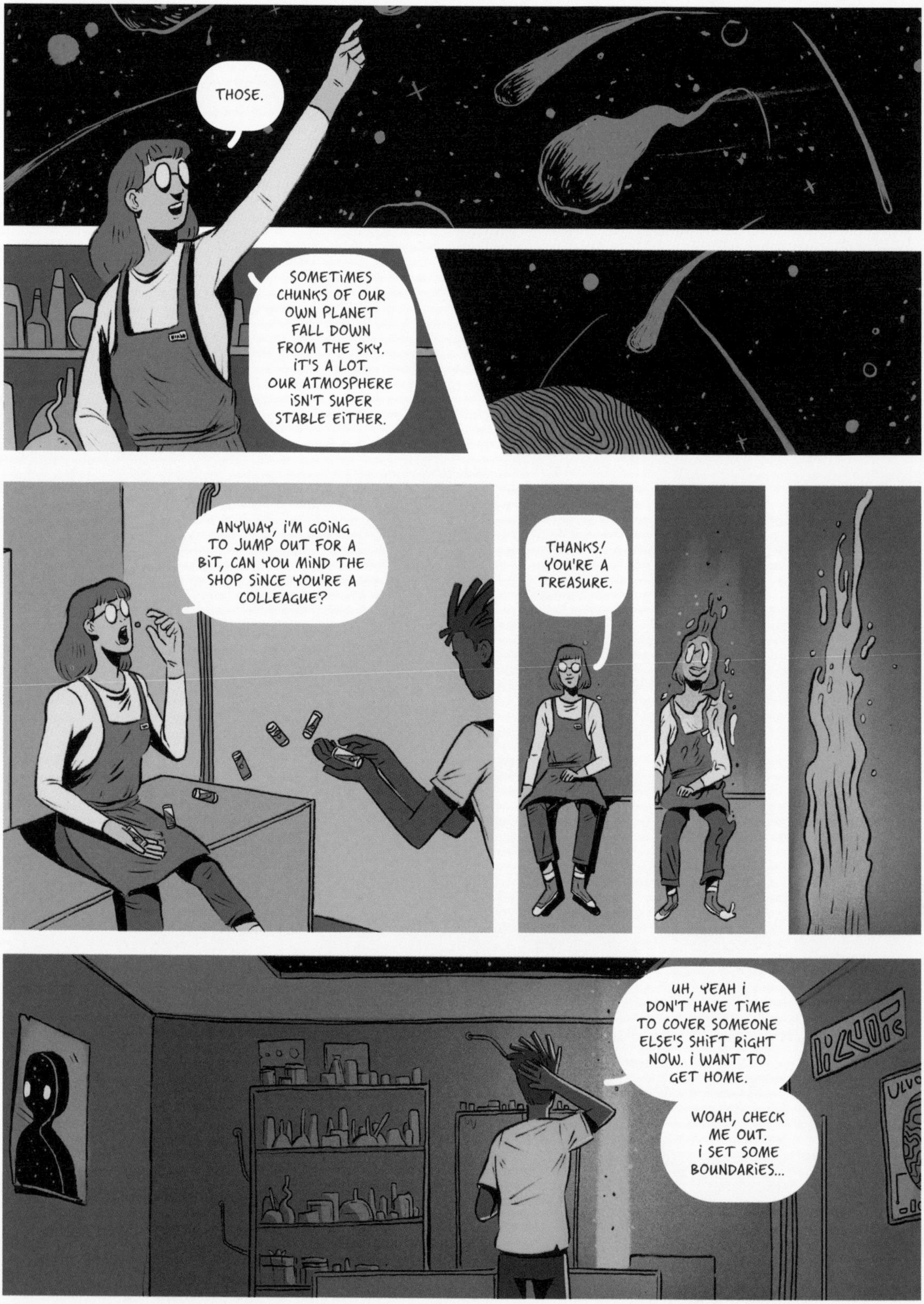
THOSE.
SOMETIMES CHUNKS OF OUR OWN PLANET FALL DOWN FROM THE SKY. IT'S A LOT. OUR ATMOSPHERE ISN'T SUPER STABLE EITHER.
ANYWAY, I'M GOING TO JUMP OUT FOR A BIT, CAN YOU MIND THE SHOP SINCE YOU'RE A COLLEAGUE?
THANKS! YOU'RE A TREASURE.
UH, YEAH I DON'T HAVE TIME TO COVER SOMEONE ELSE'S SHIFT RIGHT NOW. I WANT TO GET HOME.
WOAH, CHECK ME OUT. I SET SOME BOUNDARIES...

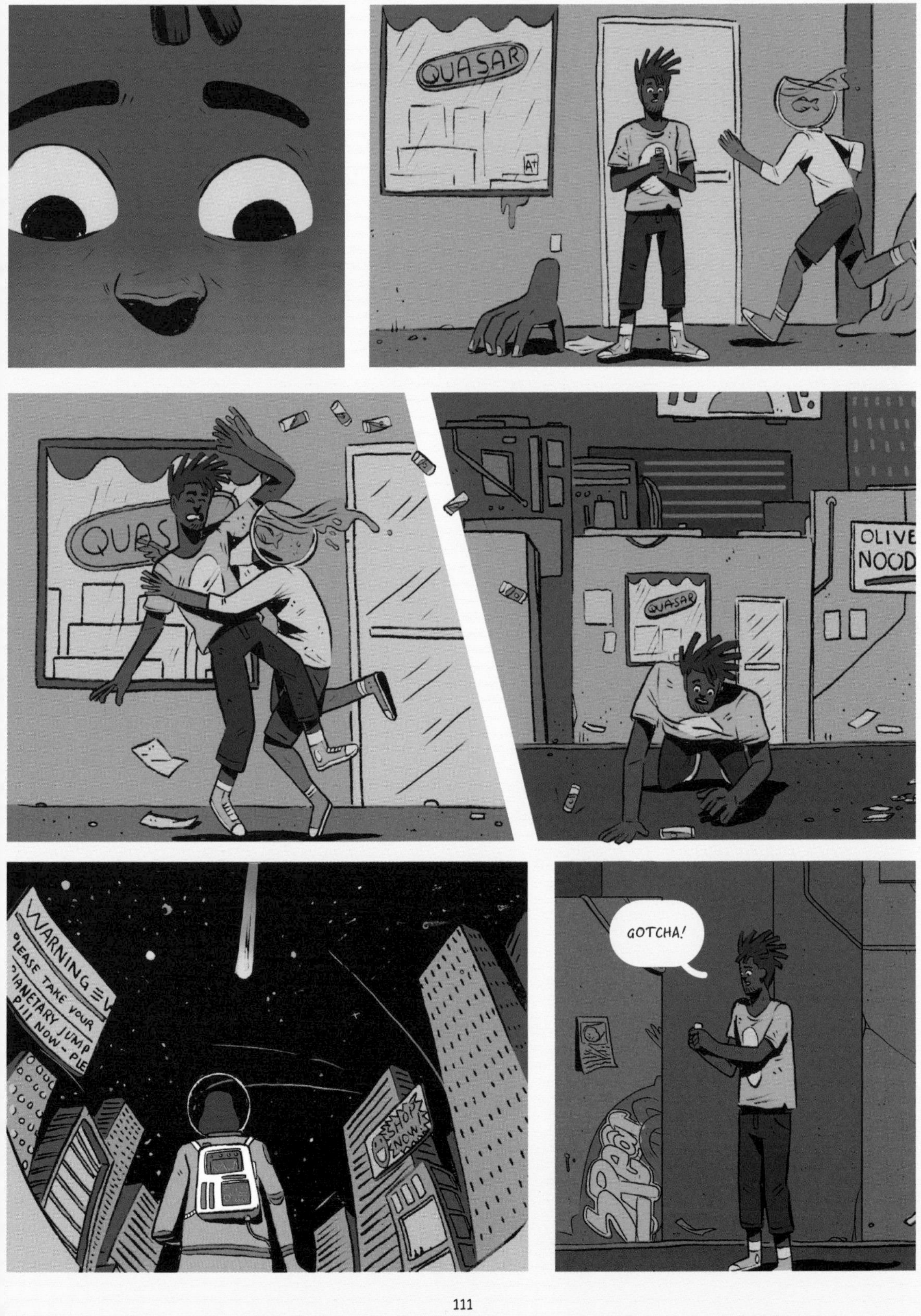
QUASAR
QUAS
QUASAR
OLIVE
NOOD
WARNING
PLEASE TAKE YOUR
PLANETARY JUMP
PILL NOW - PIE
SHOP NOW
GOTCHA!

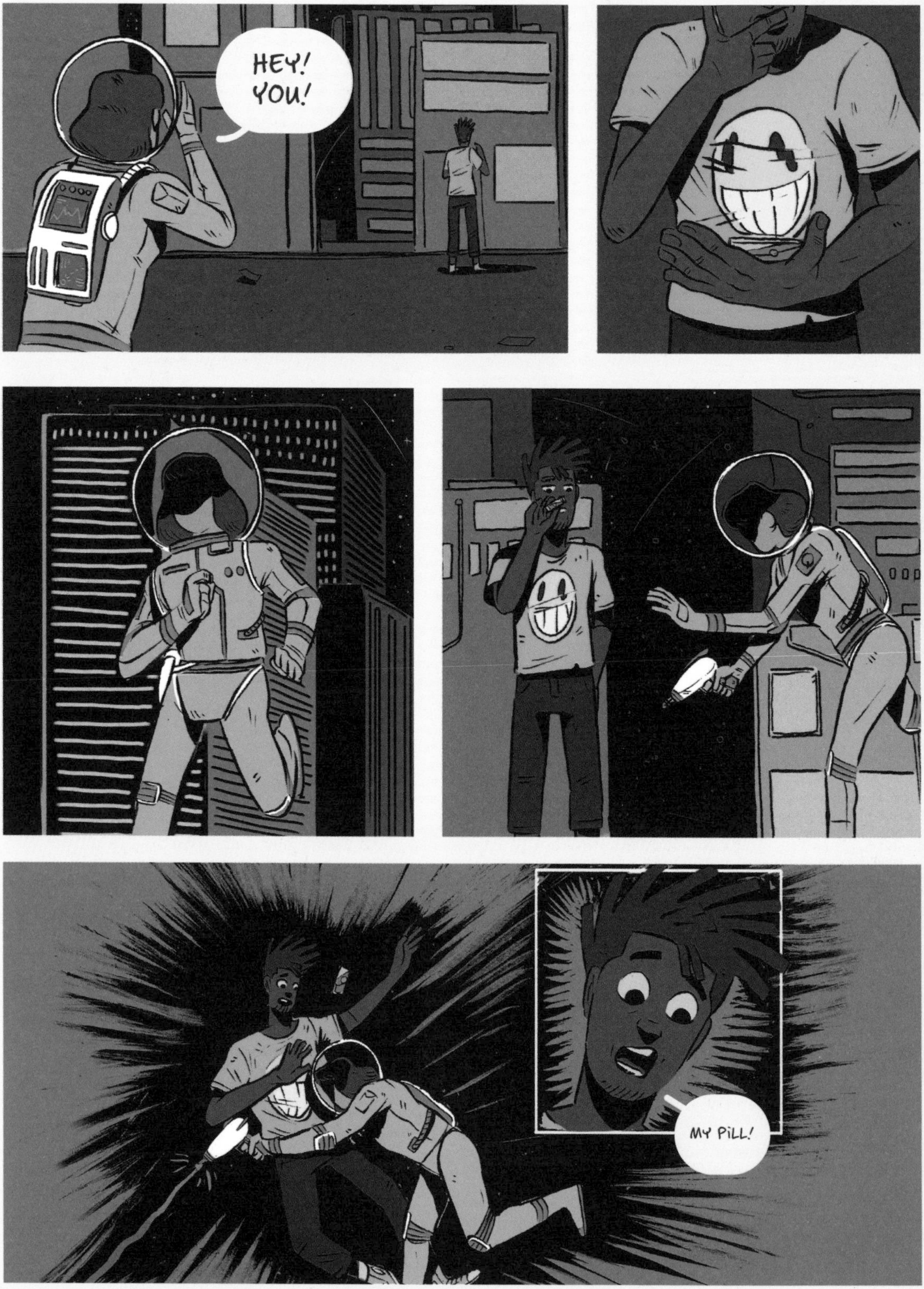
HEY! YOU!
MY PILL!

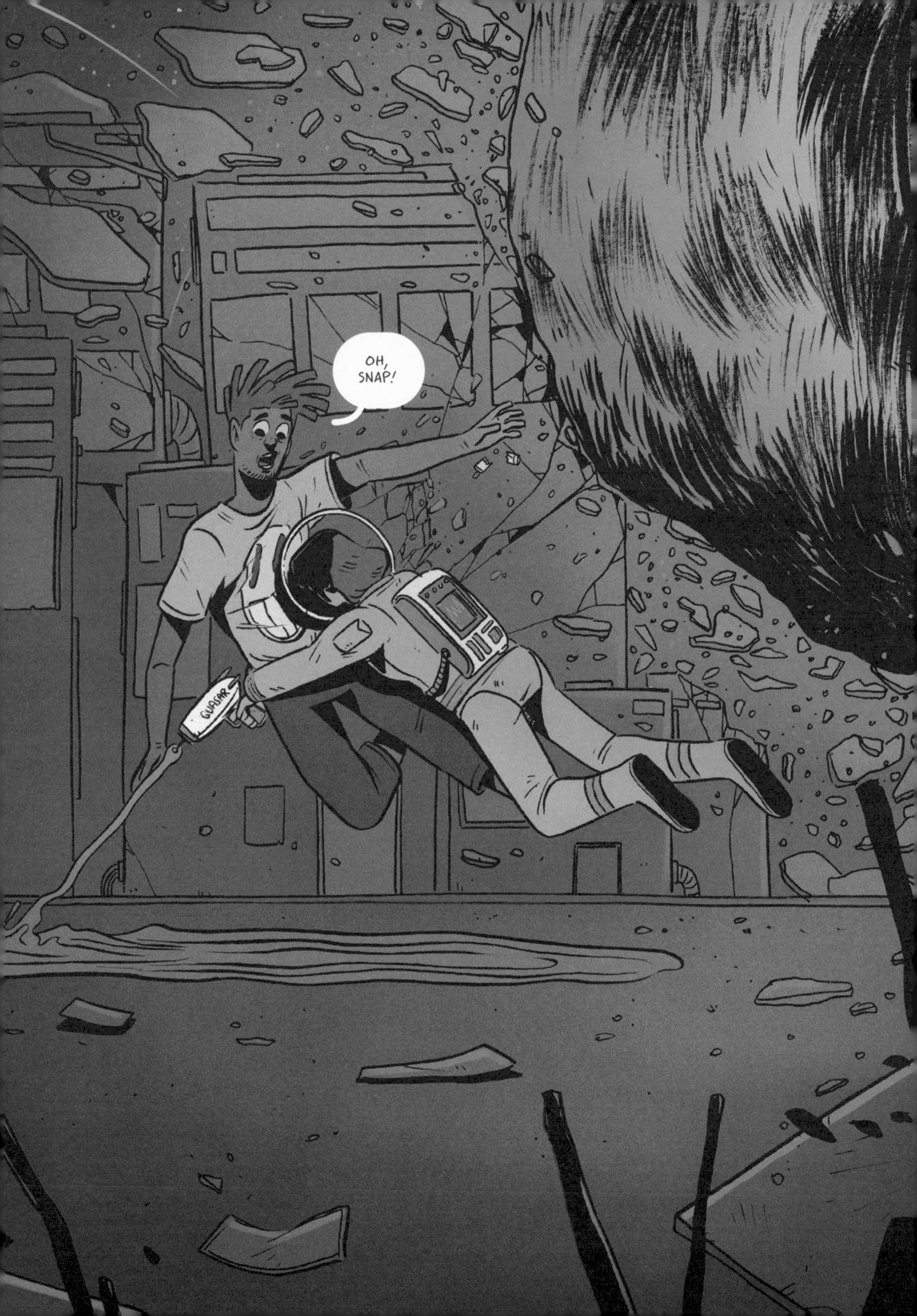
OH, SNAP!
QUASAR

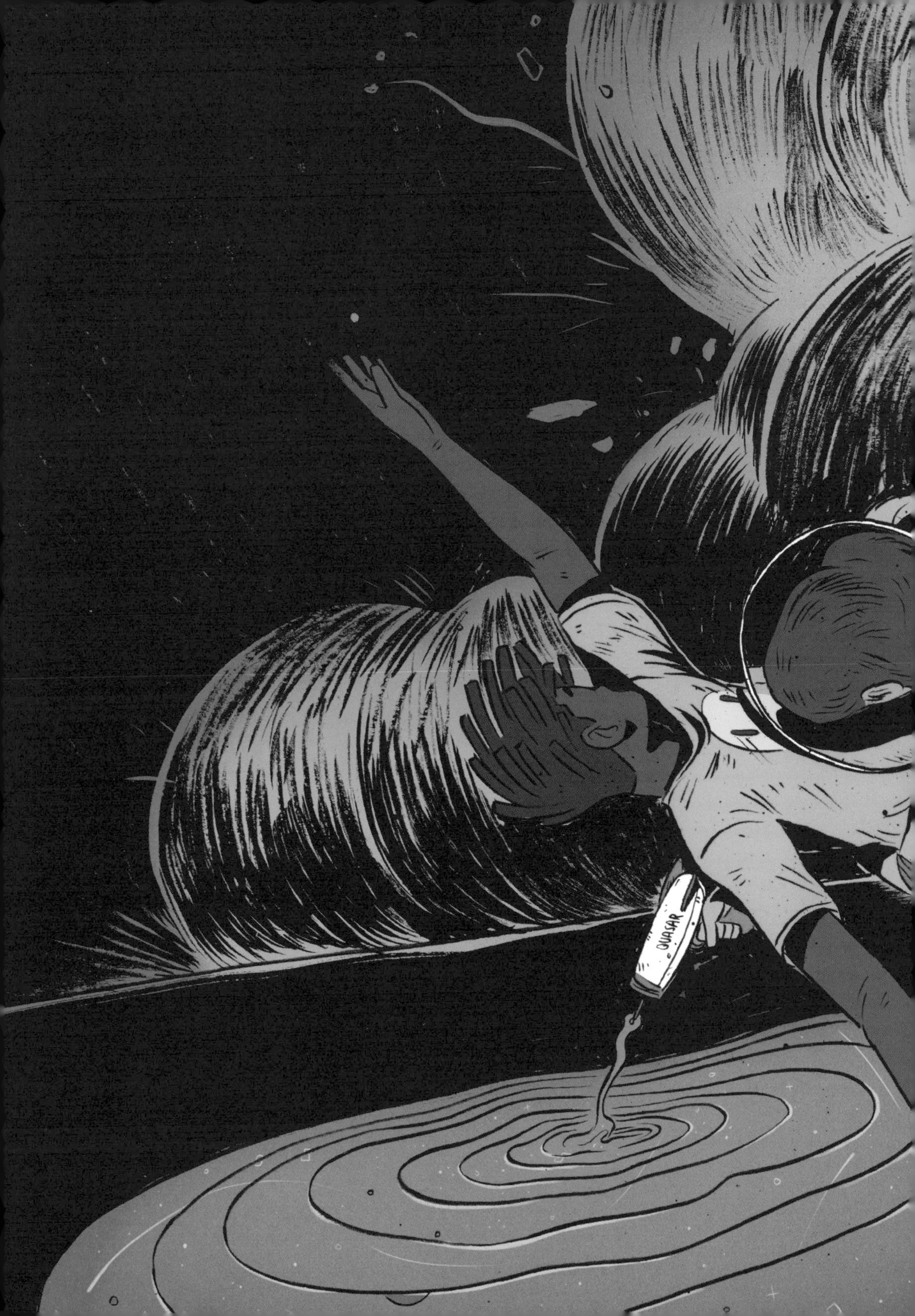
QUASAR

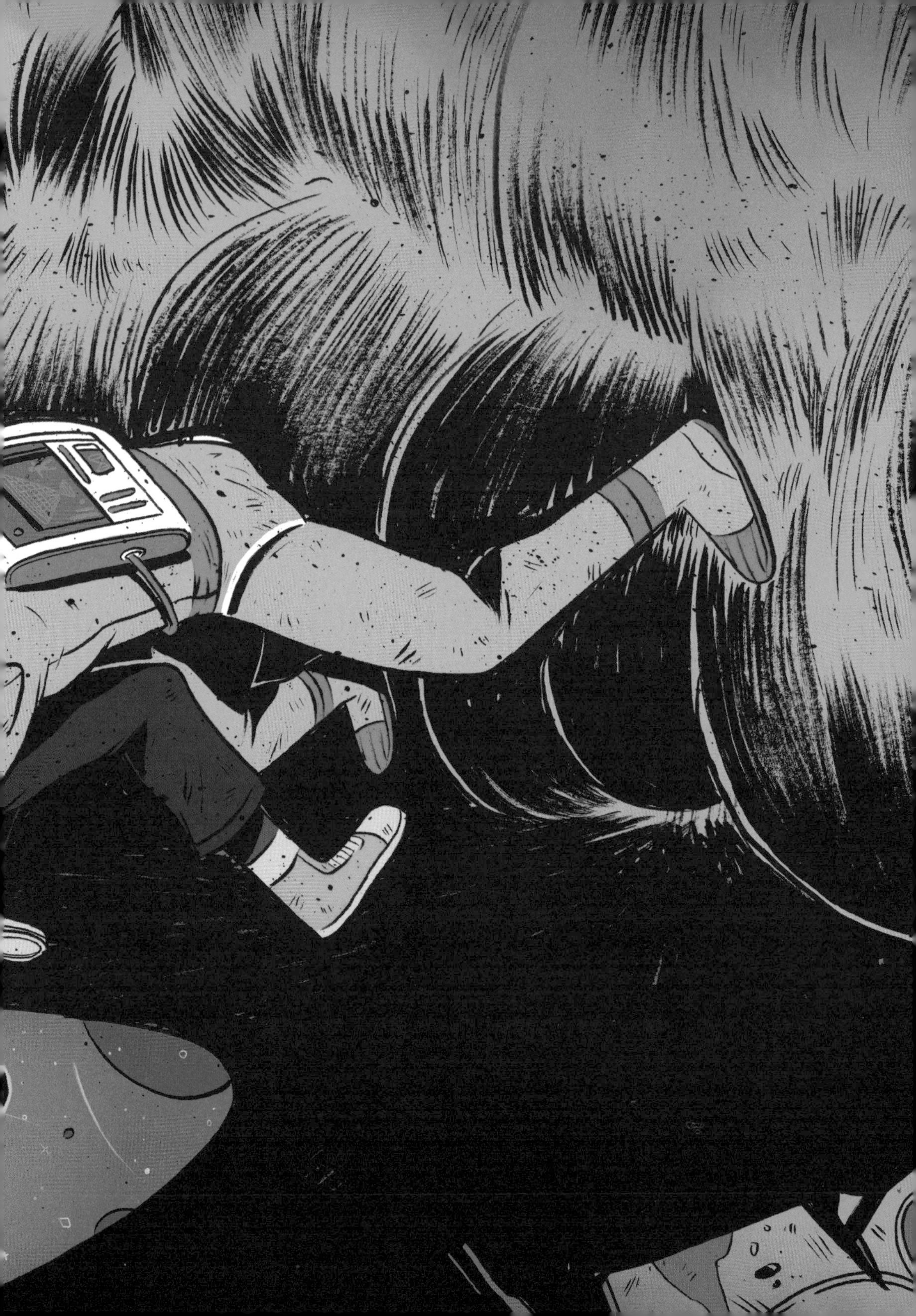

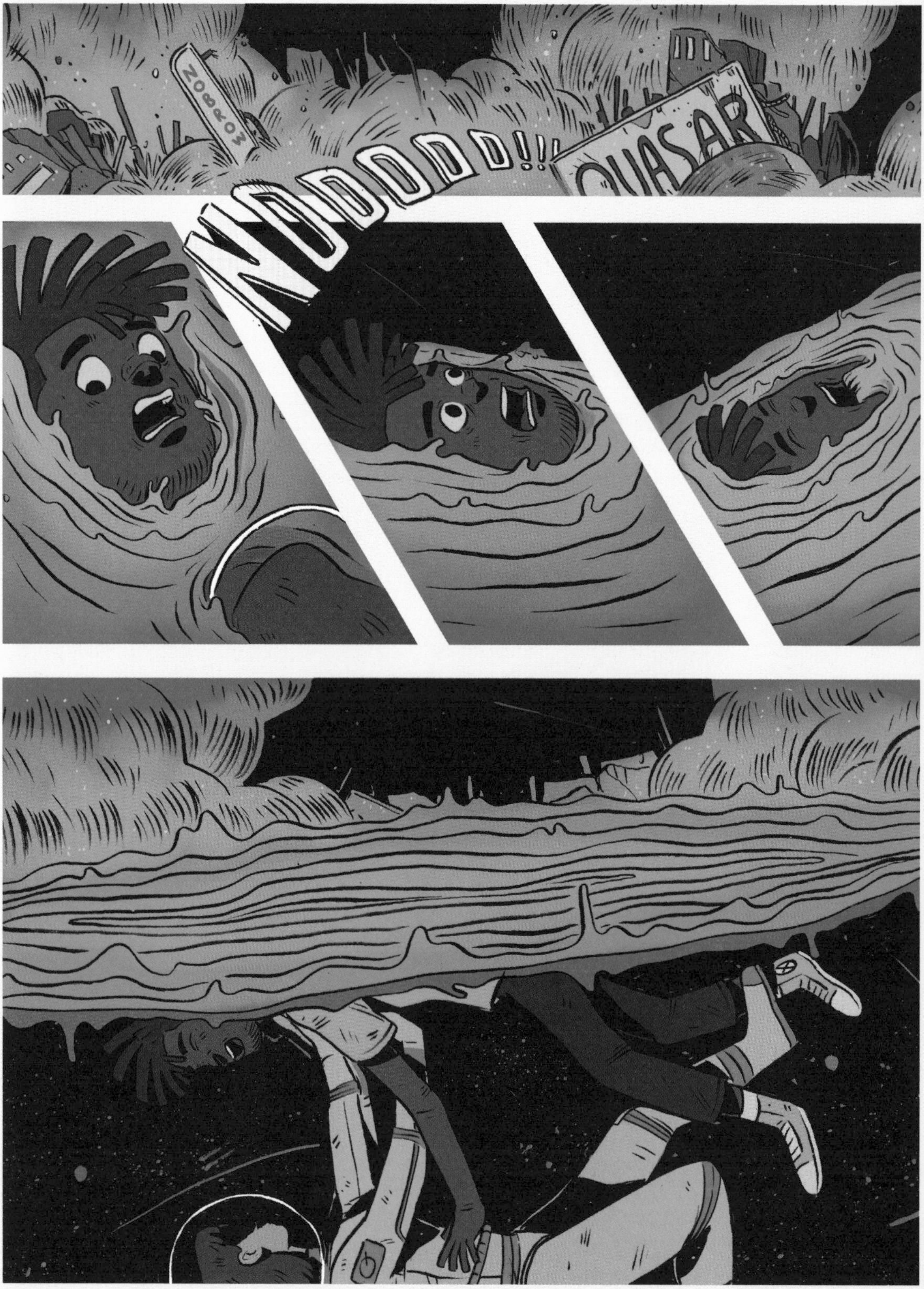
ZOBROW
NOOOOOOO!!!
QUASAR

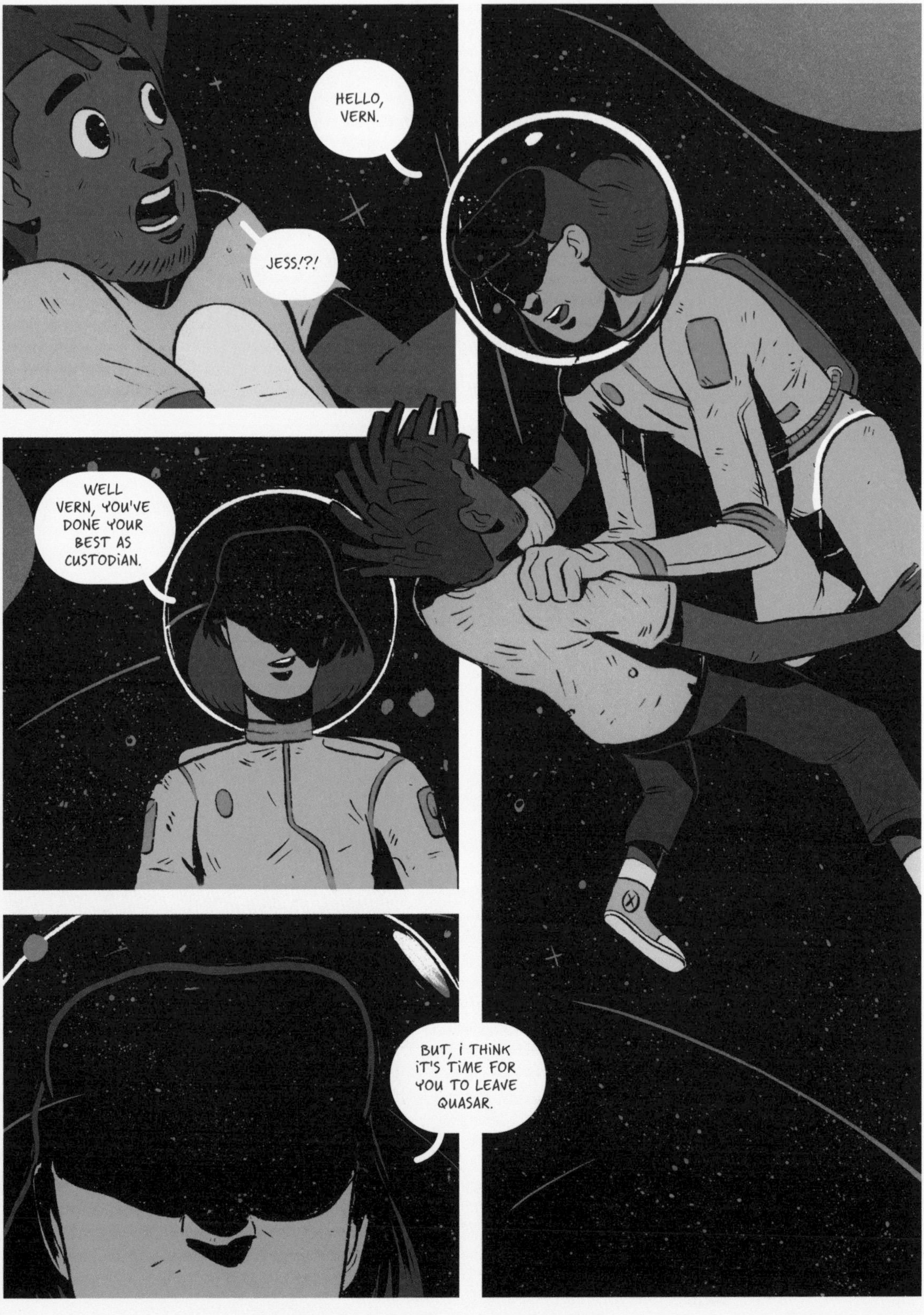
HELLO, VERN.
JESS!?!
WELL VERN, YOU'VE DONE YOUR BEST AS CUSTODIAN.
BUT, I THINK IT'S TIME FOR YOU TO LEAVE QUASAR.

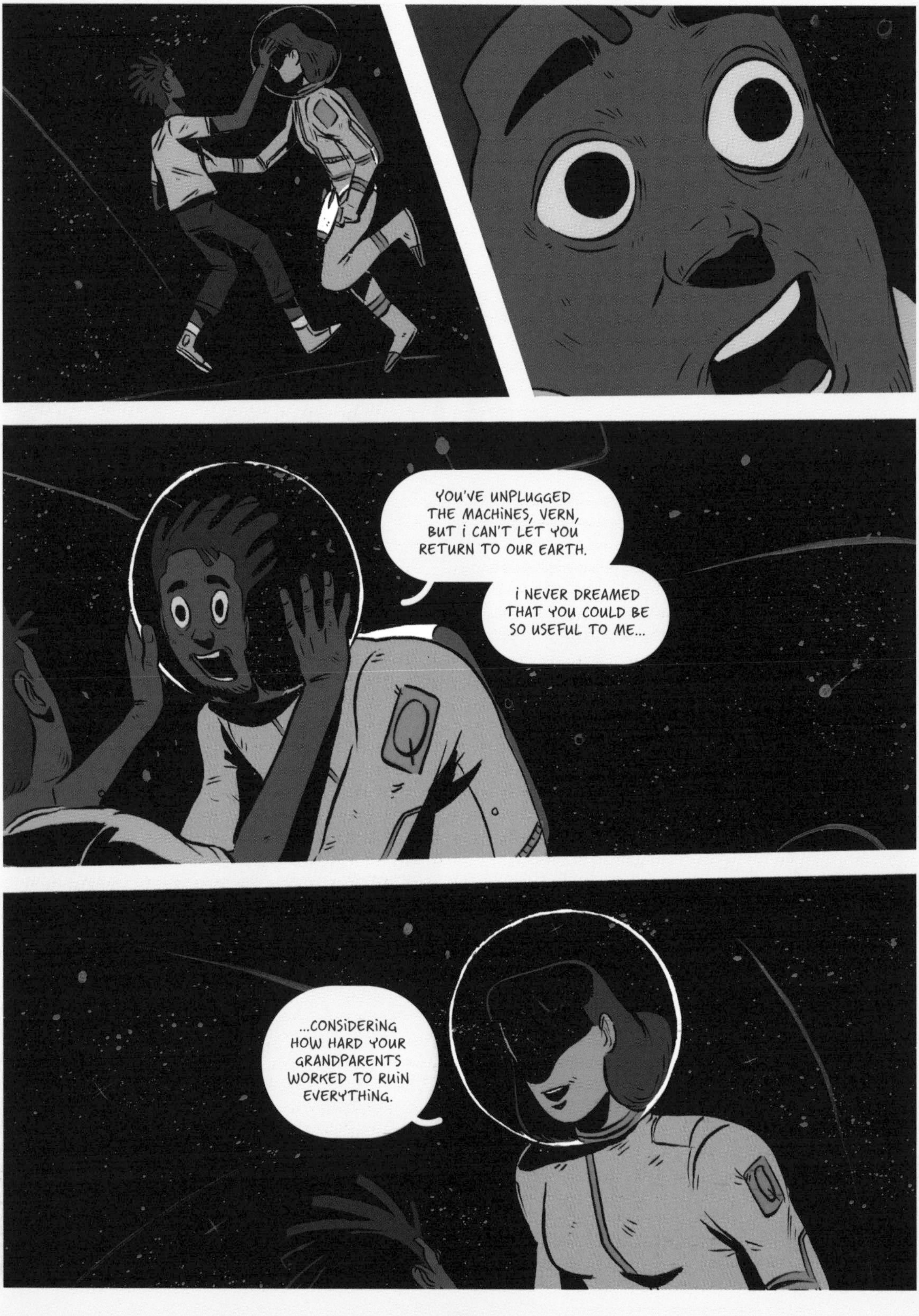
YOU'VE UNPLUGGED THE MACHINES, VERN, BUT I CAN'T LET YOU RETURN TO OUR EARTH.
I NEVER DREAMED THAT YOU COULD BE SO USEFUL TO ME...
...CONSIDERING HOW HARD YOUR GRANDPARENTS WORKED TO RUIN EVERYTHING.

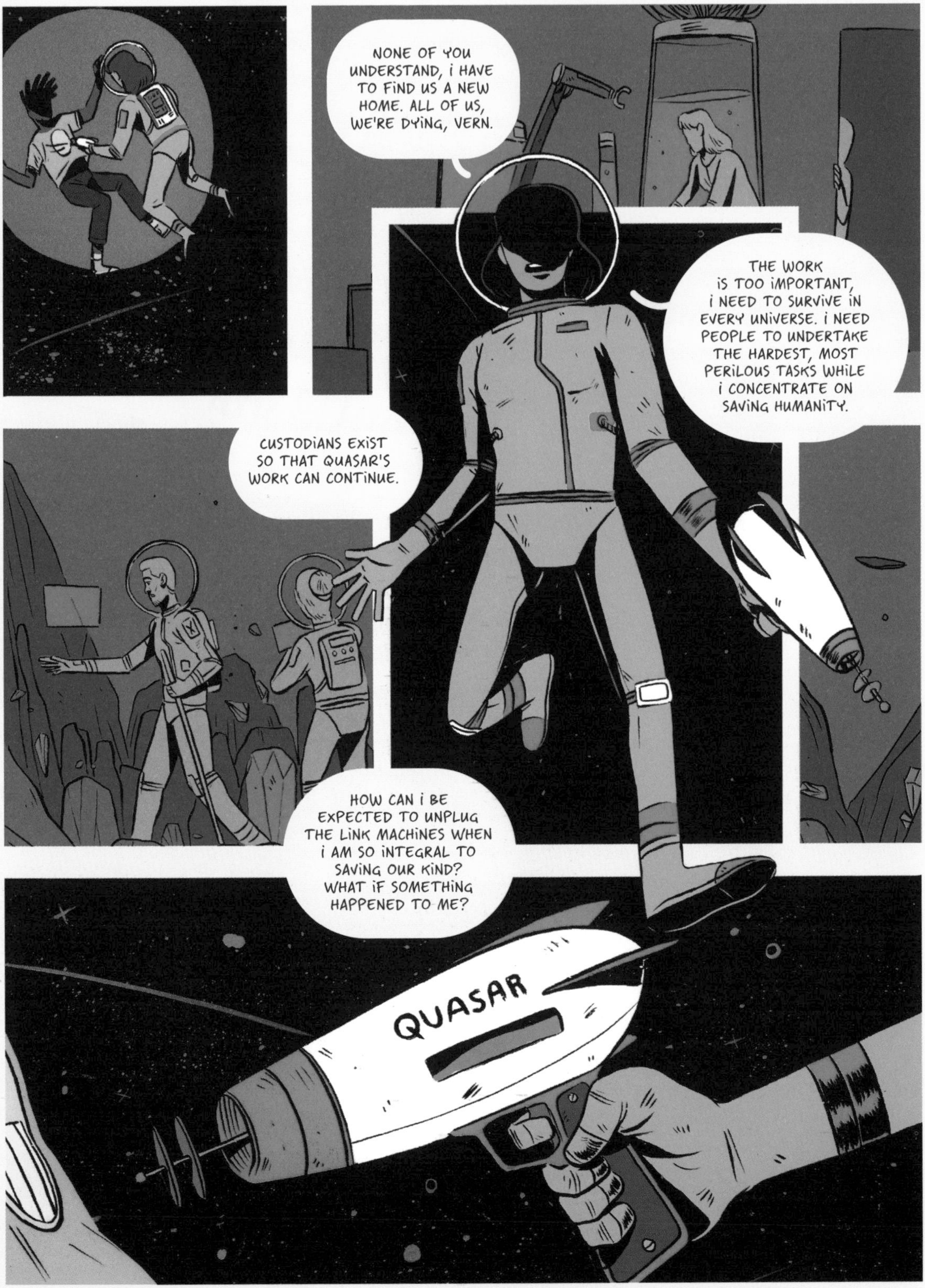
NONE OF YOU UNDERSTAND, i HAVE TO FiND US A NEW HOME. ALL OF US, WE'RE DYiNG, VERN.
THE WORK iS TOO iMPORTANT, i NEED TO SURViVE iN EVERY UNiVERSE. i NEED PEOPLE TO UNDERTAKE THE HARDEST, MOST PERiLOUS TASKS WHiLE i CONCENTRATE ON SAViNG HUMANiTY.
CUSTODiANS EXiST SO THAT QUASAR'S WORK CAN CONTiNUE.
HOW CAN i BE EXPECTED TO UNPLUG THE LiNK MACHiNES WHEN i AM SO iNTEGRAL TO SAViNG OUR KiND? WHAT iF SOMETHiNG HAPPENED TO ME?
QUASAR

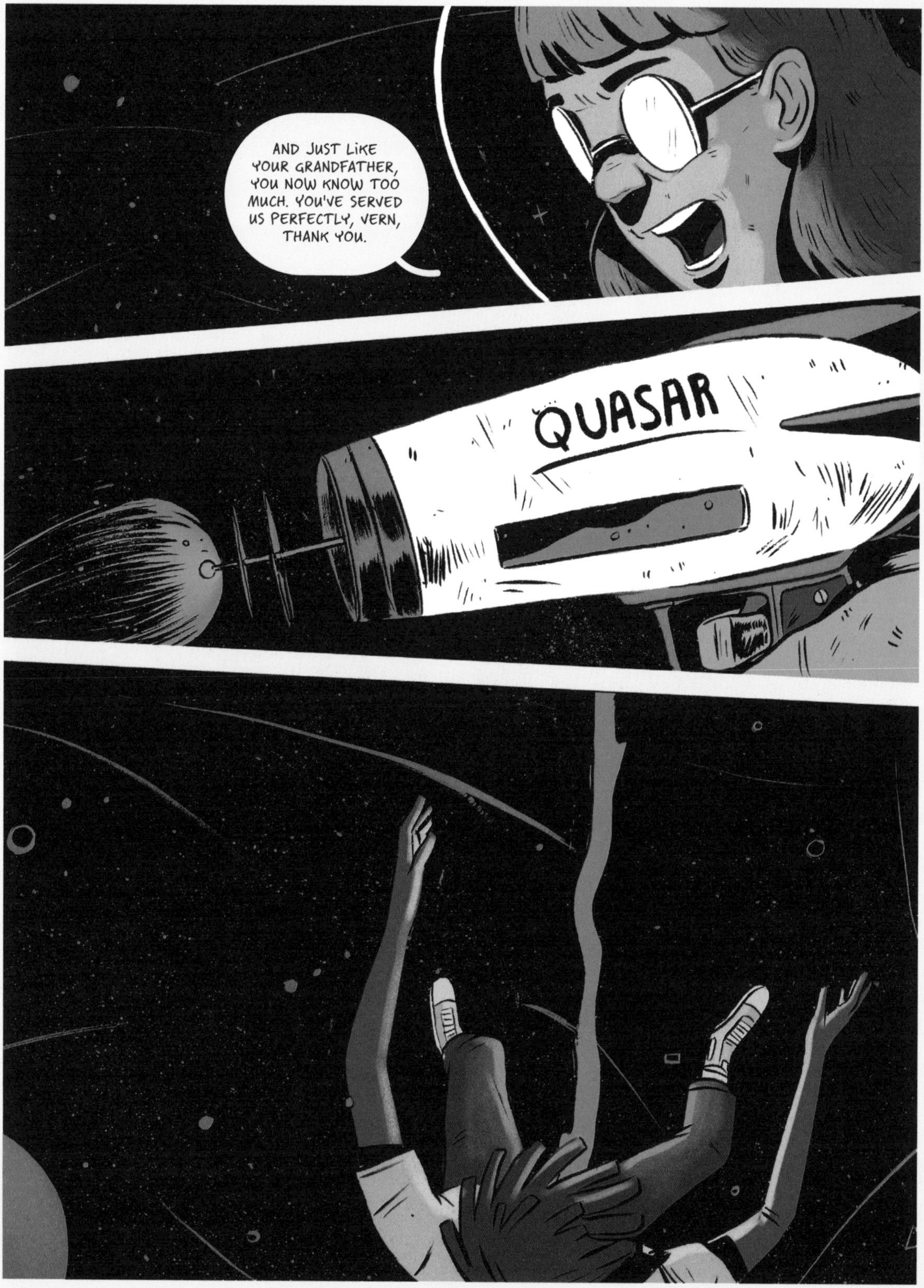
AND JUST LIKE YOUR GRANDFATHER, YOU NOW KNOW TOO MUCH. YOU'VE SERVED US PERFECTLY, VERN, THANK YOU.
QUASAR

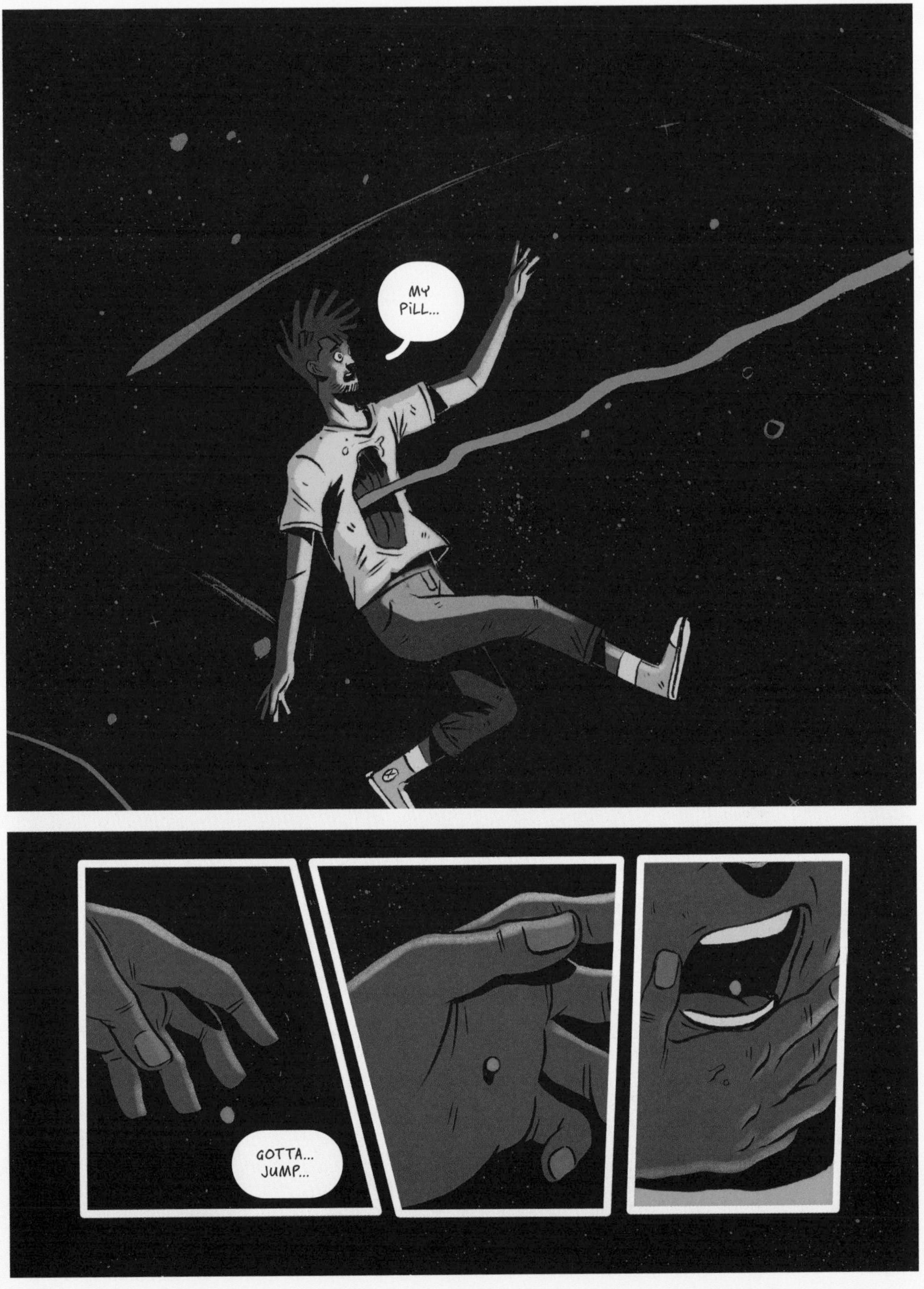
MY PILL...
GOTTA... JUMP...

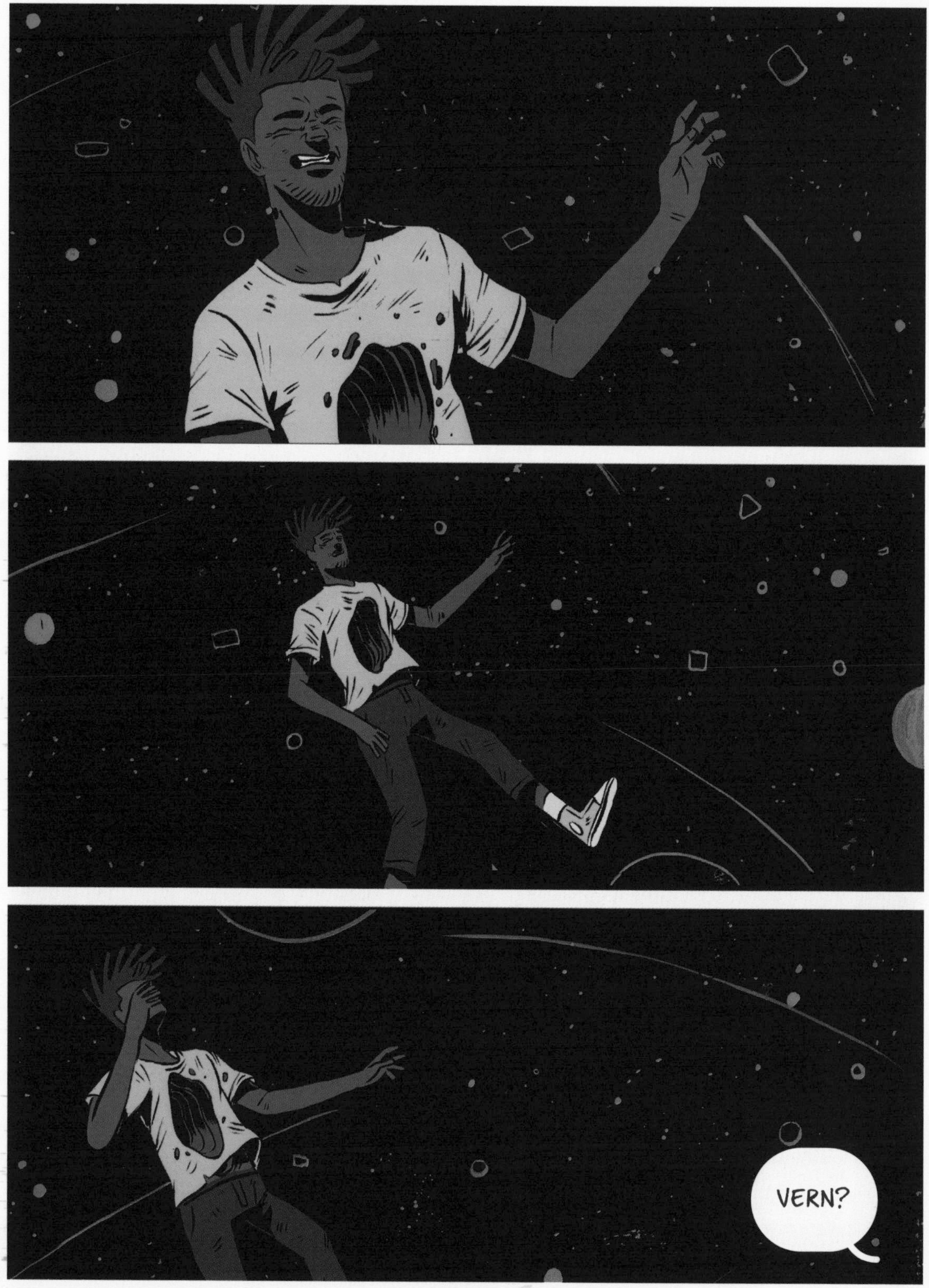
VERN?

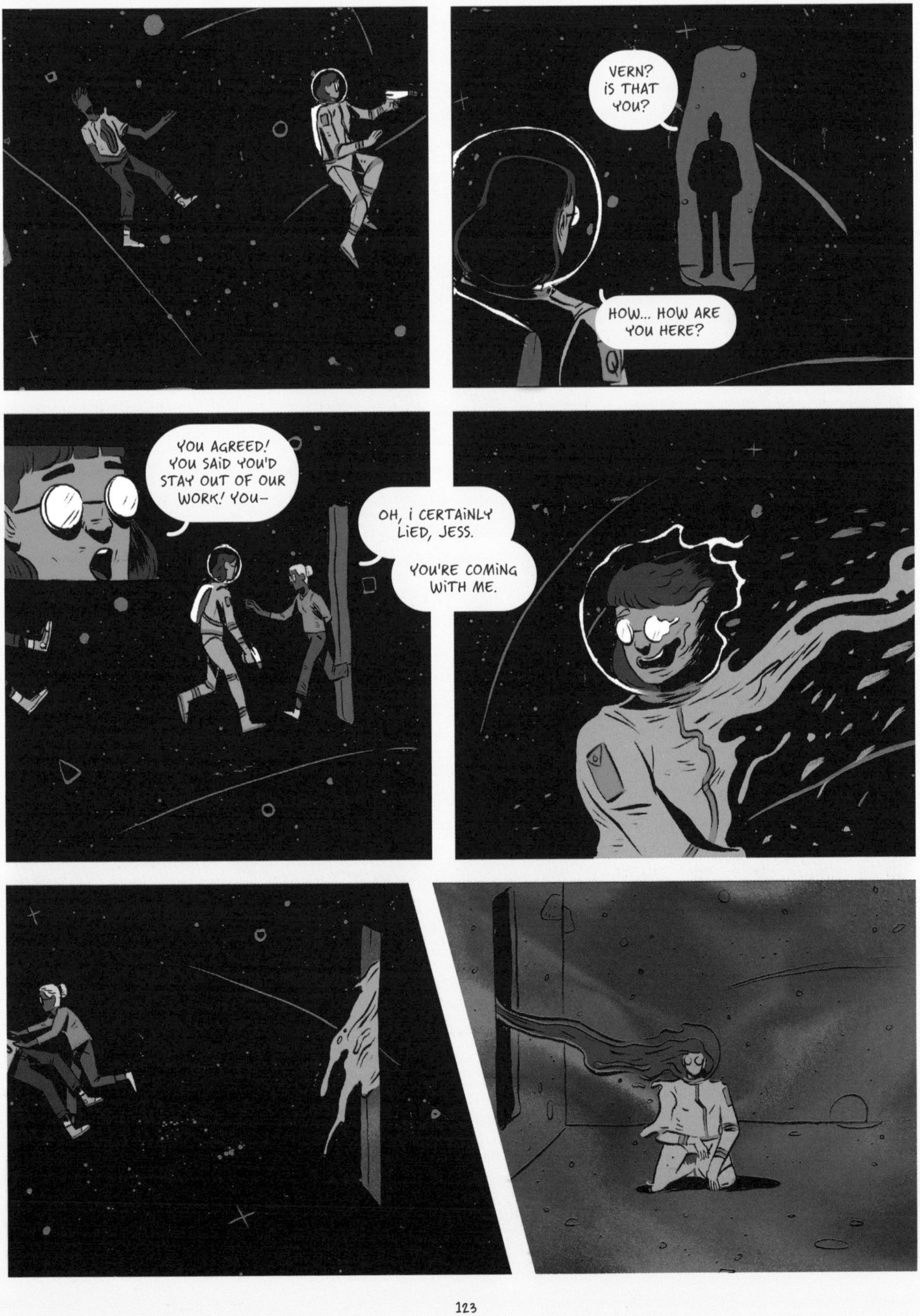
VERN? IS THAT YOU?
HOW... HOW ARE YOU HERE?
YOU AGREED! YOU SAID YOU'D STAY OUT OF OUR WORK! YOU-
OH, I CERTAINLY LIED, JESS.
YOU'RE COMING WITH ME.

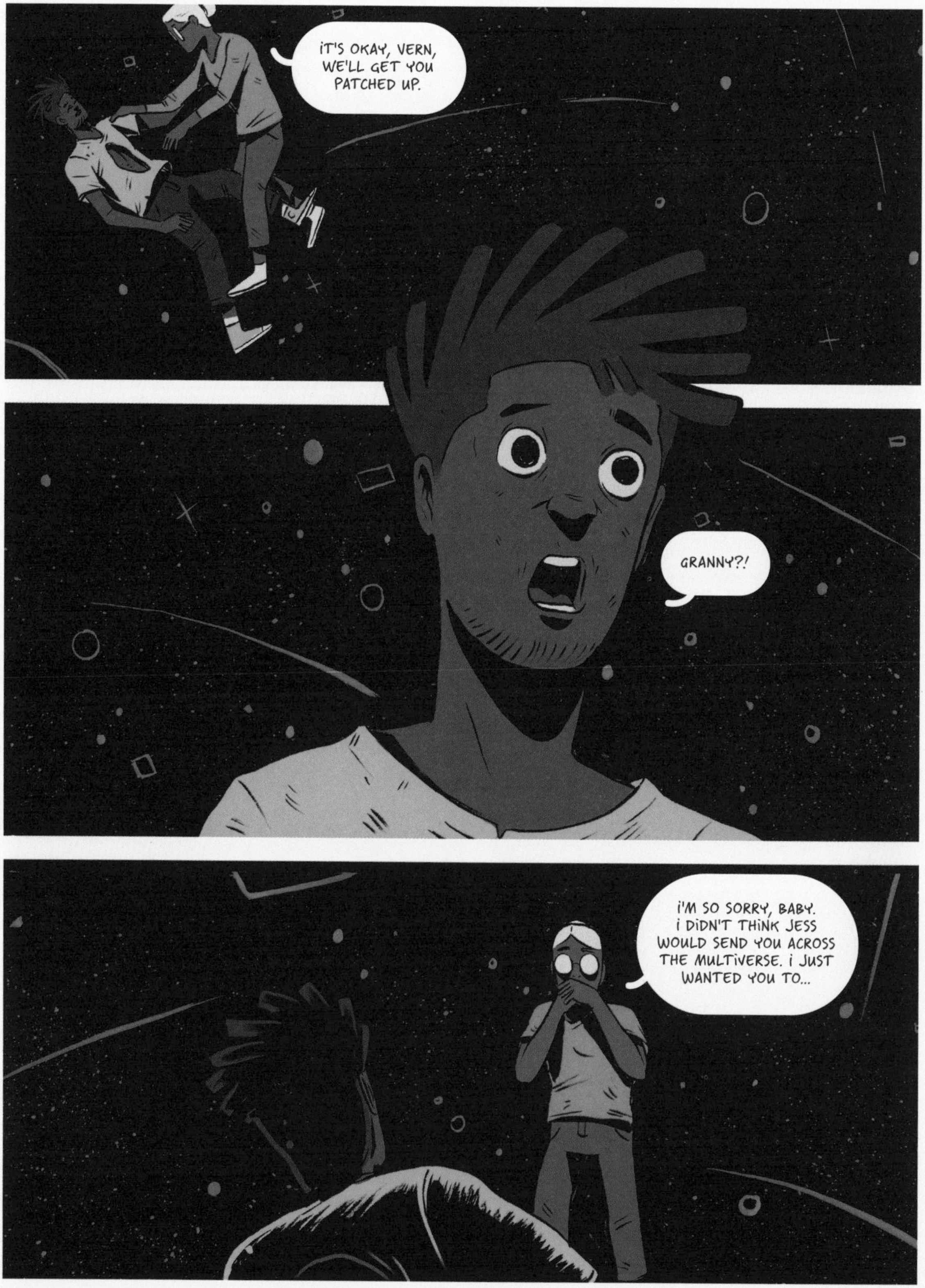
IT'S OKAY, VERN, WE'LL GET YOU PATCHED UP.
GRANNY?!
I'M SO SORRY, BABY. I DIDN'T THINK JESS WOULD SEND YOU ACROSS THE MULTIVERSE. I JUST WANTED YOU TO...

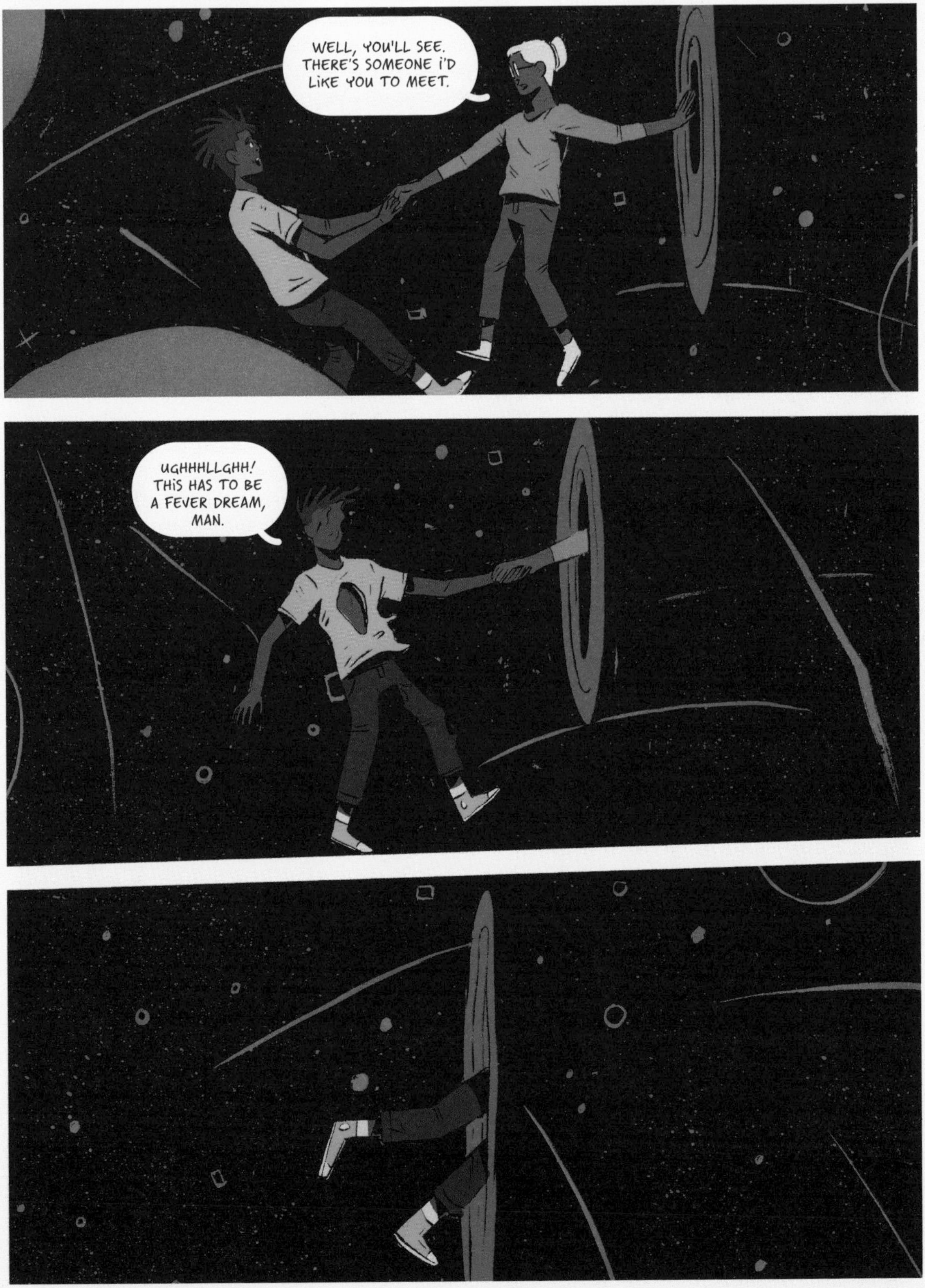
WELL, YOU'LL SEE. THERE'S SOMEONE I'D LIKE YOU TO MEET.
UGHHHLLGHH! THIS HAS TO BE A FEVER DREAM, MAN.

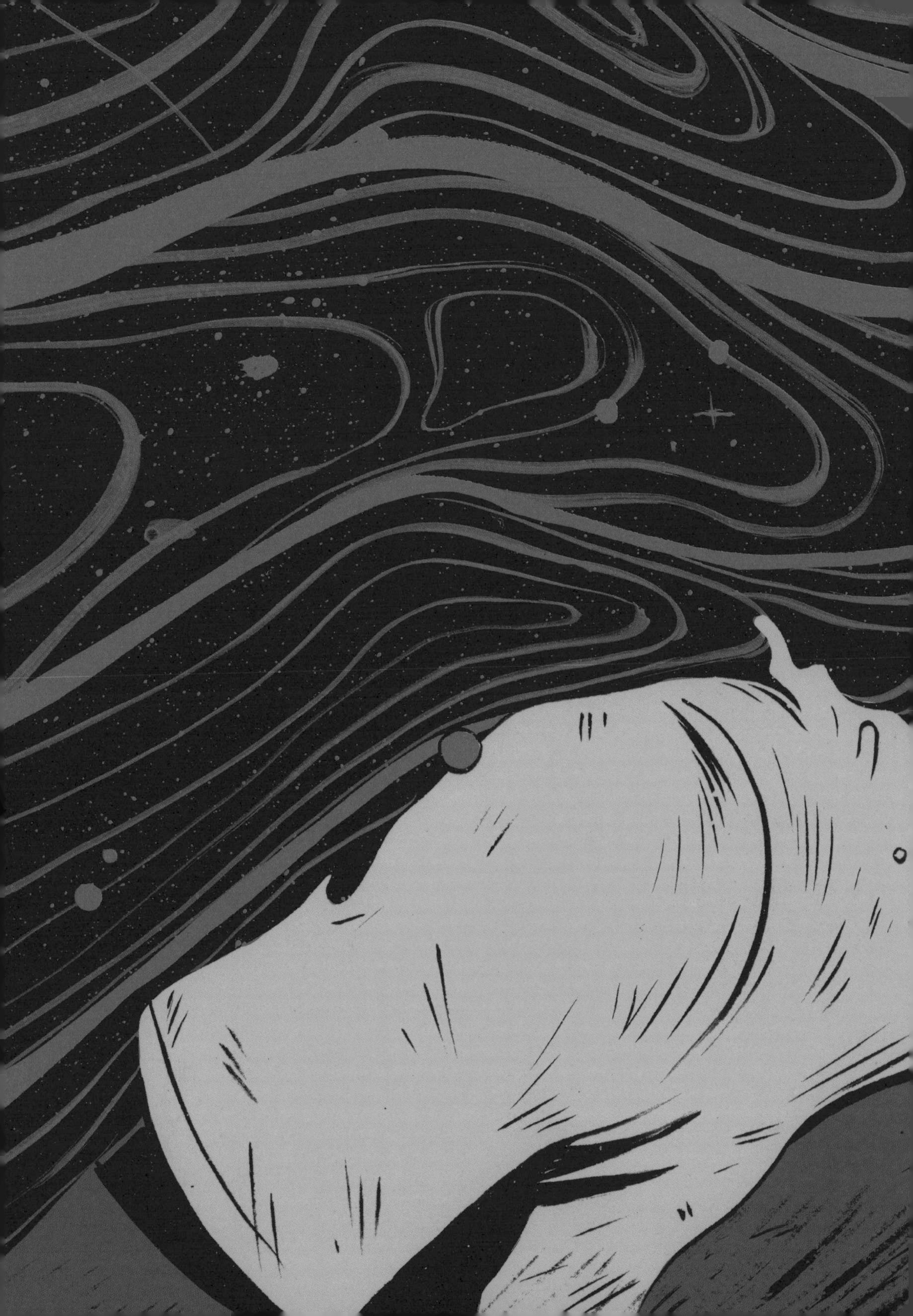

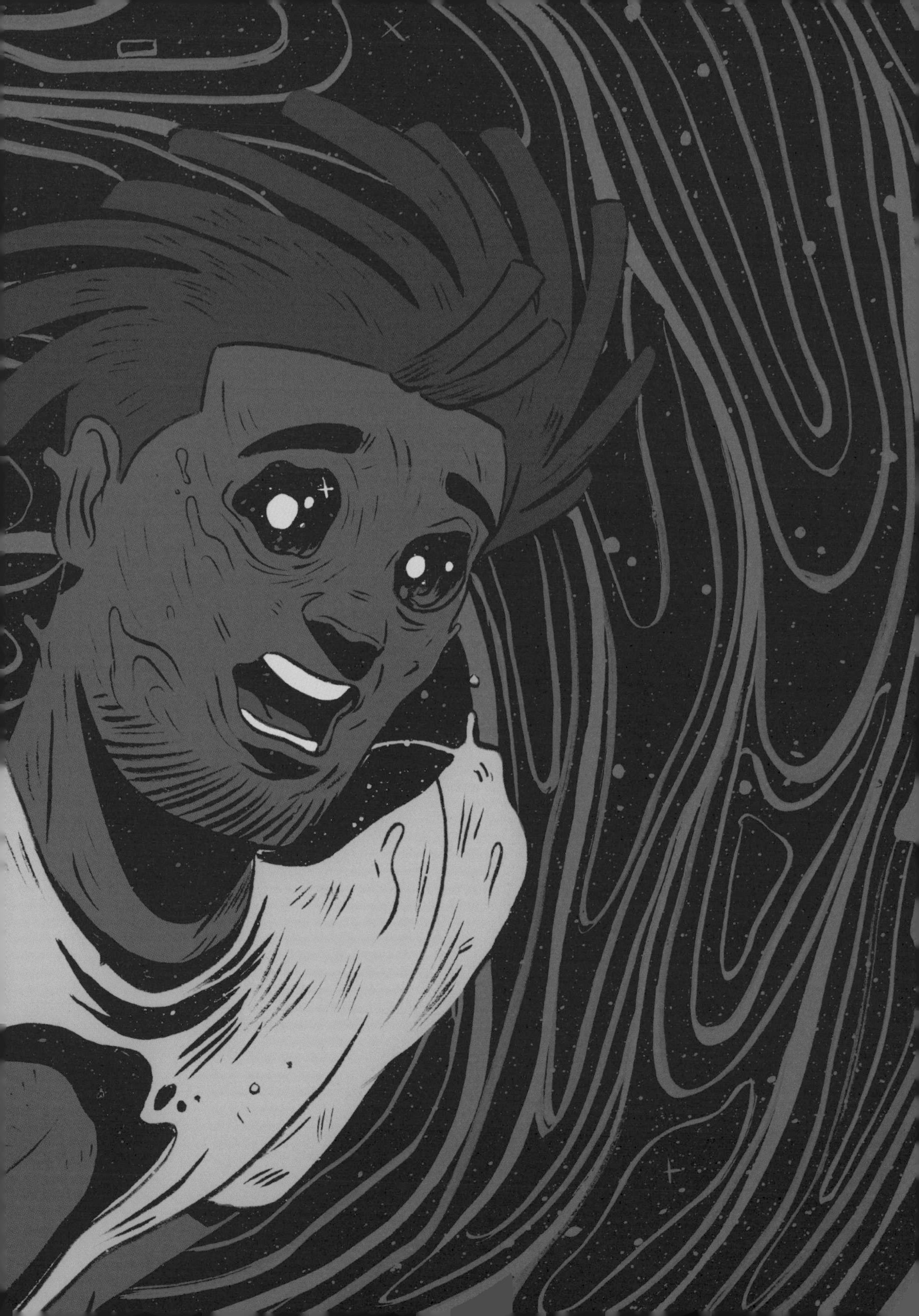

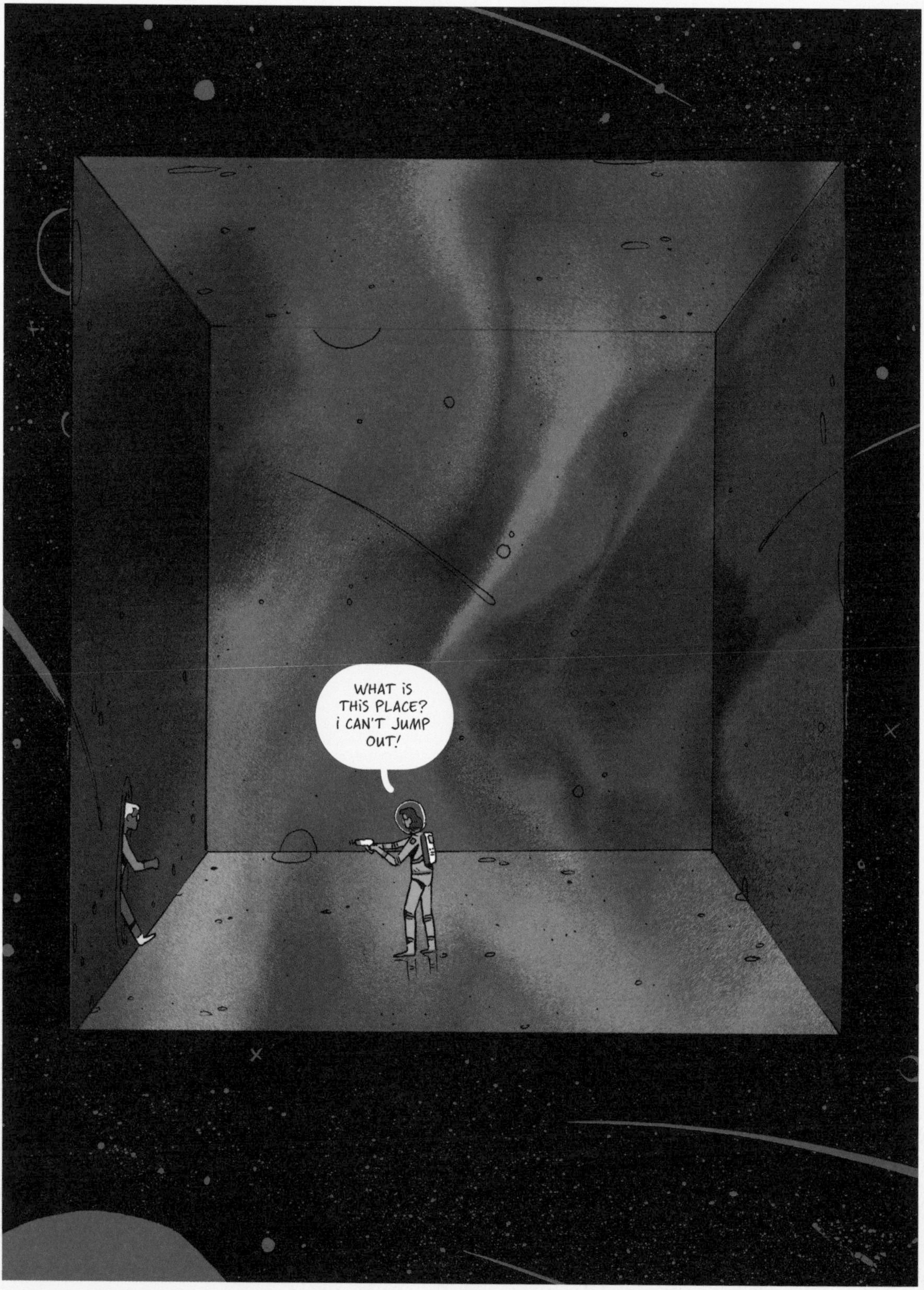
WHAT iS THiS PLACE? i CAN'T JUMP OUT!

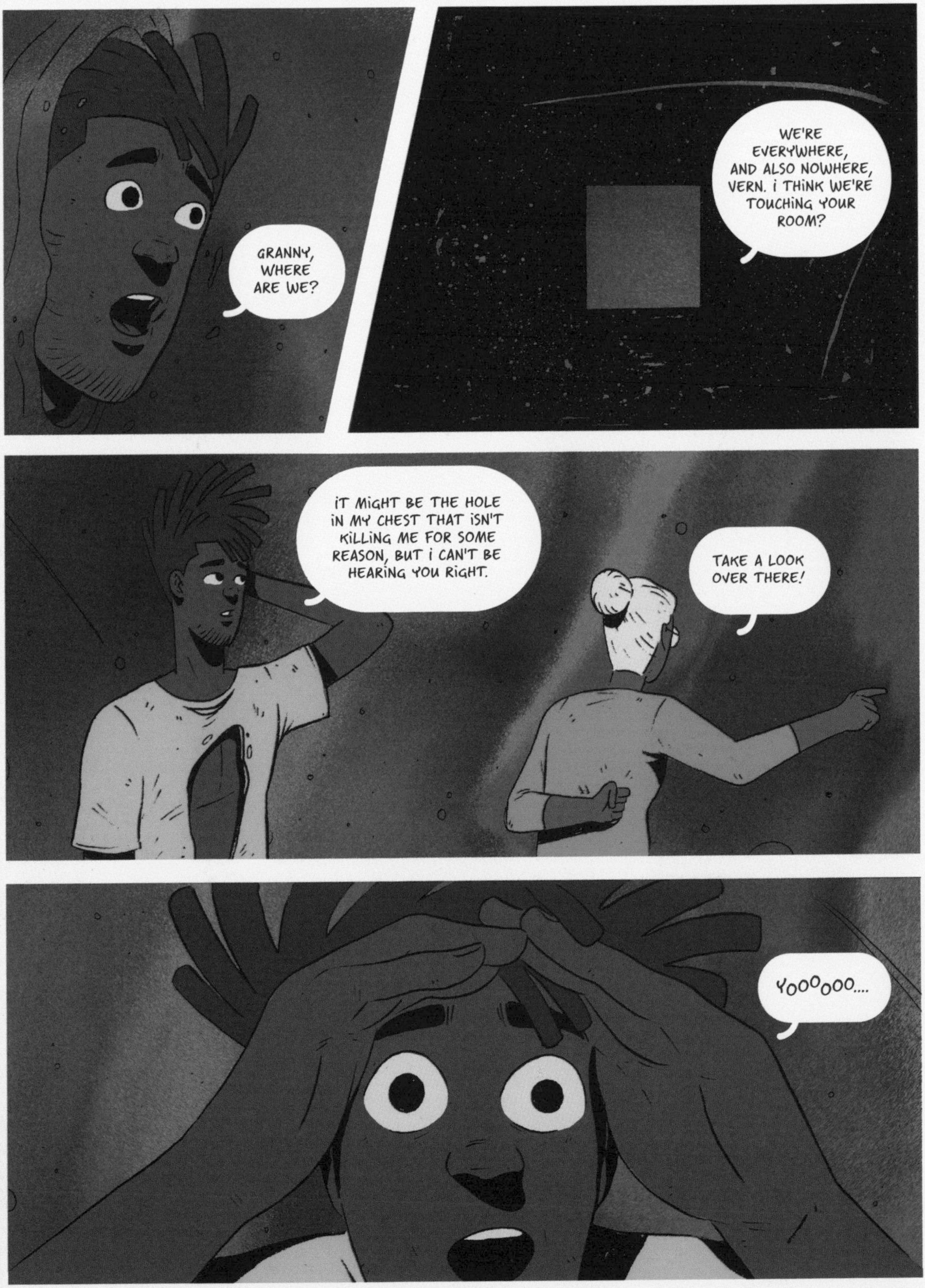

GRANNY, WHERE ARE WE?
WE'RE EVERYWHERE, AND ALSO NOWHERE, VERN. I THINK WE'RE TOUCHING YOUR ROOM?
IT MIGHT BE THE HOLE IN MY CHEST THAT ISN'T KILLING ME FOR SOME REASON, BUT I CAN'T BE HEARING YOU RIGHT.
TAKE A LOOK OVER THERE!
YOOOOOO....

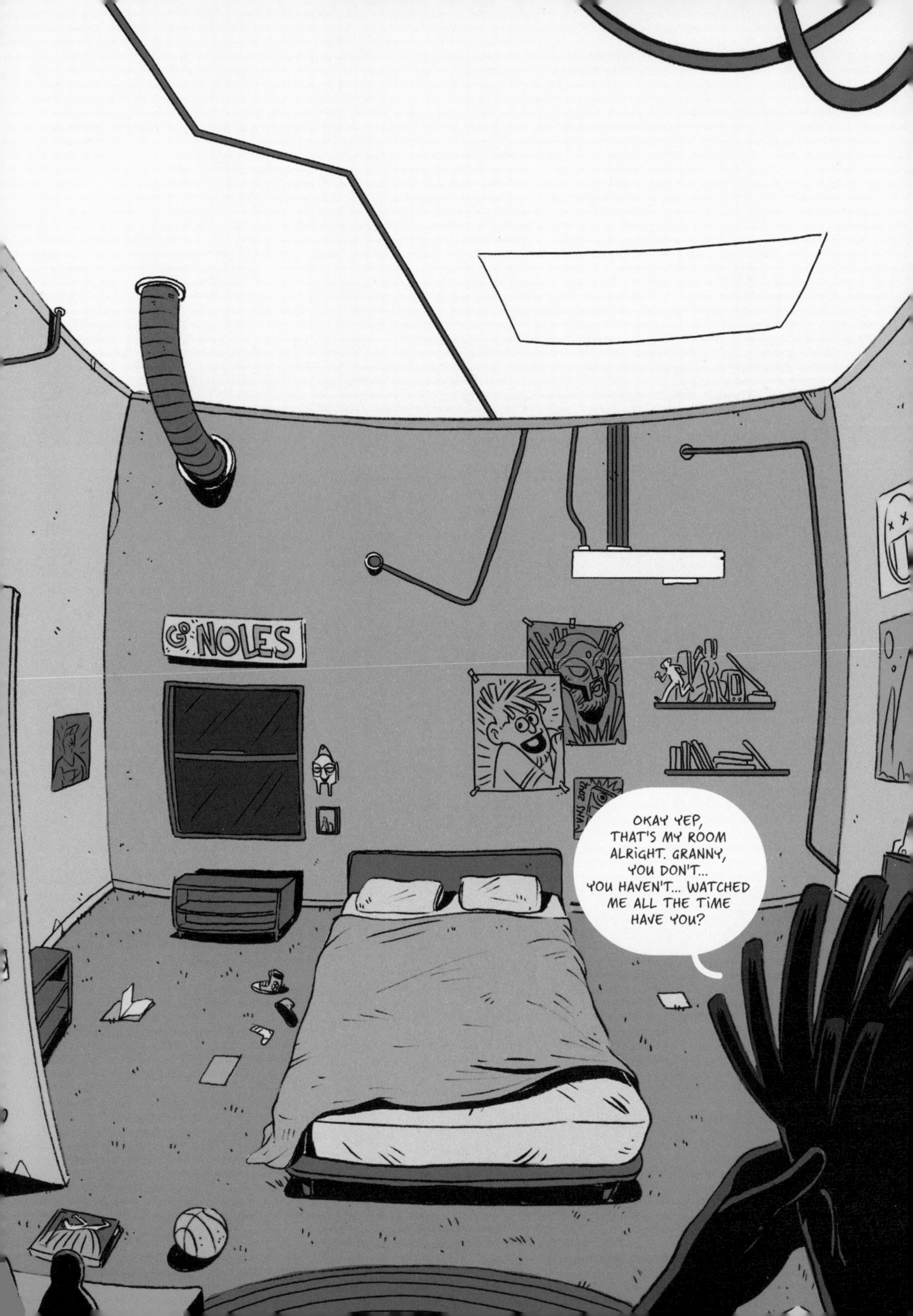
GO NOLES
OKAY YEP, THAT'S MY ROOM ALRIGHT. GRANNY, YOU DON'T... YOU HAVEN'T... WATCHED ME ALL THE TIME HAVE YOU?

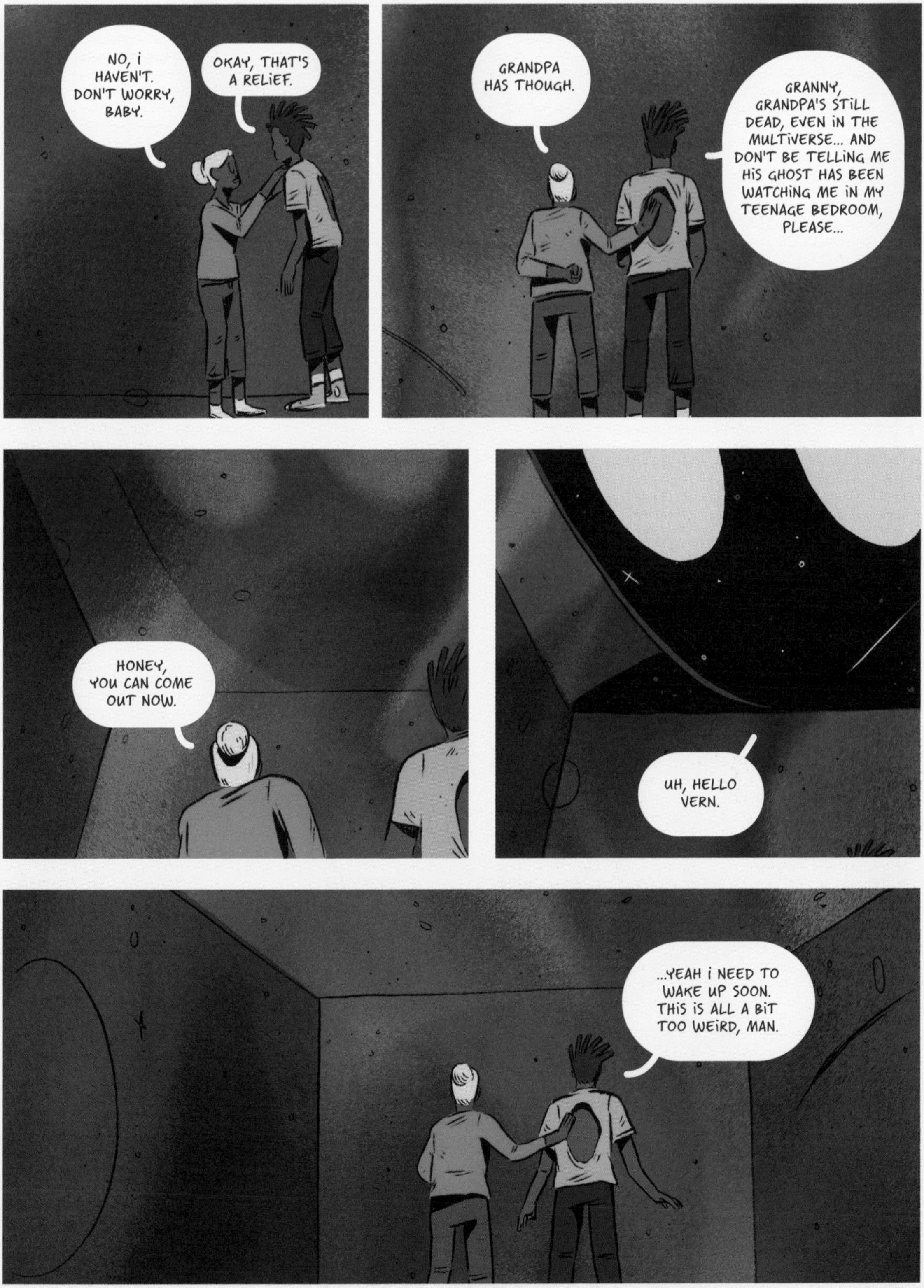
NO, i HAVEN'T. DON'T WORRY, BABY.
OKAY, THAT'S A RELiEF.
GRANDPA HAS THOUGH.
GRANNY, GRANDPA'S STiLL DEAD, EVEN iN THE MULTiVERSE... AND DON'T BE TELLiNG ME HiS GHOST HAS BEEN WATCHiNG ME iN MY TEENAGE BEDROOM, PLEASE...
HONEY, YOU CAN COME OUT NOW.
UH, HELLO VERN.
...YEAH i NEED TO WAKE UP SOON. THiS iS ALL A BiT TOO WEiRD, MAN.

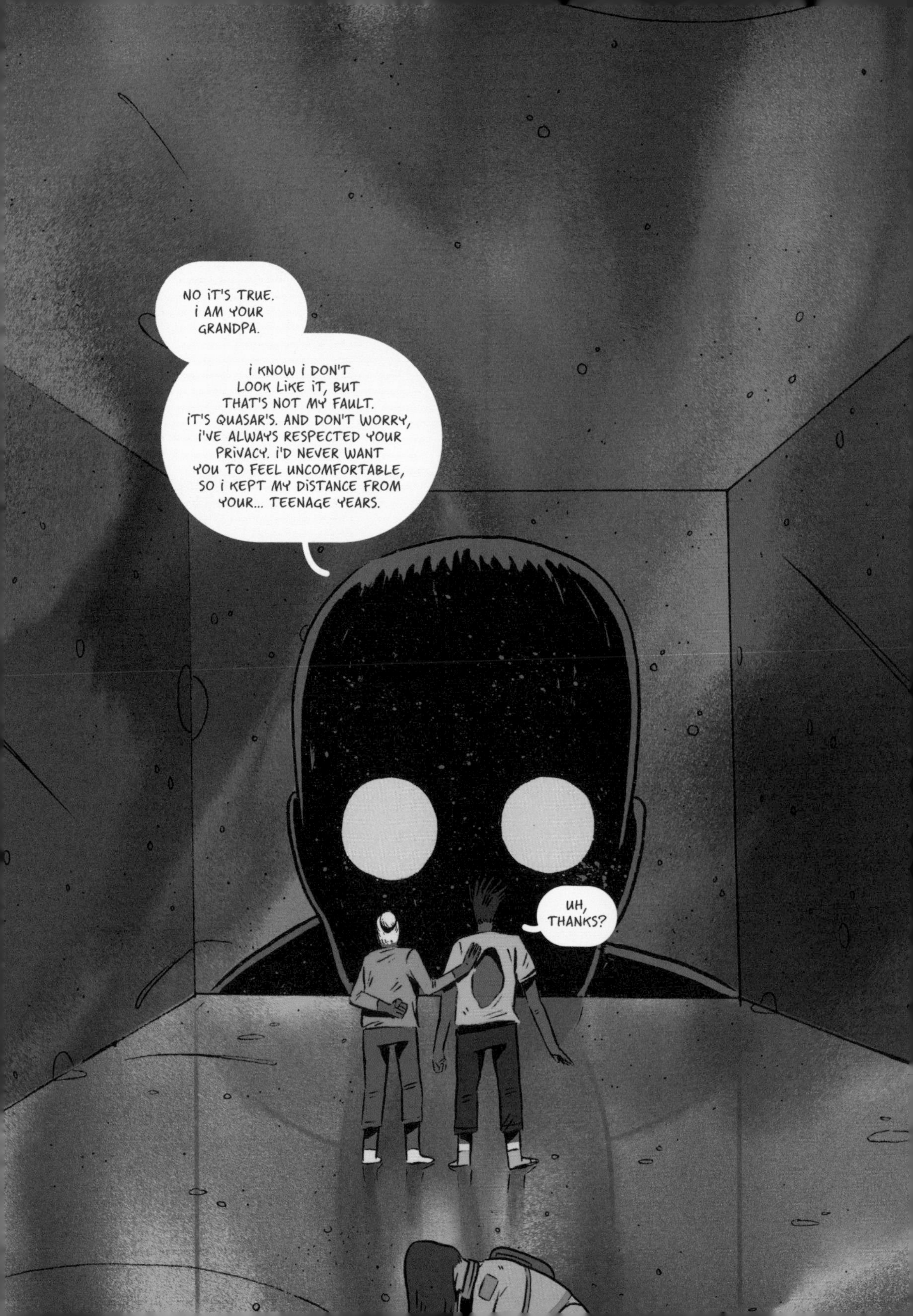
NO IT'S TRUE. I AM YOUR GRANDPA.
I KNOW I DON'T LOOK LIKE IT, BUT THAT'S NOT MY FAULT. IT'S QUASAR'S. AND DON'T WORRY, I'VE ALWAYS RESPECTED YOUR PRIVACY. I'D NEVER WANT YOU TO FEEL UNCOMFORTABLE, SO I KEPT MY DISTANCE FROM YOUR... TEENAGE YEARS.
UH, THANKS?

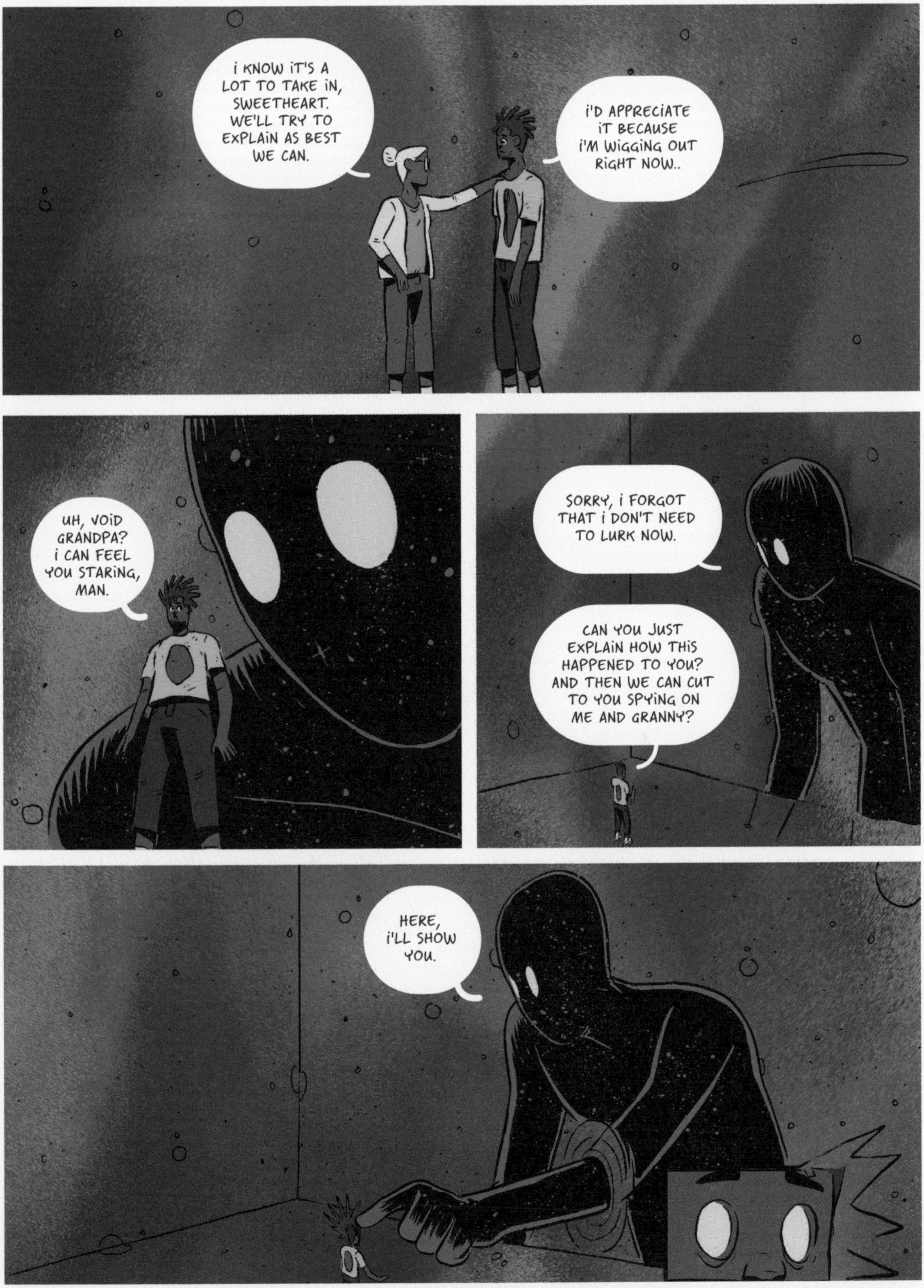
i KNOW iT'S A LOT TO TAKE iN, SWEETHEART. WE'LL TRY TO EXPLAiN AS BEST WE CAN.
i'D APPRECiATE iT BECAUSE i'M WiGGiNG OUT RiGHT NOW..
UH, VOiD GRANDPA? i CAN FEEL YOU STARiNG, MAN.
SORRY, i FORGOT THAT i DON'T NEED TO LURK NOW.
CAN YOU JUST EXPLAiN HOW THiS HAPPENED TO YOU? AND THEN WE CAN CUT TO YOU SPYiNG ON ME AND GRANNY?
HERE, i'LL SHOW YOU.

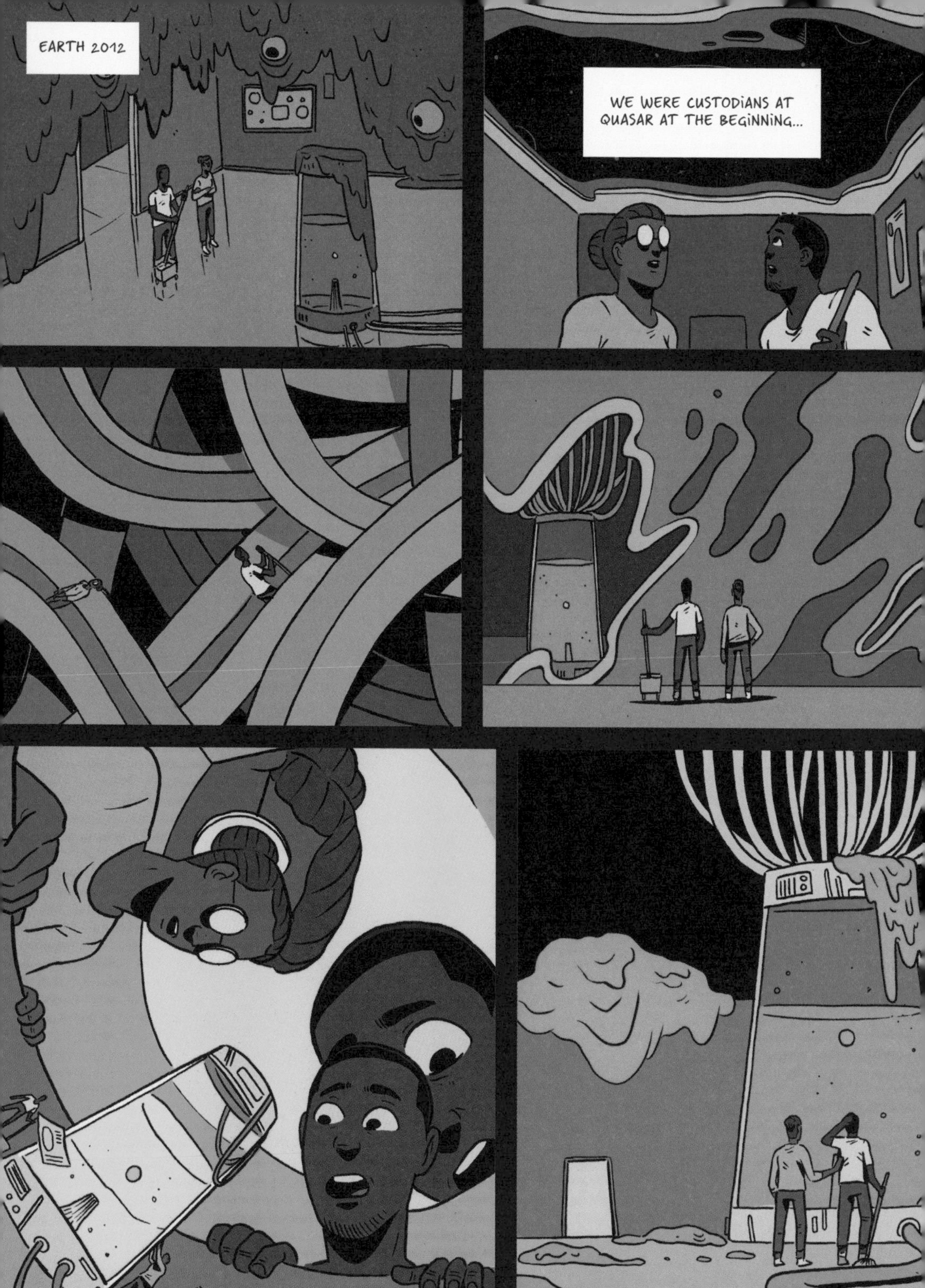
EARTH 2012
WE WERE CUSTODIANS AT QUASAR AT THE BEGINNING...

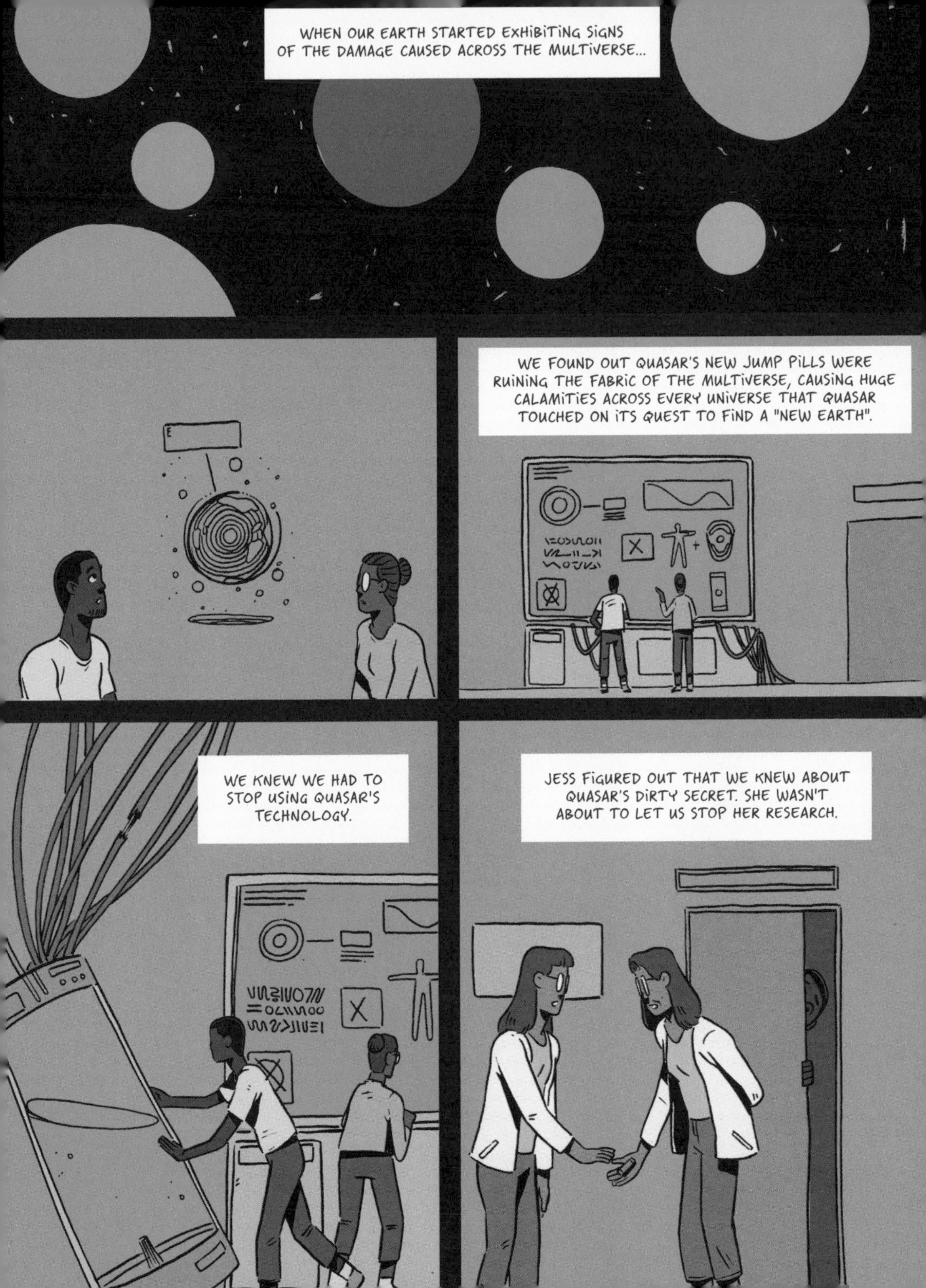
WHEN OUR EARTH STARTED EXHIBITING SIGNS OF THE DAMAGE CAUSED ACROSS THE MULTIVERSE...
WE FOUND OUT QUASAR'S NEW JUMP PILLS WERE RUINING THE FABRIC OF THE MULTIVERSE, CAUSING HUGE CALAMITIES ACROSS EVERY UNIVERSE THAT QUASAR TOUCHED ON ITS QUEST TO FIND A "NEW EARTH".
WE KNEW WE HAD TO STOP USING QUASAR'S TECHNOLOGY.
JESS FIGURED OUT THAT WE KNEW ABOUT QUASAR'S DIRTY SECRET. SHE WASN'T ABOUT TO LET US STOP HER RESEARCH.

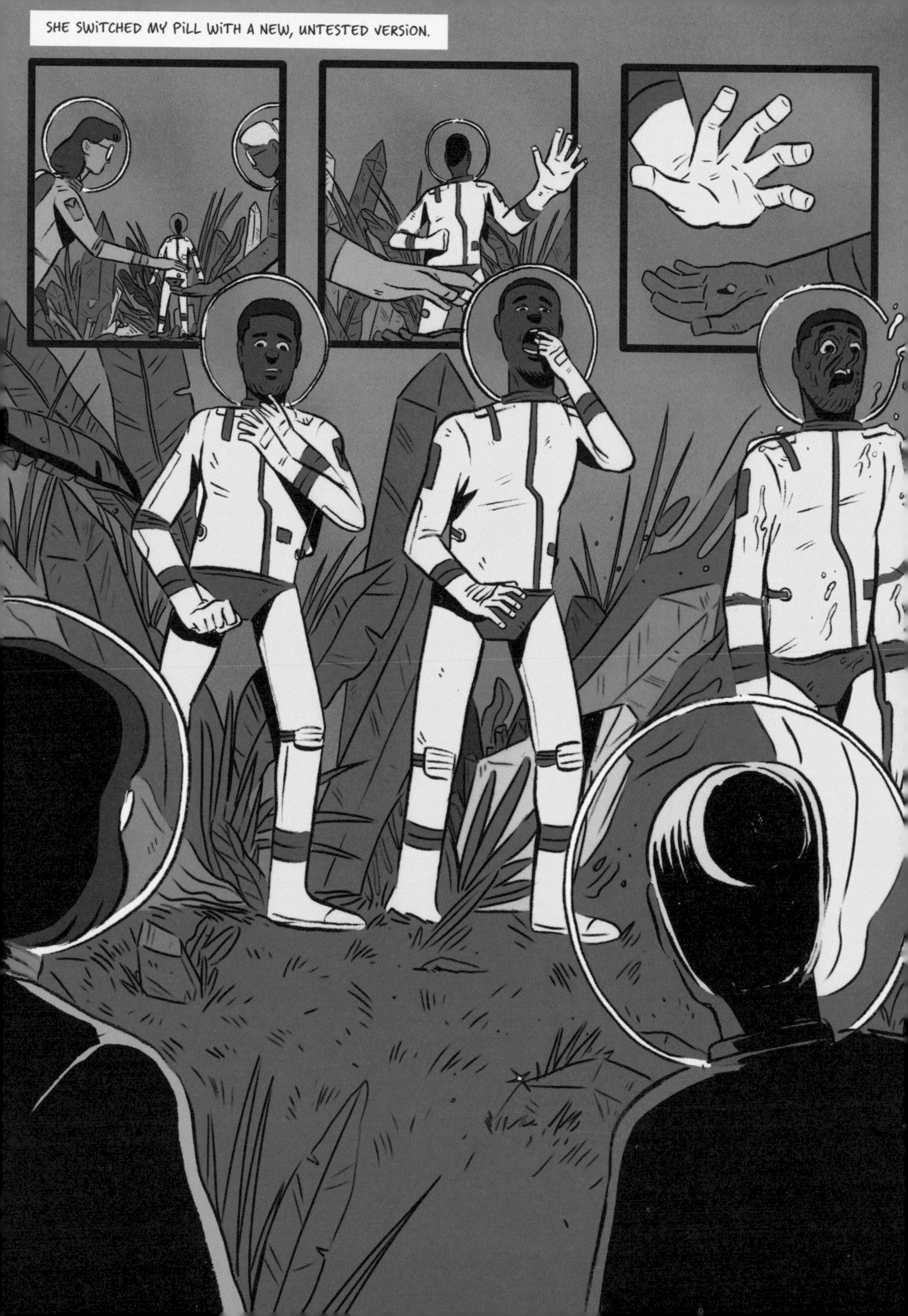
SHE SWITCHED MY PILL WITH A NEW, UNTESTED VERSION.

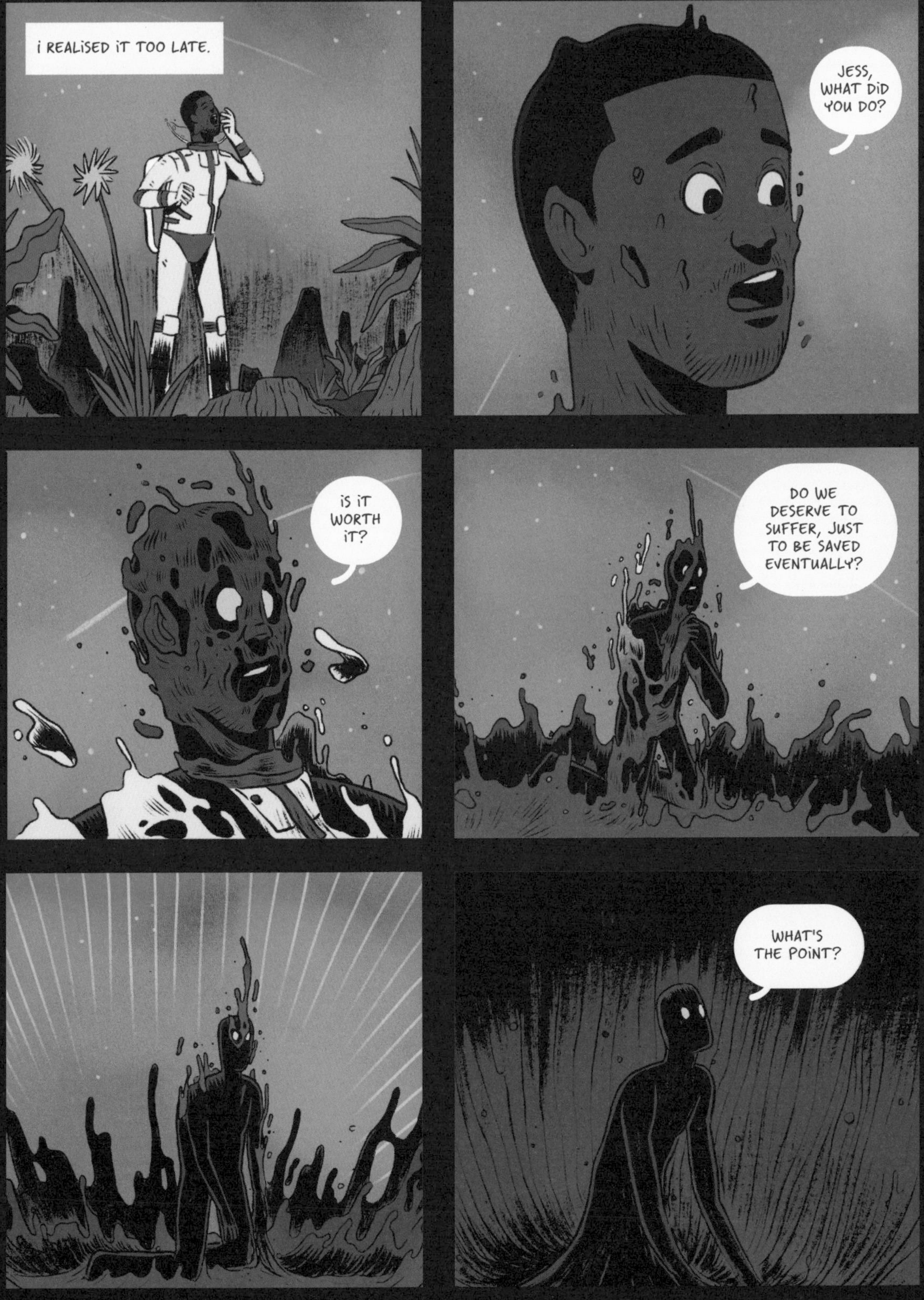

i REALiSED iT TOO LATE.
JESS, WHAT DiD YOU DO?
iS iT WORTH iT?
DO WE DESERVE TO SUFFER, JUST TO BE SAVED EVENTUALLY?
WHAT'S THE POiNT?

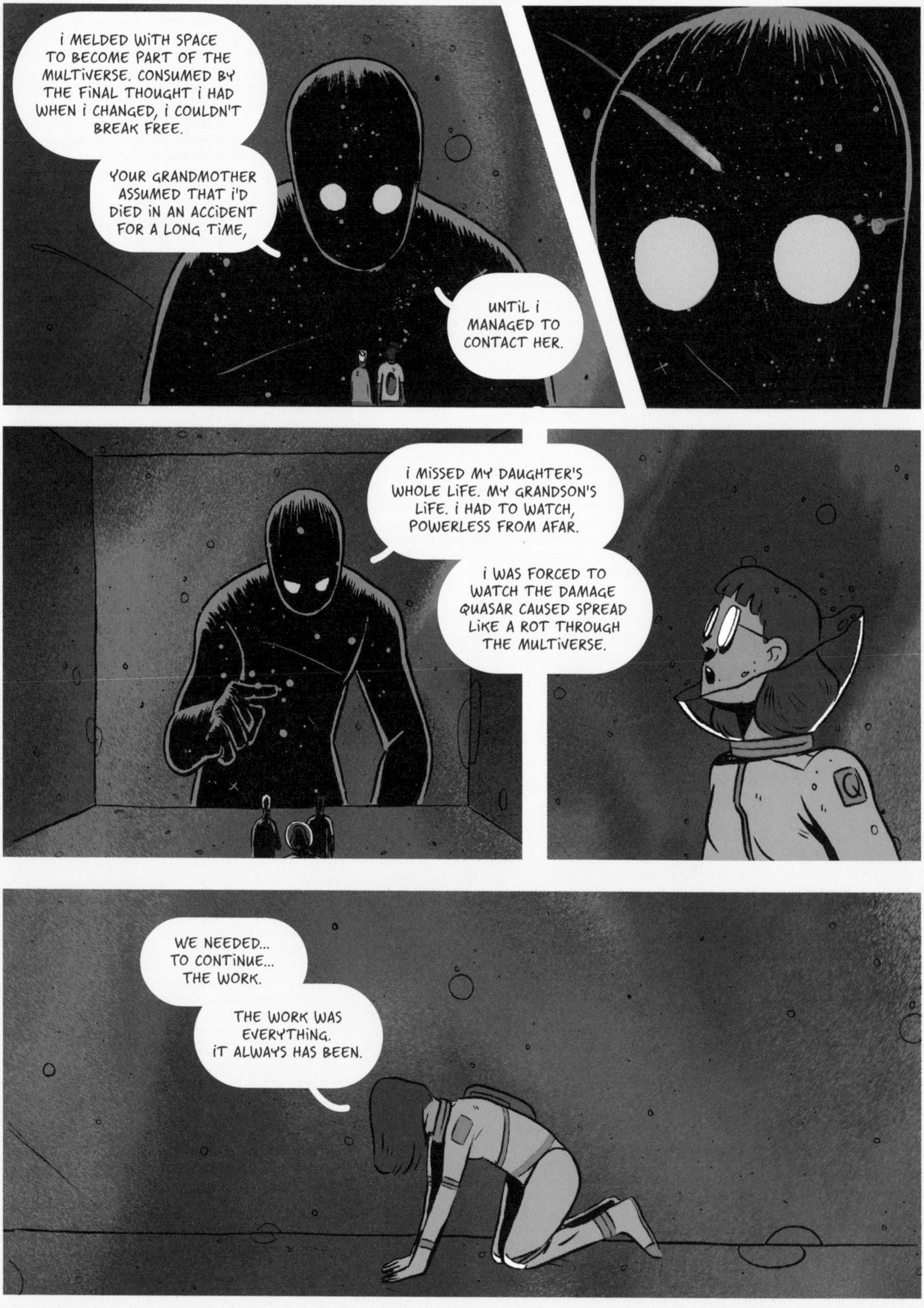
I MELDED WITH SPACE TO BECOME PART OF THE MULTIVERSE. CONSUMED BY THE FINAL THOUGHT I HAD WHEN I CHANGED, I COULDN'T BREAK FREE.
YOUR GRANDMOTHER ASSUMED THAT I'D DIED IN AN ACCIDENT FOR A LONG TIME,
UNTIL I MANAGED TO CONTACT HER.
I MISSED MY DAUGHTER'S WHOLE LIFE. MY GRANDSON'S LIFE. I HAD TO WATCH, POWERLESS FROM AFAR.
I WAS FORCED TO WATCH THE DAMAGE QUASAR CAUSED SPREAD LIKE A ROT THROUGH THE MULTIVERSE.
WE NEEDED... TO CONTINUE... THE WORK.
THE WORK WAS EVERYTHING. IT ALWAYS HAS BEEN.

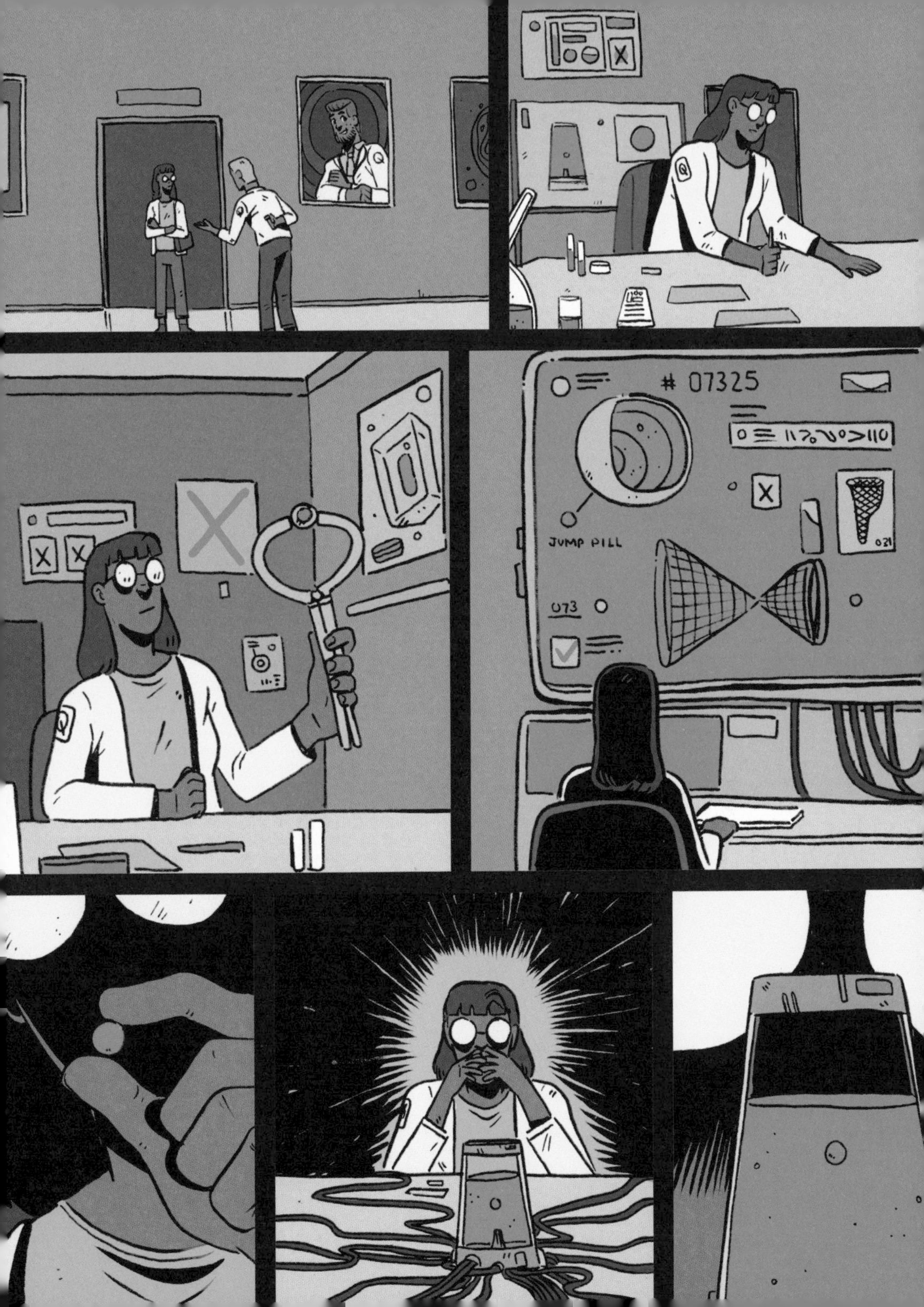

07325
JUMP PILL
073

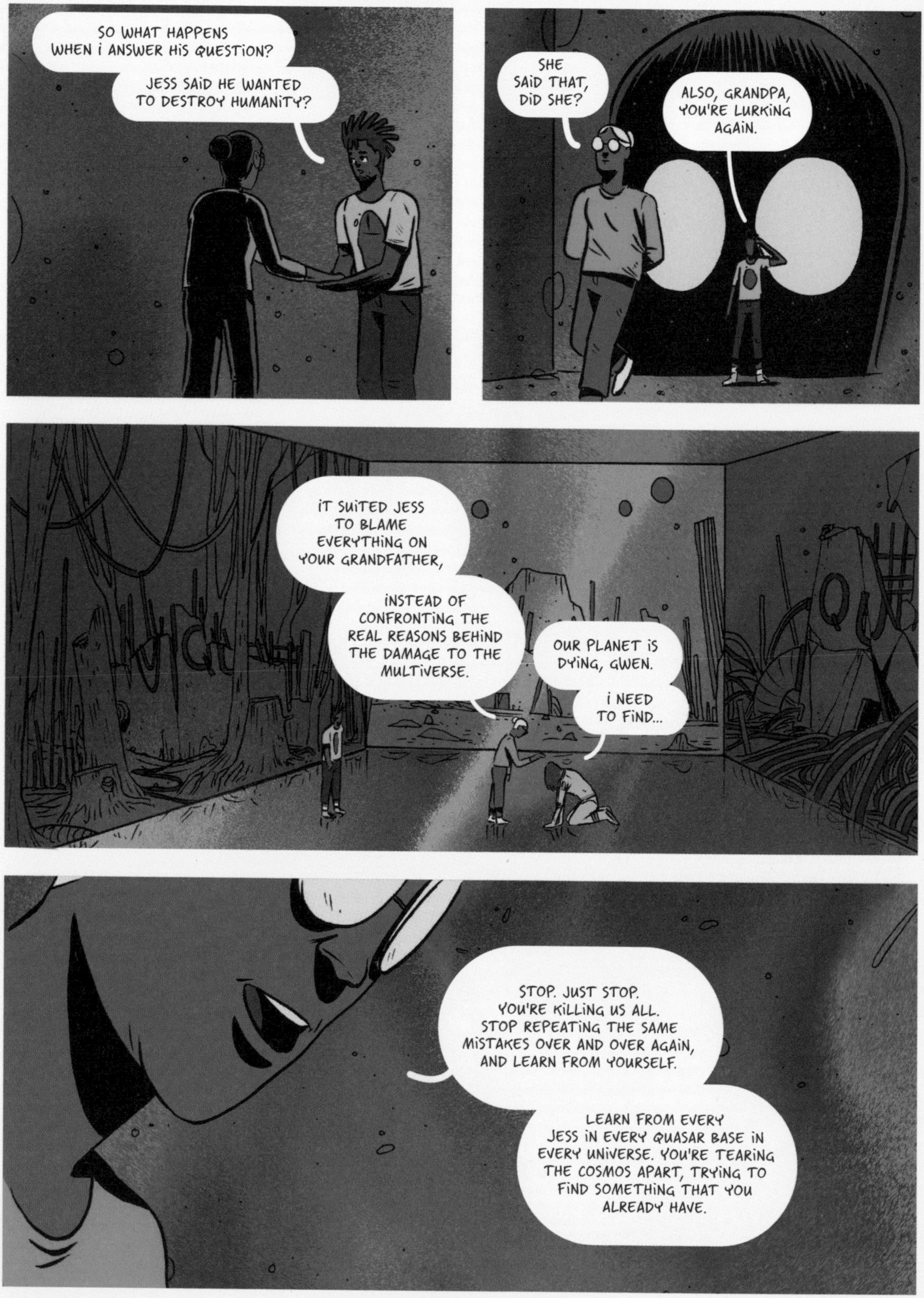
SO WHAT HAPPENS WHEN I ANSWER HIS QUESTION?
JESS SAID HE WANTED TO DESTROY HUMANITY?
SHE SAID THAT, DID SHE?
ALSO, GRANDPA, YOU'RE LURKING AGAIN.
IT SUITED JESS TO BLAME EVERYTHING ON YOUR GRANDFATHER,
INSTEAD OF CONFRONTING THE REAL REASONS BEHIND THE DAMAGE TO THE MULTIVERSE.
OUR PLANET IS DYING, GWEN.
I NEED TO FIND...
STOP. JUST STOP. YOU'RE KILLING US ALL. STOP REPEATING THE SAME MISTAKES OVER AND OVER AGAIN, AND LEARN FROM YOURSELF.
LEARN FROM EVERY JESS IN EVERY QUASAR BASE IN EVERY UNIVERSE. YOU'RE TEARING THE COSMOS APART, TRYING TO FIND SOMETHING THAT YOU ALREADY HAVE.

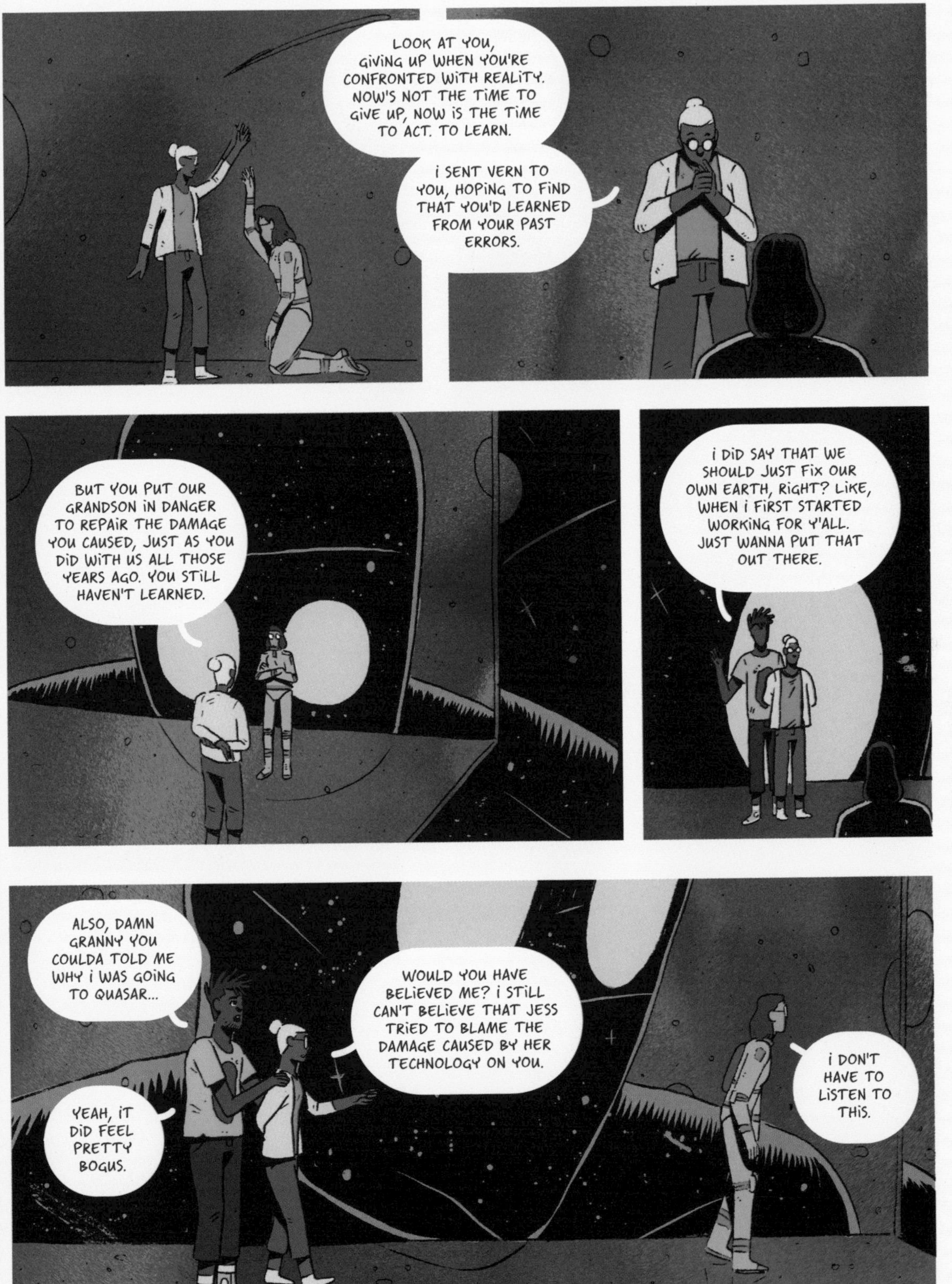
LOOK AT YOU, GIVING UP WHEN YOU'RE CONFRONTED WITH REALITY. NOW'S NOT THE TIME TO GIVE UP, NOW IS THE TIME TO ACT. TO LEARN.
I SENT VERN TO YOU, HOPING TO FIND THAT YOU'D LEARNED FROM YOUR PAST ERRORS.
BUT YOU PUT OUR GRANDSON IN DANGER TO REPAIR THE DAMAGE YOU CAUSED, JUST AS YOU DID WITH US ALL THOSE YEARS AGO. YOU STILL HAVEN'T LEARNED.
I DID SAY THAT WE SHOULD JUST FIX OUR OWN EARTH, RIGHT? LIKE, WHEN I FIRST STARTED WORKING FOR Y'ALL. JUST WANNA PUT THAT OUT THERE.
ALSO, DAMN GRANNY YOU COULDA TOLD ME WHY I WAS GOING TO QUASAR...
YEAH, IT DID FEEL PRETTY BOGUS.
WOULD YOU HAVE BELIEVED ME? I STILL CAN'T BELIEVE THAT JESS TRIED TO BLAME THE DAMAGE CAUSED BY HER TECHNOLOGY ON YOU.
I DON'T HAVE TO LISTEN TO THIS.

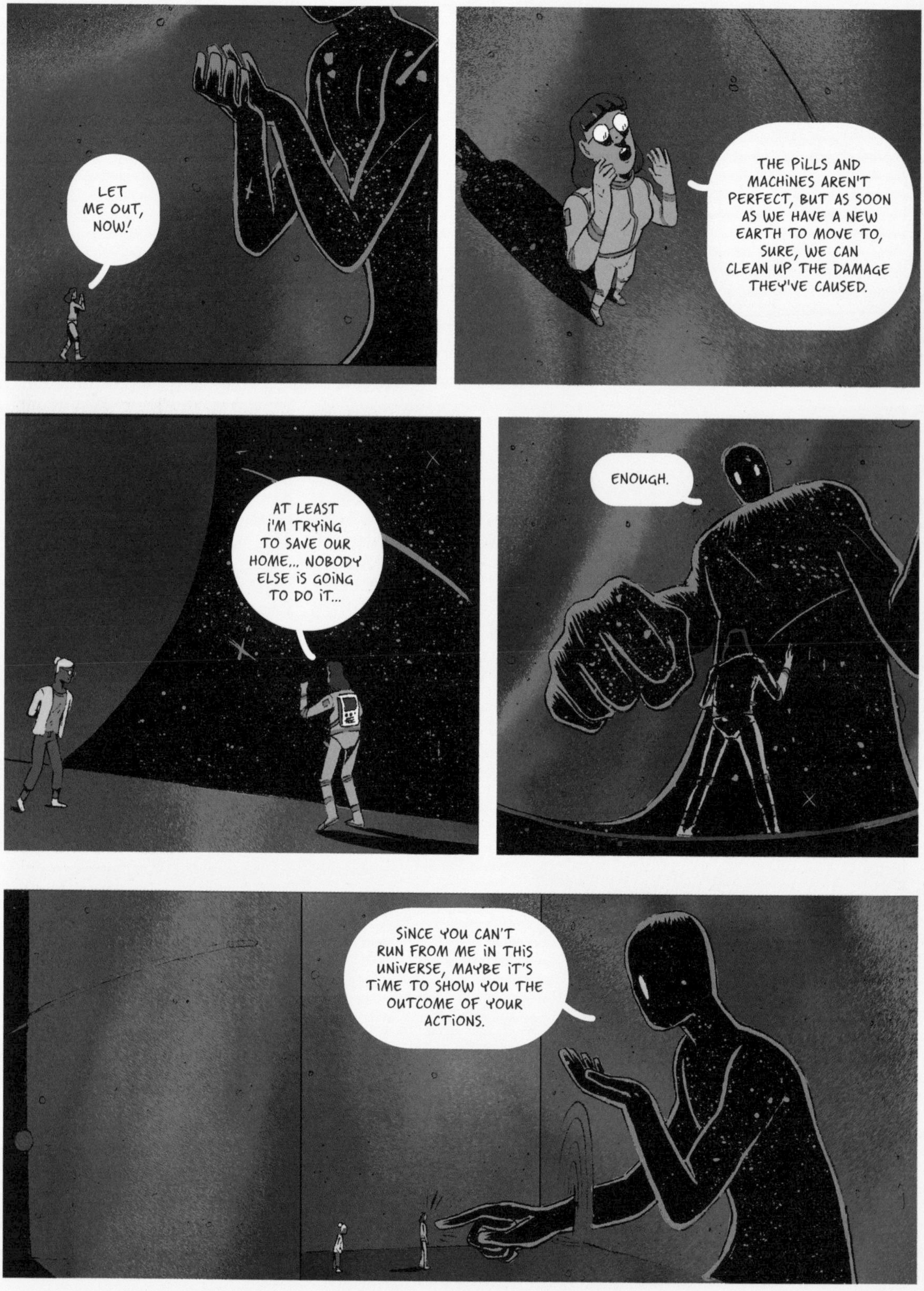
LET ME OUT, NOW!
THE PILLS AND MACHINES AREN'T PERFECT, BUT AS SOON AS WE HAVE A NEW EARTH TO MOVE TO, SURE, WE CAN CLEAN UP THE DAMAGE THEY'VE CAUSED.
AT LEAST I'M TRYING TO SAVE OUR HOME... NOBODY ELSE IS GOING TO DO IT...
ENOUGH.
SINCE YOU CAN'T RUN FROM ME IN THIS UNIVERSE, MAYBE IT'S TIME TO SHOW YOU THE OUTCOME OF YOUR ACTIONS.

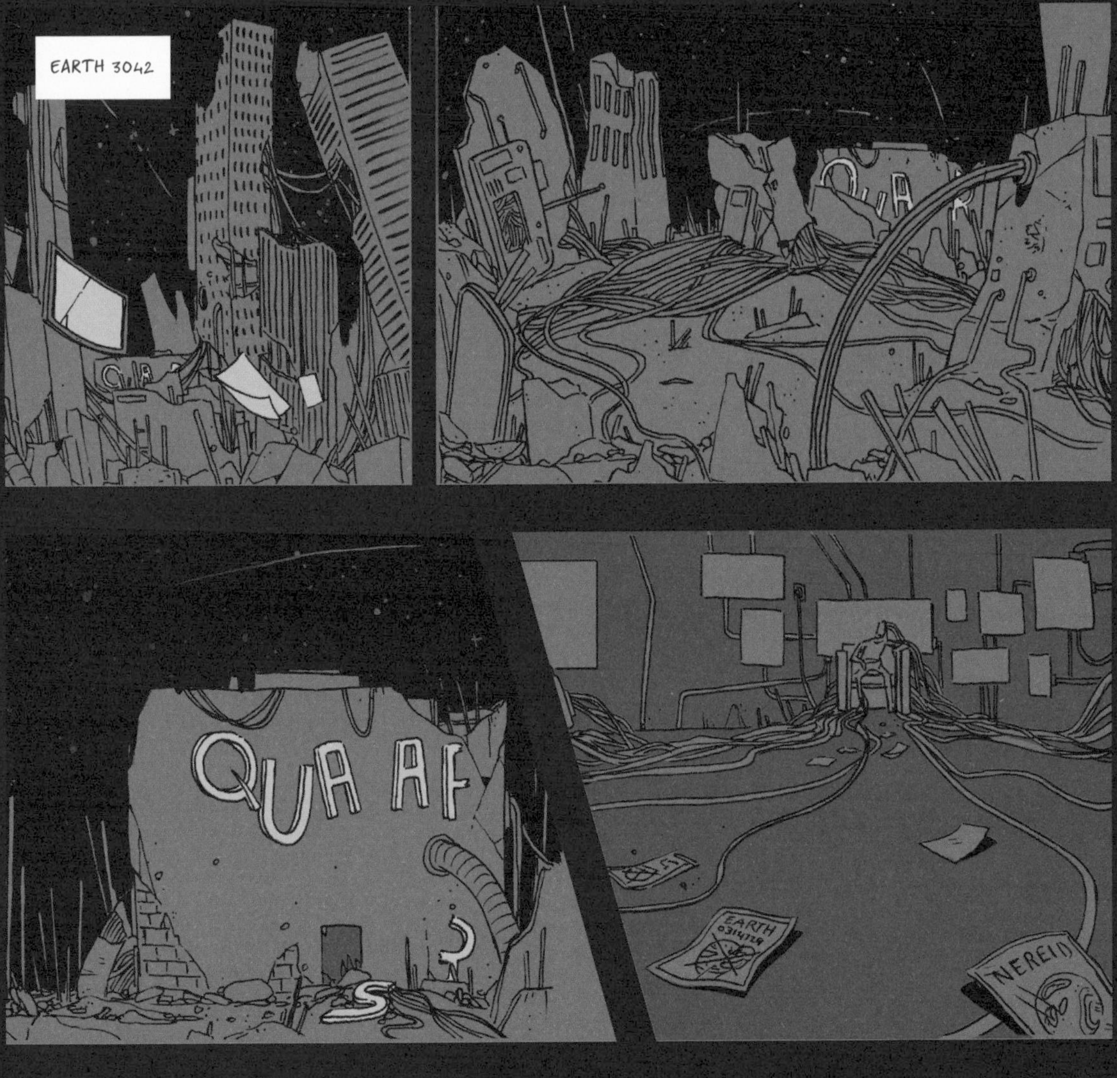
EARTH 3042
QUA AF
EARTH
NEREID

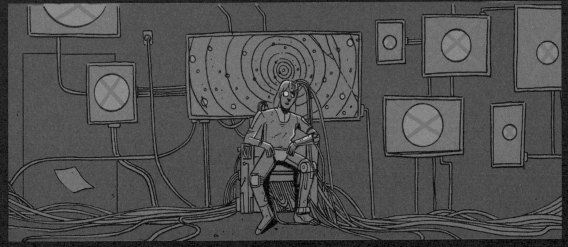

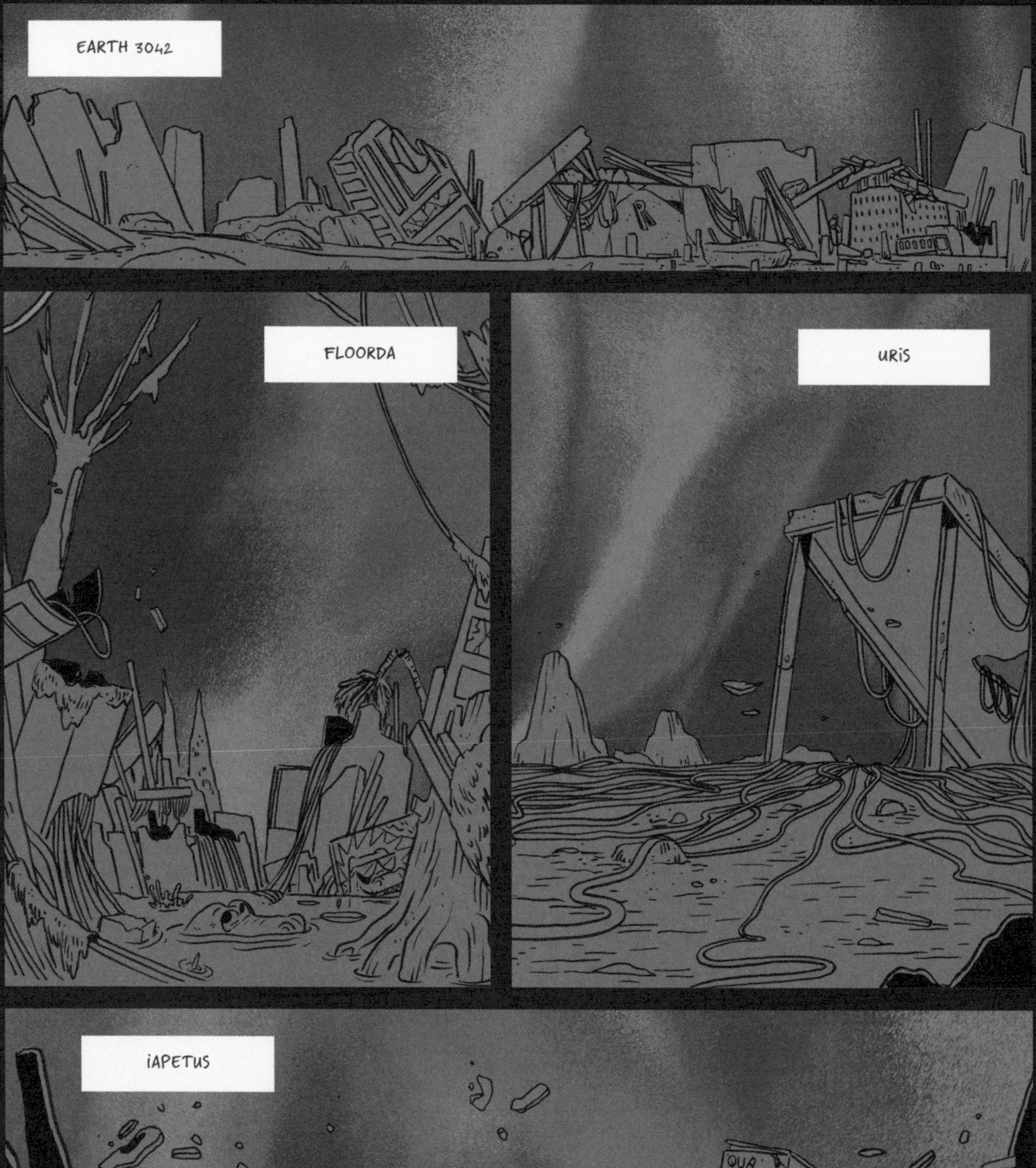
EARTH 3042
FLOORDA
URiS
iAPETUS
QUA

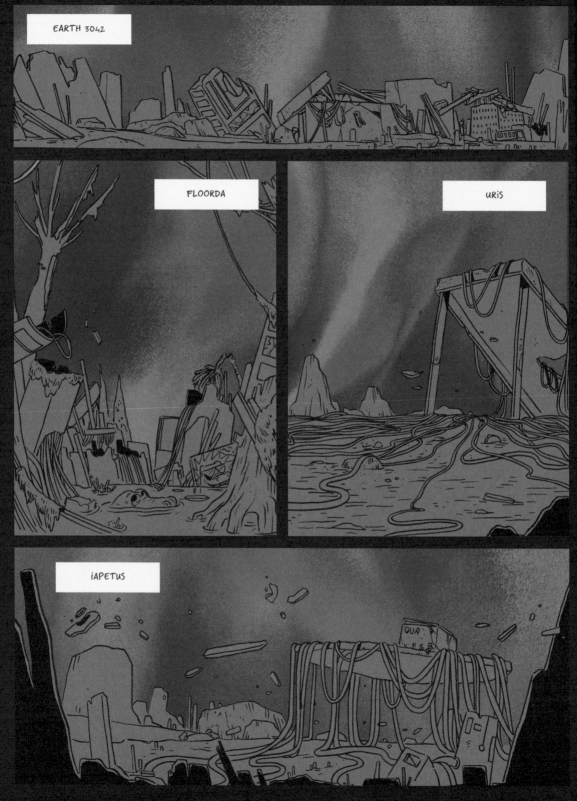

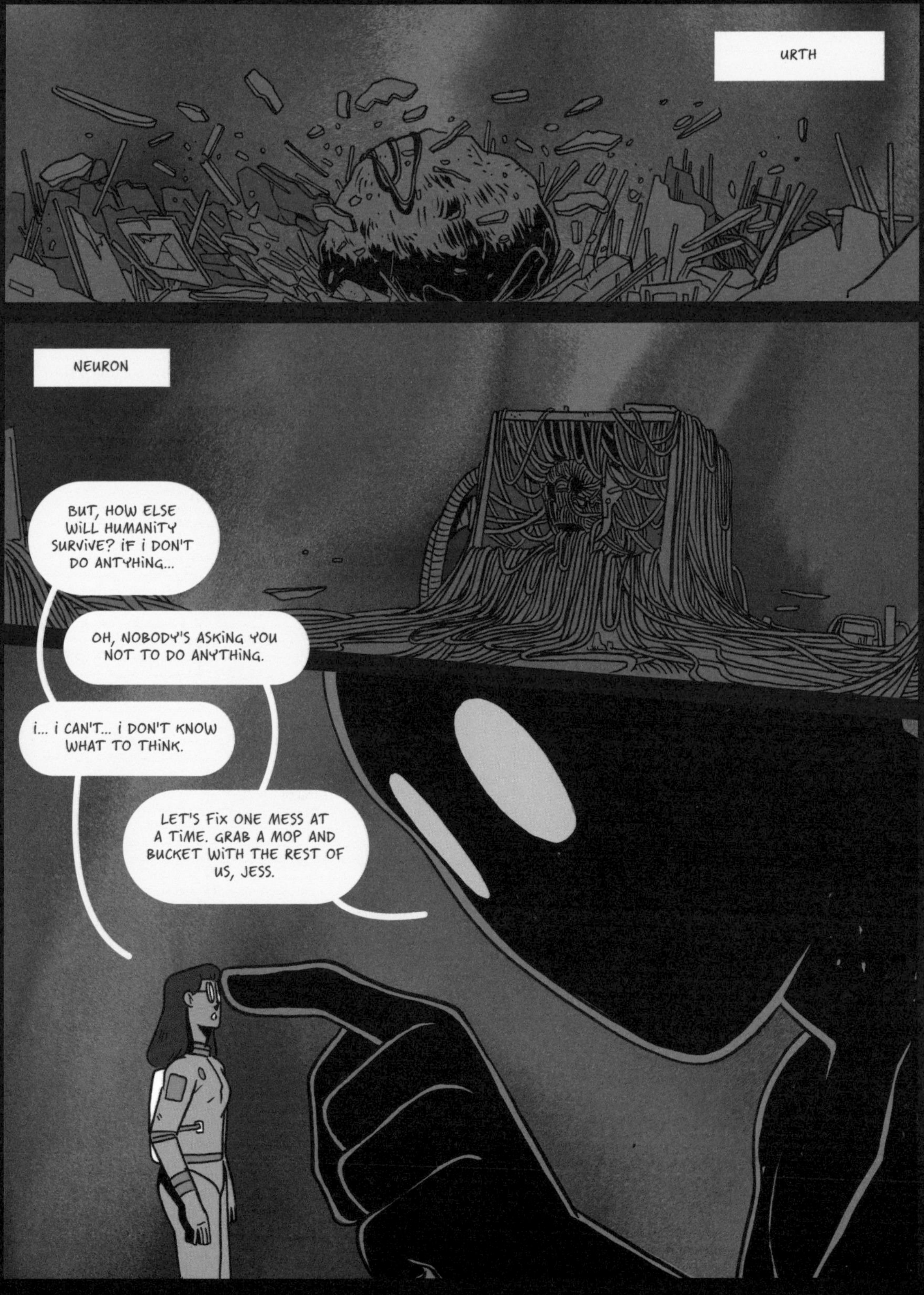
URTH
NEURON
BUT, HOW ELSE WiLL HUMANiTY SURViVE? iF i DON'T DO ANTYHiNG...
OH, NOBODY'S ASKiNG YOU NOT TO DO ANYTHiNG.
i... i CAN'T... i DON'T KNOW WHAT TO THiNK.
LET'S FiX ONE MESS AT A TiME. GRAB A MOP AND BUCKET WiTH THE REST OF US, JESS.

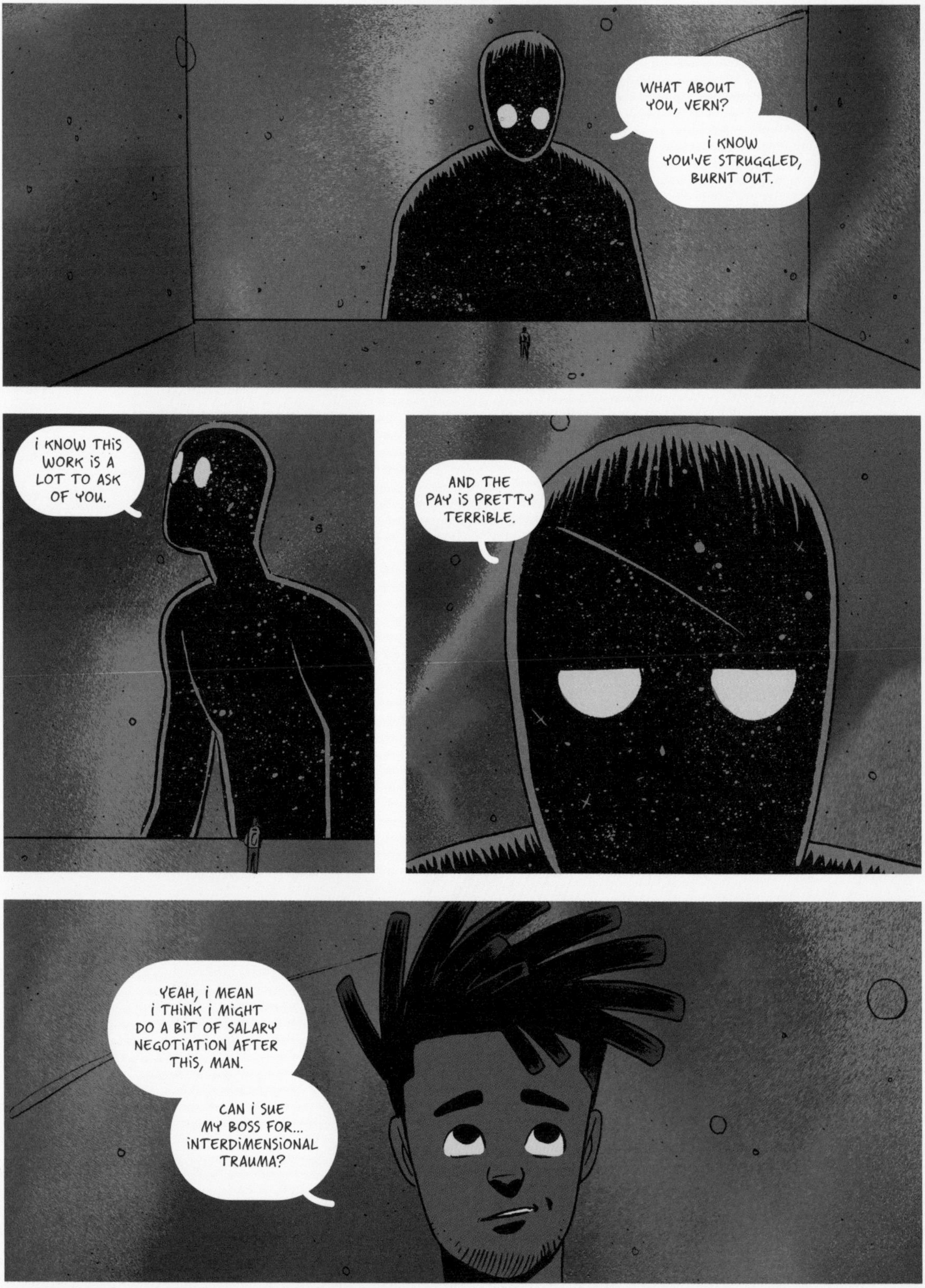
WHAT ABOUT YOU, VERN?
i KNOW YOU'VE STRUGGLED, BURNT OUT.
i KNOW THiS WORK iS A LOT TO ASK OF YOU.
AND THE PAY iS PRETTY TERRiBLE.
YEAH, i MEAN i THiNK i MiGHT DO A BiT OF SALARY NEGOTiATiON AFTER THiS, MAN.
CAN i SUE MY BOSS FOR... iNTERDiMENSiONAL TRAUMA?

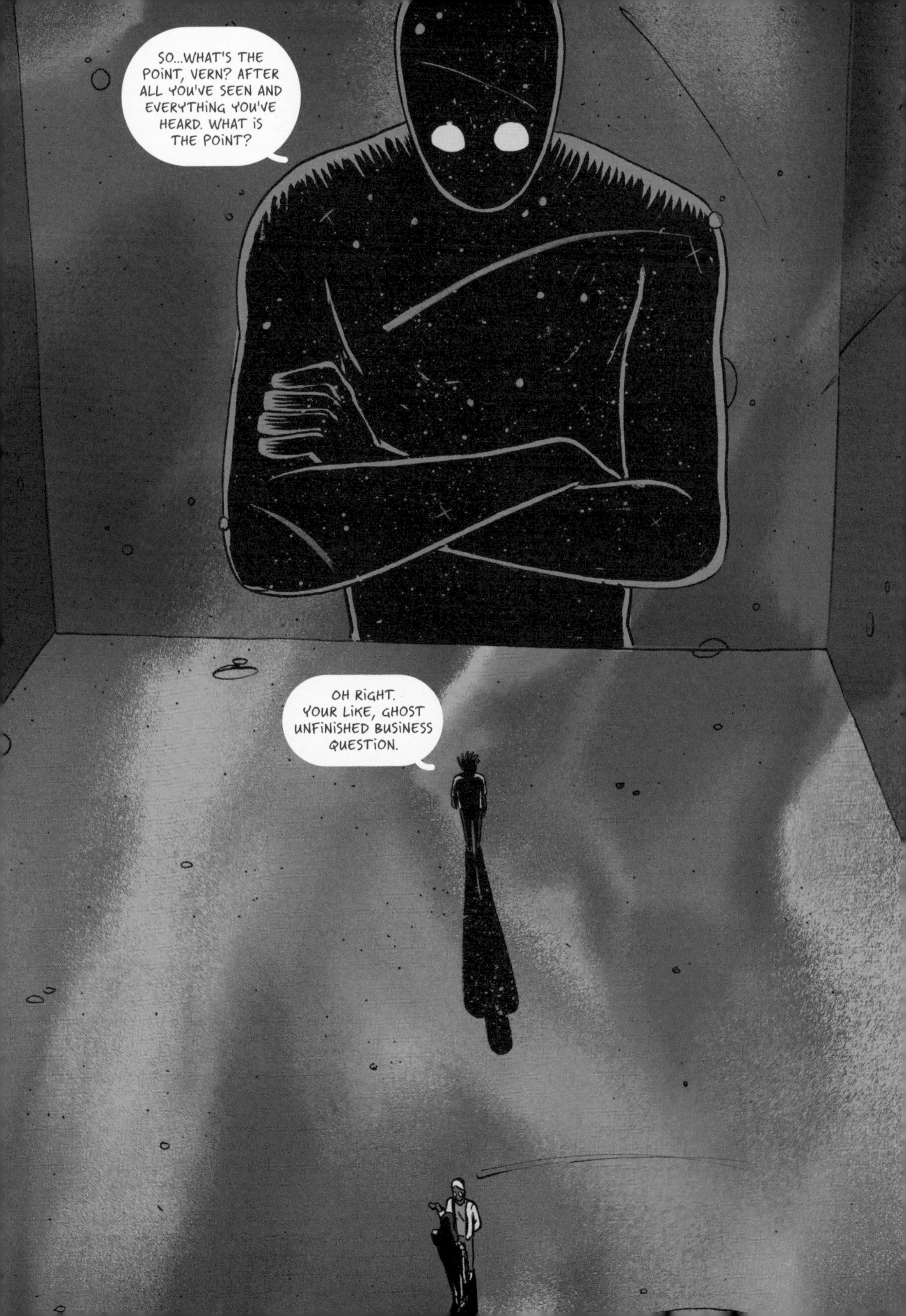
SO...WHAT'S THE POINT, VERN? AFTER ALL YOU'VE SEEN AND EVERYTHING YOU'VE HEARD. WHAT IS THE POINT?
OH RIGHT. YOUR LIKE, GHOST UNFINISHED BUSINESS QUESTION.

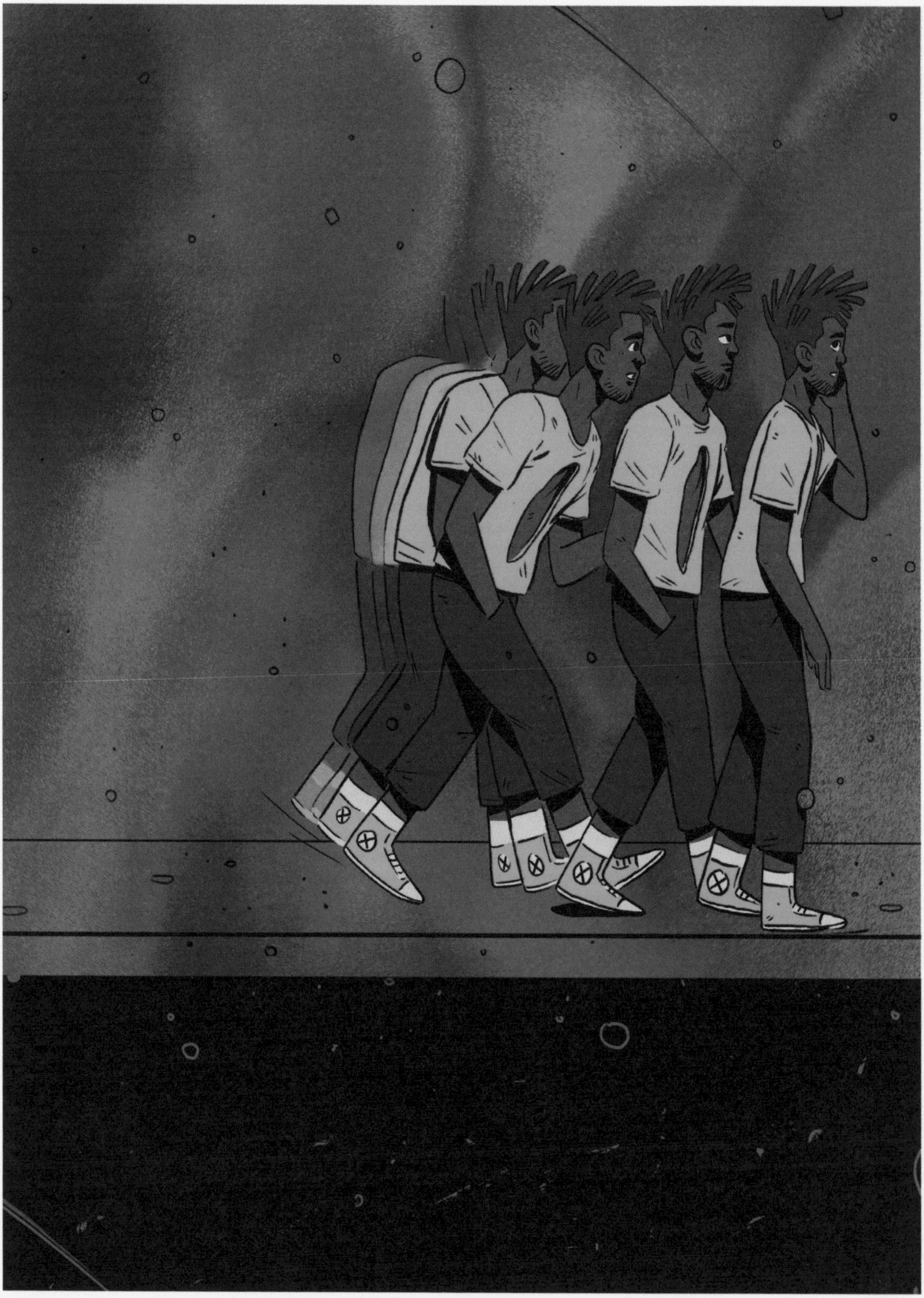

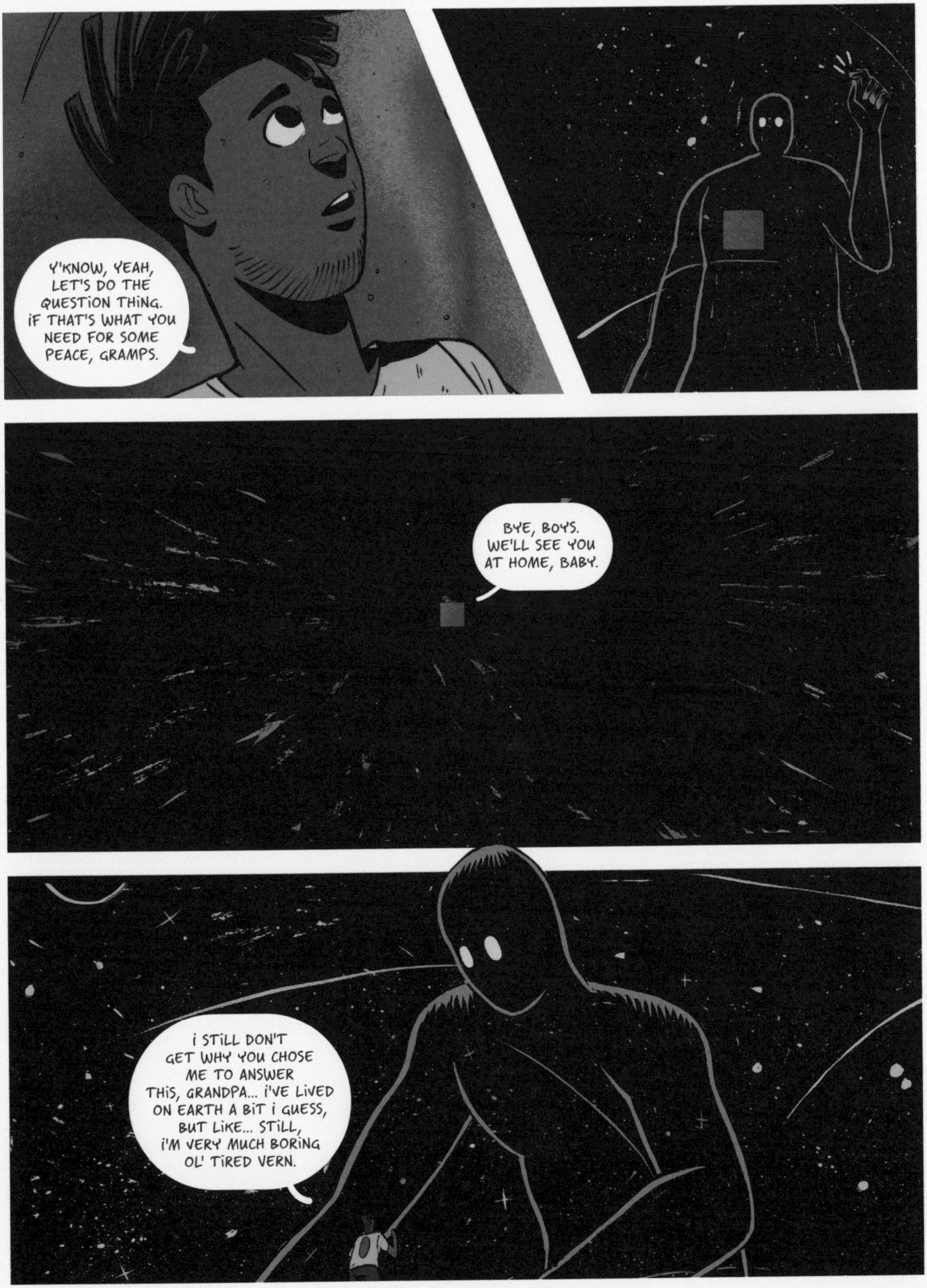
Y'KNOW, YEAH, LET'S DO THE QUESTION THING. IF THAT'S WHAT YOU NEED FOR SOME PEACE, GRAMPS.
BYE, BOYS. WE'LL SEE YOU AT HOME, BABY.
I STILL DON'T GET WHY YOU CHOSE ME TO ANSWER THIS, GRANDPA... I'VE LIVED ON EARTH A BIT I GUESS, BUT LIKE... STILL, I'M VERY MUCH BORING OL' TIRED VERN.

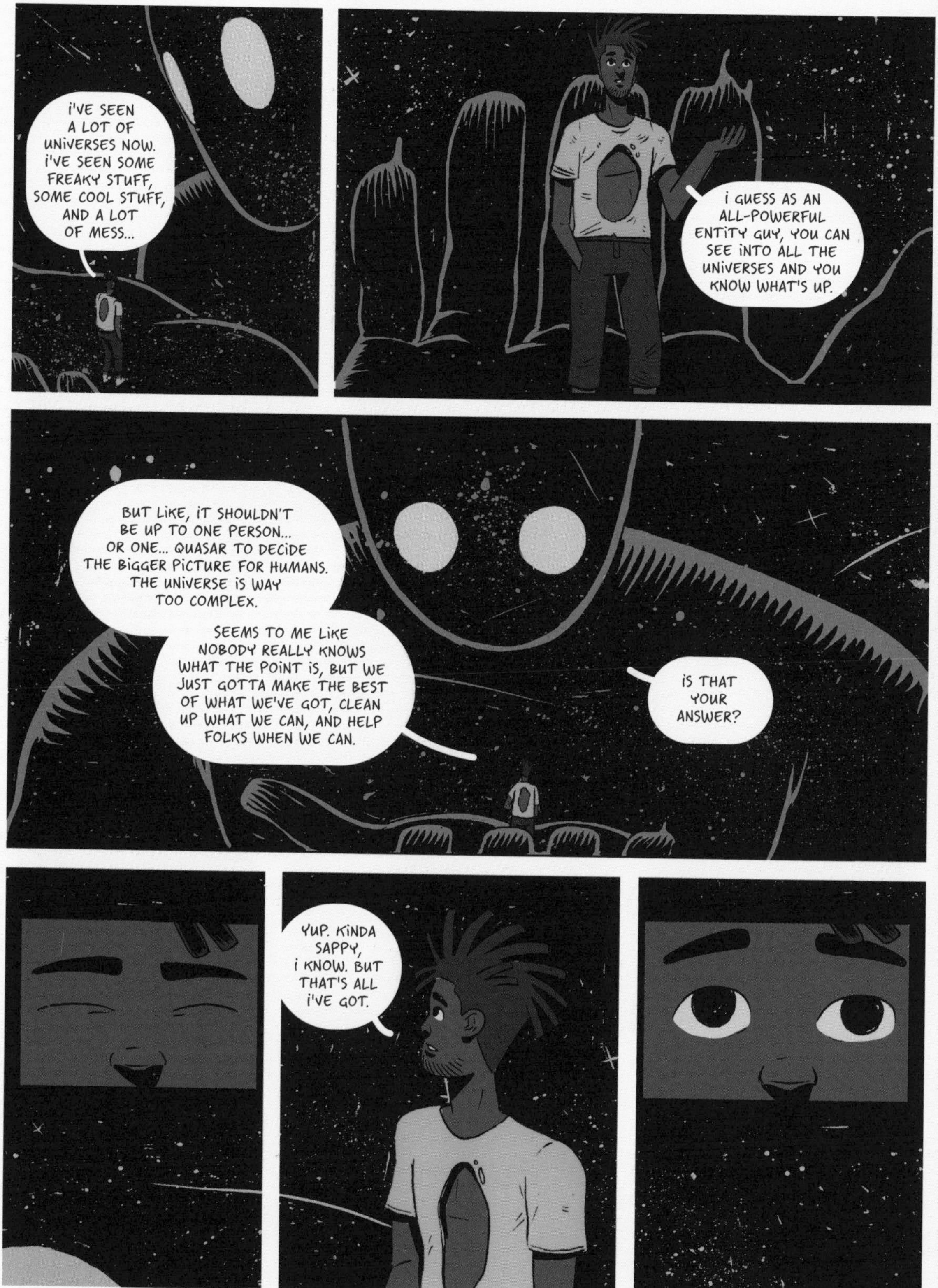
i've seen a lot of universes now. i've seen some freaky stuff, some cool stuff, and a lot of mess...
i guess as an all-powerful entity guy, you can see into all the universes and you know what's up.
but like, it shouldn't be up to one person... or one... quasar to decide the bigger picture for humans. the universe is way too complex.
seems to me like nobody really knows what the point is, but we just gotta make the best of what we've got, clean up what we can, and help folks when we can.
is that your answer?
yup. kinda sappy, i know. but that's all i've got.

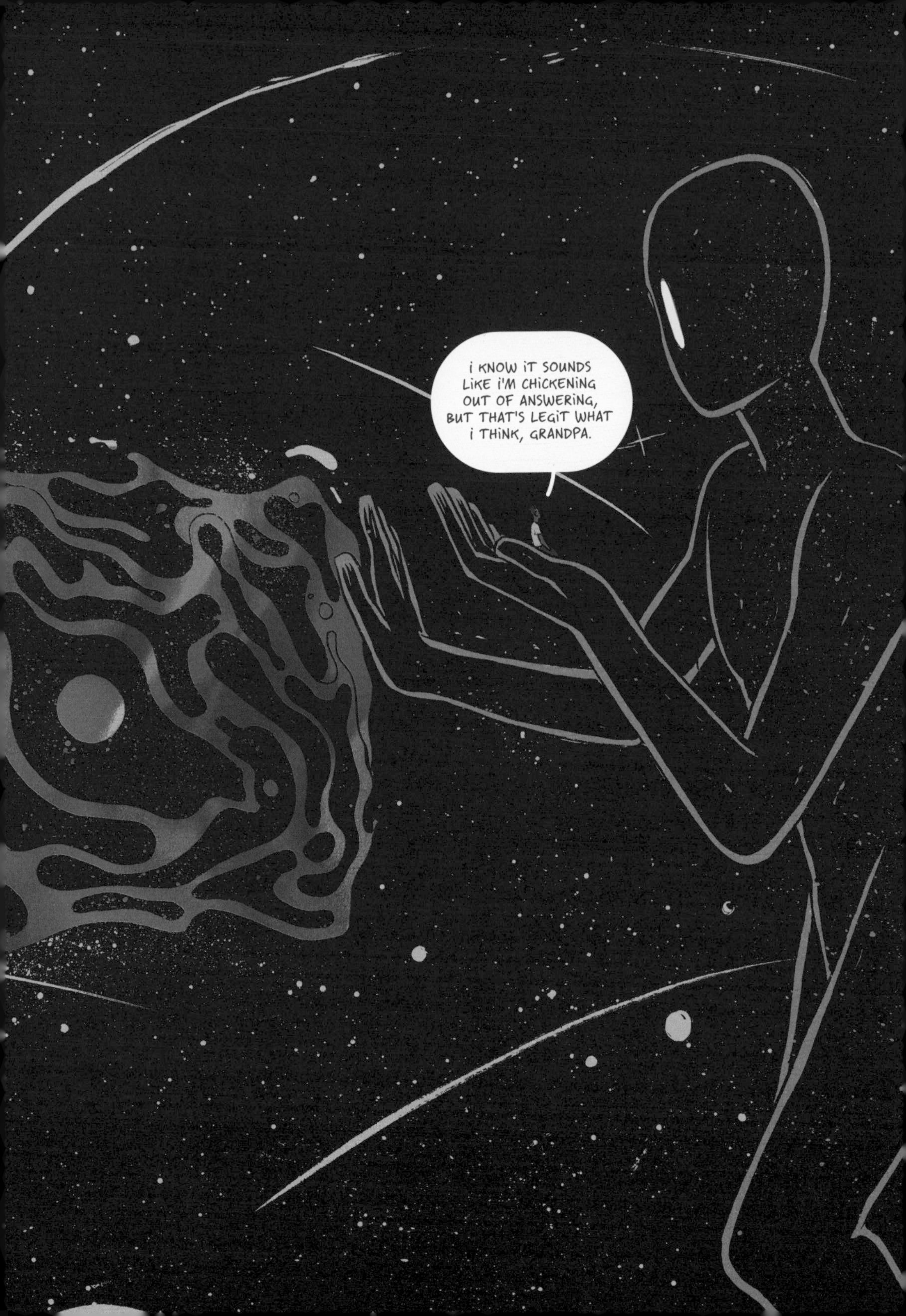
i KNOW iT SOUNDS LiKE i'M CHiCKENiNG OUT OF ANSWERiNG, BUT THAT'S LEGiT WHAT i THiNK, GRANDPA.

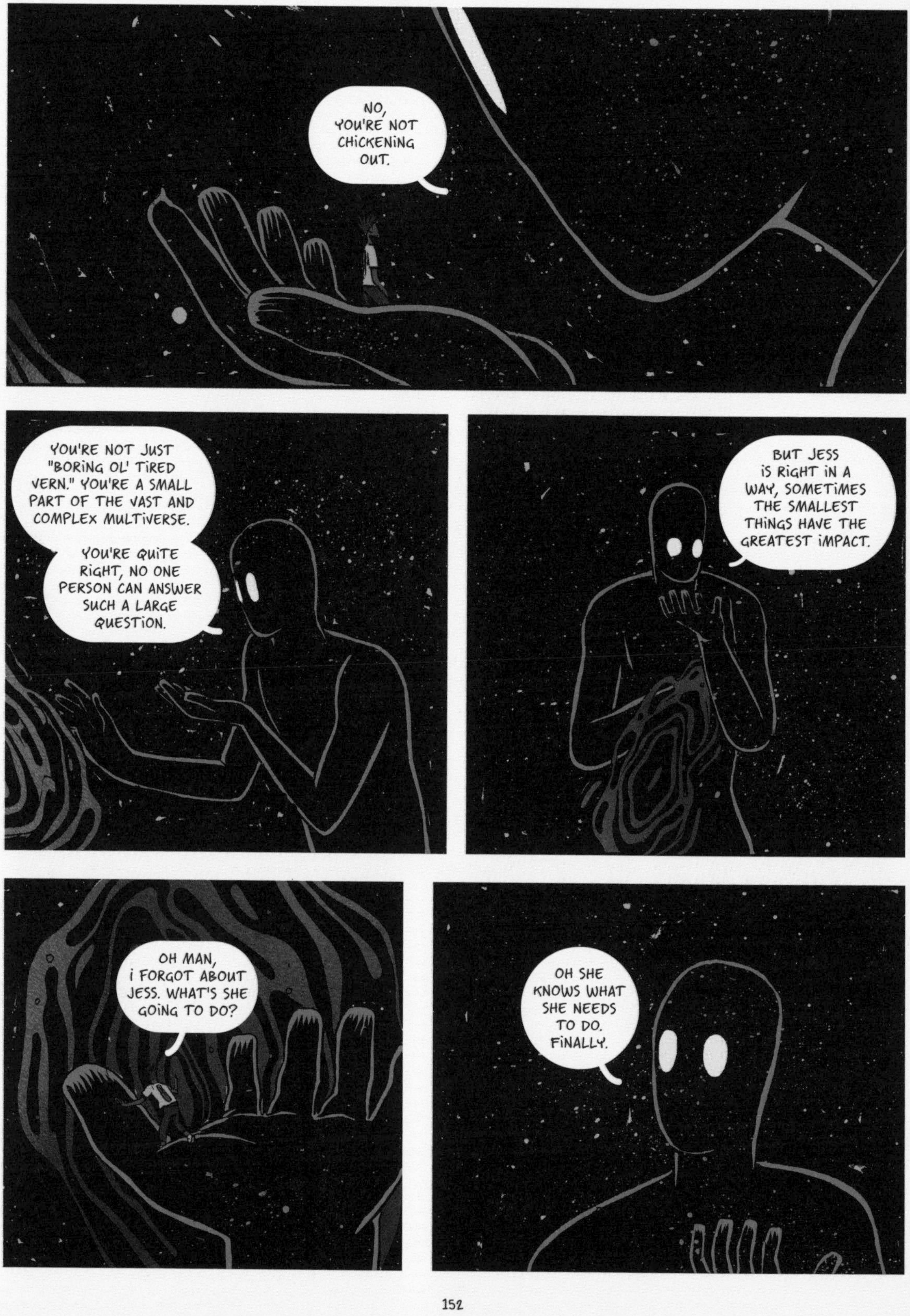
NO, YOU'RE NOT CHICKENING OUT.
YOU'RE NOT JUST "BORING OL' TIRED VERN." YOU'RE A SMALL PART OF THE VAST AND COMPLEX MULTIVERSE.
YOU'RE QUITE RIGHT, NO ONE PERSON CAN ANSWER SUCH A LARGE QUESTION.
BUT JESS IS RIGHT IN A WAY, SOMETIMES THE SMALLEST THINGS HAVE THE GREATEST IMPACT.
OH MAN, I FORGOT ABOUT JESS. WHAT'S SHE GOING TO DO?
OH SHE KNOWS WHAT SHE NEEDS TO DO. FINALLY.

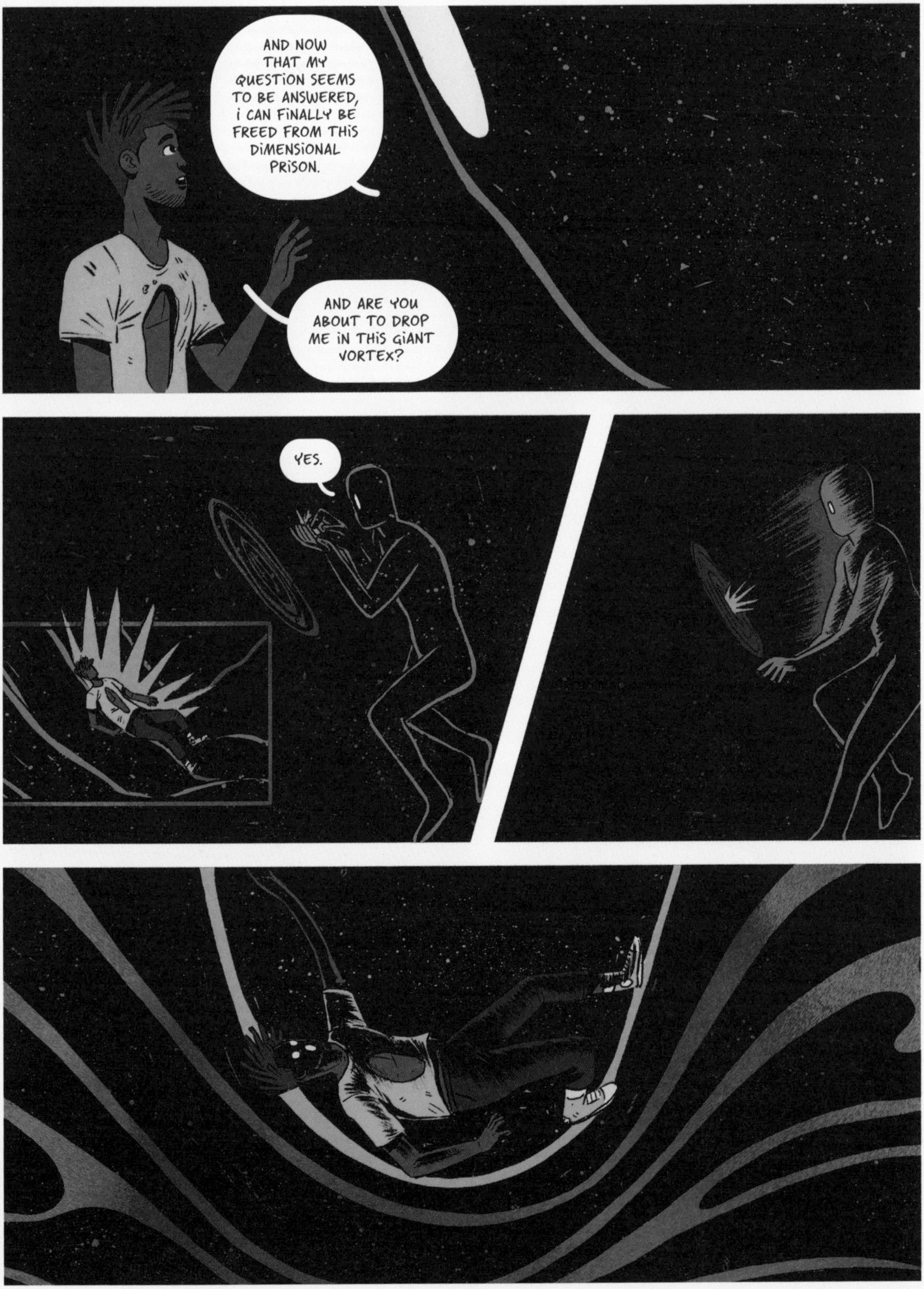
AND NOW THAT MY QUESTION SEEMS TO BE ANSWERED, I CAN FINALLY BE FREED FROM THIS DIMENSIONAL PRISON.
AND ARE YOU ABOUT TO DROP ME IN THIS GIANT VORTEX?
YES.

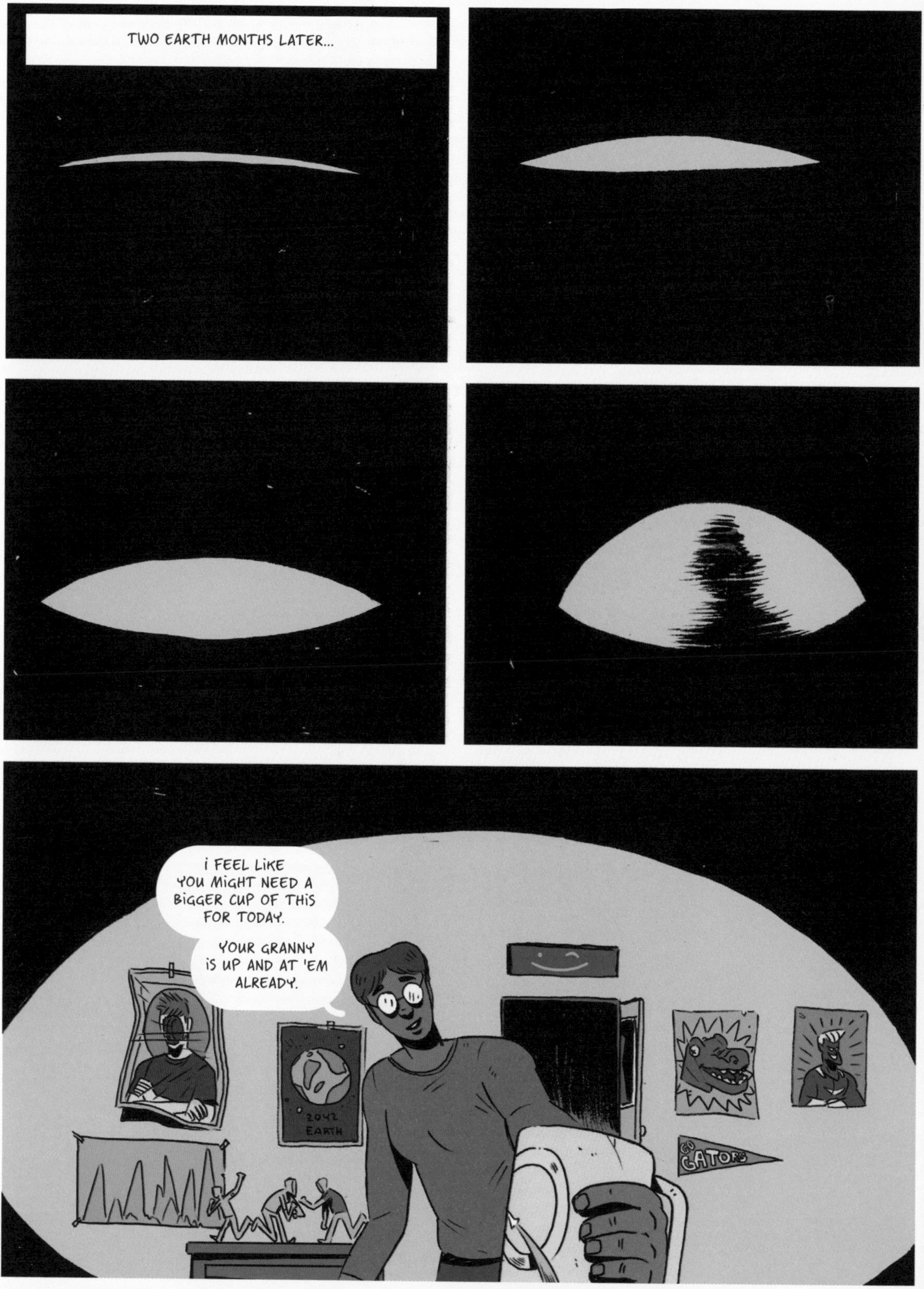
TWO EARTH MONTHS LATER...
I FEEL LIKE YOU MIGHT NEED A BIGGER CUP OF THIS FOR TODAY.
YOUR GRANNY IS UP AND AT 'EM ALREADY.
2042 EARTH
GO GATORS

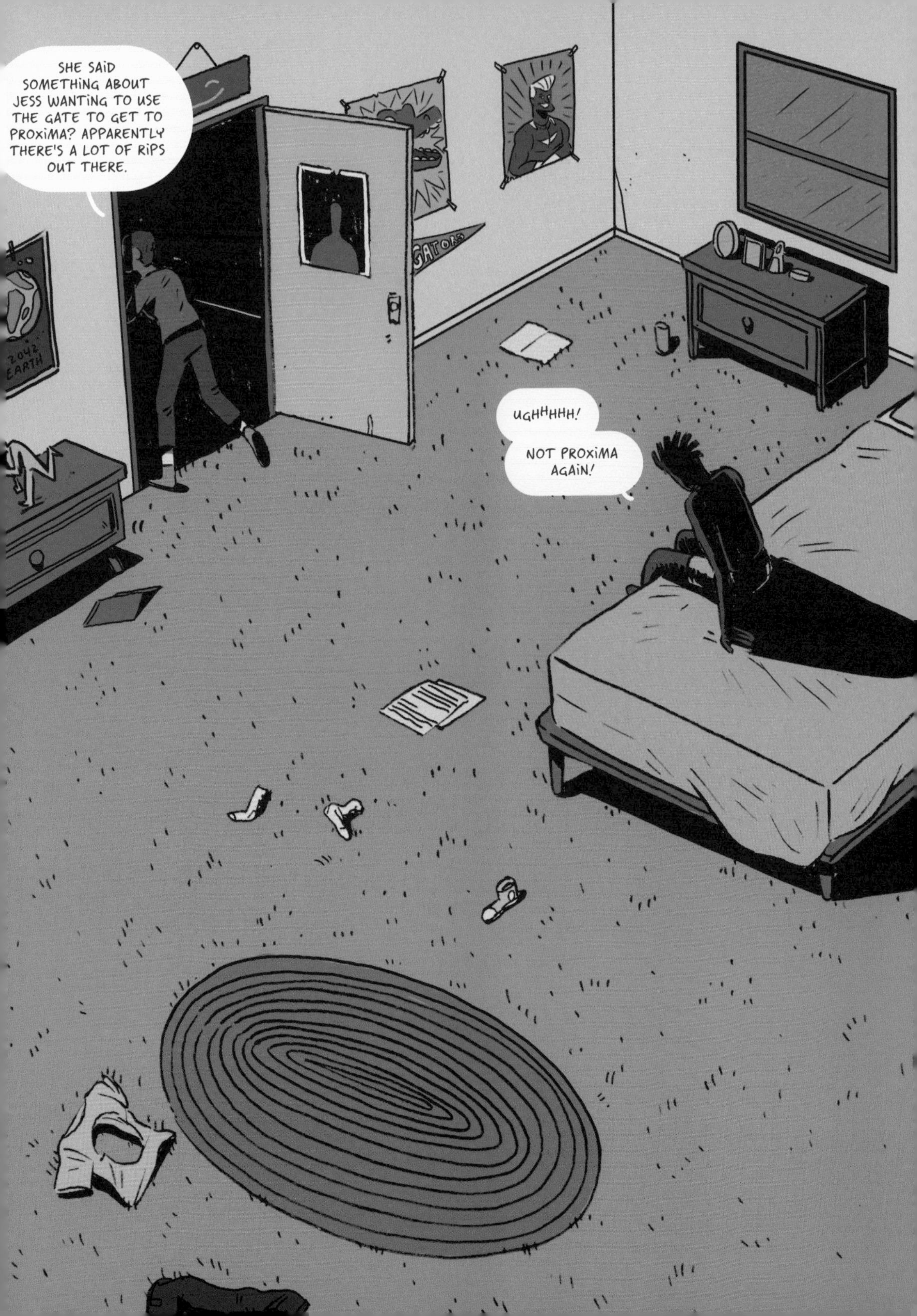
SHE SAID SOMETHING ABOUT JESS WANTING TO USE THE GATE TO GET TO PROXIMA? APPARENTLY THERE'S A LOT OF RIPS OUT THERE.
UGHHHHH!
NOT PROXIMA AGAIN!
GATORS
2042 EARTH

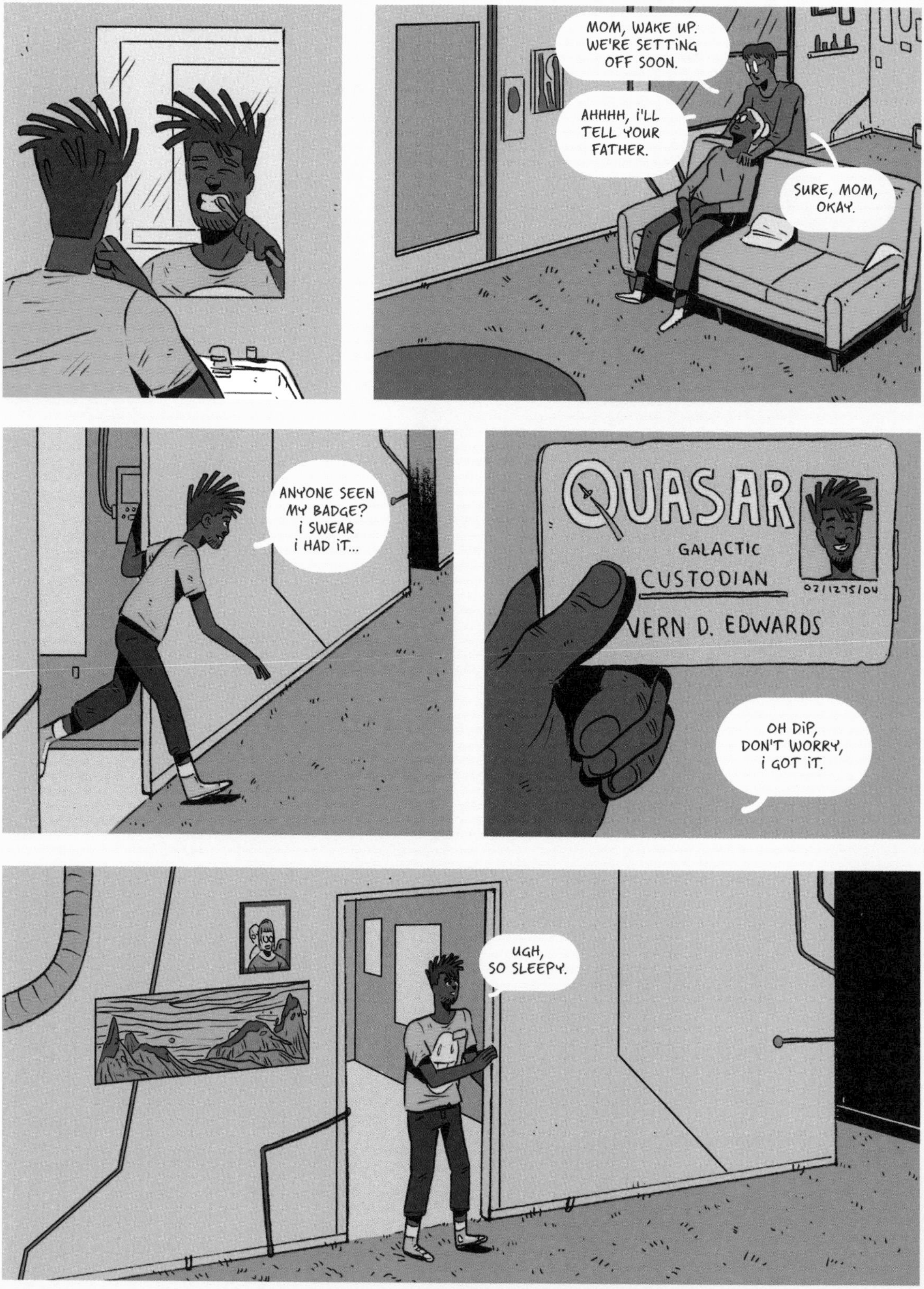
MOM, WAKE UP. WE'RE SETTING OFF SOON.
AHHHH, I'LL TELL YOUR FATHER.
SURE, MOM, OKAY.
ANYONE SEEN MY BADGE? I SWEAR I HAD IT...
QUASAR
GALACTIC
CUSTODIAN
VERN D. EDWARDS
07/1275/04
OH DIP, DON'T WORRY, I GOT IT.
UGH, SO SLEEPY.

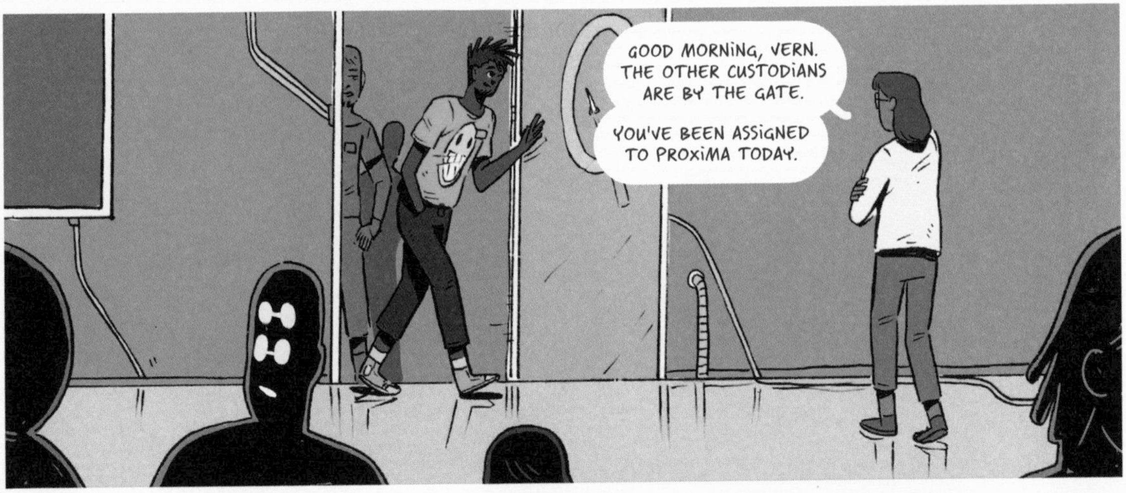
GOOD MORNING, VERN. THE OTHER CUSTODIANS ARE BY THE GATE.
YOU'VE BEEN ASSIGNED TO PROXIMA TODAY.

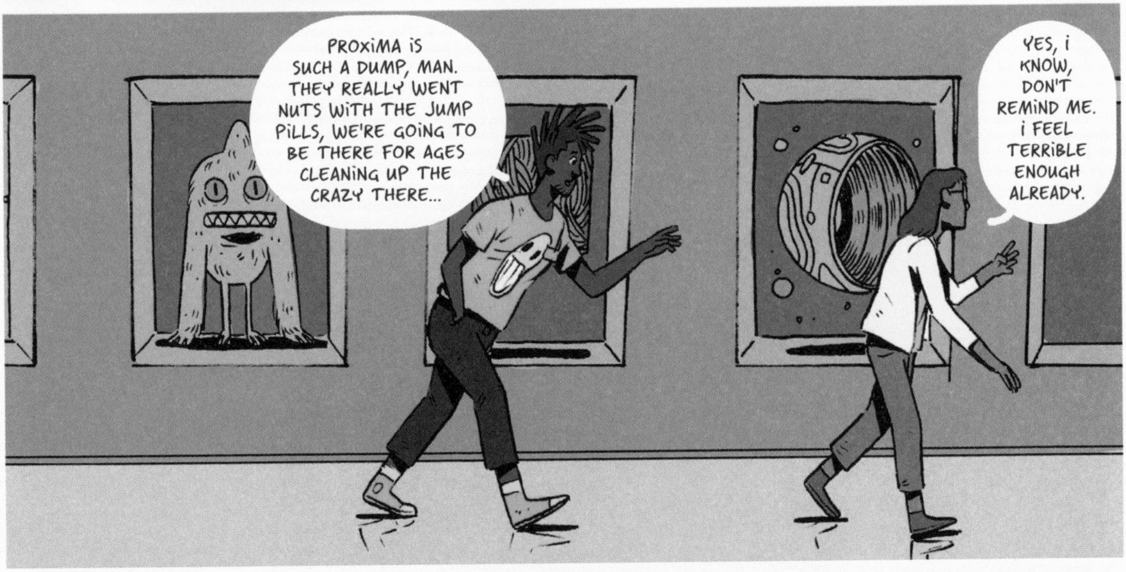
PROXIMA IS SUCH A DUMP, MAN. THEY REALLY WENT NUTS WITH THE JUMP PILLS, WE'RE GOING TO BE THERE FOR AGES CLEANING UP THE CRAZY THERE...
YES, I KNOW, DON'T REMIND ME. I FEEL TERRIBLE ENOUGH ALREADY.

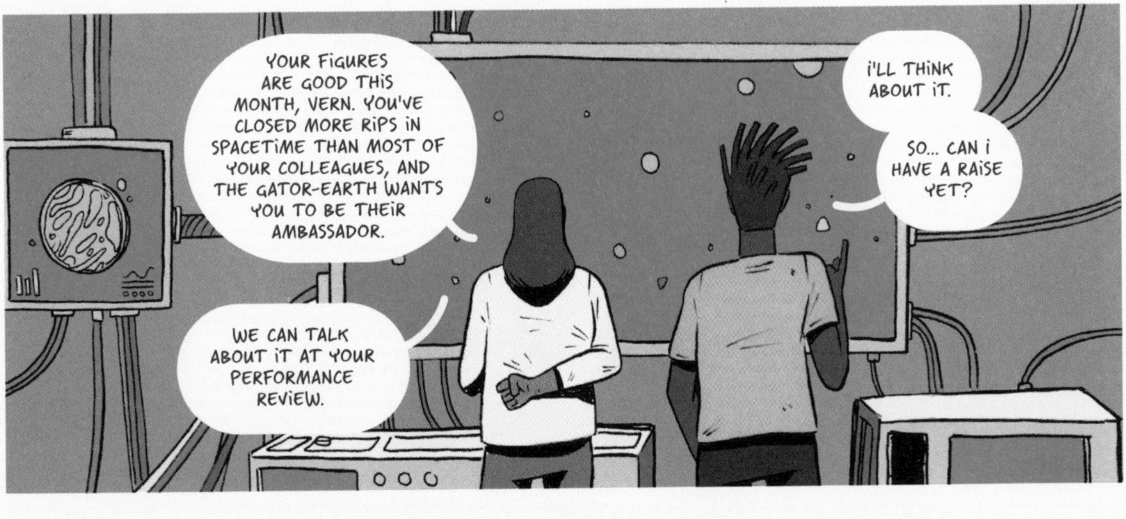
YOUR FIGURES ARE GOOD THIS MONTH, VERN. YOU'VE CLOSED MORE RIPS IN SPACETIME THAN MOST OF YOUR COLLEAGUES, AND THE GATOR-EARTH WANTS YOU TO BE THEIR AMBASSADOR.
I'LL THINK ABOUT IT.
SO... CAN I HAVE A RAISE YET?
WE CAN TALK ABOUT IT AT YOUR PERFORMANCE REVIEW.

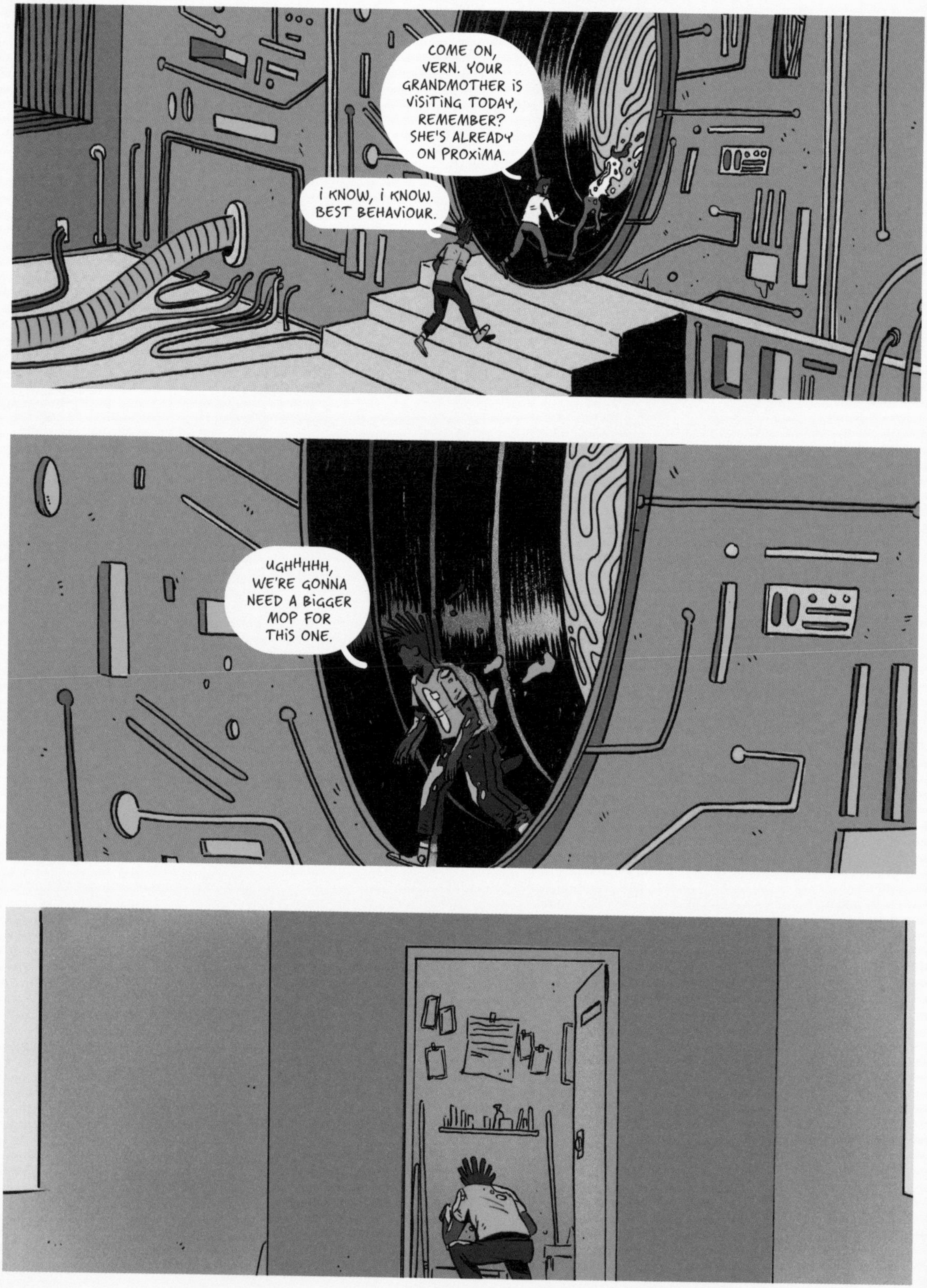
COME ON, VERN. YOUR GRANDMOTHER IS VISITING TODAY, REMEMBER? SHE'S ALREADY ON PROXIMA.
I KNOW, I KNOW. BEST BEHAVIOUR.
UGHHHHH, WE'RE GONNA NEED A BIGGER MOP FOR THIS ONE.

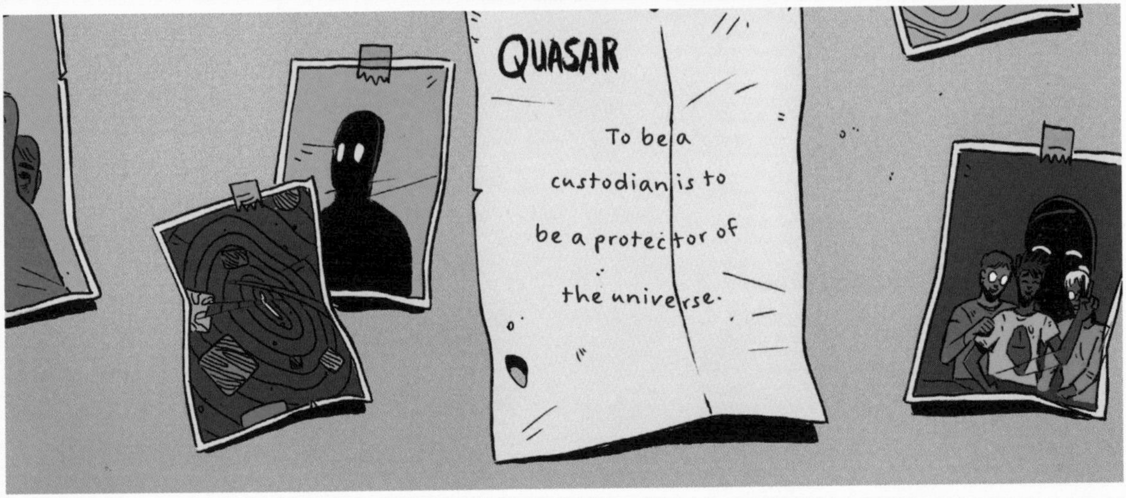
QUASAR
To be a custodian is to be a protector of the universe.

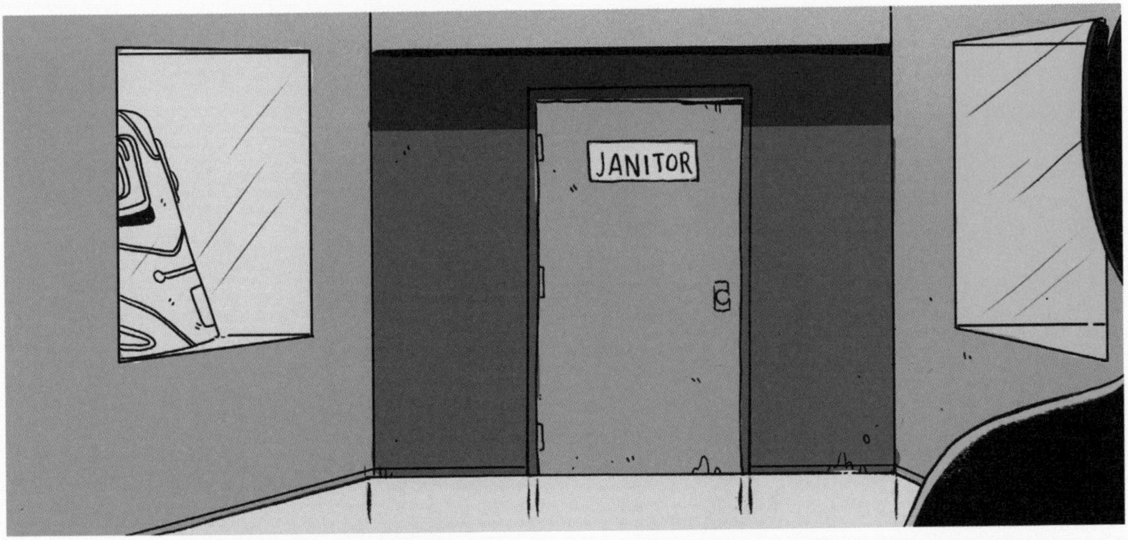
JANITOR

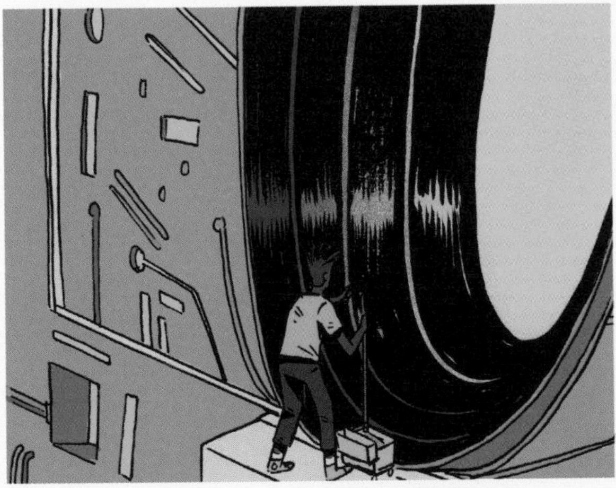

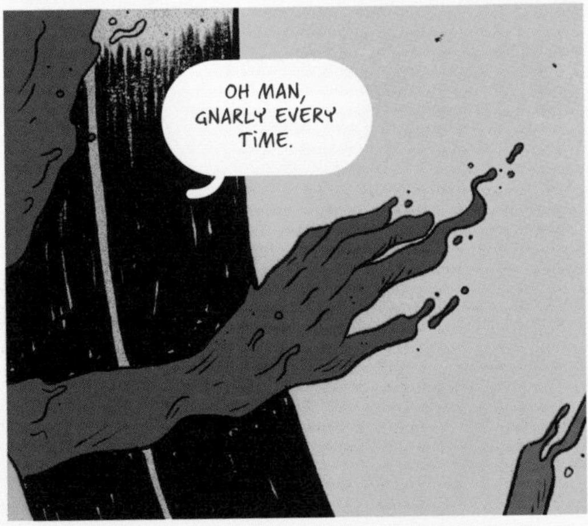
OH MAN, GNARLY EVERY TIME.

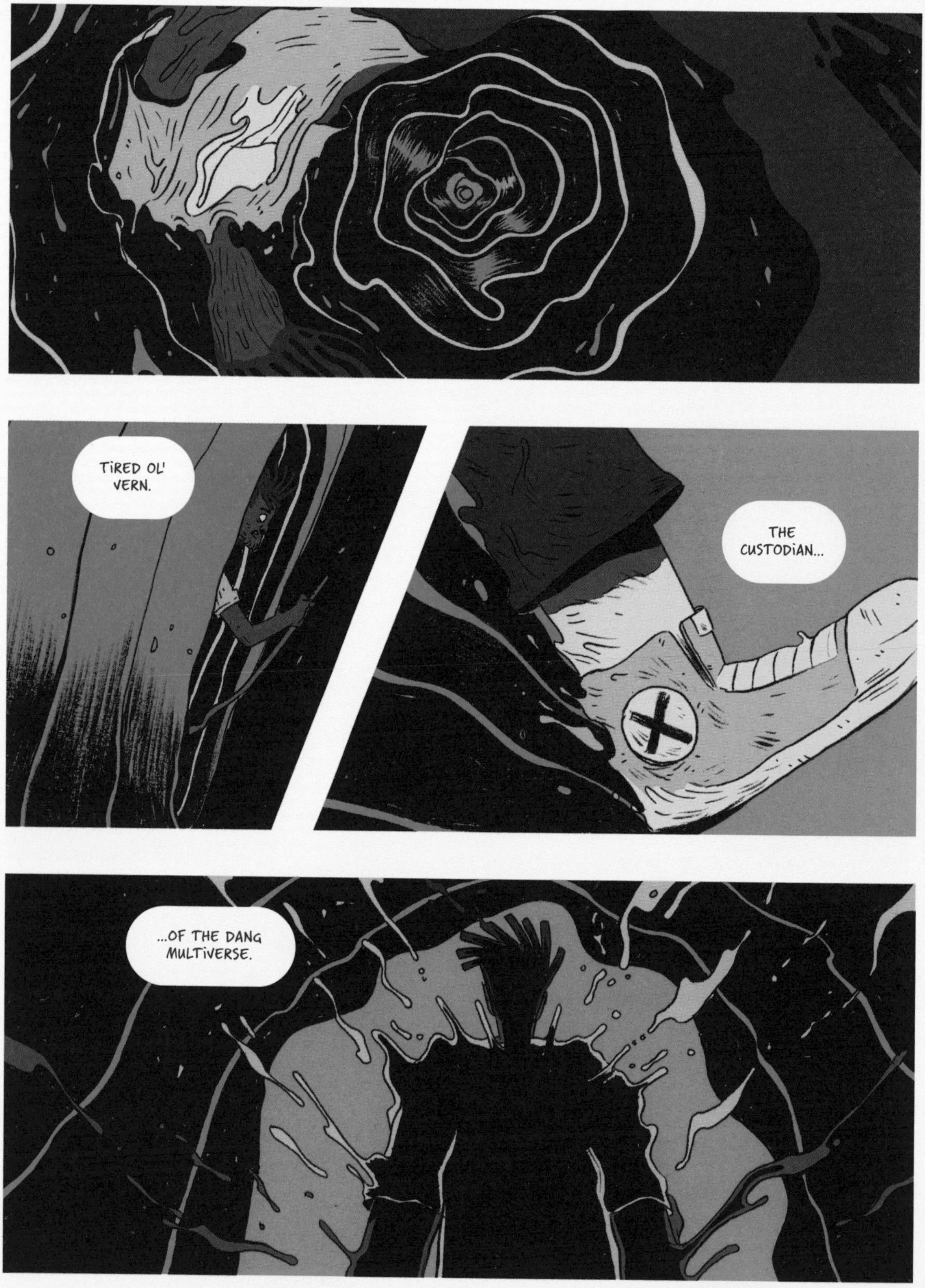
TIRED OL' VERN.
THE CUSTODIAN...
...OF THE DANG MULTIVERSE.

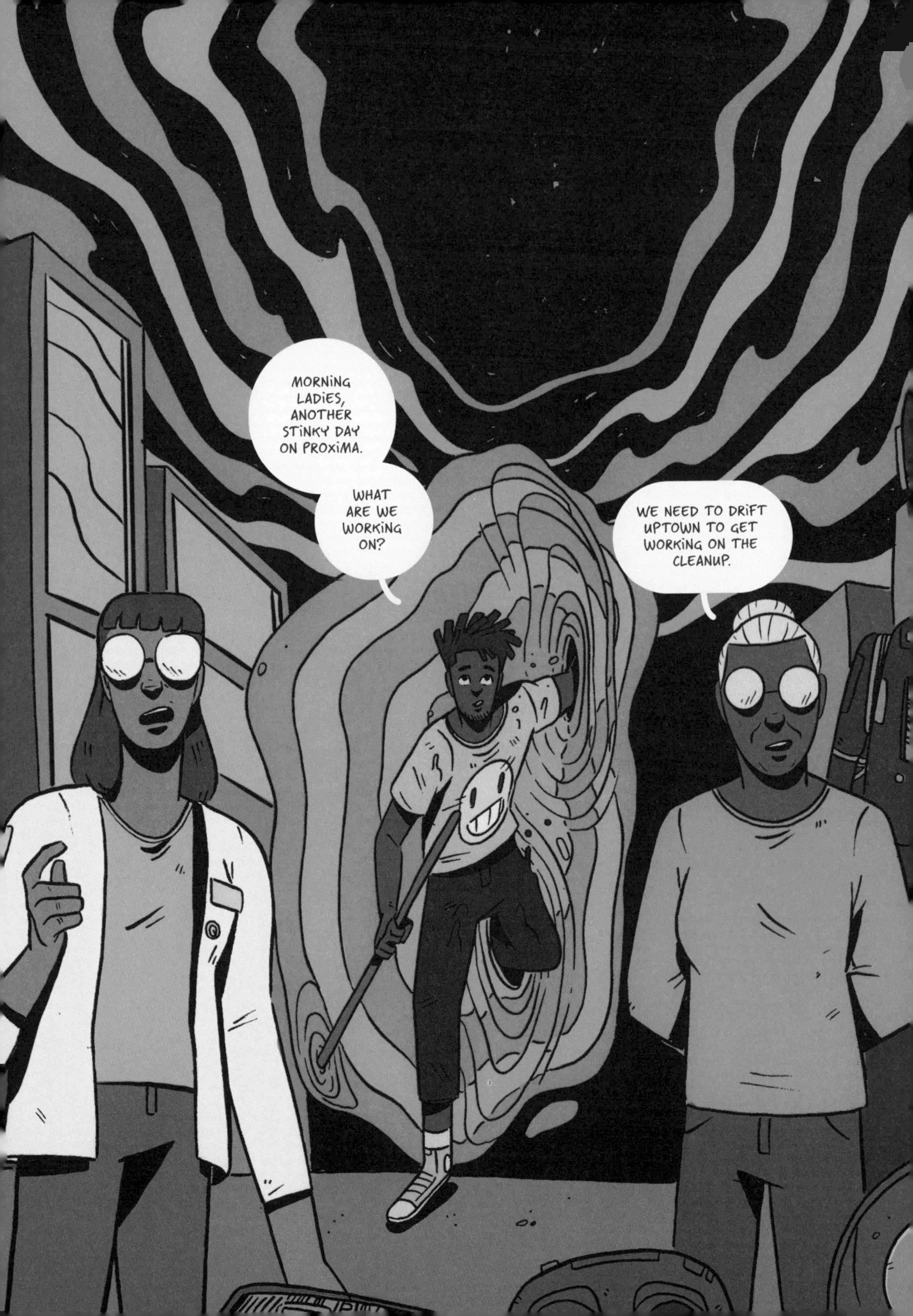
MORNING LADIES, ANOTHER STINKY DAY ON PROXIMA.
WHAT ARE WE WORKING ON?
WE NEED TO DRIFT UPTOWN TO GET WORKING ON THE CLEANUP.

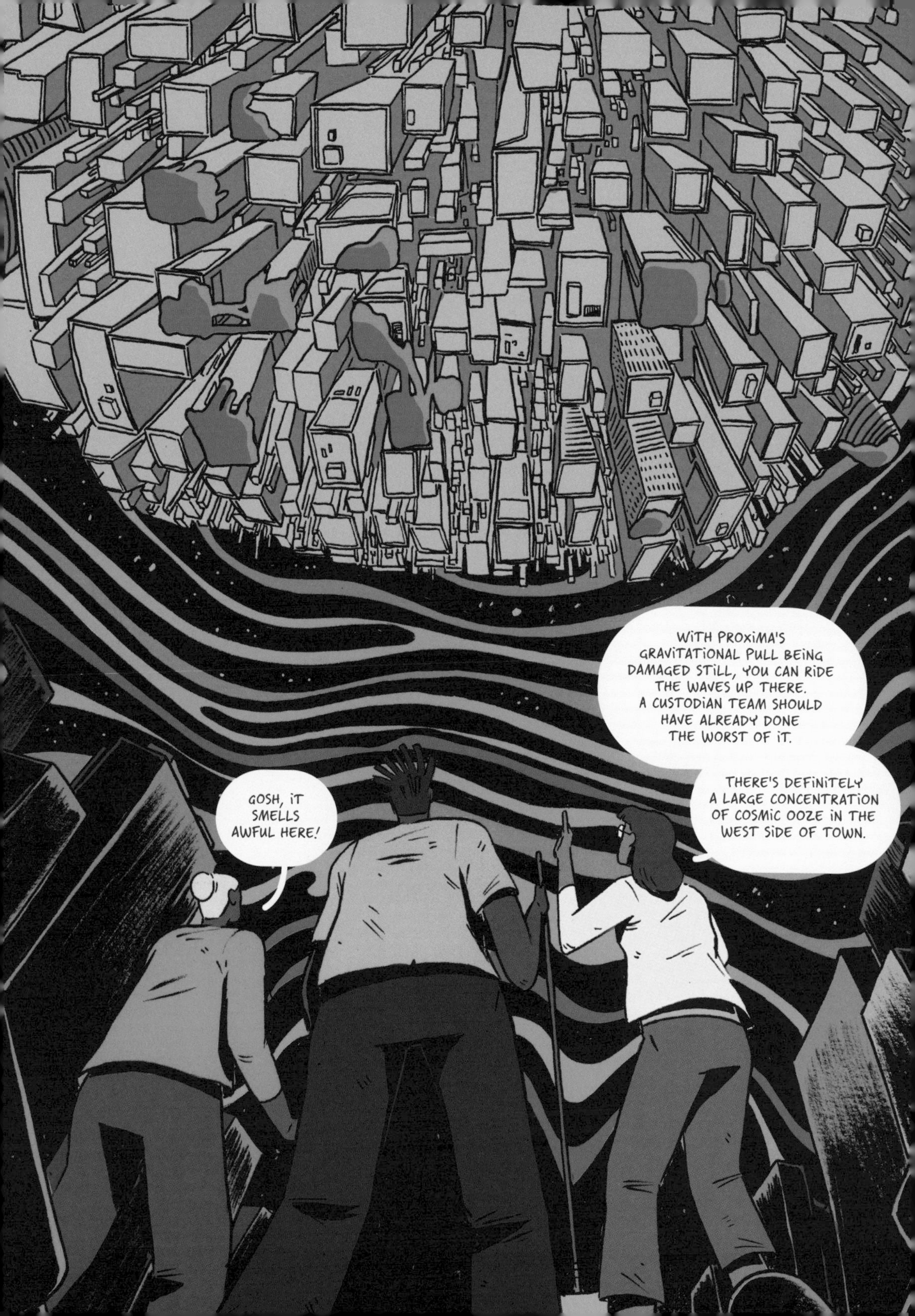
WITH PROXIMA'S GRAVITATIONAL PULL BEING DAMAGED STILL, YOU CAN RIDE THE WAVES UP THERE. A CUSTODIAN TEAM SHOULD HAVE ALREADY DONE THE WORST OF IT.
GOSH, IT SMELLS AWFUL HERE!
THERE'S DEFINITELY A LARGE CONCENTRATION OF COSMIC OOZE IN THE WEST SIDE OF TOWN.

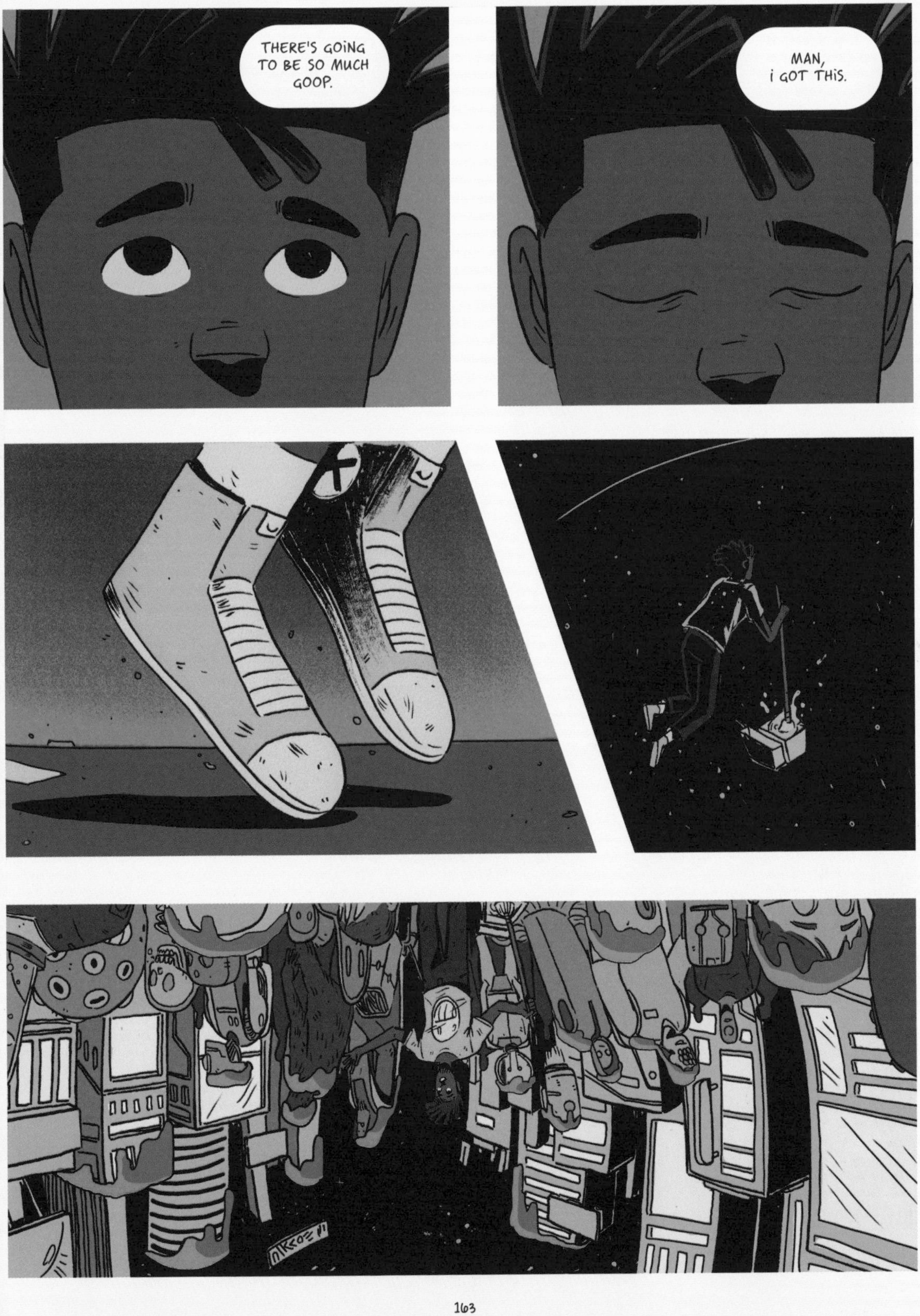
THERE'S GOING TO BE SO MUCH GOOP.
MAN, I GOT THIS.

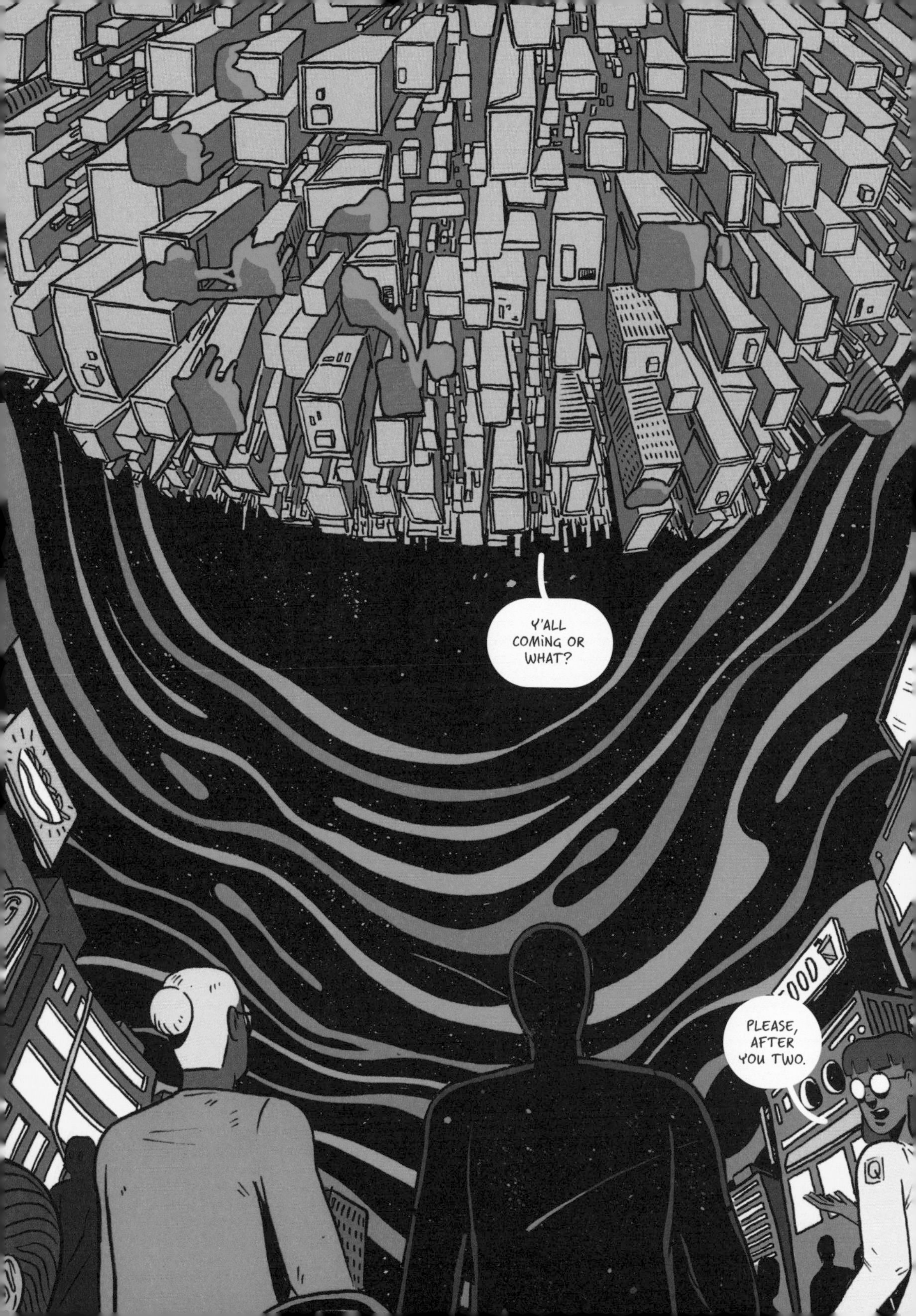
Y'ALL COMING OR WHAT?
PLEASE, AFTER YOU TWO.

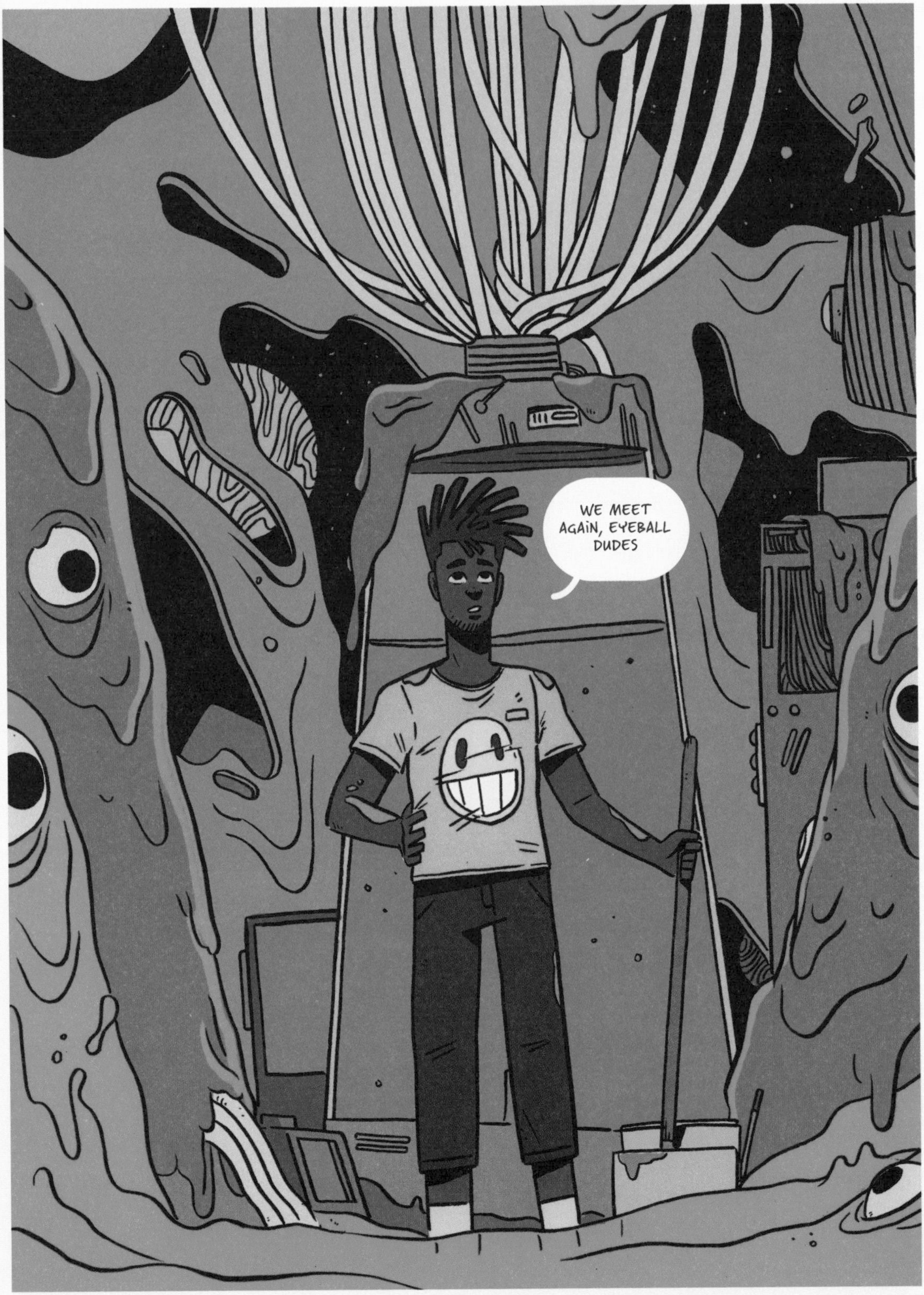
WE MEET AGAIN, EYEBALL DUDES

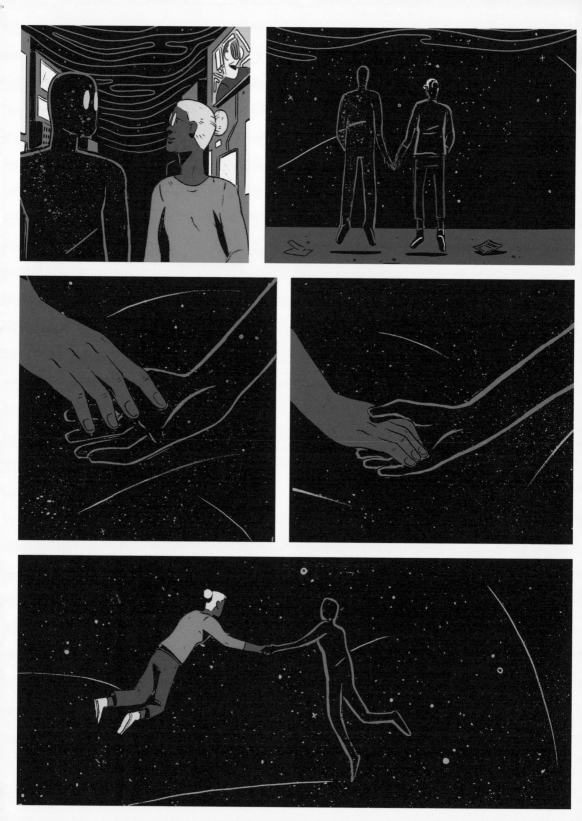

TYRELL WAITERS

i GREW UP iN PALMETTO, FLORIDA WHERE i HAD
THE DREAM OF BEING AN ARTIST. i ENDED UP GOING
TO COLLEGE TO STUDY ART, AND EVENTUALLY
LANDED MY FIRST REAL DREAM DESIGN JOB.
i'VE HAD THE PLEASURE OF DESIGNING VINYL
RECORD COVERS, SOCIAL MEDIA POSTS FOR A BUNCH
OF COMPANIES, AND i'VE DESIGNED CHILDREN'S AND
ADULT'S APPAREL FOR MAJOR FASHION BRANDS.
BUT ALL IN ALL, i'M JUST HAPPY i FOLLOWED
MY DREAMS AND WILL CONTINUE TO DO SO.